APOCALYPSE AND THE MILLENNIUM IN THE AMERICAN CIVIL WAR ERA

CONFLICTING WORLDS
NEW DIMENSIONS OF THE AMERICAN CIVIL WAR

T. Michael Parrish, Series Editor

APOCALYPSE AND THE MILLENNIUM
IN THE AMERICAN CIVIL WAR ERA

Edited by Ben Wright and
Zachary W. Dresser

WITH A FOREWORD BY MARK A. NOLL

Louisiana State University Press
Baton Rouge

Published by Louisiana State University Press

Manufactured in the United States of America
First printing

Designer: Michelle A. Neustrom
Typeface: Adobe Caslon Pro
Printer and binder: TK

Library of Congress Cataloging-in-Publication Data

Apocalypse and the millennium in the American Civil War era / edited by Ben Wright and Zachary W. Dresser ; with a foreword by Mark A. Noll.
pages cm. — (Conflicting worlds : new dimensions of the American Civil War)
Includes index.
ISBN 978-0-8071-5192-1 (cloth : alk. paper) — ISBN 978-0-8071-5193-8 (pdf) — ISBN 978-0-8071-5194-5 (epub) — ISBN 978-0-8071-5195-2 (mobi)
1. Millennialism—United States—History—19th century. 2. End of the world. 3. Millennium (Eschatology) 4. United States—Religion—19th century. 5. United States—History—Civil War, 1861–1865—Religious aspects. I. Wright, Ben, 1983– editor of compilation. II. Dresser, Zachary W., 1983– author, editor of compilation.
BR525.A74 2013
277.3'081—dc23

2013005368

The paper in this book meets the guidelines for permanence and durability of the Committee on Production Guidelines for Book Longevity of the Council on Library Resources. ♾

CONTENTS

FOREWORD

Two of the most enduring rhetorical memorials of the Civil War—documents that have been much revered by ordinary Americans and much studied by scholars—featured bold statements about God's dealings with the American people. In early 1862, the *Atlantic Monthly* published Julia Ward Howe's "Battle Hymn of the Republic" with its jubilant explanation of what warfare to restore the Union represented: it was nothing less than "the glory of the coming of the Lord." Three years later, in March 1865, at the heart of Abraham Lincoln's Second Inaugural Address was a more reflective meditation on divine purpose: "If God wills that [the war] continue, until all the wealth piled up by the bond-man's two hundred and fifty years of unrequited toil shall be sunk, and until every drop of blood drawn with the lash, shall be paid by another drawn with the sword, as was said three thousand years ago, so still it must be said, 'the judgments of the Lord, are true and righteous altogether.'"

Yet as much as Howe and Lincoln captured the providential preoccupations of the American people at the beginning and the end of the Civil War, historians have been slower to integrate the themes of providence, millennium, and apocalypse into their accounts of the conflict. Almost as much reluctance has characterized their treatment of the reform trajectories that led up to the war or the events and ideas that dominated the Reconstruction period.

The first-rate essays that Ben Wright and Zachary Dresser have collected in *Apocalypse and Millennium in the American Civil War Era* go a long way toward restoring these subjects to their rightful place in the historical record. Not only does the book offer close attention to important landmarks—for example, with discerning treatment of Julia Ward Howe's "Battle Hymn" in the editors' introduction and a fresh approach to Lincoln's Second Inaugural Address in the book's last chapter. Even more, the essays as a whole indicate how often apocalyptic and millennial thinking moved Americans to action and how often historical developments influenced the way Americans thought about the end of time "under God."

The appearance of this volume is unusually propitious. It comes at a moment when the strange reluctance to examine the religious convictions of Americans in the mid-nineteenth century has finally given way. Revealing comments found in several chapters sketch the outlines of a historiographical transformation. Gone are the days when the intense religious engagements of Americans in the Civil War and surrounding decades received only isolated scholarly attention. If some of that earlier attention was very perceptive, it was also very rare.[1] The change within the last decade or so is dramatic as a number of carefully researched monographs have detailed the important place of religion for combatants in the conflict as well as on the home front.[2] Major interpretive studies by Harry Stout and David Goldfield have in different ways made religion the key to understanding the war at its most fundamental level.[3] From George Rable has recently come an exceedingly well-researched and exceedingly wide-ranging general examination of religion in every aspect of the war.[4] Beyond the sharply focused books, many other outstanding studies have recently done much better at documenting the central place that religion occupied in the era.[5] While it is true, as Edward Blum suggests in the last essay in this book, that the treatment of religious issues trails off rapidly for the era after the Civil War, nonetheless even for that period, as testified to by Blum's own work, historians are doing better at charting the actual beliefs and religiously influenced actions of Americans for the latter decades of the century. This book, with its focused attention on themes of apocalypse and millennium, both takes advantage of a notable historical reawakening and propels that advance with its own substantial contribution.

Apocalypse and Millennium in the American Civil War Era is timely from a more contemporary angle as well. The detailed attention that responsible journalists and serious scholars are now devoting to the immense, multivalent place of religion in the modern world carries an implicit appeal to grasp more clearly the character of religion in past generations.[6] To almost the same degree as in the nineteenth-century United States, the world today is filled with contemplations of divine providence, the fear of apocalyptic cataclysm, and the hope of millennial peace. The contemporary phenomena may differ in important ways from what is described in this book, but careful historical attention to the precedents should have the spin-off effect of increased understanding, insight, and empathy for the present.

The essays that make up *Apocalypse and Millennium in the American Civil War Era* range widely. Yet unlike many essay collections, this one retains a clear, integrating focus from first to last. The strongest point of cohesion is attention to the pervasive belief that, whether directly or indirectly, an active God rules over (or at least consistently interacts with) ordinary human existence. The essays show that this belief in providence did in fact take strikingly different shapes. The providentialism of antebellum spiritualists, which is the subject of chapter 2, was very different from the providentialism of emancipated African Americans after the Civil War, a theme explored in a splendid trio of essays (chapters 8, 9, and 10). Even when observers might think that denominational propinquity would lead to similar convictions about providence, careful research shows that it worked quite differently for Associate Reformed Presbyterians in the antebellum South (chapter 5) than it did for Old School Presbyterians during and after the Civil War (chapter 7). Differences are even more striking when noticing how comparable degrees of trust in providence led to strikingly different interpretations of God's actions for Canadians shaped by their British context (chapter 4) and Americans influenced by firsthand contact with Native Americans (chapter 6).

At least two benefits flow from understanding both the wide scope of providential belief and the great diversity in applying that belief. First, we gain genuine insight into the general temper of a past era. But, second, we also see that no particular conclusion can be drawn about belief in providence until we observe closely how that belief actually functioned. Because the scholars whom Wright and Dresser assembled have excelled in bringing close research to disciplined conclusions, these and many other rewards await careful readers of this work. The book in its entirety is a model for others who seek genuine understanding of critical themes for a critical era in American history.

Mark A. Noll

NOTES

1. See, as lonely examples, Lewis G. Vander Velde, *The Presbyterian Churches and the Federal Union, 1861–1869* (Cambridge: Harvard University Press, 1932); James W. Silver, *Confederate Morale and Church Propaganda* (1957; New York: Norton, 1967); James H. Moorhead, *American Apocalypse: Yankee Protestants and the Civil War, 1860–1869* (New Haven: Yale University Press, 1978); and Gardiner H. Shattuck Jr., *A Shield and Hiding Place: The Religious Life of the Civil War Armies* (Macon, Ga.: Mercer University Press, 1987).

2. See, as examples, Steven E. Woodworth, *While God Is Marching On: The Religious World of Civil War Soldiers* (Lawrence: University Press of Kansas, 2001); Kent Dollar, *Soldiers of the Cross: Confederate Soldier Christians and the Impact of the War on Their Faith* (Macon, Ga.: Mercer University Press, 2005); David Rolfs, *No Peace for the Wicked: Northern Protestant Soldiers and the American Civil War* (Knoxville: University of Tennessee Press, 2009); and Sean A. Scott, *A Visitation of God: Northern Civilians Interpret the Civil War* (New York: Oxford University Press, 2011).

3. Harry S. Stout, *Upon the Altar of the Nation: A Moral History of the Civil War* (New York: Viking, 2006); David Goldfield, *America Aflame: How the Civil War Created a Nation* (New York: Bloomsbury, 2011). Also in this category could be Mark A. Noll, *The Civil War as a Theological Crisis* (Chapel Hill: University of North Carolina Press, 2006).

4. George C. Rable, *God's Almost Chosen Peoples: A Religious History of the American Civil War* (Chapel Hill: University of North Carolina Press, 2010).

5. Some of those studies are mentioned in Noll, *The Civil War as a Theological Crisis,* 10–11, 164–65.

6. Examples from a huge range of works include Gabriel A. Almond, R. Scott Appleby, and Emmanuel Sivan, *Strong Religion: The Rise of Fundamentalisms around the World* (Chicago: University of Chicago Press, 2003); John Micklethwait and Adrian Wooldridge, *God Is Back: How the Global Revival of Faith Is Changing the World* (New York: Penguin, 2009); Monica Duffy Toft, Daniel Philpott, and Timothy Samuel Shah, *God's Century: Resurgent Religion and Global Politics* (New York: Norton, 2011); and the three-volume series edited by Timothy Samuel Shah that includes *Evangelical Christianity and Democracy in Africa,* ed. T. O. Ranger (New York: Oxford University Press, 2008); *Evangelical Christianity and Democracy in Latin America,* ed. Paul Freston (New York: Oxford University Press, 2008); and *Evangelical Christianity and Democracy in Asia,* ed. D. H. Lumsdaine (New York: Oxford University Press, 2009).

ACKNOWLEDGEMENTS

The editors have been extremely fortunate to have found an assemblage of gracious individuals and institutions without whom this project would have been impossible. The volume began with a symposium at Rice University in the fall of 2010, made possible by the support of the History Department and Graduate Student Association of Rice University. W. Caleb McDaniel and Randal Hall offered valuable advice at each stage of the process. The editors are very pleased to recognize their shared advisor, John B. Boles, whose decades of service to Rice fostered the atmosphere of collegial collaboration that inspired the creation of this volume.

Luke E. Harlow deserves special recognition for his mentorship and assistance with recruiting contributors. Orville Vernon Burton unintentionally inspired both the conference and volume with an encouraging conversation in the spring of 2009. T. Michael Parrish has been a remarkably generous editor, and the staff at LSU Press has made the publication process efficient and pleasant. The editors assumed that such a distinguished scholar as Mark A. Noll would be unable to contribute a foreword, and we are still astonished and greatly pleased that he did. The majority of the thanks go to the outstanding scholars whose work you will find in the following pages. These authors are among the most important and innovative young voices in nineteenth-century scholarship, yet they all have been tremendously cooperative throughout the publication process.

Ben thanks Katie, to whom he is forever indebted. Zach thanks his parents, Harry and Ava Dresser, for their continued support.

APOCALYPSE AND THE MILLENNIUM IN THE AMERICAN CIVIL WAR ERA

INTRODUCTION

BEN WRIGHT AND ZACHARY W. DRESSER

On February 2, 1864, a group of dignitaries met in the hall of the House of Representatives to honor the U.S. Christian Commission, a philanthropic organization formed for the relief of soldiers after the First Battle of Bull Run. Rev. Charles Cardwell McCabe, a liberated prisoner of war and fund-raiser for the commission, rose to sing before an audience that included Speaker of the House Schuyler Colfax, Vice President Hannibal Hamlin, and the guest of honor, President Abraham Lincoln. McCabe had famously led Union captives of Richmond's Libby Prison in a celebratory rendition of "The Battle Hymn of the Republic" upon hearing of the Confederate defeat at Gettysburg, and after a series of speeches, McCabe was asked to perform the song that had gained him modest fame. In writing to his wife later that night, McCabe reveled in his execution of Julia Ward Howe's recently penned ballad. The song resonated with the assembly, including its most valued guest. McCabe reported that "the mighty audience sang in exact time. Some shouted out loud at the last verse, and above all the uproar Mr. Lincoln's voice was heard: 'Sing it again!'"[1]

From its first lines proclaiming "the glory of the coming of the Lord" to its final verse assuring that "He is coming like the glory of the morning on the wave," "The Battle Hymn of the Republic" trumpets the millennial faith that echoed in the hearts of men and women, North and South, during an era of apocalyptic turmoil. In her diary, Lucy Larcom described the election of Abraham Lincoln in 1860 as "glorious!" and rejoiced that "the millennium is not so far off as we feared."[2] Three years later, and many miles south, Mary Anne Webster Loughborough, working at a makeshift hospital during the siege at Vicksburg, wrote of a wounded soldier from Illinois sharing his breakfast with a Confederate. She joked with the two men that their cooperation marked "the dawn of the millennium," but her belief in Providence was too strong and the horrors of war were too great for her to stop at irreverent humor. She continued with a sincere wish that "the dawning was indeed with us; that brave and noble men should no more suffer, bleed, and die, but live; and in their lives grow more thankful and worthy of the Divine blood that has been shed for the removal of the fearful suffering and warfare that is all around us."[3] The sight of a young boy marching to war in February 1865 inspired William M. McLain to reflect, "I do not strain my mental vision to be able to see away yonder, in the ages that are to come, ere the millennium dawns—in the distance, and dimly foreshadowed, but yet discernible without a prophetic eye—a nation free, vigorous, educated, virtuous, religious."[4] Millennialism and providentialism have discrete theological meanings, but popular usage of these concepts spilled over definitional boundaries and soaked into the cultural consciousness in the nineteenth century. Sharp contrasts between pre- and postmillennialism and between the prewar and postwar periods obscure the flexible nuances of American religion. By examining several case studies of how Americans understood God's intervention in reform, war, and emancipation, this volume demonstrates the variable yet pervasive role of providential thinking as Americans made meaning of the national apocalypse.

As avid readers of the Bible, many nineteenth-century Americans were certain that history was approaching an end point. The sacred text did not specify the duration of that journey, but believers understood that humans were the main actors in a dramatic contest between God's forces of good and the powers of evil led by Satan. As foretold especially in the Book of Revelation, Jesus would eventually return to establish a new kingdom on earth, inaugurating a new epoch of history. For nearly all Christians, this thousand-year period known as the millennium represented the final victory of God over evil, but the timing of that eschatological era was heavily debated. Premillennialists, a small portion of Christians in the early nineteenth century, held that Christ's return would occur before the final period of history. These believers cast humanity as sinful and depraved, pointing to rampant moral failings as signs that the forces of Satan were winning the battle for this world. The severe and condemning language of premillennialism struck fear in the hearts of the soul-sick, who found meaning in personal conversion and promises of a coming divine intervention to stop the wicked ways of humankind. This psychological tension explains the popularity of William Miller's famous prediction of the Second Coming on October 22, 1844. But the disappointment of a normal day on October 23 revealed even more human frailty. Sinfulness seemed ever more dominant, and God's ways remained wholly inscrutable.

A rival and more common interpretation of the millennium, postmillennialism, held that Christ would return only after the world had been perfected. Thus, it was humanity's task to prepare the way for the Lord, ironing out moral wrinkles from the social fabric. Postmillennialists expected progress. Motivated by the spread of revivalism, the success of the American republic, and even new technology such as the telegraph, this group of believers saw human capabilities as ever-increasing, perpetually forward-moving. In both sections, reformers and evangelists were stirred by a keen sense of their agency in the divine drama of history. As Robert H. Abzug argues, a number of "religious virtuosos" in New England worked to remake the world in sacred terms.[5] Southerners also had their own vision of a perfected world based on the proliferation of slavery. According to Jack P. Maddex Jr., slaveholders articulated hopes for the gradual perfection of society and the progressive amelioration of slavery.[6] Postmillennialists believed that they alone could bring about the change in the balance of sin that would allow the Second Coming to proceed. Despite the high estimation of human capability undergirding this progressive eschatology, postmillennialists feared the flames of hell as much as their premillennialist contemporaries. Though they believed in the coming conversion of the world, they harbored no illusions that the process would be easy. In the words of historian James H. Moorhead, "If postmillennialists had one foot in the world of steamships and the telegraph, the other was still firmly planted in the cosmos of John's Revelation—a universe where angels poured out vials of wrath."[7] During the Civil War, violence replaced peaceful reform in many minds, giving the war itself a sacred character. Some ministers concluded that only death and destruction could expiate the nation's sins to meet divine satisfaction. The apocalypse was at hand, but this was a postmillennialist end of history, where humans, not God, were responsible for creating the carnage that would bring about Christ's return. Reconstruction convinced the erstwhile prophets of the end times that the thorny problems of human existence had not ended with the war. Postmillennialism did not die, but hopes for an apocalyptic end faded as it became evident that violence only begat more violence.[8]

The late-eighteenth-century rise of postmillennialist thought coincided with a new conception of God as moral governor. According to the latter theology, Christ's death was explained not as a sacrifice to an angry deity in the style of pagan ritual but instead as God's effort to ensure the maintenance of justice in the world. In the antebellum era, God was increasingly seen not as vindictive and illogical, but as compassionate and rational. Providence was recast as divine benevolence, and fears of judgment receded in the face of rising expectations of national redemption. Postmillennialism served as an extension of that doctrine of God. The gradual purification of this world reflected the divine desire to ensure that good would eventually outweigh evil. Both the moral government theory and postmillennialism reflected an increasing tendency in antebellum Americans to view existence as rational. Americans had faith that even the most mysterious of God's ways would be explained in time. As the essays in this volume demonstrate, that assumption was critically tested by the Civil War.[9]

Disagreements continued about the timing of the millennium, yet Americans nearly unanimously accepted that God did intervene in both the universe and human affairs. Since the founding of the nation, Americans had a special obsession with Providence, God's action in the world. It became commonplace to casually invoke the concept in all contexts. Theologians had labored over these ideas for centuries, culminating in precise definitions for different aspects of divine action. By the nineteenth century, clergy distinguished between a general Providence—God's ordering of the universe through natural law—and special providences. This latter category included divine acts in individual events, from the miraculous to the most mundane human actions. And these two categories were intricately connected. In the words of Robert Lewis Dabney, one of the foremost American theologians of the nineteenth century, "the general is only produced by producing all the specials which compose it."[10] In other words, a divine plan governed the entire universe, and that plan was executed through intervention in all events.

As Nicholas Guyatt has argued, it was common in both America and England to take the providential logic a step further, connecting Providence with the destinies of nations as well as individuals. Indeed, God's presence in national actions supplanted all other types of providential speculation, as individual providence came to be viewed as irrational and superstitious. According to Guyatt's model, national providentialism occurred in three guises: judicial, historical, and apocalyptic. The first category referred to God's rewarding or punishing the moral merit of a nation. "Historical providentialism" denotes the belief that God chose "a special role for certain nations in improving the world." And the final category describes the role of humanity in God's strategy for combating evil on a cosmic scale. Americans applied all of these concepts to their own society, forging their national identity around the idea that they had been divinely elected for a special purpose. Furthermore, that purpose intersected with postmillennial aims, as the United States was uniquely situated to possess both the prosperity and the piety necessary to create history's first moral society.[11]

Despite the best efforts of theologians and later scholars to parse the providential and millennial aspects of God's activity, the power of these concepts in antebellum American culture was such that the average believer entertained a vaguely conceptualized but powerfully experienced notion that Providence was behind all occurrences. Application of these ideas was not always consistent, or even coherent, but the following pages show a preoccupation that lies at the heart of nineteenth-century American culture. During the tumultuous years immediately prior, during, and after the unprecedented destruction of the Civil War, these ideas took on a greater importance as Americans struggled to make sense of the great loss, change, and promise of the period.

The latest scholarship on religion in the era demonstrates the pervasiveness of providentialism. Mark A. Noll credits sectional dissonance over Providence, along with biblical debates over slavery, as initiating an American theological crisis. In George C. Rable's recent account of religion in the Civil War, he finds that soldiers on both sides justified their actions throughout the war through references to the divine purpose. Appeal to those same sources also served to answer the hard questions brought up by the war, those questions focusing on death, loss, defeat, and triumph. Through either divine chastisement or reward, providentialism offered the succor of significance to actions that otherwise appeared increasingly bereft of meaning as the war continued. Sean A. Scott echoes these conclusions in his analysis of northern civilian religion during the war. Northerners maintained a vague sense that God controlled events and continued to hold America in esteem. Contradicting Lincoln's admonitions to the contrary in his Second Inaugural Address, northerners continued to venture readings of the will of God, even after the incomprehensible tragedy of the president's assassination. Clergy and laypeople alike construed the death of the nation's figurehead as a sign of divine favor through a "simple faith" that God "could bring good out of evil" and forge an even stronger Christian nation through the process of suffering.[12]

Although most of the scholarly literature focuses on Protestants, American Catholics joined in making these sorts of providential calculations. Catholicism did not split along sectional lines like the major Protestant churches, but Catholics proved just as susceptible to sectional thought as Protestants. Northern Catholics mostly condemned slavery, just as southern Catholics offered support, if often in a more cautious manner than Protestants. For many Irish immigrants in the North, the war represented a path to full acceptance within American culture, but those expectations soured by the time of the July 1863 draft riots in New York. While the Catholic hierarchy and those on the home front became disillusioned with the national government, a shared hope in America's providential destiny continued to unite Protestant and Catholic troops throughout the war, as epitomized by the ecumenical gathering led by Fr. William Corby before the second day of Gettysburg.[13]

Millennial notions steeled Americans to the gritty realities of waging war. The Civil War and emancipation led Frederick Douglass simultaneously to a strong identification with the nation and a corresponding understanding of the war as a moment of apocalyptic transformation. In the words of David W. Blight, wartime suffering represented a "cleansing tragedy" that would atone for the sins of slavery. The Union would then emerge from the fog of war purified and prepared to establish a new epoch. Douglass was not alone in assigning importance of apocalyptic proportions to the events of the early 1860s. James H. Moorhead's pioneering work *American Apocalypse* demonstrates the pervasiveness of postmillennial thought among the northern clergy. Death and destruction signaled only the woes of the coming of the millennium and reminded Americans of their depravity. Thus, the Civil War provided the context for "expunging the sins of the nation and preparing for the American people a victory that would fundamentally alter their relationship to other nations." After spreading American democracy to the world, surely the millennium would begin. Harry S. Stout's moral history of the Civil War shows how millennial energies paralyzed clergymen in the years prior to the war, a paralysis that did not wear off until nearly the war's end, by which time millennialism had transformed into a messianic civic nationalism, baptized in the blood of conflict. And, although theological speculation seems ill-fitted for the battlefield, those embroiled in the carnage firsthand saw millennial purpose in their work. As Chandra Manning argues, Union soldiers were "better prepared to withstand the vicissitudes of war" than were their opponents due to their understanding of the nation's role in the cosmic struggle between good and evil. The Emancipation Proclamation only stoked this motivation, as Union soldiers associated the eradication of slavery with the ultimate purpose of the war. Defeats were necessary setbacks, according to the logic of the era, in the inexorable path toward expunging the sin of human bondage.[14]

By the end of the war, the loss of so many loved ones caused some to question God's role in human affairs. White southerners, in particular, had trouble locating Providence in the widespread devastation of the landscape and in emancipation's revolutionary overturning of the social structure.[15] For most, those doubts faded in time, and God's guidance became evident in the mundane yet again. The same cannot be said for belief in the coming reign of Christ. Postmillennial dreams of effecting God's Kingdom on earth represented one of the more costly casualties of war, at least for several decades until the resurgence of reformist postmillennial thought around the turn of the century. Where visions of utopia fueled reformers' zeal in the antebellum period, efficiency and social control became the procedural virtues of wartime beneficence in elite-dominated ventures like the U.S. Sanitary Commission. According to George M. Fredrickson's classic *The Inner Civil War,* northern intellectuals came to trust the strength of government rather than the might of God to shape American destiny. Orville Vernon Burton's creative synthesis of the nineteenth century asserts that antebellum millennial energies collapsed as the upheavals of war and Reconstruction launched America into a modern age of endemic economic inequality. Drew Gilpin Faust reminds us how the shadow of death loomed over the life of nearly every American in the era. God seemed ever more distant to those who had experienced loss, and many Americans gave up hopes that the Kingdom would be established in this life. Instead, new significance was assigned to the afterlife. The popular 1868 novel *The Gates Ajar,* by Elizabeth Stuart Phelps Ward, exemplified this change by offering both northerners and southerners a comfortable vision of a reunited home in heaven rather than a hereafter filled with uncertainty and the dread of punishment.[16]

By the late nineteenth century, the traumas of the Civil War and the new ideas of Darwinism and historical criticism of the Bible pulled American believers in two opposing theological directions. The otherworldly expectation of a literal return of Christ repelled liberal thinkers who sought to make faith compatible with the new thought. Many of these same thinkers, such as Washington Gladden, had grown up in the context of postmillennialist reform and had no desire to abandon the theological focus on social perfection. Instead of viewing history as the battleground between God and Satan, proponents of a new Social Gospel argued that Christian salvation occurred on both personal and social levels. The politics of the Progressive movement meshed with a resurgent reform-oriented postmillennialism. The Kingdom of God would become realized on earth gradually, through evolutionary means, rather than in some grand cataclysm.[17] Others interpreted the signs of the times as portentous of an imminent apocalypse. The increasingly popular work of John Nelson Darby depicted the Bible as factually reliable and the key to understanding God's future dealings with humanity. By using complex scriptural calculations, Darby found that the Bible revealed the divine plan for history, and soon Christ would return to inaugurate a new era, or dispensation. In this new dispensational premillennialism, history remained a struggle between cosmic forces of good and evil in which humans were powerless to effect meaningful change.[18] Although the fin-de-siècle religious context was increasingly polarized, both extremes demonstrate the lingering importance of millennial thought repackaged to fit the demands of the times.

Yet the entropy of millennial energies took no single path. Some recast divine action as otherworldly, while others continued to trust in Providence to forge change in this world. Some looked to an imminent apocalypse, while others worked to bring about the Kingdom of God on earth. Whereas scholarship until this point has been limited to sketching these transformations in broad strokes, the essays in this volume chronicle several particular manifestations of providential and millennial belief by focusing on reform, war, and emancipation.

The abundance of interpretations found in the historiography reflects the diversity of ways in which Americans understood and deployed millennial thinking in their lives. This volume, drawn from papers presented at a symposium held at Rice University in the fall of 2010, showcases that diversity, demonstrating how millennial and providential ideas took on numerous, competing meanings as Americans worked to make sense of their lives in a period of unprecedented violence and upheaval. This volume uncovers that process by targeting three of the most important themes in the period: reform culture, the search for meaning amid victory and defeat, and the social transformation wrought by emancipation.

Providential thought involves a consideration of the future, and with the opening essay to the volume, Jason Phillips claims that the recent focus on historical memory should be coupled with the study of how historical figures imagined the future, a process he calls cultural prophecy. In what amounts to proposing a new category of historical analysis, Phillips's methodological discussion of cultural prophecy challenges historians to acknowledge how men and women in the past looked to their future. Phillips deploys this model on Edmund Ruffin's 1860 published prophecy of civil war, entitled *Anticipations of the Future,* to explain the anxieties and expectations among southern radicals on the eve of secession.

During the late antebellum period, many reform-oriented Americans looked to the future with tremendous hope rooted in a millennial expectation of national improvement. Robert K. Nelson, Ryan Cordell, Nina Reid-Maroney, and Joseph Moore all speak to the place of providential thinking in antebellum reform. Nelson's study of spirit politics, or a preoccupation among some reformers with "disembodied spirituality," locates a transformation in tactics of reform that coincided with a decline in millennial expectation among Spiritualists. Early Spiritualists sought to transform the world through spiritual practice and expected to usher in utopia on earth, but by the late antebellum period, the more disenchanted generation displaced paradise to the afterlife. This shift led the practitioners of spirit politics to engage in more practical and confrontational means of securing social change. Some Americans viewed the explosion of religion following the Second Great Awakening as evidence of the coming millennium, but Ryan Cordell uses James Fenimore Cooper's prophetic parable *The Crater* to demonstrate how many nineteenth-century Americans lamented the spirit of divisiveness among the exploding number of religious factions. For Cooper, and for many of his readers, the lack of Christian unity was holding back the nation from fulfilling its millennial destiny and instead leading the American people toward a horrifying apocalypse of civil strife. Nina Reid-Maroney asks what a narrative of national millennial destiny would look like when divorced from the American context. She shows how Canadian abolitionists and the fugitive slaves of Dresden, Ontario, modified the American and English national providential narratives to fit the daily work of the mission to fugitive slaves in Canada. Joseph Moore's study of South Carolina Covenanters, a radical, interracial Presbyterian sect, demonstrates the limits of antislavery millennialism in the heart of the proslavery South. Moore shows how black and white coreligionists adopted moderate antislavery appeals rooted in the millennial belief that colonization, in the mind of whites, and emancipation, in the mind of the enslaved, promised an end to the great sin of slavery.

Emancipation did not come without a tremendous degree of violence, and Jennifer Graber and Zachary W. Dresser illustrate how Americans were forced to make sense of both victory and defeat. North and South—and, as Graber demonstrates, East and West—Americans looked to Providence to make meaning of war. Graber's study of the 1862 Dakota War between white settlers in Minnesota and local Indians argues that this conflict fashioned a new providentialism that governed future relationships between western Indians and the federal government. Dresser tackles the particularly thorny providential problems posed by defeat and Reconstruction in an analysis of the Presbyterian Old School. There he finds that orthodox theologians maintained their belief in God's guidance in history only by redefining old categories to fit the problems posed by the postwar world.

Emancipation was undoubtedly the greatest social transformation wrought by the war, and Matthew Harper, Scott Nesbit, and Charles F. Irons reveal how Americans wrestled to understand emancipation in providential terms. Harper focuses on eastern North Carolina to explore how African Americans placed both the promises of freedom and the disappointments of Reconstruction into millennial narratives. Scott Nesbit shares Harper's theme but shows how competing providential narratives of healing through forgiveness and justice through land redistribution were both sundered by the realities of racial violence. Charles Irons challenges historians who understand the African American experience of Reconstruction solely as a process of enhanced autonomy by chronicling patterns of ecclesiastical separation, arguing that racial separation must be understood in conjunction with enduring biracial attempts at integration.

Finally, Edward J. Blum concludes the volume with a sweeping synthesis of providential thinking in Reconstruction and postbellum America. He argues that the postwar period shattered the religious world for nearly every American, requiring a reconstruction of both the polity and of Providence. Americans of all stripes—from southern sharecroppers to northern intellectuals, from Mormons to Ghost Dancers—reconfigured their understanding of God's role in the world, a process that transformed nearly every American religious tradition. Americans understood the workings of God in ways that demonstrate considerable creativity, flexibility, and diversity, but the preoccupation with Providence endured the trial of war and remained a fundamental tool through which Americans understood themselves, their nation, and their world.

Taken together, these essays reveal the ubiquity of providential thought in the era of the Civil War. Americans looked to the future with hope and dread and found comfort in the promise that God was directing the course of history toward holy ends. If we are to understand this era, we must pay close attention to the many ways that Americans looked to the glory of the coming of the Lord. Millennial zeal infused the labor of reformers and explained their successes and failures as progress toward an imminent Kingdom of God. Men and women, North and South, looked to Providence to explain the causes and consequences of both victory and defeat, and Americans, black and white, experienced the shock waves of emancipation as either a long-prophesied jubilee or a vengeful apocalypse. Religion fostered division as well as union, but while the nation tore itself apart and tentatively stitched itself back together, Americans together looked to Providence to make meaning of a world suffering "the fateful lightning of the terrible swift sword."

NOTES

1. Charles Caldwell McCabe to Rebecca McCabe, February 2, 1864, in Frank Milton Bristol, *The Life of Chaplain McCabe, Bishop of the Methodist Episcopal Church* (New York, 1908), 198–201.

2. Daniel Delaney Addison, *Lucy Larcom: Life, Letters, and Diary* (Boston, 1894), 295.

3. Mary Anne Webster Loughborough, *My Cave Life in Vicksburg: With Letters of Trial and Travel* (New York, 1864), 196.

4. William M. McLain, "Letter CCXII: An Exodus in the Nineteenth Century," in *Soldiers' Letters from Camp, Battlefield, and Prison,* ed. Lydia Minturn Post (New York, 1865), 441.

5. Robert H. Abzug, *Cosmos Crumbling: American Reform and the Religious Imagination* (New York: Oxford, 1994).

6. Jack P. Maddex Jr., "Proslavery Millennialism: Social Eschatology in Antebellum Southern Calvinism," *American Quarterly* 31 (Spring 1979): 46–62.

7. James H. Moorhead, "Between Progress and Apocalypse: A Reassessment of Millennialism in American Religious Thought, 1800–1880," *Journal of American History* 71 (December 1984), 524–42, 525.

8. James H. Moorhead, *American Apocalypse: Yankee Protestants and the Civil War, 1860–1869* (New Haven: Yale University Press, 1978).

9. Ibid., 528–29.

10. Robert Lewis Dabney, *Syllabus and Notes of the Course of Systematic and Polemic Theology Taught in Union Seminary, Richmond, Virginia* (Richmond: Shepperson & Graves, 1871), 277.

11. Nicholas Guyatt, *Providence and the Invention of the United States, 1607–1876* (Cambridge: Cambridge University Press, 2007), 5–6; Moorhead, "Between Progress and Apocalypse," 531–32.

12. Mark A. Noll, *The Civil War as a Theological Crisis* (Chapel Hill: University of North Carolina Press, 2006); George C. Rable, *God's Almost Chosen Peoples: A Religious History of the American Civil War* (Chapel Hill: University of North Carolina Press, 2010), 6; Sean A. Scott, *A Visitation of God: Northern Civilians Interpret the Civil War* (New York: Oxford University Press, 2011), 246.

13. On Catholic interpretations of Providence, see Judith Conrad Wimmer, "American Catholic Interpretations of the Civil War" (Ph.D. diss., Drew University, 1979), 234–79; Noll, *The Civil War as a Theological Crisis,* 125–32; Randall M. Miller, "Catholic Religion, Irish Ethnicity, and the

Civil War," in *Religion and the American Civil War,* ed. Miller, Harry S. Stout, and Charles Reagan Wilson, 261–96 (New York: Oxford University Press, 1998); John T. McGreevy, *Catholicism and American Freedom: A History* (New York: Norton, 2003), 68–90; and Rable, *God's Almost Chosen People,* 120–22, 191–92, 265–66, 323–25. On continued Catholic sectionalism, see David T. Gleeson, "'No Disruption of Union': The Catholic Church in the South and Reconstruction," in *Vale of Tears: New Essays on Religion and Reconstruction,* ed. Edward J. Blum and W. Scott Poole, 164–86. (Macon, Ga.: Mercer University Press, 2005).

14. David W. Blight, *Frederick Douglass's Civil War: Keeping Faith in Jubilee* (Baton Rouge: Louisiana State University Press, 1989), 101–21, 114; David W. Blight, *American Apocalypse: Yankee Protestants and the Civil War, 1860–1869* (New Haven: Yale University Press, 1978), 65; Harry S. Stout, *Upon the Altar of the Nation: A Moral History of the Civil War* (New York: Viking, 2006); Chandra Manning, *What This Cruel War Was Over: Soldiers, Slavery, and the Civil War* (New York: Knopf, 2007), 70.

15. For instance, Gertrude Thomas of Savannah wrote in her diary on October 9, 1865: "I did not know until then how intimately my faith in revolution and faith in the institution of slavery had been woven together—true i had seen the evil of the latter but if the *Bible* was right then slavery *must be*—slavery was done away with and my faith in God's Holy Book was terribly shaken. For a time I doubted God" (Ella Gertrude Clanton Thomas, *The Secret Eye: The Journal of Ella Gertrude Clanton Thomas, 1848–1889,* ed. Virginia Ingraham Burr [Chapel Hill: University of North Carolina Press, 1990], 276–77).

16. George M. Fredrickson, *The Inner Civil War: Northern Intellectuals and the Crisis of the Union* (1965; Champaign: University of Illinois Press, 1993); Orville Vernon Burton, *The Age of Lincoln* (New York: Hill and Wang, 2007); Drew Gilpin Faust, *This Republic of Suffering: Death and the American Civil War* (New York: Knopf, 2008), 176–88.

17. George M. Marsden, *Fundamentalism and American Culture* (New York: Oxford University Press, 1980), 48–51; Garry Dorrien, *The Making of American Liberal Theology: Imagining Progressive Religion, 1805–1900* (Louisville: Westminster John Knox, 2001), 266–75, 311–14.

18. Marsden, *Fundamentalism and American Culture,* 51–71.

1

THE PROPHECY OF EDMUND RUFFIN

Anticipating the Future of Civil War History

JASON PHILLIPS

Edmund Ruffin contemplated suicide on October 18, 1859. Anticipating a future of dependence and death, he concluded, "I have lived long enough" and "have no object whatever to strive for." The next day John Brown saved Ruffin's life. Newspapers for October 19 reported a failed insurrection at Harpers Ferry, orchestrated entirely by northern men. Ruffin hoped this proof of Yankee intentions would "stir the sluggish blood of the south." It certainly stirred Ruffin. He dove into the most productive and rewarding year of his life. Determined to watch Brown die, Ruffin made hasty travel plans for western Virginia and by late November was on his "way to the 'seat of war.'" Undaunted when the execution was closed to the public, Ruffin borrowed arms and a uniform from the Virginia Military Institute and marched more than four miles through winter weather to witness it. The event inspired Ruffin to write a novel, his only work of fiction. In less than two months, he finished 416 pages that foretold secession, civil war, and southern independence while the *Charleston Mercury* printed the first chapters in serial form. He titled his book *Anticipations of the Future* and considered it "the most pleasant labor of the kind that I have ever performed."[1]

Ruffin's epiphany yielded a weird book of predictions that defies simple description. Because the story kills thousands of Yankees in every conceivable fashion, it was a work of fantasy and wish fulfillment. Because it spread propaganda before the presidential election, Ruffin's book was campaign literature for the southern Democrats. Because the novel promised southern independence, it was a founding document of Confederate nationalism. Pursuing any of these descriptions yields valuable insights; however, this essay proposes a different approach, a close reading of Ruffin's work as a prophetic text. At first glance, this proposition seems risky. Ruffin opened *Anticipations of the Future* by flatly denying any prophetic power: "Though the writer of the following pages has ventured to indicate the future results of supposed and stated causes, he does not claim to possess any gift of prophecy, or extraordinary political foresight." Speaking to readers through the voice of reason, not God, Ruffin "designed to deduce correct conclusions [about the future] by sound reasoning" instead of relying on miracles or unfettered fantasy. But Ruffin's notification marked his place within, not beyond, a wide spectrum of prophetic thought in nineteenth-century America. Premillennialist Millerites and Mormons, postmillennial evangelicals, utopian perfectionists, Spiritualists, providential boosters of manifest destiny, and secular champions of scientific progress all fixated on the future and hereafter. Indeed, nineteenth-century America was obsessed with the future. Every stripe of prophetic imagination illuminated the past, present, and future in its own shade, coloring history in its hue. But this spectrum of American prophecy, like bands of light, also blended together in imperceptible places and ways. Sharp dichotomies of sacred and secular, religious and scientific, faded in the luminous and liminal world of American prophecy. When Avery Craven judged Ruffin's religion "a strange mingling of reason and faith," he described nineteenth-century American cosmology in general. A close reading of *Anticipations of the Future* as a prophetic text reveals beliefs that created Ruffin's "horizon of expectation," his world of possibilities and projects, before the war came. Stephen Toulmin writes, "Those horizons mark limits to the field of action in which, at the moment, we see it as possible or feasible to change human affairs, and so to decide which of our most cherished practical goals can be realized in fact." Ruffin's most cherished dream was southern independence, which he deemed "the one great idea" of his life. By spreading his prophecy through prose and action, Ruffin tried to form the South's present to his visions of the future. The results were deadly for thousands of Americans, including Ruffin.[2]

Ruffin acted like a prophet and appeared as one to friends, foes, and even himself. Not content to share his vision through prose alone, Ruffin traveled across the South spreading his prophecy and encouraging its fulfillment. In Columbia, South Carolina, Ruffin proselytized secession while the state legislature debated the subject. He circulated secession tracts and pamphlets and publicly debated secession in his hotel lobby. South Carolinians praised him as a prophet of disunion, honored him with a special chair at its secession convention, and serenaded him below his hotel window. Once his work was done in South Carolina, Ruffin spread the word in Georgia and Florida.

Beyond his prose and presence, Ruffin used relics to foment disunion. He famously collected John Brown's pikes at Harpers Ferry and sent one to each southern governor, requesting that the weapons "be placed in the legislative hall and exposed to the view of every visitor." Ruffin believed the relics of insurrection would "serve as a most eloquent and impressive *preacher*" in his absence. After the surrender of Fort Sumter, Ruffin cut a piece from the first Confederate flag flown over the fort and sent shell fragments from the rubble to fellow Virginians, who had not yet seceded.

Northerners noticed how Ruffin borrowed religious practices to agitate for southern nationalism. *Frank Leslie's Weekly* featured a story about him, explaining, "The old man goes from Convention to Convention a political Peter the Hermit, preaching secession wherever he goes." According to legend, Peter the Hermit, a priest from Amiens, sparked the first Crusade by traveling across France prophesying a war to reclaim Jerusalem. Ruffin liked the article so much that he kept a copy in his scrapbook. He compared himself to biblical prophets, especially Jesus Christ. In his diary, Ruffin explained his dichotomous reception in South Carolina and Virginia by paraphrasing Jesus's observation in Mark 6:4 that "a prophet is not without honor, except in his own country."[3]

Religious studies of prophecy can help historians explain how Civil War Americans imagined the future and the impact their visions had on collective perceptions and actions. As an analytical category, prophecy offers historians a temporal partner for memory. Prophecies, like historical memories, address contemporary society by telling stories of another time. As historian Elliott West explains, major events inspire people "to compose a fresh account of themselves that explains, literally, who in the world they are. . . . Such stories become guides and encouragements for living out a newly dreamed existence. Almost invariably they justify possession." West shows how two events, the introduction of the horse and the discovery of gold, inspired new visions of power and liberation among Americans on the Great Plains. In similar fashion, a major event, John Brown's raid, awoke visions of a new future within Edmund Ruffin. His prophecy also justified possession, not of land but of slaves. Religious studies of prophecy can offer historians an interdisciplinary metaphor for studying these socially constructed visions of the future. Civil War historians have focused on how people have remembered the conflict, but Americans anticipated, dreamed, and dreaded the war as intensely as they recalled it. Studying antebellum prophecies about the conflict will place historical memories within the broader timescape of past, present, *and future* that framed people's thoughts, feelings, and actions during the Civil War era. Indeed, histories of the Civil War's future perhaps point to the future of Civil War history. The linguistic turn showed how semantic systems configure reality. Perhaps a temporal turn will reveal how time conceptions order meaning as well. At the very least, this essay suggests how histories of former futures challenge current scholarship on Civil War memory. But Ruffin's prophecy must come before my own.[4]

Before the war was a memory or a fact, it was a prophecy among American foretellers. As Elizabeth Varon has shown, prophets of disunion warned about a horrific, destructive war between North and South since the ratification of the Constitution. How these prophets imagined the conflict shaped public expectations of the war for generations. Statesmen like Henry Clay prophesied disunion to encourage compromise and to channel political discourse until the specter of disunion no longer scared the sections into agreement. But while Varon analyzes prophecies of disunion as political rhetoric, this essay sees prophecies as performances that blended language and action. As political scientist Jack Turner has recently argued, antebellum radicals like Henry Thoreau sponsored "a politics of performing conscience" that not only voiced principles but acted upon them. Turner understands that this "robust" brand of politics forces scholars "to revise traditional notions of what political action is and can be." Beyond studying keywords and rhetoric, historians should emulate religious scholars of prophecy who demonstrate the links between language and action. During the sectional crisis, prophets like Edmund Ruffin and John Brown not only foretold the future, they made it. John Brown's raid failed to free the slaves, but it succeeded in raising sectional tensions, reducing the common ground required for compromise, and thus making secession and war more likely. Likewise at Fort Sumter, Ruffin tried to fulfill his prophecy. Politicians had no alternative but to react in the wake of such prophetic actions. The truism that actions speak louder than words certainly applies to the coming of the Civil War.[5]

In *Anticipations of the Future,* Edmund Ruffin is so certain of his prophecy that he conveys it to readers as a series of newspaper reports from the future. This technique gave Ruffin's future a feeling of inevitability as it appeared in the past tense. Here is his prophecy. The real trouble started in 1864, when William Seward replaced Abraham Lincoln as president. Southern radicals who expected Lincoln to attack slavery directly waited in vain for an excuse to secede. Lincoln was "praise-worthy, and respected for probity, wisdom, and firmness. . . . [V]iewing the Union as a whole, he served its general interest well, and maintained the dignity of the government." William Seward was different. He persuaded the Republican Congress to serve only northern interests. They raised tariffs and improved only northern canals and ports. They commissioned only Yankees as military officers and swelled the ranks with free-labor scum. Meanwhile, Seward packed the Supreme Court with abolitionists who overturned the *Dred Scott* decision in 1866. The value of slavery in the Border South plummeted because runaways knew this administration ignored the Fugitive Slave Law. In diplomacy, the government acknowledged the sovereignty of Haiti and Liberia. Haitians wasted no time sending a minister, "a stout, burly negro, of clumsy frame" who called himself the Duke of Marmalade. The duke professed to be a rich bachelor and courted the "fair daughters of distinguished abolitionists." All this time, southerners shouted but *did* nothing. Without bold action to back their fiery language, southern statesmen looked fierce but fragile to men across the aisle from the North.[6]

In 1867, six states (New York, Ohio, Michigan, Minnesota, Kansas, and California) voted behind closed doors to split in two, thereby adding twelve abolitionist senators and giving Republicans the three-fourths majority needed to abolish slavery. In 1868, Seward won reelection unopposed. These events finally convinced six Deep South states to secede on Christmas Eve 1868. That night South Carolina captured Fort Sumter without a single casualty. Virginia and the Upper South remained in the Union, but they warned the federal government not to tread upon their soil. When Seward sent an army through western Virginia, the Old Dominion repulsed it and seceded. The rest of the South followed, except for Texas.

The Civil War erupted in the summer of 1868. Northern armies of abolitionists invaded the South. William Lloyd Garrison captained one group of seven hundred whites and blacks who sailed five ships to Maryland. Their cargo included ten thousand muskets and five thousand pikes to arm the slaves. "If the plotters had known anything of negro human nature, they might have been sure that any such conspiracy, if confided to as many as fifty negroes, would necessarily be discovered and betrayed." Southerners knew Garrison was coming three days before he arrived. Concealed along the shoreline, defenders fired into Garrison's men after they disembarked. The Yankees who fought back died of gunshot wounds on the beach. Preachers and abolitionist lecturers who came along for the adventure fled for their boats and were stabbed to death in the surf. Southerners singled out Garrison, "the apostle of insurrection and massacre," and hanged him.[7]

A much larger abolitionist army led by Owen Brown, John Brown's son, invaded Kentucky. They butchered men, women, and children "after the infliction of still greater horrors." During their first night back in the South, Negro soldiers deserted in the hope of returning to their former masters. Apparently, escaping to slavery was their motive for enlisting with the enemy. "Like all other northerners, Brown was entirely ignorant of the peculiarities of negro nature, disposition, and character." An army of white Kentuckians surrounded Brown's dwindling force, massacred the Yankees, rounded up the remaining Negros, and returned them to bondage. Kentuckians hanged Brown and twenty-seven officers from a giant oak, leaving their carcasses for the birds. The executioners were a number of Negro prisoners "who, when invited, readily volunteered to perform the . . . duty, and appeared to enjoy" it.[8]

Meanwhile, conditions deteriorated on the northern home front. Without southern commerce, thousands of northern workers lost their jobs and took to the streets. At first they organized hunger processions to show their strength. When the war worsened, forty thousand rioters attacked New York City. The government sent four thousand regulars into the melee. One thousand fought desperately and died in the streets. Three thousand joined the mob. By nightfall the horde controlled the city and torched it. More than a million New Yorkers burned to death under "one raging sea of flame, rising in billows and breakers above the tops of the houses." Thugs attempted the same thing in Philadelphia, but reliable military forces filled the city center and slaughtered thousands by firing artillery shells into the crowds. A Boston mob proved more successful. In addition to plundering the city, they hunted down and lynched prominent abolitionists. In Washington, D.C., the government fled the capital after Virginia and Maryland seceded. The United States set up a temporary seat of power in Albany, while the Confederacy claimed Washington for its own capital. The only noticeable change in the District was a new law expelling free Negroes. Most blacks stayed in the city, however, voluntarily returning to slavery.[9]

On September 20, 1868, the North requested a truce. The terms did not recognize southern independence, but it was an established fact nonetheless. The United States was so crippled by this short, destructive war, that another wave of secession seemed imminent. In time, the West and mid-Atlantic would join the stronger Confederacy, leaving fanatical New England alone, poor, and irrelevant.

To interpret *Anticipations of the Future* as a prophetic text, this essay relies upon a seminal religious study of prophecy, Walter Brueggemann's *The Prophetic*

Imagination. Written in 1978, Brueggemann's work appeared at a time when "scriptural study was completely defined by historical criticism." "For the study of prophetic texts," this meant placing the prophets "in their presumed historical contexts and then extrapolating from that text-in-context to general thematics." By stressing "the constitutive power of imagination," Brueggemann showed how prophetic scripture spread "poetic scenarios of alternative social reality." This argument that prophets not only describe but create alternative worlds through prose, verse, and symbolic action reflected Brueggemann's grasp of Continental philosophy, particularly Paul Ricoeur's *The Rule of Metaphor* published in 1977. Brueggemann was also inspired by liberation theology, which was only beginning to influence North American religious studies at the time. "When one considers the issues of liberation and exploitation," Brueggemann wrote, "the intimate contact between biblical texts of a prophetic sort and matters of social justice, social interest, and social criticism seem to me to be incontrovertible." This political edge to Brueggemann's work and its focus on liberation dovetails beautifully with Civil War history and the visions of masters and slaves.[10]

Brueggemann defines prophetic imagination as a consciousness that topples power and liberates society by spreading alternative perceptions of reality. This definition obviously describes the works of Moses, Jesus Christ, and Martin Luther King Jr. It also depicts the labor of secessionists. The prophetic imagination of Edmund Ruffin and other "apostles of disunion" upended authority and freed a political minority by urging a radical alternative for the future. Please understand, a ring of secessionist prophets did not cause the Civil War. Slavery did, but the prophetic imagination of Ruffin and his colleagues worked beneath causes and nationalisms to shape *how* the conflict was imagined and fought. "The task of prophetic imagination," according to Brueggemann, "is to cut through the despair and to penetrate the dissatisfied coping that seems to have no end or resolution." Secessionists like Ruffin faced the same mission. Heading into the election of 1860, the country despaired of finding a solution to sectionalism. Compromises unraveled. Men of action loathed the stale air of congressional debate. Secessionists imagined a way through the political impasse and beyond southern nightmares of racial equality and political impotency. Their prophecy also "cut through the despair and penetrated the dissatisfied coping" that marked Ruffin's life at this time. Unleashing his hatred of the North, Ruffin watched in amazement while a novel poured out of his soul in mere months. When he completed the book, Ruffin confessed, "I fear this writing of mine . . . would offer to a capable judge, indications of a failing mind." Harpers Ferry inspired a prophecy that gripped Edmund Ruffin until he shared it with the world.[11]

Brueggemann argues that prophets must accomplish three tasks to escape hopelessness and inspire change. First, speak concretely about the newness that awaits society and how it will redefine the world. Second, bring public expression to people's suppressed dreams. Third, offer enduring symbols that contradict and upend prevailing perceptions of reality. Ruffin attempted all three in *Anticipations of the Future.* The novel described the new southern nation vividly and showed how it would change North America and the world. Throughout the book, he redefined America by inverting popular expectations. Slavery, not free labor, proves to be the stable, productive labor system in wartime. Negroes prefer slavery over freedom. New Orleans, not New York, becomes the commercial capital of North America. The Northeast, not the South, is politically ostracized. Washington, D.C., is the capital of the Confederate—not the United—States of America. Ruffin ends the novel with the ultimate inversion: New England, not the South, descends into an economic and political pit similar to conditions in Haiti. Brueggemann finds similar inversions in the prophecy of Second Isaiah. According to Brueggemann, "Inversions may begin in a change of language, a redefined perceptual field, or unaltered consciousness," and they challenge authority by showing people new possibilities. He explains, "When the Babylonian gods have been mocked, when the Babylonian culture has been ridiculed, and when the dethroned king is re-enthroned, then history is inverted." The same can be said about Ruffin's work: when Yankee gods have been mocked, when Yankee culture has been ridiculed, and when masters return to power in Washington, then history is inverted.[12]

Second, Ruffin publicly expressed southerners' suppressed hopes and yearnings. The novel offered a delicious fantasy for Yankee-haters. Ruffin fulfilled southern dreams for prosperity, freedom, and peace, but only after he lashed northerners with a violent reckoning. U.S. soldiers and sailors receive no quarter throughout Ruffin's war. Abolitionists are singled out and lynched not only by southerners but by irate northerners. The prophecy fulfilled secessionists' guarantee of a short war by calling a truce after months of terrible destruction. In the preface, Ruffin promised southerners that the "means for safe and perfect defence, and for full retaliation . . . , for achieving independence, and for securing the subsequent preservation of peace, and unprecedented prosperity" are "as certain as can be any events of the future." His depiction of loyal slaves also expressed white southerners' desires. Masters wanted to believe that slaves preferred bondage, their "natural" condition. As a humanitarian sensibility spread throughout the Atlantic world, southern planters professed loudly that their slaves loved them. This deep yearning is the decisive factor in Ruffin's war: the Confederacy wins because masters, not abolitionists, understand the hearts and minds of black people.[13]

Third, Ruffin spread enduring symbols that contradicted prevailing perceptions of reality. Brueggemann argues that prophets spread hope by borrowing familiar signs from collective memory and projecting them into the future. As he put it, "the prophet's promissory call" cannot rely upon "new symbols for that is wishful [thinking]." Instead the prophet must return to "the deepest memories of this community and activate those very symbols that have always been the basis for contradicting the regnant consciousness." Ruffin's prophecy accomplishes this task by evoking southern memories of the American Revolution, the fundamental symbol of America's challenge to "the regnant consciousness." The eight years when southern statesmen deliberate, form conventions, and appeal to the government for justice echo the decade when colonists sought redress from the king before declaring independence. Ruffin's war mirrors the scale and nature of the War for Independence. Armies of a few thousand campaign across the countryside while companies of minutemen rally to battles. His combat scenes replicate Lexington and Concord: "Single marksmen [fired at the enemy] from every place of concealment," Ruffin imagined, "few missed, and many were of deadly effect. . . . [H]unters . . . were shooting at soldiers for excitement and pleasure as they were accustomed to shoot deer, or bears and wolves." The novel also contains memories of a conflict that Ruffin knew firsthand as a veteran, the War of 1812. In Ruffin's war, armies burn cities and the government abandons Washington, D.C., calamities that Americans had not experienced since their last war with Great Britain. By evoking these historical memories, Ruffin tried to kindle southern nationalism by recalling a time when southern masters forged and defended their sovereignty against mighty, tyrannical powers.[14]

During his pilgrimages for disunion, Ruffin used symbolic actions as well as words to link secession to the American Revolution. Anticipating Lincoln's election, Ruffin sought a southern orator to play the part of Patrick Henry. He chose William Yancey and pointedly asked him in a long, pleading letter, "Will you be the Henry for this impending contest?" Ruffin assured Yancey, "Move in it at once, and I would stake my life on the venture that your success will not be less complete and glorious than that of your great example." As he toured the South, Ruffin wore a Virginia homespun suit, thus exhibiting his support for southern independence by literally wearing it on his sleeve. When Ruffin spotted South Carolina minutemen wearing the blue cockade of the American Revolution, he joined their ranks and had one sewn on his hat. After the South Carolina legislator voted to hold a secession convention, he convinced the editor of the *South Carolinian* to replace the state flag outside his press office with the Fort Moultrie flag as a "symbol of 'the expected Southern Confederacy.'" These actions caution us from reducing Ruffin's prophecy to political rhetoric. Whether consciously or not, Ruffin performed his prophecy throughout the South in ways that echoed Ezekiel's public expressions of his prophecy. Both men risked embarrassment by embodying their prophecies before crowds of strangers. Such activity relates to Jack Turner's description of Thoreau's "performance of conscience" as a "robust conception of political action." Ruffin's performance exuded a vigor and force that belied his age—the work of prophets and revolutionaries was physically demanding. As James Darsey has argued, "Both Old Testament prophecy and the received notion of American virtue . . . are products of a patriarchal theology that explicitly holds virtuous action in opposition to 'effeminacy.'"[15]

Studying the prophecy of Edmund Ruffin suggests how a broader timescape that encompasses past, present, and future can expand Civil War historiography. Ruffin and other Civil War Americans found meaning within their turbulent time by looking forward as well as backward. On a superficial level, each section's projections of the American Revolution can be read as attempts to legitimize secession or sanctify the Union. But beneath the surface of political rhetoric, the search forward and backward in time shows how people used the most relevant symbols, memories, and prophecies to orient a present that radically departed from the rest of experience. In other words, prophecy and memory reinforce each other by addressing a crisis from opposite directions. As Brueggemann puts it, "When the prophet returns, with the community, to those deep symbols, they will discern that hope is not a late, tacked-on hypothesis to serve a crisis but rather the primal dimension of every memory of this community." Varon argues that southerners practiced the same Janus-faced search for meaning during the political crises of the 1790s: "In every instance, Southern intimations of disunion looked backward and forward. They tapped anxieties and resentments about the founding itself, particularly anti-Federalist fears that government consolidation would undermine state sovereignty. But disunion talk also served warning that a new opposition party was consolidating, with a strong base among Southern and Northern agrarians alike, and would challenge the Federalists for control of the national government." The meeting of memory and prophecy gave meaning to the present.[16]

This interplay of remembrance and anticipation expanded as the antebellum press acquired national circulation and telegraph wires crisscrossed the continent. Widely circulated newspapers not only encouraged "imagined communities," they also changed temporality by consolidating dispersed people within a shared present and future. As the sectional crisis intensified, widening communication and transportation networks linked local experience to a national nervous system of anxiety and expectation. Simultaneously Americans could reflect each new development of the crisis through their understanding of past troubles and future forebodings. As Edward Ayers explains, "The Civil War was brought on by people imaginatively constructing chains of action and reaction beyond the boundaries of their own time and space." Newspapers made this process possible, and one of the most influential southern presses, Robert Barnwell Rhett's *Charleston Mercury,* published Ruffin's *Anticipations of the Future.* Here we begin to appreciate why Ruffin wrote the future in the past tense as a series of fictional war reports. When each fictional chapter appeared in the *Mercury,* it looked and sounded exactly like the day's news. Ruffin and Rhett gave readers the impression that they were reading the future. By obscuring distinctions between present and future, news and prophecy, the secessionists molded collective consciousness and political action. By anticipating the future, they made secession and war appear inevitable.[17]

Studying how prophecies and memories combined to shape collective perceptions will deepen our understanding of how Americans anticipated, experienced, and remembered the war. Such work could revise the scholarship of Civil War memory in a number of ways. First, by expanding the Civil War's temporality so that past, present, and future unite to shape meaning, prophecy scholarship challenges memory studies that explain remembrance as a product of the present. Similar to the French scholarship on memory that has defined the field, American work on collective memory "has demonstrated that the objects and strategies of national cultural memory at a given moment tell us just as much, if not more, about the *present doing the remembering* as they do about the *past being remembered.*" This contribution is evident in the way David Blight and other American historians use contextual analysis to show how collective memories of different groups contested for supremacy within a particular postwar milieu. According to this prevailing scholarship, Confederate memory was a highly effective propaganda campaign to cover up and reverse the meaning of the war and its emancipationist legacy. White southerners remembered a sectional conflict instead of a race war by dismissing slavery's place in the war's causes and depicting black southerners as loyal Confederates. Current scholarship frames this memory as a deliberate act of racial domination, a postwar lie created to serve white supremacy. By applying this contextual approach to the memories of subsequent generations, scholars have equated memory with racial ideology and remembrance with a never-ending struggle for contemporary power. As Alice Fahs and Joan Waugh put it, "From 1865 to the present each generation has actively reinterpreted the Civil War to support its own ideological agendas." This view of humanity reduces collective experiences, perceptions, and feelings to acts of domination or resistance that manipulate the past for the present.[18]

Contextual analysis of memories remains valuable, but it should be embedded within a broader temporality that considers how anticipations of the future shape memories of the past. One of the fascinating and important features of Ruffin's prophecy is the fact that he imagined the same wartime roles for southern blacks before the cause was lost, before it even existed. In Ruffin's war, blacks appear as loyal defenders of the Confederacy who prefer slavery. Though his prophecy failed in fantastic fashion, it anticipated white southern memory of the war with striking accuracy. Contextual analysis alone cannot explain the similarities between this antebellum prophecy and postwar portrayal of slaves. Because historians have stressed the malleability of memories, they have deemphasized how the stability of culture gives meaning to events during and after a crisis. In other words, collective memories not only reflect contemporary concerns, they mirror how people perceived the world during an event and, in Ruffin's case, before it. By providing a counterpoint to memory, prophecy can reveal the common terms people relied upon to anticipate, experience, and remember the Civil War. Memory scholars will argue that Ruffin and postwar white supremacists shared a racial ideology that emasculated black men. The political and economic contexts in which Ruffin wrote in 1860 and Thomas Nelson Page wrote a generation later differed greatly, but their works drew meaning from a common white-supremacist ideology that denigrated African Americans. Perhaps, but this point introduces a second way that prophecy studies can enhance memory scholarship.

Just as contextual analysis has strengths and weaknesses as an explanatory tool, so does racial ideology, and memory scholarship has overused it. Historians have employed racism to explain so much of Civil War memory that they run the risk of explaining nothing. Racial ideology always merits attention, but it should be placed within a broader and deeper view of the cultural sensibility that gives it shape and meaning. Obviously race affected collective memory, but that does not explain why prophecies and memories took the form they did. Ruffin (and postwar white supremacists) could have denigrated African Americans by projecting them as unfaithful hordes instead of praising them as loyal dependents. Beyond race (and gender) lies a host of elements that affected how and why Americans prophesied and remembered the Civil War as they did. Among the elements that memory scholars neglect are a culture's epistemology, ontology, theodicy, linguistics, aesthetics, disposition, temporality, and preferred modes of action. In short, ideology, power, and context *contribute* to prophecies and memories; they do not *constitute* them.[19]

Briefly exploring two of these factors—temporality and preferred modes of action—reveals how historians can enrich our understanding of the Civil War by focusing on elements that memory scholars have neglected. Ruffin's analogies to the Revolution and his decision to prophesy through a voice of reason illustrate a modern temporality. His view of time and prophecy contrasts with those of Judeo-Christian prophets who assert authority by projecting God's words and future. As Abraham Heschel explains: "In speaking, the prophet reveals God. This is the marvel of a prophet's work: in his words, *the invisible God becomes audible.*" God's prophets do not reason or prove things; they reveal Providence, God's cosmic hand on the future. As historian Reinhard Koselleck has shown, the Enlightenment created a different type of prophet, the rational prognosticator who forecasts how humanity, not God, will make the future. These more secular prophets apply experience and knowledge from the past to glimpse an empty future in which the "horizon of expectation" is shaped by men. "Henceforth history could be regarded as a long-term process of growing fulfillment which, despite setbacks and deviations, was ultimately planned and carried out by men themselves." Progress replaces Providence as time's trajectory. From its opening sentence, the Declaration of Independence exudes this rational approach to prophecy and history: "When in the course of human events it becomes necessary for one people to dissolve the political bands which have connected them with another, and to assume among the powers of the earth the separate and equal station to which the laws of nature and of nature's God entitle them, a decent respect to the opinions of mankind requires that they should declare the causes which impel them to the separation." In Thomas Jefferson's prophetic imagination, people, not God, make history and seize the future by relying on reason. For Jefferson and Ruffin, the future belongs to reasoning men who act decisively.[20]

This modern temporality ordered society for Jefferson, Ruffin, and other southern patriarchs. Neither Jefferson nor Ruffin deemed African Americans capable of intelligent, rational action. Both Virginians believed that superstition, not reason, governed slaves' thoughts. Masters frequently claimed that their slaves lacked a profound understanding of the past and the future; their bondsmen lived solely in the present. Instead of facing an empty future of limitless possibilities, slaves faced no future at all. By definition, the slave's future belonged to the master. Ruffin went farther than Jefferson, though. In Ruffin's more sectional era, he denied that northerners relied on reason and a boundless future. For Ruffin, there was no clearer sign that the South would prevail in a civil war than his conviction that reason and experience governed southerners, while religious fanaticism controlled the North. When Ruffin observed that "fanatics do not reason," he condemned his enemies to an irrelevant past. This belief supported his prophecy that New England, the Mecca of religious isms, would descend into barbarism. Only reasoning men who learned from history and weighed the consequences of actions (and inaction) could design the future. David Allmendinger explains how Ruffin's faith in reason and independence informed his racism: "His way of assessing human beings eventually confirmed his notions about race, drawing him toward contempt for blacks, in whom he could detect no apparent ambition or independence." Beyond childish slaves, a host of others lived beneath Ruffin's esteem because they lacked self-control and reason. Emotive women, drunken immigrants, fanatical Yankees, and vanishing Indians lived for the past or present but not the future.[21]

Conceiving an open future that is foreseeable through deductive reasoning encouraged Ruffin to favor anticipatory action over reactionary behavior. Southern firebrands like Ruffin are often deemed reactionary men, but Ruffin's prophecy, his agronomy, and his strategy for immediate secession were proactive, not reactive. When a South Carolina crowd serenaded Ruffin, he urged them to secede and provoke a war with the United States because "the first drop of blood spilled" would compel Virginia and every other slave state to South Carolina's side. By acting first, South Carolinians channeled the reactions of others. In *Anticipations of the Future,* Ruffin urged southerners to strike the first blow. He mocked southern Unionists and cooperationists who preferred to wait until northerners violated the Constitution. Such men were "submissionists" in Ruffin's opinion. The term teems with racial and gender connotations, but it *defines* a passive mode of action, not a racial or gender ideology. His novel begins with hundreds of pages that describe the South's tortuous passivity while the North artfully maneuvers toward abolition without giving southerners the clear insult they seek. Once the docile spell is broken, however, the South roars to life and crushes the North in a short, destructive war. Months of aggression accomplish a result that years of hesitancy nearly ruined.

The same proactive mind-set informed by reason and experience guided Ruffin's agronomy. Historians often separate Ruffin the secessionist from Ruffin the agronomist, but the same temporality and assertiveness animated his efforts in both pursuits. In his famous essay on calcareous manure, Ruffin urged farmers to shake their passive dependence on old ways and seize a more prosperous future by saving southern soil from ruin. "If we may venture to leave the sure ground of practical experience," he wrote, "and look forward to what is promised by the theory of the operation of calcareous manures, we must anticipate future crops far exceeding what have yet been obtained." As an advocate of "book farming," Ruffin believed that planters who read the latest agricultural science and applied experimental practices on their plantations would revive the soil, yield greater crops, and thus become masters of a more prosperous future. Farmers who distrusted the latest knowledge enslaved themselves to customs that doomed the land. In agriculture and politics, Ruffin dreamed of southern regeneration through independent reason and proactive agency.[22]

When Confederate defeat shattered his prophecy, it threatened Ruffin's selfhood. As scholar David Carr explains, "The sense we make, not only of ourselves but also of our world and our relations with others, is derived more from our projected future than from the past." Because expectations precede all events, even unexpected ones, what people dread or dream about the future preconditions their perceptions and memories. Projects and possibilities structure our life story, and Edmund Ruffin embodied this point. His prophetic imagination shaped his reality by presupposing the war's scale, decisive factors, and outcomes. The alternative reality he expressed in *Anticipations of the Future* affected how Ruffin interpreted events and acted during the conflict. When defeat erased Ruffin's future, it radically redefined his life's work. He told Yancey before secession and war, "I would stake my life on the venture," and he did. Defeat robbed Ruffin of his anticipated future as a founding Confederate and prophet of southern independence. The surrender of the Confederacy left Ruffin a frail old man who burdened his loved ones. Weeks later, in June 1865, Ruffin's contempt for dependence mixed with his proactive bent to form a lethal combination. Unwilling to live as a cumbrance to his children and a subject to Yankee rule, Ruffin took control and made his future. He prophesied southern ascendancy one final time and shot himself.[23]

NOTES

1. William Kauffman Scarborough, ed., *The Diary of Edmund Ruffin*, vol. 1, *Toward Independence, October, 1856–April, 1861* (Baton Rouge: Louisiana State University Press, 1972), 348 (first and second quotations), 349 (third quotation), 361 (fourth quotation), 413 (fifth quotation).

2. Edmund Ruffin, *Anticipations of the Future: To Serve as Lessons for the Present Time* (Richmond: J. W. Randolph, 1860), vi (first quotation), vii (second quotation); Avery Craven, *Edmund Ruffin, Southerner: A Study in Secession* (New York: Appleton, 1932; Baton Rouge: Louisiana State University Press, 1991), 34. Reinhart Koselleck created the term *Erwartungshorizonten,* "horizons of expectation," to explain a society's former futures in *Futures Past: On the Semantics of Historical Time,* trans. Keith Tribe (New York: Columbia University Press, 2004). Stephen Toulmin, *Cosmopolis: The Hidden Agenda of Modernity* (New York: Free Press, 1990), 1; Ruffin quoted in Craven, *Edmund Ruffin,* 194.

3. Ruffin quoted in Craven, *Edmund Ruffin,* 178 (first quotation), 179 (second quotation), emphasis added; *Frank Leslie's Weekly,* quoted ibid., 203; Scarborough, ed., *The Diary of Edmund Ruffin,* 1:505.

4. Elliott West, *The Contested Plains: Indians, Goldseekers, and the Rush to Colorado* (Lawrence: University Press of Kansas, 1998), xxiii. Writing the history of the future has its own rewards and challenges (committing to a single verb tense is difficult), but this work must be done if we hope to understand how a period and culture felt to the people who lived it. As an analytical category, prophecy links religious studies to history by showing how the prophetic imagination of the Civil War era shaped American thoughts and actions about a host of things, including politics, economics, society, and war. As such, my work joins an ongoing effort by historians to combine nineteenth-century religious history with cultural, intellectual, and political history of the period. In addition to Koselleck's work, scholarship that proposes histories of the future include Jon Cowans, "Visions of the Postwar: The Politics of Memory and Expectation in 1940s France," *History and Memory* 10, no. 2 (1998): 68–101; Roxanne Panchasi, *Future Tense: The Culture of Anticipation in France between the Wars* (Ithaca, N.Y.: Cornell University Press, 2009); and Barbara Adam, "History of the Future: Paradoxes and Challenges," *Rethinking History* 14, no. 3 (2010): 361–78.

5. Elizabeth R. Varon, *Disunion! The Coming of the American Civil War, 1789–1859* (Chapel Hill: University of North Carolina Press, 2008); Jack Turner, "Performing Conscience: Thoreau, Political Action, and the Plea for John Brown" *Political Theory* 33, no. 4 (2005), 448 (first quotation), 449 (second and third quotations), 451 (fourth quotation); Ronald G. Walters, *The Antislavery Appeal: American Abolition after 1830* (Baltimore: Johns Hopkins University Press, 1976), 25–33.

6. Ruffin, *Anticipations of the Future,* 8 (first quotation), 55 (second quotation), 56 (third quotation).

7. Ibid., 247 (first quotation), 249 (second quotation).

8. Ibid., 254 (first quotation), 258 (second quotation), 264 (third quotation).

9. Ibid., 295.

10. Walter Brueggemann, *The Prophetic Imagination,* 2nd ed. (Minneapolis: Fortress, 2001), ix (first, second, and third quotations), x (fourth and fifth quotations), xi (sixth and seventh quotations); Paul Ricoeur, *The Rule of Metaphor: Multi-disciplinary Studies of the Creation of Meaning in Language,* trans. Robert Czerny (Toronto: University of Toronto Press, 1977). For liberation theology, see Gustavo Gutierrez, *A Theology of Liberation: History, Politics and Salvation,* trans. John Eagleson and Caridad Inda (London: Orbis, 1973).

11. "Apostles of disunion" comes from Charles B. Dew, *Apostles of Disunion: Southern Secession Commissioners and the Causes of the Civil War* (Charlottesville: University of Virginia Press, 2001). Brueggemann, *The Prophetic Imagination,* 3, 63 (second and third quotations), Scarborough, ed., *The Diary of Edmund Ruffin,* 1:416. For the political climate of 1860, see William W. Freehling, *The Road to Disunion,* vol. 2, *Secessionists Triumphant, 1854–1861* (New York: Oxford University Press, 2007).

12. Brueggemann, *The Prophetic Imagination,* 3, 63, 74 (quotations).

13. Ruffin, *Anticipations of the Future,* ix. For an interpretation of Ruffin's novel as an act of wish-fulfillment, see Fred Hobson, "'Anticipations of the Future'; Or the Wish-Fulfillment of Edmund Ruffin," *Southern Literary Journal* 10, no. 1 (Fall 1977): 84–91.

14. Brueggemann, *The Prophetic Imagination,* 64; Ruffin, *Anticipations of the Future,* 186; Michael Kammen, *Mystic Cords of Memory: The Transformation of Tradition in American Culture* (New York: Knopf, 1991). Jack Temple Kirby notes that "the first Ruffin 'reform' then was the promotion of Virginia's history, wellspring of place pride," when Ruffin became a founding member of the Historical and Philosophical Society of Virginia. In the early 1850s, Ruffin drafted "The Blackwater Guerilla," a forty-three-page Revolutionary War story. This early attempt at historical fiction may have influenced the battle scenes in *Anticipations* (see Edmund Ruffin, *Nature's Management: Writings on Landscape and Reform, 1822–1859,* ed. Jack Temple Kirby [Athens: University of Georgia Press, 2000], xix).

15. Craven, *Edmund Ruffin,* 191 (first and second quotations), 196 (third quotation); Turner, "Performing Conscience," 449; James Darsey, *The Prophetic Tradition and Radical Rhetoric in America* (New York: New York University Press, 1997), xi.

16. Brueggemann, *The Prophetic Imagination,* 64. Note how Brueggemann argues that a hopeful disposition is deeply rooted within the prophet's culture; it is not propaganda or ideology fabricated for current events. Moreover, collective memory supports prophecy by reminding society of its primal sensibilities during a crisis. Here Brueggemann places prophecy within a broader timescape and a deeper sensibility than most historians consider when studying historical memory. Varon, *Disunion!,* 33.

17. Benedict Anderson, *Imagined Communities: Reflections on the Origin and Spread of Nationalism* (London: Verso, 1983); Edward L. Ayers, *What Caused the Civil War? Reflections on the South and Southern History* (New York: Norton, 2005), 141.

18. Panchasi, *Future Tense,* 4; David W. Blight, *Race and Reunion: The Civil War in American Memory* (Cambridge: Harvard University Press, 2001); Alice Fahs and Joan Waugh, eds., *The Memory of the Civil War in American Culture* (Chapel Hill: University of North Carolina Press, 2004), 4. Other historians have voiced the same criticism of memory scholarship. Fitzhugh Brundage warned that "scholars of memory also need to strive for precision in their description of historical memory and its practical effects, lest historical memory become little more than a synonym for ideology," in "Contentious and Collected: Memory's Future in Southern History," *Journal of*

Southern History 75, no. 3 (August 2009): 752–53. Stuart McConnell has worried that "studies of historical memory so often avoid the analytical forest to tend to monographic trees" (see his essay "The Geography of Memory," in *The Memory of the Civil War in American Culture,* ed. Fahs and Waugh, 265). For a brilliant critique of the new cultural history that encompasses memory scholarship, see Daniel Wickberg, "What Is the History of Sensibilities? On Cultural Histories, Old and New," *American Historical Review* 112, no. 3 (June 2007): 661–84.

19. Wickberg, "What Is the History of Sensibilities?," 678.

20. Abraham J. Heschel, *The Prophets,* Colophon ed. (New York: Harper and Row, 1962), 1:22; Koselleck, *Futures Past,* 206; Thomas Jefferson, *The Portable Thomas Jefferson,* ed. Merrill D. Peterson (New York: Penguin, 1975), 235.

21. Ruffin, *Anticipations of the Future,* 281; David F. Allmendinger Jr., *Ruffin: Family and Reform in the Old South* (New York: Oxford University Press, 1990), 22.

22. Craven, *Edmund Ruffin,* 194 (first quotation); Edmund Ruffin, *An Essay on Calcareous Manures,* 5th ed. (Richmond: J. W. Randolph, 1852), 189; William M. Mathew, *Edmund Ruffin and the Crisis of Slavery in the Old South: The Failure of Agricultural Reform* (Athens: University of Georgia Press, 1988).

23. David Carr, Review of *Futures Past,* by Koselleck, *History and Theory* 26, no. 2 (1987): 198; Craven, *Edmund Ruffin,* 191.

2

SPIRIT POLITICS

Radical Abolitionists and the Dead End of Spiritualism

ROBERT K. NELSON

On June 30, 1858, abolitionist Parker Pillsbury wrote William Lloyd Garrison and readers of the *Liberator* that he had "just returned from attending one of the largest and most important Reformatory Conventions ever held in this or any other country." In his report on the "Free Convention" held at Rutland, Vermont, Parker praised the "character and quality" and the "large brains and full hearts" of the convention participants. "The most numerous class" among these participants, he noted, were Spiritualists. Spiritualism had burst on the American scene a decade earlier, quickly attracting thousands of adherents who believed that communication and communion with the spirits of the dead was now possible. Devotees of the new religion had organized the convention to explore what they considered the pivotal role that it was playing in the various radical, perfectionist reform efforts of the day. All of the major efforts received attention during the convention: abolitionism, marriage reform, land reform, free trade, temperance, phrenology. In his letter to Garrison, Pillsbury praised the convention and the Spiritualists' perfectionist ambitions, declaring that "no convention ever held in America could have had more Millennial hope and promise in it than this," and he expressed confidence that that "hope and promise" would translate into real change: the "Convention will have a signal effect, not only upon Vermont, but also upon the whole nation."[1]

This upbeat public report on the Rutland convention was very much at odds with the frustration Pillsbury vented during the convention itself. Asked to speak on the subjects of slavery and abolitionism, Pillsbury began his speech to the convention with a rant protesting what he considered the pointlessness of what he had heard from the many Spiritualist speakers. "It appears to me," he complained, "that we have been compelled to listen to pretty long harangues, coming from this world or the other, and not always of any great practical interest to the objects of this Convention." Pillsbury did not mince words in expressing his doubt that Spiritualism had anything particularly useful to contribute to the cause of radical reform. "I will not become so enraptured with anticipations [of the heavens offered by Spiritualists] as to allow my ears to be stopped or my heart hardened against the cries and wailings of four millions of slaves," he declared. Talking ad nauseum about disembodied spirits was unconscionable when "we have vastly more important business than settling the condition of our friends in the future; and there are in our country four millions of *living* bodies" in bondage. Throughout his career, Pillsbury condemned the church as an impediment to perfectionist reform, and at Rutland, Spiritualism became the latest target for his ire against institutionalized religion. He ended his talk as he began, complaining that he was "out of patience" when "hour after hour" of the convention was taken up by Spiritualists and trance speakers, the latter of whom he derisively characterized as "lisping girls."[2]

On the one hand, we see Pillsbury applauding Spiritualism's spiritual aspirations, so pregnant with "Millennial hope and progress," on the other criticizing the movement in the language of political expediency ("practical interests" and "important business"). His schizophrenic attitude exemplifies what had always been a persistent tension in radical abolitionist thought between practical politics and utopian perfectionism. During the 1850s, the advent of Spiritualism helped amplify that tension to the breaking point among some Garrisonian abolitionists. Spiritualism drew from, even as it reworked, some of the same religious currents that sustained Garrisonian abolitionists like Pillsbury, including perfectionism—the conviction that men and women were capable of leading sinless lives and achieving moral perfection—and millennialism, the belief that they might play active, positive roles in the great cosmic drama rather than being mere spectators watching it unfold. Many Spiritualists conflated their new religion and radical reform. They insisted that Spiritualism was the missing element that would finally usher in the moral revolution for which radical reformers had spent decades fighting. This claim helped push Pillsbury and many other abolitionists to rethink the extent to which radical religious practice and radical reform activism abetted one another. It led them to question not just the political efficacy of Spiritualism per se but of "spirit" and spirituality more generally. Spiritualism became a flashpoint that led many Garrisonian abolitionists to reconsider a politics infused with spirituality and to increasingly temper their perfectionism and millennialism with political pragmatism.

In the scholarship on Spiritualism, one of the driving issues has been the religion's relationship with radical reform. How closely linked were the two movements? Did Spiritualism energize or deplete reform activism? The scholarship has come no closer to a resolution on these questions than Pillsbury did in 1858. Some historians, particularly those like Ann Braude and Molly McGarry who have focused on issues of women's rights, gender, and sexuality, have argued that Spiritualism fueled radical activism and helped sustain progressive politics both before and after the Civil War. Other historians have instead emphasized the hierarchical, conservative, and even reactionary aspects of Spiritualism. R. Laurence Moore and Bret E. Carroll each argue that Spiritualists sapped reformist energies by insisting that peace and justice would be realized in the afterlives regardless of what happened here on earth, thus robbing reform of any urgency. Robert S. Cox argues that Spiritualist politics were by no means exclusively reformist; Spiritualism found many enthusiastic adherents among the opponents of radical reform whose politics were reactionary and racist. Taken together, this scholarship reveals that Spiritualism's impact upon reform was anything but simple or consistent. For some nineteenth-century Spiritualists, it helped to generate, energize, and sustain a commitment to fight for radical social change. For others, it attenuated that commitment, redirecting time and resources into religious practice that otherwise might have been directed to reform. For many other Spiritualists—whether they were committed, indifferent, or hostile to reform—the religion did little or nothing to change their politics.[3]

The political polyvalence of Spiritualism directs us not to ask whether the religion abetted or undercut reform but to analyze the often heated debates between Spiritualism's proponents and critics within particular reform movements about the religion's political implications. Surprisingly, the relationship between Spiritualism and abolitionism has received very little sustained attention. With very rare exceptions, Spiritualism has received only the most glancing notice in scholarship on abolitionism, most often in biographies of abolitionists who sympathized with or practiced Spiritualism. For sure, almost all of the significant studies on Spiritualism consider antislavery at least in passing. But as yet no one has analyzed in any depth the conflicts and arguments that Spiritualism precipitated among abolitionists, particularly among Garrisonian abolitionists who were more likely to be drawn to Spiritualism than some of their more moderate antislavery colleagues. The debates among the Garrisonians are especially interesting and revealing because they involved questions of strategy, tactics, ideology, and spirituality—fundamental questions about the relationship between what they believed and what they did as reformers. What role did spirituality and religion play in effecting radical social change? Could they be translated into practical reform strategies? How exactly? Reform-minded Spiritualists emphatically insisted that the religion would prove instrumental in realizing radical social change. Others found these claims spurious; worse yet, these critics insisted that Spiritualism was ultimately damaging to abolitionism inasmuch as it substituted naive wishful thinking for more practical and effective strategies. The debate between abolitionist proponents and critics of Spiritualism brought into relief and amplified an ideological and strategic split within their ranks. The proponents renewed their commitment to strategies from the past that were grounded in a millennial faith in the power of spirituality and morality; the critics insisted upon exploring more pragmatic strategies and tactics.

Garrisonians debated Spiritualism intensely because it hit so close to home, involving core articles of faith that had helped shape their reform strategies and sustain their political commitment for decades. As they looked at Spiritualism, in many respects it was like looking in a mirror: they could see many of their politicized beliefs reflected back at them. That reflection, however, was far from perfect. It was distorted in ways that could sometimes be compelling but could also be disquieting. In Spiritualism, they saw magnified the faith they had placed in spirituality as a means of achieving revolutionary social and political change. By spirituality, I'm specifically referring to a recurrent preoccupation among many radical abolitionists with liberation from the material body, with the capacity of men and women to manifest themselves as pure soul. The most egregious evils of the nineteenth-century Atlantic world—racial slavery, the institutional subordination of women to men, international war—were rooted in bodily distinctions of race and sex and nation. Those evils might be eradicated if blacks and whites, women and men, Americans and foreigners could transcend their bodily differences, if they could relate to one another as undifferentiated and equal spirits. Usually this aspiration to become a disembodied spirit was clearly metaphoric; occasionally it was earnestly metaphysical. This preoccupation with disembodied spirituality and this formulation of its social implications is a leitmotif running through antebellum radical reform, a facet of the reform thought that I label *spirit politics.*

In its simplest and most powerful formulation, spirit politics offered an idiom for imagining and exploring the revolutionary social and political change that radical reformers so desperately wanted. As a number of historians, particularly Robert H. Abzug and Lewis Perry, have demonstrated, radical abolitionism emerged from and in turn further fueled profound religious innovations. Abzug argues that antebellum reform generated nothing less than a "rethinking [of] the basic theological and social foundations of Western culture." He characterizes antebellum reformers as "religious virtuosos" who engaged in "metahistorical tinkering" with the teleology of the cosmos; they first questioned and ultimately cast aside the traditional sources of authority in Christianity—clergy and the Bible—and sought to rebuild religion and theology, earth and heaven anew. Perry finds abolitionism to have been just as visionary and utopian, motivated by a desire to destroy all earthly institutions that usurped God's authority over man. While slavery was the most egregious of these institutions, the abolitionists' mission to restore the government of God led some of them to attack other institutions—church, human government, even organized antislavery societies—as well. Both Abzug and Perry stress that the millennial and utopian goals of abolitionism oriented abolitionists to rethink personal relationships. (Abzug suggests that reformers "made it their business to clarify the ways in which the most personal and most cosmic issues interconnected"; Perry that abolitionists sought to "establish new, noncoercive styles in human relationships.")[4] Spirit politics was one such reformulation—a particularly powerful one that signified the abolitionists' desire to establish godly, egalitarian, and spiritually satisfying relationships with other men and women free of the taint of the unrighteous authority, not just of institutions but of the raced and sexed earthly body as well.

We see hints of abolitionists' preoccupation with disembodied spirituality in the numerous assertions in their letters that despite being physically separated from one another, they were united in spirit. In 1843, William Lloyd Garrison voiced this aspiration in a letter to Henry C. Wright, who was then living abroad. Though their separation was a "severe trial," Garrison told Wright, it was not "incompatible with a unity of the spirit." Frederick Douglass expressed the same sentiment in a letter to Amy Post, writing her that "pleasures abroad do not turn my spirit from home." While he wished he could see her in person, he believed that "in the absence of this we may commune with our absent through the mysterious agency of thought and spirit." Radical abolitionists imagined connecting with friends and colleagues through spirit. As Garrison told another colleague, "In imagination, I am with you all, continually; for I hail you as kindred spirits." We should not dismiss the use of such language as cursory or shallowly colloquial. This language conveyed an earnest and heartfelt aspiration to connect soul to soul. These abolitionists believed that letters might serve as a proxy for their souls. In many ways, letters were a preferable way of communicating because they liberated mind and spirit from the physical body. As Ralph Waldo Emerson wrote in his 1841 essay "Friendship": "To my friend I write a letter, and from him I receive a letter. That seems to you a little. It suffices me. It is a spiritual gift worthy of him to give, and of me to receive. It profanes nobody. In these warm lines the heart will trust itself, as it will not to the tongue." Many radical abolitionists would have agreed with Emerson, preferring—in the abstract if not always in reality—disembodied warm lines to the embodied tongue.[5]

Some reformers attempted to apply this aspiration to spiritual disembodiment to level hierarchical relationships. Theodore Dwight Weld's courtship of Angelina Grimké was a particularly blunt application of spirit politics. Courting a champion of woman's rights who had argued that marriage was an institutional means for men to oppress women, Weld's strategy was to approach Grimké not as a woman but as a disembodied, genderless spirit. He fell in love with her, he told her, "not [as] a Brother nor a Sister spirit but [as an] unimbodied spirit with none of the associations or incidents of the physical nature. . . . I felt as tho *communion with your spirit* was a *law* and a *necessity* of my being." That he knew and loved her sexless soul rather than her female body was the dominant theme of his love letters. At moments Weld verged on expressing distaste and disgust with the fact that she had a sex, that she was a woman and not just a sexless spirit. The thought of her sex, her womanhood, was "an unwelcome intruder, of which the mind instinctively and instantly rids itself, feeling it to be a disturbing force, a *felt* non conductor, intercepting the progress of the soul toward the spirit that draws it and a veil dimming its vision of the loved one." Henry C. Wright expressed a similar conception of pure marriage as a communion of souls. "No man can be what he was designed to be, till, by marriage, the spirit of a woman has entered into him, to refine, beautify and strengthen his peculiar nature, and assimilate it to the divine," he declared. Likewise "No woman can be what she was designed to be, till the spirit of a man had entered into her, to purify, elevate and adorn her peculiar nature." For these abolitionists, true marriage was a union of souls and, in their most radical and politically self-conscious formulations, a union of unsexed—and thus equal—souls.[6]

Some white radical abolitionists imagined using spirit to transcend the divisions of race as well as those of sex. Sarah Grimké, for instance, asked Sarah Douglass, an African American Quaker, to explain how racial prejudice felt, telling her that she desired that "thro' the grace of God, my soul may be in your soul's stead." Grimké longed for deep spiritual empathy where she did not merely feel for African Americans who experienced the agonizing effects of racial prejudice but actually shared in that experience herself through an empathetic identification, collapsing the racial divide by connecting soul to soul. Abolitionist Thomas Earle expressed this same aspiration for spiritual communion across the boundaries of the raced body. "We must learn to put our stead in the souls of the poor African," he suggested, to "taste and drink and feel his wrongs." After being convicted of grand larceny for trying to ferry slaves from Missouri to the free state of Illinois, George Thompson reported that he went to prison "with cheerfulness" knowing that they could only imprison his body—"my spirit they cannot confine, my thoughts they cannot chain"—and that there he would be "a partaker of the *slaves'* sufferings." For abolitionists, spirit politics was at once an end and a means; it was simultaneously a figurative idealization of a postmillennial world of social equality and harmony and a strategy for realizing that world.[7]

Spiritualism reiterated, amplified, and refashioned this trope in abolitionist thought. Spiritualists claimed to have discovered the means to satisfy the desire to connect soul to soul that radical abolitionists had so passionately imagined in their letters and writings. Spiritualists believed that the physical body was not as nearly as formidable a barrier separating souls as some abolitionists feared. Far from it. For some Spiritualist mediums, the body became a tool for spiritual communion. Trance speakers and writing mediums could temporarily cede portions or the whole of their bodies to other souls, channeling those spirits and enabling them to communicate wisdom from beyond the grave. For other mediums, their bodies became little more than clothing for their souls that they could take off and put back on almost at will. These mediums could free their souls from their bodies, leaving them behind as they communed with spirits in the spiritual spheres—the heavens of the many afterlives of Spiritualist theology. In short, the liberation from embodiment that radical reformers envisaged in their writings was a central component of Spiritualist religious practice. The divisions of gender, race, space, and even time and death were attenuated, if not obliterated, in Spiritualist practice when, for instance, young white female mediums channeled long-dead male Indian chiefs.

What had been implicit, inchoate, and metaphoric in spirit politics was in Spiritualism made explicit, systematic, and literal. The abolitionists' language about communing spiritually with one another voiced a sincere and serious spiritual and social aspiration, a desire so visionary and utopian that it never was nor could be fully satisfied. Yet however earnest, this language was clearly figurative. There was nothing figurative in the spiritual communions Spiritualist mediums claimed to regularly accomplish. One of the foundational texts of Spiritualism, Andrew Jackson Davis's *The Principles of Nature, Her Divine Revelations, and a Voice to Mankind,* described a scientific process that enabled Davis to leave his body to commune with the spirits of the spiritual spheres. The procedure to accomplish this feat was more mechanistic than mystic. It required a two-person team: a magnetizee, or clairvoyant, and a magnetizer, or manipulator. The two would sit facing one another. The manipulator would perform a series of movements to magnetize the clairvoyant, placing him in a trance state. In this trance state, Davis was said to have actually accomplished what some radical abolitionists hoped to do imaginatively or figuratively: he liberated his soul from earthly, corporeal materiality, enabling him to commune intimately with others' spirits. His "mind . . . entirely freed from the sphere of the body," he temporarily became a disembodied spirit himself who could travel to the "spiritual spheres" inhabited by the spirits of humans who had died. While Davis's soul was away from his body communing with the spirits, his partner in this exercise functioned as a life-support system, sustaining Davis's empty body until his spirit returned.[8]

Displacing his materiality on to the magnetizer, Davis became all spirit. In this state, he could visit the five spiritual spheres. Davis revealed that after death each and every man and woman would be reborn in the second sphere, where they would become more spiritually enlightened before dying again to be reborn in the third sphere. This cycle of spiritual growth, death, and rebirth would repeat until a spirit reached the final, sixth sphere that orbited the "great Spiritual Sun of the Divine Mind." If radical reformers had not been yet able to realize a postmillennial world of ubiquitous peace and love on earth, Spiritualism assured them that they would find it in the afterlives. In the spiritual spheres, there existed no injustices, no wrenching social conflict. There "societies are made perfect" with all spirits united together through "a unity of feeling" and "a universal love"; there "all spirits are engaged in loving their neighbors, and advancing their welfare."[9]

The cosmology of Spiritualism literalized the connection between disembodiment, sinlessness, and sociality that had been imagined by radical reformers. As Davis moved from the second through the sixth spheres, the progressive perfection of the societies of each sphere was registered and produced by the increasing disembodiment of the spirits there. As beings moved through the five spiritual spheres, they gradually shed all bodily materiality to become pure soul. "The nearer they approach the Fount of purity," Davis reported of the spirits, "the more transparent they become, and the more do their inhabitants appear to exist as it were without body and without external and artificial habiliments." In the spiritual spheres, bodies became difficult, even impossible to see. Moving through the spheres, Davis increasingly found that the "outer body is beyond my perception, and I only see well-constituted and living spirits." As they shed their bodies, spirits became increasingly undifferentiated from one another. Social harmony was achieved through something more concrete than the spiritual communion radical reformers imagined. In the spheres, spirits literally united with one another, fusing together to such an extent that Davis had difficulty distinguishing them from one another. He reported that in the spiritual spheres, men and women "are so perfectly conjoined one with another, and their mutual affections are so absorbing and penetrating, that it requires a high degree of discernment to make a distinction between them." The social equality and spiritual communion that radical reformers had aspired to realize and imagined achieving through spirit politics were realized in the spiritual spheres.[10]

Given how much some abolitionists could see of their own spirit politics reflected back at them in Spiritualist theology and cosmology, it is little wonder that many of them would gravitate to the new religion and see it as the powerful ally they had once hoped to find in the Christian churches. The mainstream Christian denominations had all failed to embrace abolitionism. Indeed, more often than not they had been hostile to it, leading many radical abolitionists to "come out" from those corrupted churches. Spiritualism seemed to offer them an opportunity to come back in to a new religious practice, one that appeared to many to merge their sacred beliefs and their social agenda.

While many radical abolitionists sympathetically investigated or actively practiced Spiritualism—among them William Lloyd Garrison, Adin Ballou, the Grimké sisters, Henry C. Wright, Thomas Wentworth Higginson, and Sojourner Truth—arguably the most devout Spiritualist among leading radical abolitionists was Isaac Post. A resident of Rochester, New York, Post and his wife, Amy, had been active abolitionists since the late 1830s. They were founding members of the Western New York Anti-Slavery Society, close friends and supporters of many prominent abolitionists (Douglass, Garrison, and Henry C. Wright among them), and "station masters" who sheltered fugitives escaping on the Underground Railroad. Devout Quakers, they left their Hicksite meeting in the mid-1840s after being pressured by their fellow Hicksites to moderate their abolitionist activism. While they helped form a local meeting of the decidedly reform-oriented Congregational Friends, they soon became ardent Spiritualists as well. When in the spring of 1848 two young sisters whom the Posts knew heard rappings in a house in Hydesville, New York—an episode that would launch the modern Spiritualist movement—the Posts were among the first investigators on the scene. Believing the raps to be of spiritual origin, they were quick to impress the movement in the cause of reform. Isaac became a medium himself, channeling messages from the spiritual spheres. In 1852, he published a collection of messages from famed politicians, reformers, religious leaders, and thinkers such as Thomas Jefferson, Margaret Fuller, and Voltaire in a volume entitled *Voices from the Spirit World*.[11]

Voices from the Spirit World was replete with claims about the importance of Spiritualism to radical social change. All of the dead luminaries who took control of Post's hand urged reform. If they had not been reformers in life, they had become so in the spheres. Their continued spiritual progress demanded that they repent their earthly sins by aiding those still "in the body" to do better. While all were grateful to be in the heavenly spiritual spheres, some were happier than others. The earthly sins of some had cost them dearly. This was particularly true of those spirits who had been slaveholders, none more so than John C. Calhoun. Upon arriving in the spirit world, Calhoun's spirit told Post that he was "surprised" that he did not find himself among "those whose characters I had most admired." They were "far away," "in a far happier condition," while Calhoun found himself in a degraded state, lamenting that "mine is a comparatively low condition." "I should have been a leader in good, instead of evil," he now realized. "I should have been foremost in promoting liberty, instead of slavery." To make amends for his sins, Calhoun's spirit longed to broadcast his newfound wisdom about the evils of slavery—his newfound abolitionism—and convince his fellow southerners to emancipate their slaves. If they could "hear these truths from me . . . methinks they would listen, and . . . I could induce them to leave the evil of their ways, and do works meet for repentance." The spirit of George Washington communicated this same desire.

Since his death a half century earlier, Washington had spiritually progressed to the point of becoming an abolitionist from beyond the grave: "I have left the spirit that could make merchandise of my brothers far behind; I have left the spirit that could compel my brother to labor for me without wages, far behind." "I am," Washington's spirit continued, "doing what I can to loose every fetter, so that the oppressor will see the necessity of loosening the bonds that fasten him to his bondman . . . for I greatly desire to make him sensible of his great present as well as future loss."[12]

Relying upon disembodied spirits to "induce [slaveholders] to leave the evil of their ways" and to "see the necessity of loosening the bonds" linked antislavery Spiritualists of the 1850s with the abolitionists of the 1830s. The abolitionists of the 1830s had hoped to end slavery through the strategy of moral suasion. In their most idealistic, simple formulation of moral suasion, abolitionists hoped to convince the slaveholder that slavery was a sin, and once converted to antislavery, they expected him to repent by voluntarily emancipating his slaves. The Declaration of Sentiments that chartered the American Anti-Slavery Society in 1833 committed its members to this strategy, to "the opposition of moral purity to moral corruption—the destruction of error by the potency of truth—the overthrow of prejudice by the power of love—and the abolition of slavery by the spirit of repentance." The most ambitious application of the theory of moral suasion was the massive postal campaign that abolitionists organized in the mid-1830s to reach the slaveholder by flooding the South with abolitionist literature. Far from nurturing a spirit of repentance, southerners reacted by burning the mail, hanging abolitionists in effigy, calling for their extradition to the South, and threatening assassinations. In the wake of the failure of the postal campaign to nurture abolitionism in the South, many abolitionists began to retreat from moral suasion and develop and employ different tactics and strategies. Some launched antislavery political parties, others advocated disunionism, and, eventually, others embraced forceful, physical resistance to slavery. While a current of moral suasion always persisted in abolitionism, particularly among Garrisonians, beginning in the late 1830s it was largely superseded by other tactics and strategies.[13]

In the new religion of Spiritualism, some abolitionists revisited the old strategy of moral suasion. In terms of strategy, these Spiritualists were a throwback—the spirits would help accomplish reform by urging the living to repent their sins. A story in a brief article by Henry C. Wright entitled "Spiritualism—Its Bearing on Practical Reform" illustrates the renewed optimism about moral suasion among antislavery Spiritualists. Wright reported how the spirit of the late minister of a church in Plympton, Massachusetts, was visiting his former parishioners to recant the conservative religious and political positions he had championed from the pulpit. He urged them now to adopt considerably more radical religious and political views. "He told them he had taught them falsely about the Bible, depravity, marriage," Wright reported, "and he urged the people to teetotalism, anti-slavery, non-resistance, and to all practical reforms." The moral suasion campaigns of the 1830s had been directed particularly toward the conversion of leading figures in local communities: newspaper editors, politicians, and especially ministers. Abolitionists had been particularly frustrated in their efforts to convert the clergy to abolitionism. With Spiritualism, abolitionists of the 1850s were given a second chance to win to their cause these once resistant clergymen—at least those who had died. "The priests of the past are beginning to appear, here and there, to do what they can to rectify their former errors," Wright happily reported. "It is high time they did. They are sacredly bound to repentance and restitution." Perhaps with such respected figures as these repentant ministers and former slaveholders like Washington and Calhoun now on their side, moral suasion would meet with more success.[14]

Moral suasion in Spiritualism was in fact a purer version than that of the 1830s. The moral suasion campaigns of the 1830s were leavened with some political pragmatism. In the postal campaign of 1835, along with the hope of converting the slaveholder to abolitionism, abolitionists had more realistic goals in mind: generating needed publicity, stoking political controversy, and raising the national profile of the abolitionist campaign.[15] Just as Spiritualism exaggerated spirit politics, so too it produced an extreme variant of moral suasion.

This extreme, unadulterated moral suasion logic of Spiritualism as an antislavery strategy struck many abolitionists as impractical, even preposterous. It was difficult to imagine how the spirits would persuade anyone to become an abolitionist. The spirits, some abolitionists protested, were only preaching to the choir. The Calhoun who communicated his posthumous abolitionist message would not reach the slaveholding Carolinians he said he wanted to convert. His message was received by a lifelong Quaker abolitionist who published his communications from the spirit world in what was no doubt a small run through a local printer in Rochester, New York, a relative haven of abolitionism far from the slaveholding South. Anti- and proslavery Spiritualists would hear undoubtedly different messages, these critics suggested. To believe this, one did not even need to cast doubt upon spiritual communications or level charges of either fraud or self-delusion against mediums. Spiritualist theology suggested that this would be the case. Andrew Jackson Davis wrote of "the law of congeniality and affinity" that governed sociality in the spheres. There, he revealed, "every spirit has a peculiar sphere of its own," and "spirits know and associate with each other according to the quality of the sphere which is exhaled from their interiors."[16] Spirits would and could commune and communicate only with those approximating their own spiritual development. Calhoun found himself among the least enlightened spirits in the spirit world because, among spirits, "like attracts like." The same law governed communications between the living and the departed. Critics were quick to point out how much this damaged the moral suasion potential of spirit communications. A Spiritualist would hear from a spirit "corresponding with his own mental and spiritual development." Thus slaveholders would be visited by "disembodied . . . Legrees" rather than spirits preaching reform and repentance. Little wonder that there were so many proslavery Spiritualists, one critic concluded, for "Who else so well fitted to receive the messages, per spiritual telegraph, of James K. Polk and Bully Brooks."[17] These contemporary critics of Spiritualism recognized what a number of historians of the movement have noted: the varied politics of Spiritualism and its adherents. Radical spirits were no more likely to reach or convert slaveholders in the 1850s than mailed abolitionist literature had two decades earlier.

More troubling than its failure to reach the slaveholder with the message of abolitionism, critics of Spiritualism repeatedly charged that it distracted abolitionists from actively pursuing reform. Spiritualists became so enamored by the perfection of the next world that they became neglectful of and uninterested in any efforts to actively champion social justice in this one. "The general result of Spiritualism taking the hand of Anti-Slavery," one abolitionist argued, "has been, not to lead it nearer the slave, but further from him." Instead of joining in the practical work of antislavery activism, Spiritualists instead retreated "into some darkened room, to spend [their] time and energies in listening to the ravishing spiritual music of hand-bells and dinner-horns." Communication from the spirits were siren songs that, however beautiful, offered little of practical import for reform. "Too busy with peeping under the corner of the 'blanket of the dark,'" Spiritualists neglected the "needed reforms of this world." "Having a great deal to say about the spirits *out* of the flesh," another critic similarly complained, too many Spiritualists ended up being "utterly indifferent to the dearest rights of spirits *in* the flesh." After attending another Spiritualist-dominated reform convention a year prior to the Rutland convention, Parker

Pillsbury condemned “a morbid, mawkish Spiritualism” that he felt had infected abolitionism like “the potato-rot.” In Pillsbury’s estimation, however much some Spiritualists might favor reform, their faith sapped their activism because they were always “gazing away into the darkness for spirits to come and do its work.”[18]

Worse yet, by displacing the millennium into the spiritual spheres and by relying upon the guidance of departed spirits, Spiritualism undermined the perfectionism that had motivated a generation of reformers to imagine themselves and others as disembodied spirits. Despite Spiritualists’ declarations of an imminent social and spiritual revolution, their cosmology conveyed a message with deeply conservative social and political implications: perfection would not be achieved here on earth. Social and spiritual perfection were such distant goals, Spiritualism suggested, that that perfection could not be achieved in this life, nor the next life, nor even the life after that. The world of peace and justice promised by millennialism would not happen here on earth but only in a distant afterlife in the sixth sphere.

Spiritualism undermined the egalitarianism of spirit politics as well. Spirit politics had been radically egalitarian because it insisted that all souls—the souls of men and women, of whites and blacks—were inherently, eternally equal. In Spiritualism, all souls were not equal. As Bret E. Carroll has argued, the Spiritualist universe was a “cosmic hierarchy” characterized by “deferential relations between higher and lower spirits.” The spirits of each spiritual sphere were more enlightened than those of lower spheres. Even within individual spheres, infinite gradations of spiritual enlightenment separated souls from one another. Most importantly, the spirits of the spheres possessed greater spiritual insight than those still embodied on earth. The departed spirits that communicated through raps at the séance table or through speakers in trances were, for the most part, invested with the authority of angels. While certainly many Spiritualists insisted that not all spirits should be trusted and that their messages were not inerrant, nevertheless the basis of Spiritualist reform politics was the belief that the spirits were fonts of a divine wisdom that could not be found from earthly sources. They were less than God but more than man, mediating between the divine and the living. The empowering emphasis upon the soul of man in spirit politics was evacuated when Spiritualists looked to departed spirits as the source of spiritual and political direction.[19]

Because of this displacement of perfectionism and millennialism, some abolitionists who looked at Spiritualism did not see their own beliefs in spirit politics at all but only something vaguely similar that had been twisted almost beyond recognition. In the letter from Frederick Douglass to Spiritualist Amy Post (the wife of Isaac Post) quoted earlier, he made a point of distinguishing between the "mysterious agency of thought and spirit" that he was referring to and what he dismissively called "the 'rapping.'" He insisted that the former was "a higher and . . . a holier mode" than the latter.[20] Some abolitionists fought to protect the perfectionism and egalitarianism of spirit politics from being diluted or bastardized by Spiritualism. They chafed against Spiritualism's demotion of man in the cosmic order. Quaker abolitionist Richard Glazier voiced this outrage when he complained of Spiritualism's "want of faith in *man.*" In this regard, Glazier judged Spiritualism no better than the Christian denominations that many radical reformers found spiritually and politically wanting. The doctrines of both duped individuals into searching outside of themselves for salvation. "While the old religions have him sacrificing man to the 'glory of God,'" he charged, "the new will forget him while listening to the spirits." Glazier countered by reiterating some of the core premises and promises of spirit politics. Spiritualists erred in looking to the spirits and the spheres as the sources of progress and insight. The only genuine, true sources were to be found in man's own soul: "The law of growth, of unfolding, . . . is germinal—*from within, outward.*" Glazier played with and subtly critiqued the Spiritualist cosmology that pictured the Godhead as a sun surrounded by orbiting spiritual spheres that man, in his many afterlives, migrated through toward the divine source. Glazier reversed this formulation, locating man not at the periphery of the cosmic order but at its center. "All right ethics are central, and radiate thence," he maintained. That was the true "order of the moral universe." For Glazier, Spiritualism was an empty faith. However much it borrowed the trappings of spirit politics, it possessed none of its power. A Spiritualist was "a mere believer, an abstractionist, looking for that in creeds, and spirits, and coming heaven, which is only to be found embosomed in beauty and beatitude away back in the fountain sources of his own being." Instead of looking to disembodied spirits, man needed to remember "the sacredness of his fellow-man and of his own nature" and "that heaven and hell are within his own consciousness, and elsewhere only as myths."[21]

Yet if some attempted to defend spirit politics from Spiritualism, they were the exception. Spiritualism's adaptation of spirit politics was more likely to discredit spirit politics among radical abolitionists. Some critiques of the limitations of Spiritualism as an ally of reform could and did turn into broader critiques of spirit politics. This was certainly the case at the Rutland convention even with its large Spiritualist contingent. We have seen Parker Pillsbury's criticisms. More scathing was Ernestine L. Rose. She was sharply critical of the time and attention devoted to Spiritualism and religious issues at the Rutland convention. Far from aiding reform efforts, attention to spirituality or religion distracted reformers from valuable political and social activism. "I say, no matter about religion," she bluntly declared, "take it for granted that it is true; no matter about gods,—take it for granted that they exist. If they are infinite and independent, they do not need our services. But who does? You and I. We need each others' services, each other's kindness and love. . . . Let us do our duty to humanity here, and when we reach another state of existence, we will attend to the duties of that state." Spiritualists at the convention insisted that Spiritualism would advance the reform movements of the day, but Rose saw nothing more than pointless, blathering rhetoric: "If the Convention is not called for the benefit of man, it is useless; if it is, the moment we come together, the time is not ours to discuss the duties of life hereafter and neglect the life here." Invoking traditional millennialism, she called upon the conventioneers to cease talking about the heavens and instead focus their attention on "mak[ing] the heaven that ought to be here on earth." They should labor not to glimpse the beauties and happiness of the heavens from afar, but instead devote their energies to political and social reforms that might make the world they lived in now such a place that instead of welcoming their passage into the spirit world at death all could instead feel that "it is really a pity to leave this beautiful earth entirely."[22]

It is not at all surprising that Rose—who was decidedly atypical among abolitionists as an atheist and secular freethinker who had been raised Jewish in her native Poland—would condemn not just Spiritualism but religion and spirituality more generally. The even harsher criticisms of Spiritualism that were offered by Garrisonian Stephen Foster are more revealing, suggesting how Spiritualism contributed to a retreat from spirit politics among some radical abolitionists. Like Pillsbury and Rose, he too was frustrated at the amount of time devoted to discussing immortality and Spiritualism at a reform convention. Foster leveled the same charge at Spiritualists that had been so often aimed at Garrisonians: that they talked rather than acted. "I am told you are all anti-slavery here, and ready to act. In God's name, why don't you act?," he demanded of the Spiritualists at the convention. In the back-and-forth that followed this question, Foster mounted a critique not just of Spiritualism but of the faith in disembodied spirituality that served as the foundation of spirit politics. Physical violence, he suggested, would prove a more effective antislavery tactic than spiritual communion. Responding to someone who said they were ready "to give the pound of flesh, but no blood"—by which he meant they would perform the unpleasant task of voting to support antislavery but that they would stop short of employing violence—Foster attempted to turn conventioneers' attention away from the spirit to the body. "Yes; and what is that flesh?," Foster retorted, "that pound of flesh is the slave." It was their bodies that were enslaved, and antislavery advocates might have to physically confront—not just spiritually or politically confront—the slaveholder to protect fugitives. Foster did not shy away from but seemed to almost relish the prospect: "Some will say, 'This will result in blood.' Very likely it will. What of it? I ask you, is not every one ready to spill oceans of blood, if necessary, to secure his own freedom?" Foster turned the Spiritualists' belief in immediate rebirth upon death against them. If death was nothing to fear, why not die in a righteous cause? "You pretend to be Spiritualists, and believe in a future life; and yet, you are so attached to this, that you dare not repudiate the pro-slavery, man-thieving government, because it may cost a drop of blood, a scratch on the face!" Again focusing attention toward the material body ("flesh," "blood," "face") and away from the disembodied soul, Foster tauntingly urged the largely Spiritualist audience to attack slavery right now by any means necessary no matter the costs. "You believe in Spiritualism? Why, I have more Spiritualism in my little finger"—again, emphasizing the physical body—"than you have in your whole bodies. With all my non-resistance, I do not shrink from the thought of blood as you do. . . . What matters if I die, so that I die battling for the right?"[23]

As Foster had been a committed Garrisonian abolitionist and nonresistant for decades, his arrival at these positions is telling. By the late 1850s, his belief in the power of morality and spirituality had been deeply compromised, and he sought alternative strategies and tactics to fight slavery. He had long been tempering his nonresistance. Eight years earlier following the passage of the Fugitive Slave Law, he urged those who did not share his nonresistant convictions to use violence to defend runaway or free African Americans from recapture or kidnapping. Yet he insisted he would never kill anyone himself, even to defend a fugitive, reiterating his conviction that the "sword of the spirit" was mightier than the "sword of physical violence." By 1858, he was not only more forcefully advocating violence but also the use of the ballot box. At the annual meeting of the Massachusetts Anti-Slavery Society earlier that year (which featured a short but heated debate about the political implications of Spiritualism), Foster declared the Garrisonians' tactics of moral suasion—lecturing, passing resolutions, organizing antislavery revivals—"no longer sufficient" and "impracticable." Dissenting from what was effectively the Garrisonian dogma of condemning all political parties and electoral participation, Foster advocated the establishment of a new party to champion Garrisonian antislavery.[24]

Of course, Spiritualism was not the only or even the primary source of the political pragmatism that Foster and other Garrisonian abolitionists increasingly evinced during the 1850s. The dramatic events of that decade—the Fugitive Slave Law, the Kansas-Nebraska Act, Bleeding Kansas, the beating of Charles Sumner, the *Dred Scott* decision, Harpers Ferry—brought slavery to the forefront of national politics and increasingly prodded radical abolitionists to become sectional provocateurs rather than principled idealists. The mounting sectional crisis encouraged many abolitionists to gradually compromise their utopian aspirations and principles—particularly regarding nonviolence—in order to fan the flames growing between the North and the South. Perennially torn between utopian perfectionism and practical politics, these events increasingly *pulled* them toward the latter.[25]

What has not been appreciated is how Spiritualism *pushed* many abolitionists in the same direction, away from perfectionism toward pragmatism. As Spiritualists amplified and refashioned the foundational premise of spirit politics—that disembodied spiritual communions would effect revolutionary social change—they prompted radical abolitionists to reconsider the ways they had fused spirituality and activism. For a few like Isaac Post and Henry C. Wright, Spiritualism renewed and reenergized their faith in moral suasion. For others, it compromised that faith and contributed to a deep disillusionment. As they looked back at a quarter century of activism, many Garrisonians could only confess that moral suasion and spirit politics had failed to effect the revolution they had long sought. When Spiritualists proposed that what was now needed was more moral suasion—now originating from departed spirits—many abolitionists could only balk. The more Spiritualists insisted that communion with disembodied spirits would finally effect a moral and social revolution, the more unrealistic, even absurd, that idea seemed. Spirit politics appeared increasingly quixotic, and Spiritualism a dead end.

Creating the postmillennial world of peace, equality, and moral perfection no longer seemed likely or even possible. In this regard, Spiritualism's displacement of utopia into the spiritual spheres was emblematic, epitomizing a growing disenchantment among perfectionist abolitionists during the 1850s. Even as their hopes for a universal spiritual revolution dissolved, they remained committed to achieving an extraordinary social revolution by ending chattel slavery. To that end, they hesitantly accepted strategies and tactics like party politics and violence that they had once spurned as sinful. As dreams of the millennium receded ever further into other worlds and other lives, radical abolitionists found themselves increasingly willing to employ imperfect means to change an imperfect world.

NOTES

I would like to acknowledge and thank Kevin Pelletier, Robert A. Gross, Matt Cohen, Brian Geiger, Scott Nesbit, and the editors of this volume for their thoughtful and useful criticisms of drafts of this essay.

1. Parker Pillsbury, "The Convention at Rutland, Vt.," *Liberator*, July 2, 1858.

2. *Proceedings of the Free Convention Held at Rutland, VT, June 25th, 26th, 27th, 1858* (Boston: J. B Yerrinton and Son, 1858), 82, 88. On Pillsbury's lifelong critique of the church and clergy and his devotion to perfectionism and millennialism, see Stacey M. Robertson, *Parker Pillsbury: Radical Abolitionist, Male Feminist* (Ithaca, N.Y.: Cornell University Press, 2000).

3. Ann Braude, *Radical Spirits: Spiritualism and Women's Rights in Nineteenth-Century America*, 2nd ed. (Bloomington: Indiana University Press, 2001); Molly McGarry, *Ghosts of Futures Past: Spiritualism and the Cultural Politics of Nineteenth-Century America* (Berkeley: University of California Press, 2008); R. Laurence Moore, *In Search of White Crows: Spiritualism, Parapsychology, and American Culture* (New York: Oxford University Press, 1977); Bret E. Carroll, *Spiritualism in Antebellum America* (Bloomington: Indiana University Press, 1997); Robert S. Cox, "Vox Populi: Spiritualism and George Washington's Postmortem Career," *Early American Studies* 1 (Spring 2003); Robert S. Cox, *Body and Soul: A Sympathetic History of American Spiritualism* (Charlottesville: University of Virginia Press, 2003), 230–272.

4. Robert H. Abzug, *Cosmos Crumbling: American Reform and the Religious Imagination* (New York: Oxford University Press, 1994), 4, 228; Lewis Perry, *Radical Abolitionism: Anarchy and the Government of God in Antislavery Thought* (Ithaca, N.Y.: Cornell University Press, 1973), xi.

5. Garrison to Henry C. Wright, April 1, 1843, in *The Letters of William Lloyd Garrison*, vol. 3, *No Union with Slaveholders, 1841–1849*, ed. Walter M. Merrill (Cambridge: Belknap Press of Harvard University Press, 1973), 143; Frederick Douglass to Amy Kirby Post, April 11, 1848?, Post Family Papers, University of Rochester Rare Books, Special Collections and Preservation; Garrison to Elizabeth Pease, September 16, 1841, in *Letters of William Lloyd Garrison*, 3:29. Emerson, "Friendship," in *Essays: First and Second Series* (1841; n.p.: Library of America, 1990), 121; William Caleb McDaniel, "Our Country Is the World: Radical American Abolitionists Abroad" (Ph.D. diss., Johns Hopkins University, 2006), 106–53.

6. Weld to Grimké, February 8, 1838, in *Letters of Theodore Dwight Weld, Angelina Grimké Weld, and Sarah Grimké*, ed. Gilbert H. Barnes and Dwight L. Dumond (1934; repr., Gloucester, Mass.:

Peter Smith, 1965), 2:534; Weld to Grimké, March 1, 1838, in *Letters of Weld, Grimké Weld, and Grimké,* 2:581–82; Henry C. Wright, *Anthropology; or, the Science of Man: In Its Bearing on War and Slavery, and on Arguments from the Bible, Marriage, God, Death, Retribution, Atonement, and Government, in Support of These and Other Social Wrongs* (Cincinnati, Ohio: E. Shepard, 1850), 28–29; Robert K. Nelson, "'The Forgetfulness of Sex': Devotion and Desire in the Courtship Letter of Theodore Dwight Weld and Angelina Grimké," *Journal of Social History* 37, no. 3 (Spring 2004): 663–79. Donald Yacovone has argued that radical abolitionists embraced "a theory of Christian androgyny that sought to restructure American society" in his essay "Abolitionists and the 'Language of Fraternal Love,'" in *Meanings for Manhood: Constructions of Masculinity in Victorian America,* eds. Mark C. Carnes and Clyde Griffen (Chicago: University of Chicago Press, 1990), 87.

7. Grimké to Douglass, 3 April 1837, Theodore Dwight Weld, Angelina Grimké Weld, and Sarah Grimké Papers, Clements Library, University of Michigan, Ann Arbor; Thomas Earle quoted in Richard S. Newman, *The Transformation of American Abolitionism: Fighting Slavery in the Early Republic* (Chapel Hill: University of North Carolina Press, 2002), 119–20; George Thompson, *Prison Life and Reflections; or, A Narrative of the Arrest, Trial, Conviction, Imprisonment, Treatment, Observations, Reflections, and Deliverance of Work, Burr, and Thompson, Who Suffered and Unjust and Cruel Imprisonment in Missouri Penitentiary, for Attempting to Aid Some Slaves to Liberty* (1847; Hartford: A. Work, 1855), 100; Joseph Yannielli, "George Thompson among the Africans: Empathy, Authority, and Insanity in the Age of Abolition," *Journal of American History* 96 (March 2010): 979–1000.

8. Andrew Jackson Davis, *The Principles of Nature, Her Divine Revelations, and a Voice to Mankind* (New York: S. S. Lyon and Wm. Fishbough, 1852), xvii. Ann Braude has also emphasized how Spiritualism took existing traditions—in her examples, ideas associated with Transcendentalism and Quakerism—and made them "concrete" and thus, particularly in the former case, "made itself reprehensible to some of its most important philosophical forebears" by compromising the subtleties of those ideas (see Braude, *Radical Spirits,* 46). For biographical accounts of Davis's career, see Robert W. Delp's "Andrew Jackson Davis: Prophet of American Spiritualism," *Journal of American History* 54 (June 1967): 43–56; and "A Spiritualist in Connecticut: Andrew Jackson Davis, the Hartford Years, 1850–1854," *New England Quarterly* 53 (September 1980): 345–62.

9. Davis, *Principles of Nature,* 672, 650, 655.

10. Ibid., 669, 647, 663.

11. Braude, *Radical Spirits,* 10–16; Nancy A. Hewitt, "Amy Kirby Post: 'Of Whom It Was Said, "Being Dead, Yet Speaketh,"'" *University of Rochester Library Bulletin* 37 (1984): 5–21; Caitlin Powalski, "Radical Transmissions: Isaac and Amy Post, Spiritualism, and Progressive Reform in Nineteenth-Century Rochester," *Rochester History* 71, no. 2 (Fall 2009): 1–27.

12. Isaac Post, *Voices from the Spirit World, Being Communications from Many Spirits* (Rochester, N.Y.: Charles H. McDonell, Printer, 1852), 87–90, 33.

13. "American Anti-Slavery Society," *The Abolitionists: or Record of the New England Anti-Slavery Society,* December 1833; James Brewer Stewart, "Peaceful Hopes and Violent Experiences: The Evolution of Reforming and Radical Abolitionism, 1831–1837," *Civil War History* 17, no. 1 (December 1971): 293–309. Studies of the development of alternative strategies to moral suasion within abolitionism beginning in the mid-1830s are numerous. A classic, insightful, and influential study is Aileen S. Kraditor, *Means and Ends in American Abolitionism: Garrison and His Critics on Strategy and Tactics, 1834–1850* (Chicago: Dee, 1967).

14. Henry C. Wright, "Spiritualism—Its Bearing on Practical Reform," *Liberator*, July 29, 1853.

15. Bertram Wyatt-Brown, "The Abolitionists' Postal Campaign of 1835," *Journal of Negro History* 50, no. 4 (October 1865): 227–38.

16. Davis, *Principles of Nature*, 647–648.

17. Richard Glazier, "Reply to 'Justice,'" *Liberator*, December 18, 1857.

18. J. A. H., "'Justice' to All Parties," *Liberator*, December 18, 1857; E. R. Place, "Spiritualism and Anti-Slavery," *Liberator*, July 23, 1858; Pillsbury, "Progress of Disunionism at the West," *Liberator*, October 23, 1857.

19. Carroll, *Spiritualism in Antebellum America*, 63, 75. Carroll has suggested that Spiritualists "sometimes sounded almost Calvinistic in suggesting that the people of earth were incapable of improving themselves and required help" (101). Ann Braude has offered a different argument: Spiritualism may have displaced perfection in the spiritual spheres, but it still emphasized human perfectibility. People might die morally imperfect, but they would continue to grow toward perfection. By compromising perfectionism—the most extreme departure from Calvinistic doctrines of predestination, God's grace, and man's innate depravity—she suggests that Spiritualism actually salvaged it (Braude, *Radical Spirits*, 36–37). On the problematic issue of authority in Spiritualism, see also Perry, *Radical Abolitionism*, 218–22.

20. Douglass to Post, April 11, 1848.

21. Glazier, "Reply to 'Justice.'"

22. *Proceedings of the Free Convention*, 13, 31; Carol A. Kolmerten, *The American Life of Ernestine L. Rose* (Syracuse, N.Y.: Syracuse University Press, 1999), 204–7.

23. *Proceedings of the Free Convention*, 97–99.

24. "Anti-Slavery Convention at Valley Falls, R.I.," *Liberator*, October 11, 1850; "Annual Meeting of the Massachusetts Anti-Slavery Society," *Liberator*, February 5, 1858; Troy Duncan and Chris Dixon, "Denouncing the Brotherhood of Thieves: Stephen Symonds Foster's Critique of Anti-Abolitionist Clergy," *Civil War History* 47 (June 2001): 97–117.

25. James Brewer Stewart, *Holy Warriors: The Abolitionists and American Slavery*, rev. ed. (New York: Hill and Wang, 1997), 151–80; Valarie H. Ziegler, *The Advocates of Peace in Antebellum America* (Bloomington: Indiana University Press, 1992), 116–48; John L. Thomas, "Antislavery and Utopia," in *The Antislavery Vanguard: New Essays on the Abolitionists*, ed. Martin Duberman (Princeton, N.J.: Princeton University Press, 1965), 240–69.

3

"THIS FLATTERING MILLENNIUM THEORY"

Denominationalism against Millennialism in James Fenimore Cooper's *The Crater*

RYAN CORDELL

James Fenimore Cooper's late novel *The Crater* (1847) begins as an optimistic retelling of *Robinson Crusoe.* Cooper's young Crusoe, Mark Woolston, is stranded with one companion on a barren volcanic island, about a mile in length, in the Pacific. Woolston cultivates his new home with tools and seeds found in the ruins of his ship—originally packed by its Quaker owners to help the crew in "civilizing the people of Fejee." Woolston literally builds the landscape, packing together a combination of ashes, hog and goat feces (from animals that survived the shipwreck), and guano scraped from the island's rocks. Soon an underwater eruption helps his construction project, substantially expanding Woolston's island home and bringing into view another, much larger, nearby island with a high mountain peak. By the time Woolston is rescued midway through the novel, the volcanic soil has nourished his crops and livestock so fruitfully, and the island become so bountiful, that Woolston decides not to leave, but instead to bring settlers from the United States and reshape his prison into a new colony.[1]

Cooper's narrator notes that Woolston was born "in 1777 . . . only ten days before the surrender of Burgoyne," which signals the national allegory this protagonist and his colony will embody in Cooper's novel. The colonists build the primary buildings of Woolston's new colony on the side of Vulcan's Peak—the larger island's central volcanic mountain—making the new settlement quite literally "a city upon a hill." Like the Puritan John Winthrop, Woolston perceives a divine mandate guiding his colony: "The mysteries of our condition here on earth, with the double connection between the past and the future . . . tend to the belief in an existence of a vast and beneficent design." Cooper's narrator, however, warns that "the only thing that can be termed stable is the slow but sure progress of prophecy," and he warns that "the signs of the times are not to be mistaken."[2]

When, late in the novel, the pride of the colonists begins to overwhelm the noble ambitions on which the colony was founded, the signs of their times point toward apocalypse rather than millennium. Lakshmi Mani describes how "the tranquil picture of Eden in the first half of the novel stands in sharp contrast to the feverish activity of the second, the period in which the simple agrarian paradise becomes transformed into Sodom and Gomorrah."[3] In the novel's final pages, the volcano that built the island erupts and annihilates colony, colonists, and the island itself, an event that "is meant to be an object lesson in humility for America, whose career seemed to Cooper very similar to that of the Craterinos. God's grace is infinite, but since man is innately depraved, Cooper concludes, he will continue to "corrupt the fairest of Edens."[4] The Craterinos are doomed because of their uncritical modernization: technological, political, and spiritual. Critics have overlooked the latter, but Cooper's narrator equates religious modernization with the new colonists' other evils. In fact, Cooper's religious concerns in *The Crater* line up with those of many contemporary Protestant eschatologists, who argued in pulpits and periodicals that sectarianism refuted the millennialism happily espoused by many contemporary preachers and theologians.

One mainline pastor serves the spiritual needs of all the Crater's first colonists: Mr. Hornblower, an Episcopalian. Some of the colonists, especially the Quaker Bob Betts, question Hornblower's methods, including his liturgical prayers and dress. Betts quips, "Friends doesn't hold, at all, to dressing and undressing in church time; and I think, myself, books is out of place in praying to God." Betts and the other antiformalist Protestants on the island suspect the formality of the Episcopal liturgy—a whiff of Catholicism—which contrasts sharply with the spontaneous, emotional worship to which they are accustomed. "As to praying from the book," Betts explains to Woolston, "quite half of our people think it is not any better than no praying at all. A little worse, perhaps." Despite these concerns, however, Betts concedes that most of the colonists "came to the conclusion that Episcopalian ministrations were better than none." Forced into theological intimacy, Cooper's colonists enact a denominational truce and worship together in relative peace.[5]

As the colony prospers and expands, however, sectarian tensions begin to strain religious, social, and political bonds. Indeed, Woolston—now the colony's governor—confesses to his wife: "I am more uneasy on the subject of religion than on any other. . . . I took great pains to sound the people on the subject, and I found a much greater variety of opinions, or rather of feelings, among them than I could have believed possible." When Woolston learns that a new ship full of colonists will bring with it "a Methodist and a Presbyterian clergyman," he wonders, "It is extraordinary that, as there is but one God, and one Saviour, there should be more than one mode of worshipping them!" Cooper's narrator interjects here to warn that these denominational debates will be "the form in which the serpent of old was about to visit this Eden of modern times." When the ship arrives, not two, but four new clergymen step off the boat: "one was a Presbyterian, one a Methodist, the third was a Baptist, and the fourth a Quaker." These new divines—with the possible exception of the Quaker—symbolize the fractured denominational landscape of American religion in the 1840s. After the new colonists arrive, Cooper's island colonists begin to divide among the major mainline (Episcopalian, Presbyterian) and evangelical (Baptist, Methodist) religions that divided Cooper's countrymen and -women in 1847.[6]

THE DENOMINATIONAL CONTEXT OF *The Crater*

In 1777, the year Cooper assigns for the birth of his hero, Woolston, 55 percent of those Americans who belonged to a church belonged to a Congregationalist, Presbyterian, or Episcopal congregation. "It seemed certain" to many Americans, Roger Finke and Rodney Stark contend, "that these groups would continue to be the 'mainline' for the foreseeable future."[7] As late as 1822, Thomas Jefferson predicted that the liberalizing and secularizing trends within those three mainline faiths would continue to shape American religion: "The present generation will see Unitarianism become the general religion of the United States."[8] Unitarianism was the most liberal and secularist offshoot of Congregationalism, so much so that many antebellum religious commentators, such as Robert Baird in *Religion and America* (1844), refused to categorize it as Christianity at all. Nevertheless, Jefferson believed that American religion would continue to grow less fervent and less supernaturalist. By the 1840s, however, the reality of American religion was far different from what Jefferson had imagined. In the wake and aftermath of the Second Great Awakening, membership in the mainline churches, and in more liberal offshoots such as Unitarianism, stagnated or declined precipitously. At the same time, as Finke and Stark show, "the Baptists achieved very substantial growth, through conversion, and the Catholics grew rapidly, through immigration," both happening alongside "the meteoric rise of Methodism." This last rise was dramatic: "In 1776 the Methodists were a tiny religious society with only 65 churches scattered through the colonies. Seven decades later they towered over the nation. In 1850, there were 13,302 Methodist congregations, enrolling more than 2.6 million members—the single-largest denomination, accounting for more than a third of all American church members."[9] Mark Noll points out that "identifiably evangelical churches by 1860 made up [at least 85 percent] of American congregations," and further specifies that "perhaps as many as three-fifths" of those evangelicals were "frankly sectarian, emotional, apocalyptic, and determinedly conversionist."[10]

Beginning in the 1830s, the major evangelical churches in America balanced on a peak between their radical roots and mainline futures. Methodism's "meteoric rise," for example, was accomplished largely through the efforts of untaught, lay, itinerant preachers. Through the 1830s, however, Methodist colleges began opening around the country.[11] In the 1840s, the Methodists developed a "uniform course of study for all conferences" and began to build seminaries around the country.[12] During this same period, Methodist bishops began assigning more of their pastors to static home churches, and a few Methodist churches even began charging parishioners for pews like their mainline contemporaries.[13] Despite these movements toward acceptance and influence, however, in the antebellum period neither Methodism nor its evangelical counterparts were the faiths of America's elite. They were still seen by the most prominent divines of the day, such as the Beechers, as too enthusiastic, unrefined, or radical.

But sects, as theologian Reinhold Niebuhr argues, have a natural half-life of one generation, as "the children born to the voluntary members of the first generation begin to make the sect a church"; that is, to reshape it from a radical movement into "an educational and disciplinary institution."[14] During the antebellum period, the United States' newly powerful evangelical churches were already showing signs of stress. Indeed, the large denominational categories included a quickly multiplying host of subgroups, sects within sects, each insisting on the sanctity of particular social, political, or theological distinctions. Perhaps most importantly, in 1845 the dominant Baptist and Methodist denominations in the United States both split along geographic lines, into northern and southern conventions, over slavery.

In *A Secular Age,* Charles Taylor argues that "a denominational identity tends to separate religion from the state" because "a denomination cannot be a national church, and its members can't accept and join whatever claims to be the national church." Instead, "denominationalism implies that churches are all equally options, and thrives best in a régime of separation of church and state," where the denomination can "organize so much of their member's lives" that they become "the focus of often intense loyalty, a sentiment akin to nationalism."[15] Contemporary observers of antebellum American faith recognized the way that American religion inspired such devotion. European observers worried that this democratic religion would lead inevitably to conflict. In her travel memoir *Domestic Manners of the Americans* (1832), Frances Trollope—mother to British novelist Anthony Trollope—worried about the ferocity of American sectionalism:

> The whole people appear to be divided into an almost endless variety of religious factions, and I was told, that to be well received in society, it was necessary to declare yourself as belonging to some one of these. Let your acknowledged belief be what it may, you are said to be *not a Christian,* unless you attach yourself to a particular congregation. . . . [E]ach . . . assumes a church government of its own; of this, the most intriguing and factious individual is invariably the head; and in order, as it should seem, to show a reason for this separation, each congregation invests itself with some queer variety of external observance that has the melancholy effect of exposing *all* religious ceremonies to contempt.

Trollope urges her American readers to "recognize the advantages of an established church as a sort of headquarters for quite unpresuming Christians, who are contented to serve faithfully, without insisting upon having each a separate banner."[16] Another foreign observer of antebellum American life, Alexis de Tocqueville, asserts in *Democracy in America* that "general ideas pertaining to God and human nature are, therefore, of all ideas, the ones most appropriately shielded from the usual action of individual reason, and in which there is the most to gain and least to lose in recognizing an authority." Without such authority, Tocqueville worries, "individuals become accustomed to making do with confused and fluctuating notions about the matters of greatest interest to themselves and their fellow men. They defend their opinions badly or give them up altogether." This danger, he warns, "is especially true of men living in free countries."[17]

Modern historian Daniel Walker Howe argues, in essence, that Trollope and Tocqueville saw rightly the relationship between American denominationalism and American republicanism. Howe notes that denominational religion both fostered and intertwined with the perceived sanctity of Republican government: "Religion . . . was reinvigorated and reawakened in the life of the American republic. Religious denominations and religious action organizations multiplied beyond number. Americans of this generation [1830s and 1840s] experienced widespread direct democracy through the creation, administration, and financing of churches and other voluntary societies."[18] America at the beginning of the nineteenth century experienced a denominational explosion, a theological revolution based on and rivaling in scope the political revolutions that defined the eighteenth century.

DENOMINATIONALISM AS A "SIGN OF THE TIMES"

These revolutions deeply concerned many religious writers in the 1840s and 1850s. Denominationalism was often derided as a species of sectarianism, a term that could describe various sorts of disunion, both religious and political. Using Google's recently released Ngram Viewer, we can quantitatively chart a heightened concern with sectarianism during the 1840s and 1850s.[19] The Ngram Viewer searches for words and phrases in the Google Books corpora, and graphs their frequency within a selected corpus. Searching for the word "sectarian" within the "American English" corpus between the years 1800 and 1900, we find that use of the word spiked during the decades just before the Civil War. "Sectarian" appears in approximately 0.000025 percent of the books and periodicals in the corpora that were published in the United States in 1800. Over the next decades, however, use of "sectarian" steadily increases. By 1850, "sectarian" appears in 0.000375 percent of the books in the corpora published in the United States. In other words, books and periodicals in 1850 used "sectarian" more than ten times more frequently than books in 1800: an increase of an order of magnitude. Use of "sectarian" declined rapidly after 1860 (though never back to 1800 levels).[20] Granted, these data do not tell how "sectarian" was used in these texts. Some of them, as will be shown in the examples below, defended sectarianism or dismissed others' concerns about it. However, we can see in these data that interest in denominational disunion spiked during this period. Delving into some textual examples, we will see that religious commentators frequently and explicitly framed sectarianism as an eschatological issue: a crisis of apocalyptic significance.

Though evangelical groups were largely responsible for breaking up the influence of the nation's established denominations, nonetheless many evangelical believers saw the nation's doctrinal Babel as a telling sign of the times, ample proof of impending judgment for the nation rather than millennial paradise. The Adventists—better known by many scholars as Millerites[21]—expressed these anxieties with particular force in their newspapers, tracts, and sermons. During the 1840s, the Adventists were not yet a denomination as such. William Miller, the movement's founder, was deeply concerned about the divisive effects of denominationalism, and he urged his followers to remain in their predominantly Baptist, Methodist, and Presbyterian churches, which they did until the final year before the Great Disappointment. Indeed, many modern religious historians argue that, aside from setting such a precise date for Christ's return, the Adventists "were essentially orthodox."[22] J. F. C. Harrison notes that "Millerism" was so popular in large part because Adventist teaching did not claim any special revelation, or modify the basic tenets of American evangelical belief. Indeed, he argues that Adventist doctrine "accorded well with the dominant Protestant orthodoxy of the time, and Millerism in this respect was only a rather unusual version of evangelical and revivalist religion."[23]

Because of their broad appeal to contemporary evangelicals, Adventist literature offers a uniquely interdenominational view of the debate over denominationalism during the period of *The Crater*'s publication. In 1843, the Adventist newspaper the *Midnight Cry!* couches a discussion of slavery in a critique of denominationalism. The article begins by listing an "inventory of the slave property of American Churches" specifically by the denominations of slave owners. The article takes umbrage at the 204,000 slaves owned by American Methodists; 125,000 by Baptists; 70,000 by Presbyterians; 80,000 by Episcopalians; 100,000 by Campbellites; and 25,000 by "other smaller denominations." The author frets more, however, over the interdenominational squabbling and division that slavery has engendered than over slavery itself. After noting that "every Christian's arm" should be "nerved to bold and zealous action to clear the sanctuary of this abomination," the article asks pointedly, "While such facts exist, what are the churches doing?" What they are doing, the author decides, is wallowing in petty doctrinal squabbles: "One half of the Presbyterian churches are contending that the other half are not good Presbyterians. But the Episcopalians reject them all as not belonging to the true church, and say it is 'a profanation' for Presbyterians, or other '*dissenting*'!! [*sic*] ministers to administer the sacrament. The Evangelist retorts, that such principles are '*heathenish*.'" The *Cry*'s writer closes with exasperation, "How long will it take these divided and belligerent churches to convert the world to unity in the apostolic faith, when a great portion of them scorn the apostolic faith, on the subject of Christ's second coming, and despise those who hold it?"[24] The implied answer is that the denominations will take as much time as God allows them—which, the Adventists believed, would not be long.

In the abolitionist *North Star* paper, Henry H. Garney wrote about the members of "The Liberty Street Presbyterian Church of Troy, N.Y." who renounced their denomination altogether because "sectarianism is at variance with the spirit and letter of the Gospel, and is the end foundation of all ecclesiastical oppression, a most prolific source of wars and slavery." The church resolved, "We shall hereafter be known as 'The Church in Liberty Street, Troy, N.Y.' and that we shall acknowledge no other creed than the Bible."[25] Like the editors of the *Cry*, many abolitionist writers and editors frequently decried denominational infighting as complicit in the continuation of slavery in the nation. In an article from the *Herald of Freedom*, reprinted in William Lloyd Garrison's *Liberator*, the author calls "sectarian worship . . . the Chinese Wall in the way of the peaceful abolition of slavery." The article ends with an apocalyptic warning: "Friends, beware how you circumvent yourselves with this meeting-house religion. It will fail you like the spider's web. Not when you die merely, it will fail before. It *fails you now*. You feel no support in it—no confidence—no consolation. It is not christianity [*sic*]—under whatever denominational name you may follow it. Its teachers are 'blind leaders' and 'of the blind,' if *you* follow them."[26]

In these examples, both the *Cry* and its abolitionist contemporaries dismiss the belief of millennialists, exemplified in this passage from the *New York Evangelist*, that a time was fast approaching "when all hearts shall be brought under the spiritual influence of the religion of Christ; when all men shall be truly born again of the Holy Spirit; when all wrong shall cease, and the ties of brotherhood shall be universally recognized, then will this world again appear as it did on that bright morning when, at its birth, all the sons of God shouted together for joy."[27] For apocalyptic thinkers, widespread Protestant disunion demonstrated the inconsistency or unfeasibility of millennialist theologies. In fact, for many antebellum eschatologists, the proliferation of dissent within and among Protestant denominations during the period was a primary sign of time's imminent end. In June 1843, the *Midnight Cry!* wrote, "While the

Church is self-complacently quoting the promises which they apply to a millennium, there are certainly no very encouraging indications that they are approaching the state in which the watchmen will see eye to eye." The *Cry* then quotes at length an article about disputes between the General Association of Congregationalist ministers and the New School [Presbyterian] General Assembly, concluding: "The 'orthodox' churches of the United States are divided into three great parties which are scarcely on speaking terms with each other. With pain and heart-sickness we ask if these churches will convert the world."[28] The *Cry* here takes America's mainline churches specifically to task, and asks how Christianity could become "*the* religion" of the world when it has ceased to be *a* religion at all?

Many evangelicals shared the Adventists' concerns about the terrible consequences of denominational disunion. In June 1847, the Baptist *Christian Review* argued in dramatic fashion:

> To say, that still, thus separated, the disciples might preserve the unity of the spirit, and so fulfil [*sic*] the law of love, and present one front against the common enemy, is to beg the whole question.... For two or three centuries we have been trying how the plan would work—the plan of multiplying forms of church organization to meet the endlessly varied and ever shifting demands of the human intellect. Our best and wisest men have superintended the experiment. And how has it worked? Let the rent and bleeding body of our Lord reply. The appearance of unity has been totally destroyed. Sectarianism has entered and fed upon the heart of the church.[29]

Likewise, in an 1854 sermon the Methodist pastor T. H. Stockton called sectarianism "that professed friend, but real enemy, of the gospel" that "ministers to Infidelity" and would be "the way by which Mohammedanism and Paganism should be, and might be, conducted to the Cross."[30] Both the *Christian Review* and Stockton argue, much like the *Midnight Cry!*, that sectarianism refutes millennialist idealism. Rather than a unified Christian world, they see a weakened Christian body, vulnerable to incursion from within and without.

Likewise the *Millennial Harbinger*, the flagship newspaper of the Campbellite movement, frequently printed articles and sermons outlining the evils of denominationalism. This is perhaps unsurprising: a core tenet of the Restoration Movement was the unification of Protestant Christians under one church. The language used in the *Harbinger*, however, further demonstrates the apocalyptic significance that many Americans saw in denominational discord. The *Harbinger*'s "Prospectus"—printed in the newspaper's first issue—claims, "This work shall be devoted to the destruction of Sectarianism, Infidelity, and Antichristian doctrine and practice." The *Harbinger* hoped to help speed the arrival of the millennium, but insisted on "the incompatibility of any sectarian establishment, now known on earth, with the genius of the glorious age to come."[31] A decade later, the *Harbinger* continued to name sectarianism as heresy: "As to the evils of heresy, or sects, they are well defined. Sectarianism, first, prevents the spread of Christianity at home; second, the spread of Christianity abroad; third, it corrupts the first principles of religion in the heart; forth, it produces a distorted character."[32] Like the Adventist editors of the *Midnight Cry!*, these contemporaneous evangelical thinkers worry that denominational disunion will lead to the diminishment of Christian influence in the world, rather than millennial paradise.

There were, of course, critics of such unification movements. In March 1843, for instance, the Freewill Baptist's *Morning Star* argued that groups like the Campbellites fought "against sectarian names" rather than against sectarianism: "just as though, if sectarian names were given up, the differences which those names denote, would cease." The *Morning Star* notes wryly—and, as it turns out, rightly—that the names "Christians," "Disciples," and "Campbellites" will simply become, in time, new denominational names. Nonetheless, even this article concedes that a sectarian name does "no more harm than in any other name which defines that which ought not to exist," conceding that, ideally, denominational differences would not persist.[33]

Some mainline commentators also bemoaned the denominational divisions that split American Protestantism. In 1843, the *Oberlin Evangelist* printed a sermon by Henry Cowles, one of the Presbyterian college's founding professors, who argued that Protestants should "let sectarianism therefore die. There is no brotherhood in it." As "a great many sects have become powerful, proud, and popular," Cowles preached, "Christianity [has] gained thereby only the more sectarianism, bitterness, vanity, and show, but has lost in point of humility, Christian charity, and sympathy with Christ."[34] In 1847, the Congregationalist *New Englander* noted, "It is one of the auspicious signs of the time that Christian union is so prominently occupying the thoughts, the prayers, and efforts of God's children." The *New Englander*, like these other commentators, names sectarianism as an evil, and proceeds to outline its causes and propose solutions, concluding that "the church must address herself in earnest to the work of discovering and removing the causes of disagreement, and must return to the simplicity that is in Christ, if our desires for Christian unity are ever to be realized."[35] While most mainline commentators took a more measured stance than their evangelical counterparts, they, too, worried that a lack of Protestant unity would damage the cause of Christianity in the United States and the larger world.

As these examples show, religious writers fervently debated the issue of Protestant unity during the 1840s and 1850s. While some saw religious difference as an essential outcome of religious freedom—a necessary evil, perhaps—most agreed that interdenominational discord was not the ideal expression of Christianity. Indeed, many religious thinkers across the denominational landscape portrayed denominational discord as a hurdle to the coming of millennium. In other words, for many Americans in the 1840s and 1850s, denominationalism was an issue with eternal, and potentially apocalyptic, consequences.

THEOLOGICAL REVOLUTION IN *The Crater*

In *The Crater,* Cooper's critique of millennialism—focused as it is on denominational strife—echoes critiques made by his religious contemporaries. The new Baptist, Methodist, Presbyterian, and Quaker pastors arrive on the novel's island colony "with a thousand professions of brotherly love, and a great parade of Christian charity," professing "that they had emigrated in order to enjoy a higher degree of religious liberty than was now to be found in America, where men were divided into sects, thinking more of their distinguishing tenets than of the Being they professed to serve." But the pastors' declarations of denominational peace are short-lived. Within a few paragraphs, the narrator describes how "these men set to work, immediately, to collect followers and believers after their own peculiar notions." In other words, each sect campaigns for its own "distinguishing tenets" under the banner of unity, casting their own dogmas as fundamental and untainted by sectarianism, and their opponents' protests as merely sectarian. Even the meek Episcopal priest Parson Hornblower "buckled on his armor, and took the field in earnest." Cooper's narrator depicts competing shepherds branding their flocks—"one clipped an ear, another smeared the wool (or drew it over the eyes) . . . so that his sheep might be known by their outward appearance" and "the sheep of one flock should not be mistaken for the sheep of another." The narrator identifies denominational debate as wool drawn "over the eyes" of willing sheep, as the debates that spring up over minor points of doctrine quickly destroy the tenuous religious peace the colonists had made under Hornblower.[36]

These turf wars, Cooper argues, exemplify not real religious or millennial zeal, but human pride. Here, too, he echoes the ideas of contemporary apocalyptic thinkers. On New Year's Day, 1841, the *Signs of the Times* (a sister publication to the *Midnight Cry!*) began a series of articles arguing that Christ's Second Coming was "at hand . . . without a previous millennium." In these articles, the editors of the *Signs* insist that "the doctrine of a temporal Millennium, or spiritual reign of Christ with his saints in this world" was "the greatest of all barriers in the way of spreading the gospel of this kingdom already at hand." They characterize millennial thinking as prideful, even sinful: "This flattering millennium theory, though now very common in the church, is, according to ecclesiastical history, and the established creeds of the churches, of very modern origin."[37] By using the word "flattering," the *Signs* here implies that millennial, progressivist theology reflects not meaningful societal change, but rather the collective pride of American Christians. For many antebellum believers, then, millennial thought flattered believers into seeing their age as sufficiently good to deserve God's approval rather than God's grace.

Cooper argues just this in the final pages of *The Crater.* As denominations proliferate on the novel's island colony, "the subtleties of sectarian faith smothered that humble submission to the divine law by trusting solely to the mediation, substituting in its place immaterial observances and theories which were much more strenuously urged than clearly understood." The religious life of the colony becomes consumed by "discussions on 'free grace,' 'immersion,' 'spiritual baptism,' and the 'apostolical succession.'" The narrator notes, "The birds sang as sweetly as ever, and their morning and evening songs hymned the praises of their creator as old." In one of the novel's best lines, however, the narrator insists, "not so was it with the morning and evening devotions of men. These last began to pray *at* each other." Religion, in short, has been trumped by religious politics among the colonists.[38]

The rise of denominationalism on the island leads toward spiritual disunion and, ironically, a kind of secularity, as material and procedural concerns supplant the purely spiritual worship of the island's earliest colonist. The trajectory of *The Crater* closely mirrors Charles Taylor's model of secularity in the nineteenth century. Taylor traces the shift not from a society of hegemonic blind faith to one of enlightened atheism, but rather from "a society in which it was virtually impossible not to believe in God, to one in which faith, even for the staunchest believer, is one human possibility among others," and "belief in God is no longer axiomatic. There are alternatives." In Taylor's model, a modern, secular society is not necessarily one with fewer religious practices or practitioners than in times past. A secular society for Taylor is one in which any particular configuration of beliefs is widely understood as personal: one potential configuration among myriad others, one model of human flourishing. Taylor argues that the secularization process of the United States pivoted on the growth of denominations, beginning in the eighteenth and rapidly proliferating in the nineteenth century.[39]

Cooper's religious narrative in *The Crater* mirrors this secularization process, but frames it explicitly as a decline. It begins with Mark Woolston's pure and uninhibited communion with nature, moves through a tacitly united "church" under Parson Hornblower, and finally disintegrates into a full-blown battle for bodies—not souls, Cooper's narrator insists over and again—in the pews of warring denominations. As spiritual union dissolves, so too does the political union of the colony's earliest inhabitants, who fled to the island to escape similar divisions in the United States. The Craterinos quickly follow their home countrymen and women by exchanging the colony's millennial promise for immediate, short-term religious gains. In *The Crater*, moreover, these religious wars coincide directly with political strife. Echoing the sectionalist strife that led, for example, Baptists and Methodists to split into northern and southern conventions in 1845, Cooper's narrator notes, "Nor did the accession of law and intelligence help the matter [religious strife among the colonists] much." Though living in what has been a utopia, the Craterinos "were soon convinced that they had hitherto been living under an unheard-of tyranny, and were invoked weekly to arouse in their might, and be true to themselves and their posterity."

These political debates do not center on slavery, though the specter of slavery does emerge throughout the novel. The notion of enslaving native people from a nearby island is first proposed midway through the novel and is quickly dismissed by Woolston and his governing council, who "would not lend itself for an instant" to "this scheme." Interestingly, in the novel's final pages the narrator notes that most of the native people left the Crater colony late in its history because the colonists had "begun to oppress them by exacting more work than was usual, and forgetting to pay for it." The novel hints, then, that "this scheme" of slavery was never entirely abandoned.[40] Although these mentions of slavery are fleeting, when the colony's newspaper argues "that the majority of any community had a right to do as it pleased," these ideas certainly evoke antebellum sectarian debates about who should decide the direction of the nation. Cooper's narrator condemns "the false reasoning and exaggerations of the demagogue [the newspaper's editor] and his deluded, or selfish followers"—in words that could be read as critiques of northern or southern editorial writers or political activists. Cooper's narrator worries that "if a majority has a right to rule, in this arbitrary manner, it has a right to set its dogmas above the commandments, and to legalize theft, murder, adultery, and all the other sins denounced in the twentieth chapter of Exodus."[41]

These political worries are explicitly theological worries; political power may lead to moral turpitude. And, as Mark Noll argues, antebellum sectarian debates can be read precisely as theological debates over the correct interpretation of the Bible's "commandments." Indeed, Noll reads the Civil War itself as a "theological crisis" over nuances of biblical interpretation.[42] In his preface to *The Crater,* Cooper seems to worry about just such an outcome: "If those who now live in this republic, can see any grounds for a timely warning in the events here recorded, it may happen that the mercy of a divine Creator may still preserve that which he has hitherto cherished and protected."[43] Implicit in Cooper's "if" is a warning that begins, "if not."

Here, too, Cooper insists that *The Crater*'s political crisis—and by extension, the United States' political crisis—is, at heart, a theological crisis. Indeed, Cooper's narrator speculates that "religion, under these influences, had quite as much to do with the downfall of the governor . . . as politics, and the newspaper." Again echoing the sectarian debates of the 1840s and 1850s, Cooper's narrator recounts how "the whole colony was divided into parishes, which exercised in themselves a few of the minor functions of government." These parishes metaphorically mirror the American states, just as the island mirrors the United States. Within each of these parishes, new politicians opposed to Governor Woolston introduce laws "to require the people to vote 'yes' or 'no,' in order to ascertain whether there should, or should not be, a convention to amend the constitution." When only "one-fourth of the electors" attend these meetings—because most citizens "believed the whole procedure not only illegal, but dangerous"—the measure passes. In the ensuing constitutional convention, the colony's laws are altered "to cause power and influence to pass into new hands."[44]

Cooper's narrator explicitly ties these sectarian and political maneuvers to denominational strife: "Religion had a word to say in these changes," the narrator argues: "that the governor was an Episcopalian reconciled many devout

Christians" to deposing him. This argument, the narrator warns, "renders religious faith secondary to human institutions." Indeed, in *The Crater,* the colony's political and religious disputes become explicit condemnations of millennial optimism, which insists that humanity can improve itself. Cooper's narrator notes that "self-righteousness, the inseparable companion of the quarrels of sects, took the place of humility, and thus became prevalent that most dangerous condition of the soul of man, when he imagines that *he* sanctifies what he does."[45] In short, the denominational fervor of the colony in *The Crater* enables the sectarian disputes that lead to political disunion. Cooper insists that the nation's spiritual and political destinies are inextricably tied, and that from both quarters his nation drives toward its own annihilation.

Pages before Cooper's narrator consigns the colony itself to the ocean's floor, he describes how "religion was running riot" as "next-door neighbors hated each other most sincerely, because they took different views of regeneration, justification, predestination, and all the other subtleties of doctrine." Even Parson Hornblower, for whom the narrator maintains considerable sympathy, exacerbates the colony's descent: "The Rev. Mr. Hornblower . . . took a course which had a tendency to aggravate, instead of lessening the strife among the sects. Had he been prudent, he would have proclaimed louder than ever 'Christ, and him crucified,' but he made the capital mistake of going up and down, crying, with the mob, 'the church, the church!'" Cooper's narrator speculates when Hornblower is first introduced that his name is "no bad appellation, by the way, for one who had to sound so many notes of warning," and his final "crying . . . up and down" serves as the colony's last trump, its midnight cry, as it "advanc[es] slowly but unerringly toward that great consummation." His "notes of warning" are drowned out by the "yells and clamor" of the colony's denominational squabbling, which the narrator calls "profane," comparing "the shouting and declamatory parts of religion" to "evil spirits growling and yelling before they are expelled," which "must not be mistaken for the voice of the Ancient of Days."[46]

In *The Crater,* the colonists' increasingly punctilious doctrinal disagreements overwhelm and begin to destroy the political and social bonds between the Craterinos. They forfeit any sense of cohesive nationality to smaller religious labels. The end result is both political and spiritual apocalypse. Mark Woolston, "naturally much mortified at the turn things had taken, decides to leave the colony with his wife for a trip home to America. While there, Woolston stubbornly "remembered it [the island] as he found it, a paradise in the midst of the waters, wanting only in man to erect the last great altar in his heart, in honor of its divine Creator."[47] Woolston insists upon the metaphor of "a city upon a hill" when thinking about his colony, even when evidence points to another metaphor: the corrupt and doomed Babylon of Revelation, with which contemporary apocalyptic writers often compared cities such as New York, Boston, or Philadelphia. George Lippard's popular but largely forgotten 1845 novel *The Quaker City,* for instance, condemns Philadelphia as both the birthplace and the graveyard of freedom. In one chapter of Lippard's novel, a chorus of ghosts presides over the apocalyptic destruction of the city. The chapter is punctuated by the refrain, "Wo Unto Sodom!," and as Philadelphia sinks into the earth at the chapter's end, the ghostly chorus shrieks: "Look and behold the Massacre of Judgments! The Sacrifice of Justice! The wrongs of ages are avenged at last! At last the voice of Blood crying out from the very stones of the idolatrous city, has pierced the ear of God. Look beneath, and look upon the wreck of the Doomed City!"[48]

It is this image that Cooper invokes at his novel's end, and when Woolston returns to his colony, he finds that it has suffered a similarly apocalyptic fate. Only "the summit of the peak" remains above the water, as "the remainder of his paradise had sunk beneath the ocean!" Cooper's narrator makes no secret as to why this happened: the colony experienced "blessings, so long as it pursued the right" and "curses, when it began to pursue the wrong." The colonists "substitute[d] the voice of the created for that of the Creator"—including substituting the "subtleties of doctrine" for the worship of God. "As soon as a man begins to *shout* in religion," Cooper warns, or to pray *at* his fellow Christians rather than *with* them, spiritual decay and destruction will quickly follow.[49]

Through his portrayal of denominational squabbling in *The Crater,* Cooper argues that the explosion of Protestant sects in the country makes the idea of the United States as a divinely approved "city upon a hill" untenable. Cooper shared these concerns with many apocalyptic thinkers who saw the discord within the American church as the country's preeminent spiritual crisis—and, thus, the country's preeminent crisis of any kind. Cooper yokes Christian disunion with a host of modernizing ills, a primary cause of religious atrophy, even of secularization. In the novel's final paragraph, Cooper warns "those who would substitute the voice of the created for that of the Creator; who shout 'the people, the people,' instead of hymning the praises of their God" to beware a similar fate to the Craterinos. It is difficult not to see an echo of the Constitution—"We the people"—in the faith Cooper denounces—"the people, the people." Cooper denounces the idea that "the masses are sufficient for all things" when, Cooper insists, those masses "are but mites amid millions of other mites."[50] If, as Jenny Franchot argues, "Those antebellum citizens who converted to one or another denomination of Protestant Christianity were both leaving the world and subscribing to one of their culture's most prized values,"[51] Cooper seeks in *The Crater* to undermine that value, to demonstrate how it imperils the nation. Such values, Cooper argues, produce secularized religions whose adherents are compelled not by the truth of the Christian message but by political one-upmanship.

Alexis de Tocqueville posited that two opposing but powerful forces defined American religion in the antebellum period. On one hand, "men who are similar and equal readily conceive of the notion of a single God who imposes the same rules on each of them and grants them future happiness at the same price." Most antebellum religious commentators, mainline and evangelical, millennialist and apocalyptic, agreed that the ideal Christianity would be unified by common belief in a common God. But straining this idealism was the fact that "while equality brings the world much that is good, it also opens the door to some highly dangerous instincts . . . it tends to isolate people from one another, so that each individual is inclined to think only of himself. It also leaves their souls inordinately vulnerable to material pleasures." Tocqueville even claims, "For my part, I doubt that man can ever tolerate both complete religious independence and total political liberty, and I am inclined to think that if he has no faith, he must serve, and if he is free, he must believe."[52]

In other words, political and religious freedom leads inexorably toward dogmatic disagreement and division. Antebellum eschatologists discussed denominational difference in opposite ways, often within the same texts. Apocalyptic thinkers described the venom of sectarian debates as damaging to American Christianity, a primary cause and dire sign of God's impending judgment. At the same time, religious leaders quickly denounced any one group's claims to speak with authority for all Christians. The democratic ideals of the denomination—its insistence on religion as the choice of an individual, based on his or her conscience—were celebrated and defended against any hint of catholicity.

In *The Crater,* Cooper dramatizes the anxiety that denominationalism sparked in eschatological thinkers in the United States. For those inclined to millennial visions of the church or the nation, the bickering of Protestant sects made that vision far more difficult to realize, even in the imagination. The signs of the times, that is, could easily be seen as pointing away from a millennial future for the United States—the "city upon a hill" seen as collapsing. Apocalyptic thinkers argued that American risked becoming a beacon not of millennial promise, but of God's judgment. In the closing pages of *The Crater,* Cooper assumes a strident, prophetic voice—consciously opposing the "*flattering* millennium theory" that, for him and other skeptics, encapsulated the dangerous pride of American Christians.

NOTES

1. James Fenimore Cooper, *The Crater: or, Vulcan's Peak,* in *The Works of James Fenimore Cooper,* vol. 16, ed. Susan Fenimore Cooper (New York: Houghton, Mifflin, 1884), 101. *The Crater* was originally published in 1847. Between 1876 and 1884, Cooper's daughter, Susan Fenimore Cooper, wrote introductions to the Household Editions of the *Works of J. Fenimore Cooper.* I use the edition of *The Crater* published in this series here, as no scholarly edition of *The Crater* yet exists.

2. Ibid., 3, 142, 143.

3. Lakshmi Mani, *The Apocalyptic Vision in Nineteenth Century Fiction: A Study of Cooper, Hawthorne, and Melville* (Washington, D.C.: University Press of America, 1981), 117.

4. Ibid., 19.

5. Cooper, *Crater,* 391, 316.

6. Ibid., 408, 409, 410, 453. Of course, Cooper's island does not include *all* major denominations. For instance, no Congregationalist immigrates to Cooper's utopia, but after their 1801 "Plan of Union," Presbyterians and Congregationalists were closely associated. For instance, one of the most famous antebellum preachers, Lyman Beecher, pastored both Presbyterian and Congregationalist churches during his career. These events happen in *The Crater* around the year 1800—Cooper refers to "more than 40 years ago" in several places—but Cooper's colonial ministers more closely mirror the denominational makeup of the United States in 1847—the year of *The Crater*'s publication—than they do the year of its setting.

7. Roger Finke and Rodney Stark, *The Churching of America, 1776–2005: Winners and Losers in Our Religious Economy* (New Brunswick, N.J.: Rutgers University Press, 2005), 55.

8. Jefferson to James Smith, 8 December 1822, in *Jefferson's Extracts from the Gospels,* ed. Dickinson W. Adams, *The Papers of Thomas Jefferson,* 2nd ser. (Princeton: Princeton University Press, 1983), 409, quoted in Mark A. Noll, *America's God: From Jonathan Edwards to Abraham Lincoln* (Oxford: Oxford University Press, 2002), 161.

9. Finke and Stark, *The Churching of America,* 56.

10. Noll, *America's God,* 170, 176.

11. Noll identifies seven Methodist "institutions of higher learning" that opened in the 1830s: Randolph-Macon (1832), Dickinson (acquired by Methodists in 1833), Allegheny (acquired by Methodists in 1833), McKendree (1834), Emory (1836), DePauw (1837), and Wesleyan Female College (acquired by Methodists in 1839) (*America's God,* 354).

12. Finke and Stark, *The Churching of America,* 165.

13. Ibid., 164.

14. H. Richard Niebuhr, *Social Sources of Denominationalism* (New York: Henry Holt, 1929), 17–19.

15. Charles Taylor, *A Secular Age* (Cambridge: Belknap Press of Harvard University Press, 2007), 471–72.

16. Frances Trollope, *Domestic Manners of the Americans* (London: Whittaker, Treacher, and Co., 1832), 99.

17. Alexis de Tocqueville, "How Religion Uses Democratic Instincts in the United States," in *Democracy in America,* ed. Olivier Zunz, trans. Arthur Goldhammer (Library of America, 2004), 502–3.

18. Daniel Walker Howe, *What Hath God Wrought: The Transformation of America, 1815–1848* (New York: Oxford University Press, 2007), 165–66.

19. The Google Books Ngram Viewer can be found at http://ngrams.googlelabs.com. For more on the potential value of this tool to historical and literary research, see Geoffrey Nunberg's article "Counting on Google Books," in the *Chronicle of Higher Education,* December 16, 2010.

20. The word "sectarianism" follows a similar trajectory. To see the data for both "sectarian" and "sectarianism," follow this URL: http://ngrams.googlelabs.com/graph?content=sectarian%2Csectarianism&year_start=1800&year_end=1900&corpus=5&smoothing=3.

21. Contemporaries usually called them "Millerites" after William Miller. They called themselves "Adventists," "Second Adventists," or "Believers in Christ's Kingdom Close at Hand." I will use the former throughout most of this study, unless compelled otherwise for reasons of clarity. My reasoning is simple: I prefer to use the label that an actual follower of William Miller would have used.

22. David L. Rowe, "Millerites: A Shadow Portrait," in *The Disappointed: Millerism and Millenarianism in the Nineteenth Century,* ed. Ronald L. Numbers and Jonathan M. Butler (Bloomington: Indiana University Press, 1987), 13.

23. J. F. C. Harrison, *The Second Coming: Popular Millenarianism, 1780–1850* (New Brunswick, N.J.: Rutgers University Press, 1979), 199. Perhaps the earliest scholarly argument for Adventist orthodoxy can be found in Whitney R. Cross, *The Burned-Over District: The Social and Intellectual History of Enthusiastic Religion in Western New York, 1800–1850* (New York: Harper and Row, 1950), 291. Cross argues that William Miller and his followers "achieved no startling novelty. His doctrine in every other way [from the precise date he set] virtually epitomized orthodoxy."

24. "Is This a Christian Land?," *Midnight Cry!* (New York), March 10, 1843, 40–41.

25. Henry H. Garney, "Renouncement of Sectarianism," *Rochester (N.Y.) North Star,* April 7, 1848.

26. "Sectarian Worship," *Boston Liberator,* November 26, 1841, 192.

27. John S. C. Abbot, "The Signs of the Times, V," *New York Evangelist,* June 11, 1846).

28. "Disunion in the Church," *Midnight Cry!,* June 15, 1843.

29. "Perfect in One," *Christian Review* (Boston) 12, no. 46 (June 1847): 169.

30. T. H. Stockton, "The Claims of the Gospel," in *Sermons for the People,* 5th ed. (Pittsburgh: A. H. English & Co., 1854).

31. "Prospectus," *Millennial Harbinger* (Bethany, Va.) 1, no. 1 (January 4, 1830).

32. "Sectarianism Is Heresy," *Millennial Harbinger* (Bethany, Va.) 4, no. 6 (June 1840), 260.

33. "What Harm Is There in a Mere Sectarian Name?" *Dover (N.H.) Morning Star,* March 23, 1843, 190.

34. Henry Cowles, "The Peace and Prosperity of Zion," *Oberlin (Ohio) Evangelist* 5, no. 18 (August 30, 1843): 137.

35. S. H., "Cause and Cure of Sectarianism," *New Englander* (New Haven, Ct.) 17 (January 1847): 78, 90.

36. Cooper, *Crater,* 453–54.

37. J., "Christ Second Coming at Hand; Without a Previous Millennium, No. 1," *Signs of the Times* (Boston) 1, no. 19 (1 January 1841), 146.

38. Cooper, *Crater,* 454.

39. Taylor, *A Secular Age,* 3, 461.

40. Cooper, *Crater,* 455–56, 353, 483.

41. Ibid., 459.

42. Mark Noll, *The Civil War as a Theological Crisis* (Chapel Hill: University of North Carolina Press, 2006).

43. Cooper, *Crater,* viii.

44. Ibid., 462.

45. Ibid., 463–65, 470.

46. Ibid., 462, 316, 468, 470.

47. Ibid., 476.

48. George Lippard, *The Quaker City; or, the Monks of Monk Hall,* ed. David S. Reynolds (Amherst: University of Massachusetts Press, 1995), 393.

49. Cooper, *Crater,* 480, 483, 469.

50. Ibid., 484.

51. Jenny Franchot, *Roads to Rome: The Antebellum Protestant Encounter with Catholicism* (Berkeley: University of California Press, 1994), 280.

52. Tocqueville, "How Religion Uses Democratic Instincts in the United States," 505, 503.

4

MILLENNIALISM AND THE CHURCH OF ENGLAND'S MISSION TO FUGITIVE SLAVES IN CANADA

NINA REID-MARONEY

The story of millennialism in the Church of England's Mission to Fugitive Slaves in Canada begins with an ending: the conclusion to Harriet Beecher Stowe's *Uncle Tom's Cabin.* Addressing her readers directly, Stowe steps out of the fictional world she has created and ends her book with a call for the destruction of slavery and for the education of emancipated slaves. Both goals are set out in prophetic language, laced with the hope that there was still a day of grace in which to act: "This is an age of the world when nations are trembling and convulsed. A mighty influence is abroad, surging and heaving the world, as with an earthquake. And is America safe? O, Church of Christ, read the signs of the times! Is not this power the spirit of Him whose kingdom is yet to come, and whose will to be done on earth as it is in heaven?"[1] Most interesting in this concluding address to Stowe's readers is the dual charge—first, to America ("both North and South have been guilty before God"), and then to the Christian church. Calling both nation and church to account in the same breath, Stowe draws attention to the ways in which millennial expectations were at once anchored in a national narrative of fall and redemption and set loose beyond America in that "mighty influence" that Stowe described as "surging and heaving" through a wider Christendom.

The double strand of millennial expectation—tied to the American national experience, but also pulled outward in other directions—is at the center of my inquiry into the nature of providential religion and the ways in which it defined the antislavery culture of nineteenth-century Canada. On the Canadian side of the slavery question, millennial hopes and fears remained recognizably linked to the question Stowe asks—What will become of America?—even as the answer to that question was complicated by its decidedly global implications. Perched at the edge of the British Empire and teetering on the moral precipice of someone else's civil war, antislavery communities in Canada were shaped by the millennial expectations of those abolitionists who helped to found them. It is an important and neglected aspect of the history of Canadian antislavery movements, which derived much of their meaning from the part they were to play in the struggle for abolition in the United States. Even less familiar is the story of Canada's antislavery communities at the nexus of American and English providential narratives, both of which focused, though in different ways, on the end of slavery. During the era of the Civil War, the Anglican presence in the established antislavery communities of Canada West meant that millennial thought of both American and English origins found expression in the daily work of the Mission to Fugitive Slaves in Canada.

One of the most ideologically important black abolitionist communities in Canada West grew up on the on the banks of the Sydenham River in the County of Kent. The self-emancipated slave Josiah Henson and the Reverend Hiram Wilson, Lane Seminary rebel and graduate of Oberlin College, established a settlement for fugitives from American slavery. Their experiment centered on the founding of a sawmill and school: the British American Institute (1842). Steeped in Oberlin perfectionism and in the reformist understanding of the moral and intellectual value of manual labor schools, the British American Institute became the nucleus for the agricultural community of the Dawn settlement.[2] By 1859, the school had closed and the formal organization of the Dawn settlement remained embroiled in controversy, but the black pioneers of the region remained, and continued to invest in land, businesses, and civic institutions, shifting the community's center to the nearby village of Dresden. In the midst of ongoing court battles challenging the poorly funded and racially segregated schools that were established in the district under the protection of the provincial Common Schools Act of 1850, black abolitionists convinced the local committee of the Church of England's Colonial Church and School Society (CCSS) to send them a schoolmaster. The CCSS agreed, and in July 1859, an English missionary named Thomas Hughes arrived to open a school and minister to the families of the village, black and white alike.

Celebrated among his black parishioners as "a man who knew no complexional distinctions," Hughes left a rich record of his years in the abolitionist community of Dresden. The records include printed reports published annually by the CCSS home office in London, the manuscript minute books of the local Corresponding Committee for the Mission in Canada West (particularly valuable because much of the original correspondence was lost during the bombing of London during World War II), and the remarkable diary he kept between 1861 and 1874. In the Dresden example, we can see something of the web of connection, sympathy, and implication that bound the millennial vision of Stowe's signs of the times to the religious life of Canada West.[3] We can also see that Canadian antislavery work, shaped by both American and English narratives of moral redemption and political imperatives, became a new creation. The Church of England men who sent Hughes into the mission field and the network of American abolitionists who met him once he arrived in Canada made it clear to Hughes that the mission carried millennial possibilities as part of the wider struggle against slavery. Yet even as he used a sense of providential direction and evangelical purpose to strike at racial prejudice wherever he found it—from pew to classroom to burial ground—Hughes came to understand that the Mission to Fugitive Slaves opened up the possibility of profound disappointment. Hughes remained convinced that his mission among the people of Dresden was part of the broader redemptive work that had fired his religious imagination while he was still a settled schoolmaster in a little town in Staffordshire, but he also seems to have emerged from the Civil War years having modified his millennial expectations. This modification was a consequence of scale. Through his daily pastoral experience, he came to know the general horrors of chattel slavery and the general hope of human liberation.

Of all millennial pronouncements that the 1850s produced on slavery and abolition, Stowe's charge to the readers of *Uncle Tom's Cabin* to emancipate and to educate was the one most immediately connected to the Church of England's Mission to Fugitive Slaves in Canada and the events that brought Thomas Hughes to the remote Canadian village in the long summer of 1859. On a wave of celebrity that followed the publication of her novel, Stowe traveled through Britain on a speaking tour during the winter of 1853. She was frequently joined on the antislavery lecture circuit by the former slave and black abolitionist Samuel Ringgold Ward. Both Stowe and Ward were drawn into the powerful currents of the English antislavery movement that still defined the moral life of the Church of England's Evangelical Party. The two celebrated American antislavery authors helped to revive English interest in practical antislavery work.

Their message found an especially keen audience in the Church of England's Evangelical Party, the self-conscious heirs of the abolitionist tradition going back to William Wilberforce and the abolitionists of the Clapham Sect.

In the face of the deepening political crisis over slavery in the United States, both Harriet Beecher Stowe and Samuel Ringgold Ward proposed that their English hosts might have a substantial effect in the fight against slavery if they were to open schools among the growing black population of Canada. Schools established on the doorstep of the American republic would serve a political purpose by challenging the logic of slavery. Within a few months of framing the plan for education as an act to expose the inhumanity of slavery and to reveal the providential blessings of liberty, Stowe and Ward had secured the support of the "People's Earl," Lord Shaftesbury, the best-known reformer of the British aristocracy. Stowe's novel, as Shaftsbury noted, had a sense of "destiny" about it. "It left me long troubled in spirit," he wrote in his diary, "and moved me to my heart's core." Shaftesbury's diary entry for Good Friday, 1853, was simple: "Began a movement for the evangelization of the fugitive slaves settled in Canada. It is a natural, necessary and becoming consequence of our movement for emancipation."[4] Shaftesbury served as the president of the Mission to Fugitive Slaves in Canada for the life of the organization.

The better-known result of the alliance between Stowe, Ward, Shaftesbury, and his aristocratic friends was the "Stafford House Address," a letter penned by Shaftesbury and sent out to the press under the name of the Duchess of Sutherland. The letter called on the women of the United States to turn against slavery. It drew intense criticism, including a heated reply from Karl Marx and a chilly letter from Julia Tyler, wife of the president of the United States. The latter prompted a reply of its own—the first published work of Harriet Jacobs was her response to the proslavery sentiment of Julia Tyler.[5] Meanwhile, Frederick Douglass and Martin Delany held an open debate on what aid to the abolitionist cause could possibly come from members of the British aristocracy through Harriet Beecher Stowe, whose proposals to aid and educate the fugitive slaves of Canada were, for Delany at least, still tainted by Stowe's early support for Liberian colonization.[6] In the context of this war of words over who did or did not have the moral authority to call for an end to American slavery, English reformers invested great hope in the practical plan to open schools through the Mission to Fugitive Slaves in Canada.

Even before it began, the mission was cast as part of a larger abolitionist strategy that would link the day of grace to the beneficent and providential workings of the British Empire. In 1854, a few weeks before first CCSS missionary sailed from Southampton for Canada West to seek out a suitable site for the first school, the Church of England's bishop of Sierra Leone, Owen Emeric

Vidal, used the occasion of his departure from England for Africa to pray for the Mission to Fugitive Slaves in Canada. Recalling the imaginative power of Stowe's image of Eliza crossing the ice floes in the Ohio River to freedom on the other side, the bishop reminded his English audience that the fugitive slave need only make "the one sublime leap that places him on English ground and he is free." It was then up to the church to provide the newly emancipated with "gospel liberty for their souls as well as the charter of liberty for their persons."[7]

The address from the bishop is worth examining in some detail because it describes the Church of England's evangelical position on the Mission to Fugitive Slaves in terms that are strikingly familiar to those attuned to the language of American millennialism. "God in his gracious providence," Vidal wrote, "has raised our country above all the world, and given her prominence among the nations, and this power was committed to her as an invaluable trust, of which she should give account to him who gave it. The moral state of England is of immeasurable importance to the whole human race. God has placed her in a position to advance or retard the highest interests of our species, such as nation never occupied before." Through such images, the bishop evoked the power of a "redeemer nation" whose moral life and imperatives were of God's choosing—but this chosen land of immeasurable moral importance for the future happiness of the human race was England, not the United States. Lifted from the American setting and placed in an English one, the language of freedom, and the moral power of the overthrow of slavery was a message delivered to a postemancipation audience. It was thus untrammeled by any sense of paradox. Claiming moral leadership legitimized by his representing of an emancipated empire, the bishop played with the language and imagery of providential history. In the bishop's formulation, England already *was* the promised land, and in taking on work among the fugitives from American slavery, the church had sent out her children "from a land flowing with milk and honey to a waste howling wilderness." Recent historians of British abolition note the general gloom of second thoughts developing in the 1850s among some Britons, who worried about the wisdom of their emancipation enacted twenty years before.[8] If this were the rising mood, then the Church of England's antislavery work must have been crafted to restore a sense of urgency to the cause. In the bishop's address, antislavery missions became part of a providential future driving relentlessly not toward moral progress alone, but toward the ultimate resolution of the deeper problem of human freedom.

The effect was to give the Mission to Fugitive Slaves in Canada a contested identity—part wilderness, part promised land—and it is this ambiguous, shifting, symbolic geography that lent the mission much of its peculiar character in relation to the millennial imagination invested in it. From the English side, however, there was no doubt of the millennial expectations attached to the mission in relation to American slavery. The familiar trope of an empire on which the sun never sets was turned to the bishop's purpose in striking twists of language woven through the description of the Canadian mission: "We have been taught to feel that as our evening sun recedes from view behind the waters of the wide Atlantic, he rises upon many a scene of unutterable anguish, lighting the miserable victims of chains and slavery to labour and toil and sorrow without cessation and without hope." The point is not simply that the language of empire is equated with the language of hope; it is rather that British antislavery men and women used a cosmic narrative of English-ness and empire in ways that paralleled the American narrative of abolition as atonement for the original sin of slavery. The Canadian mission was bathed in the light of this providential story and placed at its center. In the narrative that framed the mission, the sin was assuredly American; redemption belonged to England.

On board the ship that bore him back to the See of Sierra Leone, Bishop Vidal died before reaching Africa, almost at the same moment as the first teachers bound for the Mission to Fugitive Slaves sailed from Southampton, carrying with them the hopes that the bishop had attached in a most singular way to the Canadian mission. Those hopes found a practical application and a fresh layer of providential interpretation at the hands of the Reverend Benjamin Cronyn, then rector of St. Paul's in London, Canada West. Cronyn opened the church premises to the first mission school, and much of its early success in London can be linked to his support.[9] By 1856, Cronyn was at the head of the local Corresponding Committee of the CCSS, and he assumed a direct role in shaping the expansion of the Mission to Fugitive Slaves across the region, from the village of Oro on the shore of Lake Simcoe to the southwestern communities of Windsor and Sandwich along the Detroit River.

At the same time, Cronyn and his friends of the CCSS in England were engaged in a movement to create the Diocese of Huron—a vast sweep of evangelical territory wrest from the control of the High Church bishop of Toronto in 1857. Benjamin Cronyn was chosen as the first bishop of Huron. At its founding, the promise of the new diocese was bound up with that of the Mission to

Fugitive Slaves, thanks to Cronyn's influence. Awaiting his Lambeth Palace consecration in 1857, Benjamin Cronyn made the point by attending CCSS meetings. There, before the ardent antislavery men of the CCSS, he "exhibited a map of Canada and traced thereon the boundaries of the Diocese of Huron." With a palpable sense of satisfaction and promise, the founders of the mission saw the happy implications for their own work in the region and looked forward to a "preponderance of Evangelical men" in Canada West who would "perpetuate a guarantee for the election of evangelical Bishops in succession to the See of Huron for all time to come."[10]

Thomas Hughes came to all of this from the sympathetic fringes of the antislavery movement in England. Family tradition holds that he was inspired to apply for the posting in Canada through the same process that had moved Lord Shaftesbury to found the mission: his reading of *Uncle Tom's Cabin.* It is almost certain that Hughes would have known of Stowe's speaking engagements in Birmingham in 1853, and that he understood the wider context of social reform that animated people such as Shaftesbury. Before he came to the school in Walsall, Hughes taught at a National School in Birmingham. The National School movement carried core assumptions about uplift of the poor through education, and formed an important backdrop for Hughes's work. At the time of his application to the CCSS in Christmastime, 1856, Hughes was thirty-six years old, a husband and father with an established career. Staffordshire, where Hughes worked as a schoolmaster, may not have been the land of milk and honey, but the distant mission school in Canada was surely a wilderness by comparison.

As soon as he made his application for the post, Hughes came under the influence of men who saw the Canadian mission in the same light—men such as Benjamin Cronyn and Bishop Cronyn's friend Reverend Isaac Hellmuth, general superintendent of the Colonial and Continental Church Society for British North America. Hellmuth interviewed Hughes for the mission job, and was reportedly "very favourably impressed by his conversation and manner."[11] It was a sign that Hellmuth considered Hughes to be on the right side of the High Church/Evangelical divide. For Isaac Hellmuth, the work of the CCSS in Canada was part of an evangelical movement preparing for the return of Christ, a matter which Hellmuth engaged both in very broad dispensationalist terms and in quite personal ones related to his own conversion from the Judaism of his rabbinical family in Breslau to the Christianity of Church of England missionaries. From this starting point, Hellmuth was inclined to view the Church of England's evangelical work less as evidence that "moral state of England is of immeasurable importance" and more as evidence for the final "dispensation which shall extend the empire of Christ over every climate and region of the globe."[12] This context is particularly important to the understanding of Hughes's spiritual formation because it was under Hellmuth's guidance that Hughes turned toward the priesthood. Shortly after he arrived in Canada to teach at the CCSS school in London, he took up the study of holy orders with Hellmuth. He was priested in December 1859, six months after he opened the mission station in Dresden. "Thank God," Hellmuth wrote of his new priests heading out into the mission field, "they are all converted men and experimental Christians!"

Both of Hughes's mentors in Canada West spent the latter part of the 1850s thinking about the links between their plan to expand the mission to fugitive slaves in ways that would connect the work most logically to the antislavery movement in the United States. Together they boarded the London train to visit abolitionist leaders of the Detroit Vigilance Committee at the Second Baptist Church in Detroit. They entertained Bishop Daniel Payne of the African Methodist Episcopal Church during his visit to the mission school in London in 1857. They cultivated connections to the Evangelical and antislavery party of the Episcopal Church in the United States. And in the early months of 1861, Isaac Hellmuth made a trip to New Orleans to see slavery for himself, dispatching reports of the horrors of the slave markets, and writing of his own sense of fear that his antislavery sentiments might place him in danger.[13]

At the first Diocesan Synod in 1859, Cronyn had been at pains to set out the political significance of the work of the mission. "So long as slavery is upheld by the laws of the neighboring republic," he told the assembled clergy and teachers from the London school, "so long will the degraded and enslaved African, who hears of Canada as a land of freedom and a refuge from cruelty and oppression, seek to escape from a country in which the first rights of manhood are denied him." Elizabeth King, an English teacher at the London school in 1859, reported on the bishop's confirmation of black children in terms that evoke the sense of interconnection between the personal and the political. The bishop, we are told, gave the children "a beautiful little address before they left the communion rails, reminding them and all present, in a very nice manner, that all are one in Christ Jesus, and that 'there is neither Barbarian, Scythian, bond, nor free.' He then preached a beautiful and suitable sermon, just such an one as he can give, from the text, 'If any man be in Christ, he is a new creature,' and, as he expressed it, a new creation: thus through the whole striking at the very root of the American prejudices."[14] Later that summer, on the anniversary of Emancipation in the British West Indies, a thousand people marched through the streets of London to Bishop Cronyn's church to hear the preaching of the Reverend Robert Gordon, a black abolitionist and Episcopal missionary working for Cronyn and the CCSS. Gordon warned of the coming judgment, the "retributive sword of Justice," and a bath of blood that would submerge "the resplendent head of liberty" and sweep away the whole republican experiment if slavery were allowed to run its course.[15] Set out in these terms, there was no question that the charitable activities of the mission's teachers and priests carried the sharp edge of millennial purpose.

Once the war began, Bishop Cronyn and (now Archdeacon) Hellmuth set the Mission to Fugitive Slaves against the backdrop of the wider politics of the church. One of their closest American allies in the Episcopal Church was Charles P. McIlvaine, bishop of Ohio, who shared the antislavery conviction of his Canadian colleagues. In 1861, Abraham Lincoln dispatched Bishop McIlvaine to England on a diplomatic mission to gain English support for the Union. During the strained period of the Trent Affair, McIlvaine met with Lord Shaftesbury and other supporters of the Canadian mission, adding moral credibility to the Union cause.[16] Isaac Hellmuth and Benjamin Cronyn kept up close ties with McIlvaine during the war years, and largely adopted the same view on its meaning: war was retribution for the sin of slavery (made worse because it was committed in what was supposed to be the "palladium of liberty," as Archdeacon Hellmuth put it). In turn, the end of the war and the end of slavery would mean, in McIlvaine's words, "deliverance from all of the evils engendered by slavery against the whites and the colored—and the beginning of a new era of prosperity, happiness, peace, godliness to all."[17] In late 1863, two weeks after the Gettysburg Address helped refashion the frame of providential history set around the war, Bishop McIlvaine was invited by his Canadian friends to deliver the founding address at Huron College, the seminary founded by Benjamin Cronyn and Isaac Hellmuth. Given that Bishop McIlvaine was their closest contact to the American church, it not surprising that McIlvaine's Canadian brethren saw the Civil War largely from his point of view.

From every side of the antislavery movements, both British and American ones, that informed his life and recent entry into the priesthood, Hughes heard the message that his new posting in the tiny village of Dresden flowed into the great themes of redemption and the coming of the kingdom of Christ. But even as he arrived in the mission field in 1859, Hughes found that his new home was well established as a center of abolitionist activity, and possessed of its own history as a repository of hopes for a Promised Land. Both Benjamin Cronyn and Thomas Hughes already knew Dresden's most celebrated resident, Josiah Henson, founder of the British American Institute and the inspiration for much of the character of Stowe's "Uncle Tom."[18] They also knew that the settlement and surrounding rural community were invested with a complex of associations that had played for years in the American abolitionist press. A generation of abolitionists of every sort—moral reformers, Quakers, Lane Hall Rebels, Oberlin graduates, Baptists, AME bishops, feminists, radicals, Liberty Party supporters, Frederick Douglass, John Brown—had picked up on the "unavoidable symbolic value" of the crossing from slavery into the "Canadian Canaan."[19] Thus, the Quaker abolitionist Lucretia Mott, traveling through Dresden on her way to the Seneca Falls Convention in 1848, wrote of the practical challenges faced in the Canadian wilderness, and of the way in which the challenge was being met by black pioneers "in the giant forests of their Canaan-land. . . . They cheerfully toil on and submit to their present privations, seeing a 'good land and a large' before them."[20] To Frederick Douglass, black settlers to Canada West were "clearing the land, converting the wilderness into fertile fields and causing the very earth to rejoice in their presence."[21] It was difficult to find an abolitionist description of the place that did *not* use biblical language and identify this part of Canada as the promised land.

The same framework was used by black settlers themselves—some fugitives from slavery, others free when they chose to emigrate—to cast the Canadian alternative in providential terms, and to use those terms to shape their experience of freedom. The fact of the Canadian context alone made a difference to the political and theological implications of providential thought attached to the work of building a home, clearing the land, or sending children to school. Ordinary life was to be understood in sacred terms; things sacred were understood to carry a dimension that was inescapably political. For Hughes, this could be, at first, a troubling diversion from what he considered to be proper religious exercises, particularly when the political dimension of worship included children. At a summer celebration in a small black community Sunday school soon after he arrived, Hughes was surprised to find that all "references to anything of a sacred character" were subsumed in the language of emancipation. Even the inscriptions on the festive banners—"'Union is strength,' 'We will progress,' 'Our march is onward'"—which Hughes found "appropriate enough perhaps for political or emancipation meetings, but decidedly out of place at a gathering of Sunday-school children," spoke of the identification of things sacred and secular in the black abolitionist community.[22] From the vantage point of Philadelphia or London, Cincinnati or Port-au-Prince, black settlements of Canada West were most readily defined by the language of the promised land, but for those who lived here, there was no separation of that sense of higher purpose from the simplest events of ordinary life. All of this is to say that the Mission to Fugitive Slaves in Canada was linked to millennial hopes in both the United States and Britain, but was also under a peculiar set of pressures that collapsed the distance—in both time and space—between the "promised land," a product of religious imagination, and the promised land as an ordinary place.

The point was brought home through the community's connection to John Brown and the raid at Harpers Ferry. In the spring of 1858, while Thomas Hughes was still teaching in London and studying for holy orders, John Brown had held his "quiet convention" in the town of Chatham, a short stage-ride away from the village of Dresden. One of the members of Brown's convention and a signatory to the provisional constitution for a free republic was Alfred Whipper, a member of one of the most prominent black abolitionist families in Pennsylvania. John Brown's body had been in the grave but three months when Hughes hired Whipper to take over as schoolmaster at the Dresden mission. The premises for the school and for Hughes's church were the "upper room" of a grocery store owned by another black abolitionist family with deep connections to Whipper's abolitionist brother William Whipper and his friends in the Philadelphia Vigilance Committee.[23] In this setting, the raid at Harpers Ferry, the martyrdom of John Brown, and the war itself all reached to the heart of the mission as clear and present shocks. For Hughes, the effect was extraordinary. The millennialist language of retribution and justice, fire and redemption, had quit the pages of novels and sermons and found its way into the most mundane aspects of his professional life. News of the war poured into the village through American newspapers. Hughes reported the avid reading of the *New York Tribune* among his flock; his choirmaster in the spring of 1861, a Philadelphian, arranged for the delivery of Forney's *War Press*.[24] In turn, news of the work in Dresden was always reported alongside news from the American scene—first in the form of accounts of slavery and escape, then in the accounts of the Civil War. Sharing space in the CCSS report with the "American War" only heightened the sense that the history of one was bound up with the history of the other in the working out of a providential design.

To the extent that the language of millennialism had the effect of drawing this small place into a larger drama, it provided an important aspect of the culture of evangelicalism that made the Canadian antislavery movement work and made it possible for the mission to expand and cross the boundaries of race. The erasing of racial barriers was one point at which the kingdom of Christ seemed closest to Hughes, even in the middle of the war and its uncertainty. The reputation forged by Hughes and his schoolmaster, Alfred Whipper, provided encouragement to black abolitionists elsewhere, including the prominent abolitionists Isaac Shadd and Amelia Freeman Shadd, who appealed to the CCSS Corresponding Committee and received financial support for their school in Chatham in 1860 and 1861. Whipper's schoolroom in Dresden was at the vanguard of the society's expanding mission field across Canada West in stations from Toronto to Windsor, and through the years of the Civil War, the school's supporters dwelled within the larger sense that they were part of an historic turning point at which, as Shaftesbury had said, "God interposes for his people." During the most encouraging hours of their work, it may well have appeared that Shaftesbury had it right when he wrote of the whole problem of slavery, that "the thing is drawing to a close."[25]

Notably absent from Hughes own work in the war years, however, is the sustained assurance that anything much was drawing to a close at all. This did not in any way lessen the sense of a general providential direction, but it is likely that black congregants taught him to view events with a full measure of caution. For white antislavery reformers at a distance, the mission operated at the level of clear symbolism and unequivocal values—the death of slavery equaled freedom. For those closer to the action, the war and the prospect of the end of slavery were hedged about with a keen awareness of contingency of human life, even in the promised land.

The sense of vulnerability comes through clearly in some of the incidents Hughes reported to the erstwhile men and women of the CCSS in England. A good example comes in his account of his first year in the mission field. A cruel autumn, a blighted harvest, and a bitter winter brought unexpected privation. One bitter February night in 1861, Hughes answered a knock at his door. A letter to his supervisors described the late-night encounter with the two visitors, a "poor man and woman" from Hughes's congregation. The couple had walked some five miles in the cold to Hughes's home, "wretchedly clad" in quilts and worn-out boots "affording scarcely any protection against the weather." The man's hands were frostbitten, and as Hughes noted in horror, "his sufferings had evidently affected his mind, for though quiet and subdued in his manner, he was continually raving about some strange beings that, he said, infested his shanty, and were 'sucking his blood from the ends of his fingers.'" Hughes and his wife did what they could, offering warm clothing, food, and money to buy more, but the encounter was clearly unsettling.[26] Among Hughes's extensive reports to the English agency that supported his work at Dresden's Mission to Fugitive Slaves in Canada, this episode stands out for its stark portrayal of human suffering in the "promised land" of Canadian freedom. None of his parishioners within the settlement, Hughes hastened to add, wanted those abroad to hear any hint of such privation lest it be attributed to a failure to live up to freedom's promise. The rest of the letter goes on to describe the successes of the year's work overall. But to Hughes, this particular moment, complete with its element of the gothic, carried a peculiar and revelatory force. Even in Canada, where the beneficent light of freedom was supposed to have long ago banished shadows bred in the nightmare world of the tormented man on Hughes's doorstep, the horror was there.

Peering into this nightmarish world through the eyes of those who had lived it, Hughes of course felt that the war to end slavery cut very close to home, and resonated in obvious ways with the millennial pronouncements with which the CCSS mission had begun. The mission was removed, however, from the most immediate concern with the war's implications for the idea of American nationhood. This affected Hughes's sense of timing. The collapsing of distance between the promised land *imagined* and the promised land *lived* had a temporal dimension; one did not have to wait for the death of American slavery to usher in the kingdom of Christ. Hughes felt this as fresh urgency, recognizing that the mission in Canada must have had something akin to a head start. At the same time, he developed his own measures of progress. Emancipation of American slaves would not be enough. Instead, he turned to the argument that there could be no ultimate victory over slavery without addressing the problem of racial prejudice. Noting the complex social conditions that made up everyday life in his community, Hughes had long indicted those who would profess antislavery views without digging out the roots of racial prejudice in their own hearts:

> What makes the matter more shocking is this, that all branches of the Christian Church give way to it! Ministers, both in the states and in Canada, being for the most part dependant on their congregations for support, are in no position to set themselves against the general feeling. While,

> therefore, numbers are to be found loud and eloquent enough in their advocacy of the abolition of slavery, and denouncing in the strongest terms the cruelty of the slave-owner; yet hardly a minister of the Gospel can be met with who will take the free-colored man by the hand and treat him as a friend and brother.[27]

Hughes was thus in the position of having his sense of optimism that "the thing is drawing to a close" run up against experience in the muddy village streets—where whites refused to worship or enter into communion with the black members of his congregation, where white landowners refused to sell a building lot for a church that was racially integrated, and where Hughes felt the sting of prejudice for his open views and practice. In 1865, he went so far as to refer to the long-awaited abolition of the institution as "the mere destruction of slavery."

Of course, Hughes had no monopoly on a sense of disappointment. Samuel Ringgold Ward had memorably described Canada as the "great moral lighthouse for black people on this continent," but he had also written of "Canadian Negro Hate—incomparably meaner than the American article."[28] What is interesting about Hughes is the way in which his role as missionary forced him to live through that tension from the beginning of his work in Canada until the day he died in 1876. Hughes was at once borne up by the millennial expectations of others, and pressed down by the weight of his own experience. As a result, his diary and his reports to his supporters maintain a careful balance between his ability to recognize small signs of the kingdom in human relationships—in the success of children at the school, in the confirmation of new communicants—and to cope with being let down. One of the many reports that eloquently expressed Hughes's dilemma came in his account of the year 1867. Under the depressing influence of continued racial prejudice, Hughes wrote to his London employers: "Can it be surprising that comparatively little progress is made, or that your missionary, alone and unsupported, should sometimes give way to feelings of despondency. This is indeed 'the day of small things' with us."[29]

Samuel Ringgold Ward had hoped that when "placed side by side with a country that boasted of a freedom it did not possess," the Mission to Fugitive Slaves in Canada might "work out most important results."[30] Hughes was sustained by moments of a more optimistic turn when it appeared that those important results were close at hand. One such occasion came when Benjamin Cronyn visited Hughes's mission in September 1865. At the time, Hughes's

Dresden congregation still met in the small upstairs quarters of a grocery store. The effort to find a building site for a church had been thwarted for years by racial prejudice in the village. Cronyn preached "in our humble upper room at Dresden," from Romans 5:1, and confirmed thirteen candidates—eleven of whom were black and two of whom were white (members of Hughes's family).[31] The sharing of the small room by the bishop of Huron and the black abolitionists of Hughes's school serves as a reminder of how deeply the mission's evangelical concept of freedom and its political concept of freedom—"gospel liberty for their souls and the charter of liberty for their persons"—were intertwined. This reading of events, however, depended on the contrast, as Ward noted, that came with placing the mission "side by side with a country that boasted of a freedom it did not possess."[32] Once emancipation came to the United States, those who were long practiced in reading the signs of the times turned their gaze back to the American side.

The "day of small things" seems a long way from the day of grace that provided Stowe's readers with a way forward through the tumult of the 1850s, but it is also an appropriate metaphor for Hughes's sense of his life's work, and like the passage in Zechariah from which the reference is drawn, Hughes's use of the image carries a complexity that belies the simple reading of the day of small things as disillusionment. It would be too easy to conclude that in nineteenth-century Canada, under the "beneficent sway of Victoria's scepter," the cosmos may have cracked, but was seldom given over to crumbling. The Mission to Fugitive Slaves shows us what happened when millennialism was unloosed from its moorings in an American narrative of national identity and redemption and drifted into deep backwaters. There are all sorts of ways to explore what this meant in the subsequent life of theology in Victorian Canada. The day of small things, after all, was not to be despised, and in this particular place, the millennialist visions of the promised land managed to unsettle established hierarchies of race and gender for at least a generation. The first ordained woman in Canadian ministry was an African Canadian baptized as an infant by Thomas Hughes in the church her father had helped to build in the 1860s.[33] The appearance of such "lively stones" in the landscape created through the CCSS mission offers new terrain for study; for the moment, it will be enough to think about the ways in which Hughes shows us a powerful and pervasive millennial vision perplexed by experience, though not, in James Moorhead's terms, "reduced to a metaphor of perpetual improvement."[34] In Canada West, as in the United

States, there was no easy solving of what Mark Noll has called the "theological puzzle of the Civil War."[35] It is possible, though, that under the constant pressure of having to look for the millennium by concentrating on the foreground, the evangelical tradition that Hughes represented learned to live with the "day of small things" and to conceptualize a millennial hope the more resilient for its modest scale.

NOTES

1. Harriet Beecher Stowe, *Uncle Tom's Cabin, or Life among the Lowly* (Boston: John P. Jewett & Company, 1852), 629.

2. Josiah Henson, *The Life of Josiah Henson, Formerly a Slave, Now an Inhabitant of Canada, as Narrated by Himself* (Boston: A. D. Phelps, 1849). On the Dawn settlement, see the accounts in William H. Pease and Jane H. Pease, *Black Utopia: Negro Communal Experiments in America* (Madison: State Historical Society of Wisconsin, 1963); Allen Stouffer, *The Light of Nature and the Law of God: Anti-Slavery in Ontario, 1833–1877* (Baton Rouge: Louisiana State University Press, 1992); and Robin Winks, *The Blacks in Canada* (New Haven: Yale University Press, 1991). On the fate of the Dawn settlement and the controversy over white leadership and control, see Peter Ripley, ed., *Black Abolitionist Papers,* vol. 2 (Chapel Hill: University of North Carolina Press, 1992), 106–7 nn. 2–7, hereafter cited as *BAP*; and Jane Rhodes, *Mary Ann Shadd Cary: The Black Press and Protest in the Nineteenth Century* (Bloomington: Indiana University Press, 1998), 104–6. See also Henson's letters, printed in *BAP,* and the *Provincial Freeman,* September 8, 1855, September 22, 1855, on Mary Ann Shadd's and William Newman's relationship with the Dawn leadership. On Hiram Wilson, see William H. Pease and Jane H. Pease, *Bound with Them in Chains* (Westport, Ct.: Greenwood, 1972), 115–39; Pease and Pease, *Black Utopia,* 63–82; *BAP,* 2:159n. On the movement for manual labor education as part of the reform impulse among American abolitionists, including Hiram Wilson, see Milton Sernett, *Abolition's Axe: Beriah Green, the Oneida Institute and the Black Freedom Struggle* (Syracuse, N.Y.: Syracuse University Press, 1986).

3. Thomas Hughes Diary, manuscript, Diocese of Huron Archives, London, Ontario; Minute Book of the Colonial Church and School Society MG17-B4 reel A-23, National Archives, Ottawa. A brief account of the Mission to Fugitive Slaves in Canada is found in Winks, *The Blacks in Canada,* 236–38.

4. Edwin Hodder, *The Life and Work of the Seventh Earl of Shaftesbury, K.G.,* vol. 2 (London, 1887), 395–98. See also Georgina Battiscombe, *Shaftesbury: A Biography of the Seventh Earl* (London: Constable, 1974), 238–39; and Geoffrey B. A. M. Finlayson, *The Seventh Earl of Shaftesbury, 1801–1885* (London: Methuen, 1981), 344–45.

5. Stowe's account of these events in the spring of 1853 is recorded in her *Sunny Memories of Foreign Lands,* vol. 2 (Boston, 1854), Letters to Calvin Stowe, 84–89; 134–42. See also Samuel Ringgold Ward, *Autobiography of a Fugitive Negro: His Anti-Slavery Labours in the United States, Canada and England* (London: John Snow, 1855), 289–90; and William Wells Brown, *Narrative of William Wells Brown, a Fugitive Slave, Written by Himself* (Boston: Anti-Slavery Office, 1847). Brown's ac-

count of Stowe and the Duchess of Sutherland is found in a letter to William Lloyd Garrison, noted in Harriet C. Frazier, *Runaway Freed Missouri Slaves and Those Who Helped Them* (Jefferson, N.C.: McFarland, 2004), 21.

On the Address to the Women of America, Harriet Beecher Stowe, the Duchess of Sutherland, and Julia Tyler, see Evelyn Pugh, "Women and Slavery: Julia Tyler and the Duchess of Sutherland," *Virginia Magazine of History and Biography* 88 (1980): 186–202. Harriett Jacobs's response is described in Jean Fagin Yellin, *Harriett Jacobs: A Life* (New York: Basic Civitas, 2004), 122–23. On Marx and his critique of the Duchess of Sutherland's family connection to the evicting of tenants from family landholdings in the Scottish Highlands, and for an excellent discussion of Stowe's connections to the "Stafford House Address," see Sarah Meer, *Uncle Tom Mania: Slavery, Minstrelsy and Transatlantic Culture in the 1850s* (Athens: University of Georgia Press, 2005), 167–69.

6. The exchange between Douglass and Delany is reprinted in Robert S. Levine, ed., *Martin R. Delany: A Documentary Reader* (Chapel Hill: University of North Carolina Press, 2003), 226–30.

7. *Sermon, Delivered at St. Dunstan's Church, Fleet Street . . . by the Lord Bishop of Sierra Leone* (London, 1854).

8. David Brion Davis, *Inhuman Bondage: The Rise and Fall of Slavery in the New World* (New York: Oxford University Press, 2006), 231–33.

9. West London Branch of the Colonial Church and School Society, Occasional Paper no. 4, London, October 1855.

10. Minute Book of the Corresponding Committee of the Colonial Church and School Society, 1856, Diocese of Huron Verschoyle Philip Memorial Archives, London; Minute Book of the Colonial Church and School Society, October 1857, Colonial and Continental Church Society Records (microfilm), MG17-B4, reel A-23, National Archives, Ottawa.

11. General Minute Book, Colonial Church and School Society, December 30, 1856, February 3, 1857. CCSS records of support to the Mission to Fugitive Slaves in Canada for the year 1855 list Walsall as the only town in Staffordshire in which substantial donations were collected (*Mission to the Free Colored Population in Canada,* Occasional Paper of the West London Branch, Colonial Church and School Society [London, 1855], 23).

12. Isaac Hellmuth, *The Divine Dispensations* (Toronto, 1866). A recent reassessment of Hellmuth's conversion from Judaism to Christianity is found in Monda Halpern, "'This Ambitious Polish Jew': Rethinking the Conversion and Career of Bishop Isaac Hellmuth," *Ontario History* 99, no. 2 (Autumn 2007): 221–48.

13. Minute Book of the Corresponding Committee of the Colonial Church and School Society, 1856, Diocese of Huron Verschoyle Philip Memorial Archives, London; Minute Book of the Colonial Church and School Society, October 1857, Colonial and Continental Church Society Records (microfilm), MG17-B4, reel A-23, National Archives, Ottawa; *Mission to Fugitive Slaves in Canada; Being a Branch of the Operations of the Colonial Church and School Society, Report for the Year 1860–61* (London, 1861).

14. *Mission to Fugitive Slaves in Canada; Being a Branch of the Operations of the Colonial Church and School Society, Report for the Year 1859–60* (London, 1860), 18–19.

15. Robert Gordon, *A Sermon preached on the morning of the first of August: by a black clergyman, the Rev. Robert Gordon, in St. Paul Cathedral, London, Canada West on the occasion of the celebration of the twenty-first anniversary of the West Indies emancipation, by the coloured citizens of London, and several other places* (London, 1859).

16. Kara M. McClurken, "For Love of God and Country: McIlvaine's Mission," *Anglican and Episcopal History* 69 (2000); William Carus, ed., *Memorials of the Right Reverend C. P. McIlvaine* (New York, 1882), 234–36.

17. C. P. McIlvaine, in Diana Butler, *Standing against the Whirlwind: Evangelical Episcopalians in Nineteenth-Century America* (New York: Oxford University Press, 1995), 167.

18. On Henson and Stowe, see the biographical note on Henson in *BAP,* vol. 2, *Canada.*

19. For a recent assessment of the abolitionist culture of Canada West in its transatlantic context, see Heike Paul, "Out of Chatham: Abolitionism on the Canadian Frontier," *Atlantic Studies* 8 (June 2011): 165–88.

20. Lucretia Mott to Edmund Quincy, August 24, 1848, in *Selected Letters of Lucretia Coffin Mott,* ed. Beverly Wilson Palmer (Urbana: University of Illinois Press, 2002), 165–66.

21. *Frederick Douglass' Paper,* August 18, 1854.

22. Thomas Hughes, in *Mission to the Fugitive Slaves in Canada: Report for the Year 1861–62* (London, 1862), 25–26; Diary of Thomas Hughes, MS, Diocese of Huron Archives, London, ON.

23. William Whipper's account of his work giving safe passage to fugitives is found in William Still's *The Underground Railroad* (Philadelphia, 1872), 735–40. Julie Winch, *Philadelphia's Black Elite: Activism, Accommodation and the Struggle for Autonomy, 1787–1848* (Philadelphia: Temple University Press, 1988), 102–3; see also Richard McCormick, "William Whipper, Moral Reformer," in *The Elite of Our People: Joseph Willson's Sketches of Black Upper-Class Life in Ante-Bellum Philadelphia,* ed. Julie Winch (State College: Pennsylvania State University Press, 2000), 102–7.

24. Parker Smith to Jacob C. White, April 5, 1862, Jacob C. White Papers, Howard University.

25. Amelia Shadd to the Corresponding Committee, Letter Book, MS, Diocese of Huron Archives; Shadd to the Colonial Church and School Society, in *Mission to the Fugitive Slaves in Canada: Report for the Year 1860*, 46.

26. Thomas Hughes, in *Mission to Fugitive Slaves in Canada; Being a Branch of the Operations of the Colonial Church and School Society: Report for the Year 1859–1860* (London, 1860), 29.

27. Thomas Hughes to the CCSS, February 3, 1862, in *Mission to the Fugitive Slaves in Canada: Report for the Year 1861–62,* 33.

28. Samuel Ringgold Ward, in *BAP,* 2:224–37.

29. Hughes to the CCSS, October 1868, in *Mission to the Coloured Population in Canada* (London, 1869), 12.

30. Colonial Church and School Society Occasional Paper no. 1, London, February 1854.

31. *Mission to the Coloured Population of Canada, late Fugitive Slave Mission; Being a Branch of the Operations of the Colonial and Continental Church Society* (London, 1865), 8–9.

32. Ward, *Autobiography of a Fugitive Negro,* 289–90.

33. N. Reid-Maroney, *The Reverend Jennie Johnson in African Canadian History, 1868–1967* (Rochester: University of Rochester Press, 2012).

34. James Moorhead, *World without End: Mainstream American Protestant Visions of the Last Things, 1880–1925* (Bloomington: Indiana University Press, 1999).

35. Mark Noll, *America's God: From Jonathan Edwards to Abraham Lincoln* (New York: Oxford University Press, 2002).

5

COLONIZATION AND THE LIMITS OF ANTISLAVERY IN UPCOUNTRY SOUTH CAROLINA

JOSEPH MOORE

South Carolina's antebellum Associate Reformed Presbyterians (ARP) pursued the return of Christ with evangelistic action. But it was slavery, more than biblical prophecy, that provided the intellectual and spiritual creativity that energized the ARP encounter with millennialism. Emancipation and the eschaton informed one another for both white and black members. This essay examines two interwoven case studies emanating from the ARP religious community in Abbeville District, South Carolina. These cases possess overlapping themes: the moral dilemma of slavery, providential deliverance, and millennial mission. These themes are not unique in the Civil War–era South. However, the failed attempts by this interracial religious sect to find a moral middle ground on slavery raise important questions about the nature of antislavery thought in the heart of the proslavery South.

The first message was spoken to celebrate Independence Day, but its reception was far from warm. An ARP minister struggled to explain to a hostile white audience that the slow eradication of slavery could bring about Christ's return to earth. The second address was preached to a crowded black audience in a kitchen and proclaimed a coming deliverance that was at once imminent and painfully far off. Despite their differences, these two statements had common connections in content and context that shed light onto the awkward and eventually failed attempts at creating a moral middle ground on the slave question in South Carolina. They reveal how messages spoken into interracial communities crossed the line between freedom and slavery with both continuity and transformation.

The Associate Reformed Presbyterians were the American hybrid of two closely related Scottish religious traditions called Covenanters and Seceders.

These groups, often referred to in Britain as "Phanaticks," comprised the militant fringe of Presbyterianism in the Atlantic world. They had a long tradition dating back to the 1637 National Covenant and 1643 Solemn League and Covenant that bound Scotland, Britain, and all future generations of Presbyterians to uphold a godly government that would acknowledge the headship of Christ over church and state. Over the course of the eighteenth century, Covenanter rhetoric on religious and civil liberty intermingled with that of Enlightenment radicals as the sects participated vigorously in both the American Revolution and the 1798 Irish Rebellion. By the early nineteenth century, most of their adherents clung to a Whig interpretation of their own history that portrayed themselves and their ancestors as zealous advocates for the rights of churches to live out the Bible as the primitive church without interference from the state. As part of this tradition, Covenanters had been avowedly antislavery since 1644, when Covenanter Samuel Rutherford lashed out against slavery as a violation of God-given civil liberties in his tract *Lex, Rex.* Most Covenanter households contained a copy of that book, and children were weaned hearing it quoted in devotionals and sermons. The slavery issue took on increasing importance for those Covenanters who moved into the American South. Equally important in understanding their southern experience was the fact that the superstructure of the movement had long been based in a network of cell-like religious groups that were led by laity. These groups met weekly for prayer, Bible and devotional readings, and psalm singing. Male and female, young and old were expected to be literate. When slavery spread to the Carolina backcountry to which they had immigrated in the late eighteenth century, many Covenanters left rather than join their Presbyterian neighbors in slaveholding. Those who remained tempered their antislavery rhetoric but insisted that slaves held the same rights as other Christians, that slavery was evil, and that a righteous community would include literate blacks as well as whites in the regular religious devotionals that involved reading the Bible out loud to one another.[1]

The ARP battled with the state over slavery more than any other group in post-Nullification South Carolina because of their long-standing emphases on civil liberties, religious rights, and literacy. Covenanters protested South Carolina's debate to reopen the international slave trade. They pushed for the recognition of slave marriages as legitimate and as a buffer against sales that broke up families. Perhaps most importantly, they petitioned the South Carolina legislature, nearly alone, against the slave literacy laws and pledged not to obey the law. These laws struck at the heart of Covenanter piety: the evening family devotionals in which alternating members of the family would read Scriptures, discuss their meaning, and sing the Psalms. These petitions highlighted two distinctions between Covenanters and their other Protestant neighbors. First, they demanded that every church member be literate in the Bible and Westminster Confession of Faith. This emphasis on literacy and religious discussion opened doors for informal family devotional times in which blacks and whites interacted on religious questions together, and provided an opportunity for religious ideas to germinate outside of traditional church structures. Second, the ARP sang only the Psalms, believing hymns to be human corruptions of pure, biblical worship. Thus, biblical literacy was at the core of the Covenanter religious tradition, and ARP slaves needed this civil liberty in order to exercise their religious liberties. This seemingly arcane detail would assume great importance in the years ahead.[2]

The other way the ARP uniquely confronted slavery was through colonization. Despite its popularity elsewhere, colonization was anathema in the Palmetto State. After the early 1820s, the only prominent antislavery Presbyterian ministers left in the South, John Holt Rice of Virginia and Robert Hall Morrison in North Carolina, believed that even discussing abolition in the South made the problem of slavery worse. Public statements by clergymen on the issue "retard the mark of public feeling in relation to slavery," Rice argued. The southern ministers who felt uncomfortable with slavery kept their opinions out of the public sphere. Those who could not, simply moved away. In Greensboro, North Carolina, Presbyterian minister Eli Caruthers remained closeted in his antislavery views until 1861. Upon voicing those views, he was promptly removed from his pulpit by the church elders. Southern emancipation efforts in the antebellum period were more important for the impact they had on northern abolitionists than for any success in converting southern neighbors. The few southern antislavery movements that did occur have traditionally been seen as either the product of an aging revolutionary generation manumitting through wills or a conflicted set of gradualists confined exclusively to the Upper South.[3]

The colonization movement, spearheaded by the national organization called the American Colonization Society (ACS), occupied the complicated middle of the slavery debates of antebellum America. Its advocates came from a variety of persuasions and positions. Most were antislavery gradualists, others proslavery southerners intent on eliminating the anomaly of free blacks living near enslaved ones, and still others racist northerners fearful of miscegenation. The ACS had a brief but important role in the northern antislavery scene, and colonization was a favored position for political moderates like Abraham Lincoln.[4]

Most antebellum southern evangelicals, especially in the Upper South, held a favorable opinion of the American Colonization Society. Many viewed colonization as the answer to the twin problems of social meddling from northern abolitionists and the economic hegemony of elite slaveholders. South Carolina, however, proved uncompromisingly hostile. Baptist minister Richard Fuller made a carefully guarded plea for the movement as a middle ground only after leaving South Carolina for Baltimore. Upon meeting fierce resistance in public and in print, he quickly back-pedaled and emphasized that he "as fully as ever identified with the South." Reform-minded southerners concerned with moral issues like temperance, revivalism, and slavery risked guilt by association with radical abolitionists. For this reason, South Carolina remained the only state in the South without a chapter of the ACS prior to the Civil War.[5]

Even in South Carolina, many proslavery evangelicals advocated for moral reforms to the institutions of slavery. Yet colonization remained a bridge too far for almost all South Carolinians in the wake of the Nullification Crisis. In South Carolina, no one was debating abolition. In the state capital of Columbia, there was a $1,500 reward for the capture of any person distributing pamphlets on the slavery issue. Colonization was lumped together with the dangerous abolitionist message, as evidenced in 1833, when Francis Goulding was forced to suspend his Sabbath school for slaves because it was discovered he had colonization sympathies. South Carolina lawmakers and judges waged a sustained war against colonization in the early antebellum period by pushing against federal support of the ACS and by restricting the right to manumit slaves through testamentary liberation in 1841. The blame was placed at the feet of "fanatic" evangelicals and dangerous black preachers.[6]

Covenanters rejected the prevailing sentiment and championed colonization, in part by making direct financial contributions to the national organization of the American Colonization Society. The ACS received $4,410.13 from South Carolinians prior to the Civil War. Of this, only around a quarter was sent from the ARP-heavy Upcountry. However, individual acts of giving for Charlestonians tended to be for larger sums, while smaller gifts characterized the generally poorer populations of the upstate. There were only 68 acts of giving from the Lowcountry, compared to 129 separate contributions from the Upcountry. Many of these, on both sides, were regular contributors. Of Upcountry colonization donations, 63 percent came from ARPs. The numbers rose slightly with the Nullification Controversy, when nearly 67 percent of donations came from ARP churches, pastors, and laymen. By the final antebellum decade, the numbers were striking. Between 1850 and 1861, 88 percent of the money raised in the upstate came from identifiably ARP sources. The final gift before the war, in February 1860, was twenty dollars, raised in a collection in the ARP church in Due West Corner, Abbeville District.[7]

Twenty years earlier in Abbeville District, ARP minister William Hemphill presented his "Address on Colonization" at the 1840 Fourth of July celebration as an attempt to win over his neighbors to the colonization cause. He began by applauding colonization as a "benevolent undertaking" and a "Heaven born enterprise." Why, then, were there so few followers within their own region? Undoubtedly, it was because "some of those in the South who are opposed to Colonization pretend to believe that it is the same as Abolitionism." Nothing, he tried to convince his audience, could be further from the truth.[8]

The essence of abolition, Hemphill emphasized, was its conception of slavery as a "moral evil or sin under any and every circumstance" and, of great importance for his distinction, "that sin of any kind ought not to be indulged even for a moment, consequently slavery ought to be abandoned immediately, and the slaves turned loose into society." Abolition's emphasis, then, was on *immediacy*. Abolitionists wanted slavery gone now, and slaves freed "to do anything and everything that ignorance and hunger and depraved nature might prompt them to perform." He insisted that this was not colonization at all.[9]

Colonization's aim was "to journey to Africa such free coloured persons as are willing to go, and settle them down comfortably on the soil of their ancestors." Here Hemphill turned to the paternalistic argument against abolitionism, stating that the ACS plan "does not propose to transport any coloured person to Africa who is not willing to go." In other words, colonization took into consideration the desires of black men and women. Abolitionism, he continued, did not. The abolitionists' aim was "to liberate all the slaves at once without the consent either of master or servants." Hemphill insisted that the ACS did not desire to emancipate slaves against their masters' will, or to force immediate abolition on anyone.[10]

In pointing out that every state in the Union had an ACS auxiliary chapter except South Carolina, he contrasted the radical, fearmongering, conspiracy-theory-driven political leadership of his own state with "the most distinguished men" of other states: "Presidents Madison + Munroe [*sic*] (and Jefferson too)." He argued that Liberia was not the deathtrap it had been portrayed as and offered statistics to argue that the death rate of Liberian immigrants was 6.9 percent, far lower than that of the English at Jamestown.[11]

There would be moral benefit as well. Colonization, he argued, would have "the good instrumentality in suppressing the *slave trade.*" That "nefarious, infernal traffic" would have a formidable American enemy on the coast of Africa with which to contend. There would also be economic gains. A black American colony would "be very reluctant" to turn against American financial interests, he insisted. But there was also the basic interest the white evangelical conscience felt in the black condition: "If any nation on earth ought to feel interested in any scheme that would better the condition of Africa, it is the people of this nation. We have long had in possession her sons + her daughters + have grown rich as a people by the process of the proceeds of their industry, and a few dollars every year to restore to her soil, those of her children who are free + willing to go, is not only a benevolent contribution but a just and righteous act."[12] Hemphill had arrived at his millennial theme.

Hemphill concluded his discussion with a pan-evangelical message about the coming millennium and the role of missions. Colonization was full of "vast advantages that have and will yet result to earth and Heaven from this Heaven born enterprise." "As christians," he urged, "we cannot but desire the universal spread of the Gospel; we look forward with joyous anticipation to the coming Millennium." This millennium required that "Africa then must be converted to God, must embrace the Gospel before the thousand years of Sabbath shall commence upon earth." This would require that Africa be "enlightened and Christianized before the millennium can be fully introduced." This was supported by Psalm 68:31, "Ethiopia must stretch forth her hand unto God," and Matthew 24:14, that the Gospel must be preached to all nations before the end could come.[13]

Arguing that the international slave trade had forever robbed white men of an honest audience with the people of Africa, Hemphill suggested that only blacks could preach to native Africans with any kind of moral authority. Thus, "Every Christian man or woman sent to the African colonies will exert a missionary influence upon some portion of native Africans whether directly or indirectly." Every dollar of support to the ACS was, de facto, a dollar to the foreign missionary fund. It was also "a dollar to establish on another continent the principle of civil liberty; a dollar to suppress the slave trade and prepare the way for a trade of an innocent and important character. In a word, to advance the cause of colonization by money or otherwise is to promote the best interest of both heaven and earth."[14]

What was good for Africa was good for the world, and southern whites' role in the slave trade loaded them with a special burden in bringing about that good. "What then is the best method of sending the tidings of salvation to the people of that continent," he asked. "Shall we send them the Bible and Missionaries by the slave ships that sail from Boston and the free states?" He doubted that Africans would "receive without suspicion the word of salvation from a white man no matter in what way he had been conveyed to them?"[15]

In this emphasis on Africa, Hemphill was straddling various impulses in southern life beyond his own peculiar Atlantic religious sect, especially the millennial evangelical spirit growing among both northern and southern Protestants. Colonization was a means of resolving evangelical qualms over slavery, uplifting the backward cultures of the non-Western world, and redeeming the world for Christ in one fell swoop. This appeal cut across denominational lines in the antebellum South. Central to the proslavery southern position was a sense of world history. Slavery had always existed and, in the hands of a providential God, could serve purposes that were ultimately for the good. Southerners could be conservative on slavery while retaining a liberal spirit because slavery was historically ubiquitous and part of the onward march to spiritual freedom. Such a message was rife with contradictions but appealing at every level for evangelicals who saw in the world the workings of ultimate deliverance.[16]

Liberian minister E. W. Blyden painted just such an image of an Africa redeemed in soul, culture, and society to a Maine audience in 1862. He looked forward to the day when black Americans were roused by "their duty to Africa" and rushed "to bless that benighted continent." By building "Temples to the Most High," they would ensure that "science again establish her sway in Africa" as well as the "hand of culture . . . Genius, and learning, and skill" that would "revolutionize the land." Northern reformers like the Tappan family imagined Liberia at the confluence of commerce, culture, and conversion as late as the 1830s. Colonization was a form of cultural imperialism.[17]

The mission impulse to Africa was intimately wound up in the idea of exporting Western culture, economics, technology, and religion. Traditionally, this has been seen as a post–Civil War phenomenon in American churches. With slavery over and native peoples pushed beyond the general purview, an increasingly wealthy American Christianity began to look beyond the seas with its humanitarian impulses. Yet the ideal of international conversion antedated the sectional crisis by many decades. The American Board of Commissioners for Foreign Missions (ABCFM) had a long and ongoing network of Protestant missionaries in Africa and Asia from the 1830s through the 1850s. As Clifton Jackson Phillips has pointed out, only commerce superseded missions as an international operation in the popular mind during the antebellum period. A globalized Christian Protestantism was very much in the consciousness of antebellum Christians. Such impulses were not confined to the North. In 1833, North Carolinian Melville B. Cox was considered by many Methodists to be the first American missionary to Africa. In 1834, three members of the first American missionary team to South Africa were ministers or physicians from the American South. J. Leighton Wilson, a South Carolinian, was a missionary to Africa and a slave owner by marriage who sought to emancipate his slaves and colonized them all in Liberia. Africa was already firmly planted in the religious imaginations of Hemphill's audience.[18]

The mental map of Africa for antebellum Christians had been taking shape for decades prior to the Civil War, and Hemphill's message was part of an ongoing process of creating and invoking that ideation. Edward Griffin preached in 1817 that black missionaries could save "bleeding Africa." Griffin's sermon fit a particular genre of sermon: the "Plea for Africa." Ministers throughout the North preached such sermons addressing colonization, African evangelical missions, and the problems of slavery. These sermons were typically preached on the Fourth of July and almost always addressed the prophecy that Ethiopia would lift up its hand to God from Psalm 68:31. They featured discussions of the evils of the slave trade, the moral call American whites must feel for Africa as the beneficiaries of slave laborers, and the providential opportunity to send black Christians to redeem another continent. That land, it was said, was not unlike America. "It is a country varied, like our own fair land, with mountains and forests," and "abounding in all the resources that might minister employment or sustenance to a civilized and happy population." Africa was as wild as America had been in the seventeenth century. It was a promised land of opportunity for black Christian civilization.[19]

The mission to Africa, though, was not only about geography. It was also about race. Specifically, it was an effort for "the improvement of the African race." Leonard Bacon's address in Connecticut quoted Proverbs 31:9, asking God to "plead the cause of the poor and needy." Africa was discussed as a land of tribal peoples, impoverished, ignorant of civilization, but infinitely capable if given the correct tools. African plea sermons emphasized the mental acuity, industriousness, and general innate equality of African Americans. African American slaves, when adequately educated, were hailed as morally upright civilizing agents. Freed slaves could be the extension of Western whiteness to Africa.[20]

Hemphill's compassion for Africa was unique in that it was given in the heart of the proslavery South. For Hemphill, the moral response of colonization was instrumental in bringing about God's final intervention. By engaging the Africa of the evangelical imagination, the moral problems of slavery could be slowly resolved while bringing about a greater moral good. This response also insulated him, his followers, and his skeptical listeners from what he had styled in a letter to a friend as "the dangers of immediacy." Action now in favor of a moderate solution like colonization dissolved the need for more radical action, actions more in keeping with the rest of his religious brethren outside the South and with his own personal principles. In short, the peace of the moment could be maintained without abandoning the better peace of the future.[21]

Hemphill's advocacy failed. No Abbeville slaves were manumitted or sent on the mission to Liberia. Several families in neighboring Edgefield District did emigrate to Liberia, though local freedmen and -women experienced an equal pull to Arkansas in the postwar period. For many blacks, it was the religiously charged idea of exodus *from* a persecuting land rather than any particular draw *toward* a different land that fueled the religious and social appeal of colonization. Meanwhile, local whites pushed back against the ARP for their support of colonization and threatened to apply the ban on abolitionist literature passing through the mail. Hemphill had been donating a copy of the ACS newspaper, the *African Repository*, to Erskine Seminary in Due West. A friend noted that receiving the *Repository* was "beginning to work mischief through the *gentleman of the Post office*." Local sentiments were too tense for such political tensions in the life of the school. "For the sake of peace, and this alone, I have concluded with much *reluctance* to suggest to you the propriety of discontinuing the paper for the present." Hemphill had succeeded only in making things worse.[22]

Colonization offered a window to the millennium for white ARPs. For black ARPs, meanwhile, emancipation was a millennium all its own. Although his colonization efforts shared an emphasis on cultural exportation and an idealized African frontier with other evangelicals, William Hemphill was also motivated by specific Covenanter devotional societies. Interacting daily with highly literate, religiously devout slaves in study and prayer, white ARP southerners confronted black suffering more regularly and forcefully than neighboring whites. For Hemphill and the ARP of Upcountry South Carolina, the role of missionary outreach to Africa loomed large in their religious and social imaginations in large part because Christian slaves were ever-present in their religious realities. This was an important part of how Hemphill articulated his support for colonization and probably a strong motivation for ARP financial contributions. This evangelical millennial impulse met colonization at the confluence of other imperatives, especially the long-standing Covenanter antislavery rhetoric that dated back to the 1640s. Their motivations were unique among South Carolinians and, in many respects, other southern colonizationists.[23]

Other Christian zealots who were exposed to interracial devotional experiences also became great supporters of African missionary outreach. The white George Thompson so identified with slaves that he came to see himself as nearly black himself and traveled to Sierra Leone in 1847 as a missionary. Joseph Yannielli has argued convincingly that such humanitarian sensibilities and sympathetic blackness lay at the heart of the "fragile attempts at interracial cooperation" that Thompson and Hemphill tried to achieve. Yet this mutual interactivity went in more than one direction. Just as whites who intimately engaged blacks could reflect back a different sentiment regarding slavery and missions, so too blacks who interacted at these levels with whites could be absorbed into older, non-African Atlantic religious traditions like those of the Covenanters.[24]

Historians have long argued that southern slaves successfully synthesized elements of white culture into enduring African traditions. Models of family, religion, gender norms, and work ways were the product of the blending of many African and white traditions into workable solutions to the challenges of slave life. These were often interpreted as the process of more dominant white ways being superimposed on less sustainable but nonetheless vibrant Old World traditions and a corresponding assimilation of various African folkways into a new Afro-American tradition; these experiences varied by region and were often visible in areas of Christian religious belief. More recently, historians have argued that African culture endured longer and more strongly than previously believed, and that slaves were not nearly as active in Christianity as once thought. Some have even argued that the emphasis on slave Christianity might be overblown by indicating that only around 30 percent of slaves actively embraced any form of Christianity prior to emancipation.[25]

However enduring African traditions may or may not have been, the racial reciprocity of antebellum southern religious culture largely has been seen, quite fairly, as an uneven and especially unfair cultural interaction. In such debates, key words have included syncretization, survival, retention, adaptation, assimilation, power, and loss. The products of this discussion have been a black evangelicalism that offers both a challenge to and an amelioration of oppression as well as a white evangelicalism that left behind its radical past to become a model of social order and racial control. Room for discussion remains because black and white evangelicalisms did not always operate in separate spheres. The one was not always submerged or in hiding, and the other was not always unconscious of its transformative social and political tendencies.

Historians are increasingly aware of another important concept, that of intertwining. In some ways, of course, this insight is far from new. As Donald Mathews noted, "the two religious modes of southern Evangelicalism—black and white—cannot be understood apart from one another." But even Mathews went on to make lines of clear demarcation between white and black evangelicalisms. There were borders between these two religions, but they were borders with many checkpoints frequently crossed.[26]

Historians of northern abolition have increasingly focused on the interracial nature of antagonism toward the peculiar institution. Recent studies of Washington, D.C., and Virginia have discovered the centrality of interracial relationships to southern antislavery sympathizers as well. Charles Irons has located the motivations for white theorizing on slavery first and foremost in the relationships they shared in religious life with slaves. African American Virginians, meanwhile, exerted considerable determining agency over what whites believed and said through interreligious relationships. In general, the closer white and blacks were religiously, the more whites struggled to reconcile the conflicting aspects of Christian religion and agrarian slavery, and the more influence blacks held on the day-to-day negotiations of life. In religious terms, slaves' choices regarding to which religion they would adhere were the most powerful factors in forming biracial religious communities. The more authentic slaves judged a particular form of the Gospel to be, the more likely they were to engage that denomination and form relationships of spiritual mutuality with whites.[27]

Antebellum cultures, religious and otherwise, were not simply the products of white ways eroding older African traditions, nor were they solely the function of African traditions surviving the process of forced migration and social subjugation. They were also the process of mutual cultural exchange through interracial work, worship, and interaction. In peculiar instances like the South Carolina ARP, those exchanges may have been more acutely intimate and cooperative than previously assumed.[28]

Their interracial, literacy-driven devotional system brought the ARP into conflict with their neighbors. Abbeville itself represented the mainstream of southern society. Abbeville District bordered Georgia on one side, the Appalachian foothill districts on another, and the more burgeoning cotton districts of the South Carolina Piedmont to the southeast and down the Savannah River. John C. Calhoun was raised in the area, and his family remained one of the region's most politically prominent. A battleground district in the Nullification Controversy, Abbeville later became a black majority population and experienced the radicalization of politics and personified the paternalism of religion that dominated southern life over the next decades. Local communities represented strong pockets of influence for the Methodist and Presbyterian faiths, and missionary efforts to slaves focused on religious conversion and piety without biblical literacy. In 1838, fifty-three citizens of Abbeville District wanted the government to shut down local church schools "wherein a Number of Negros are Instructed to read." These were the local ARP devotional groups. By 1860, the first district to vote in favor of a secession convention was Abbeville. In the course of the ARP experience in this region, Abbeville transformed from a moderate backcountry into the epicenter of the Civil War. Confrontation between paternalistic South Carolinians and their heterodox neighbors was inevitable.[29]

The most volatile confrontation, however, was the product of a black Covenanter, not white ones. Hemphill's next-door neighbor was Rev. Robert C. Grier, who ran a small college and seminary in Abbeville District. Robert Grier, a Pennsylvanian, had married a southern woman from a slaveholding family and, of mixed opinion about the morality of slaveholding, appears to have kept several slaves in the family and hired them out to local farmers. One of these slaves was a twenty-five-year-old carpenter named George Grier. George Grier was hired out to an Abbeville farmer named Lemuel Reid in June 1850. One evening, Reid heard loud talking coming from his kitchen building, and sneaked around the back to hear what was being said.[30]

Reid later gave a deposition on what he heard. He stated that he had rightly suspected that George Grier would be speaking "on the subject of religion," indicating that George Grier was known for speaking on religious matters and may have operated as a preacher within the slave community. He recorded hearing nine sentences of George Grier's message before breaking up the assembly.

> The first thing I heard him distinctly say to my negroes, was, that they ought not to be discouraged on the account of their difficulties. There was no reason why they were in the situation they were, only that God permitted it to

> be so. That God was working for their deliverance. He was working by secret means, and would deliver them from their bondage as sure as the children of Israel were delivered from the Egyptian bondage. That the question had been in agitation for the last fifty years. That those who were working for them did not know exactly how long it would be before they would be set free. There was no doubt that it would be soon. That they ought to pray for, and their prayers would go up before God and be answered. That the smartest men in the United States——. At this point of his conversation I could not stand any longer to listen to any such conversation, and permit him to talk in that strain to my negroes. I did not hear him finish the sentence.

What Reid had heard led to a heated dispute between local Presbyterians and ARPs over whether slavery was, as Rev. Robert Grier claimed in discussions with Reid afterward, "a moral evil."[31]

The sermon itself contained several interesting interpretive points. The obvious point of theological comparison is with African American sermons promising deliverance from slavery. The very different interpretations of Providence and slavery posed by George Grier and other religious slave leaders like Nat Turner in Virginia and the freeman Denmark Vesey in Charleston, South Carolina, is insightful. Instead of urging slaves to personally live out God's power to overthrow slavery, George Grier vested the deliverance of his people in God's working through "secret means." The Israelite deliverance from the Egyptian captivity made their own deliverance sure. As in that case, it was God who performed the miracles and, critically, it had been a nonviolent insurrection that happened only when God intervened into human affairs. Instead of rising up, the slaves ought to pray, "and their prayers would go up before God and be answered." This deliverance they were not only right in wanting but sure in trusting it would come.[32]

After being confronted by the slaveholding Reid, George Grier repeatedly did two things. First, he insisted he had not meant to stir up an insurrection or discontent among Reid's slaves. Second, he did not go back on his message, insisting, according to the deposition, that people talked that way "about town," by which he meant the town occupied by ARPs rather than mainline Presbyterians. George Grier would later be tried for seditious speech, lashed thirty-nine times, and exiled from South Carolina for repeating what whites were saying in their private homes and in churches "about town."[33]

It was in this critical distinction that George Grier's complicated religious tradition became clear. He claimed the identity not of a black evangelical, but of an Old World, Atlantic, Scottish radicalism that other whites understood as fundamentally different from mainstream southern religion. By claiming membership within a community different in origin and belief than Reid's, George Grier was claiming the protection of sanctuary that might be offered to a group that had been openly uncomfortable with slavery for many decades while nonetheless living productively in the South. Even more telling in this regard is what George Grier had been saying to fellow slaves. The issue turned on what seemed an antiquarian and irrelevant point to the discussion of slavery, colonization, and world evangelism. That small point is simply that Covenanters sang only the Psalms.

During George Grier's trial, a slave in the audience was called as a witness. Abram Reid was asked what Grier had been discussing before being overheard. He stated, "George had been talking a good while—a half hour—talking about singing, praying, and churches." It is impossible to know what side Grier took in the seemingly miniscule theological debate regarding the use of hymns and Psalms in worship. His subject matter is more important than his stance. George Grier was expositing on the divisions within white churches. What divided the ARPs in his community and the Presbyterians in Abram Reid's community was precisely "singing, praying, and churches," that is to say, denominations and how they worshiped. George Grier was explaining the differences in his community and theirs.[34]

This message would crescendo with the disagreements regarding slavery. Slavery was, indeed, a moral evil. This was a point Rev. Robert Grier, George Grier's owner, supported to the enraged Lemuel Reid. For proslavery whites, slavery had ceased to be an evil institution, but rather an amelioration of other evils of race and civilization. But for Covenanters, it was an evil requiring desire and prayer to overcome. It wasn't abolition, but it was a start. And it was a division. George Grier was talking about the fault lines in white Abbeville District society. There was space, small, tight, but critical space between the ideology of one white community and another. Into this space slaves could find useful room to discuss the end of slavery and with emphasis on God's intervening power on a divine, mystical but sure timeline. George Grier had gathered these insights from night after night of religious devotions, literacy education, and catechizing.

These two moderate approaches to the slave problem, from two very different perspectives, nonetheless had common roots in Covenanter religious life. George Grier was almost assuredly literate, in violation of the law, because he participated in the devotional life of this peculiar sect of Presbyterianism. In those discussions, all manner of religious insights and social dilemmas could have been and probably were, formally or otherwise, discussed: the biblical manner of singing in church, the obligation to learn to read the Bible and catechism, and moderate visions of the end of slavery.

From these interracial discussions on the nuances of an awkward moderation on slavery came intraracial discussions on where the space to believe in a peaceful resistance might be. That these visions ultimately failed is on abundant display. The failure to gather ACS support, George Grier's trial and banishment, and the seemingly inexorable march to war in 1861 cast doubt that these moderate visions offered solutions with any chance of success. Yet the fact that they existed at all suggests that the march to war was only *seemingly* inevitable; there were those, like the ARP, who worked in unpopular causes and across racial boundaries for other ways out of their generation's greatest moral dilemma.

George Grier was likely a slave preacher. Slave preachers were a common phenomenon in southern culture, but had been severely curtailed in South Carolina after the Denmark Vesey and Nat Turner plots. Slave preachers often emphasized narratives of deliverance, prayer, and emancipation expectation, either overtly or covertly. George Grier's was a discussion of religious differences, but in its context this religious discussion was fundamentally political. As J. G. A. Pocock noted, political language prescribes "what we might say and how we might say it." The rhetorical space between Presbyterians and ARP, though tight, was filled with radical possibilities for George Grier and his listeners.[35]

The confluence of literate black evangelicals like George Grier and sympathetic white coreligionists still holding to older, Atlantic forms of radical religion was rife with potentiality. The ARP in Upcountry South Carolina could have become, indeed almost became, subversive communities in the South as did similar biracial groups in Washington, D.C. Instead, in a comparison they would have abhorred, the ARP became far more like the North Carolina Quakers: they resisted slavery even as they made peace with it.[36]

Hemphill and the ARP supporters of colonization were atypical southern Christians. But they demonstrate that colonization allowed at least some southern evangelicals to envision a manifest destiny of the Kingdom of Christ that offered spiritual and physical freedom. Colonization was well suited to this republican millennialism because it flattened out the contractions of American slavery and freedom by promising to advance the cause of freedom in a larger phalanx against global darkness. Social and political ills of all kinds, in all places must be confronted to bring about the Kingdom of Christ. Colonization could hasten the end of days. Even racism, then, could serve a providential purpose. The South, through her slaves, could reach out her hand to Africa. In turn, "Ethiopia" would soon "stretch out her hands to God."[37]

Colonization, as historian Lacy Ford has rightly noted, was an Upper South solution to the social problems of slavery rather than an abolitionist impulse in the South per se. In the Lower South, this answer was rejected in favor of an ideological reconfiguration of slavery into a paternalistic trope of republican virtue. The Covenanter supporters of the ACS might, then, be easily explained as Upper South thinkers living in a Lower South world. Yet even in Virginia, whites who manumitted their slaves were subject to social pressures and, in some cases, severe beatings. Such an explanation would also miss the key peculiarities of the Associate Reformed Presbyterian tradition that had been maintained across the Atlantic world.[38]

Colonization in Upstate South Carolina was entirely the product of ARP agitation and therefore the product of several factors. First, it grew out of a long Atlantic tradition of radicalism rooted in lay teaching that had been antislavery since 1644. Second, it came from the interracial religious encounters that forced those sensitive to antislavery sentiments not to give in to the proslavery culture in which they lived. Without the active presence of slaves like George Grier in their regular daily society meetings, the ARP would more easily have assimilated themselves to dominant cultural values. Third, ARPs were increasingly moving within the mainstream evangelical umbrella, and they envisioned a world won over from darkness to light. No continent fit that metaphor, with all of its racial overtones, more clearly than Africa. Fourth, it was a product of all of these conflicting rhetorics of radical tradition, racial comity, missionary imaginations, and their neighbors' proslavery conservatism. The ARP needed a language that would honor their older traditions but not lose a hearing from their Upcountry neighbors. As Irons has noted, "moderately antislavery white evangelicals had few strategies available through which to assist enslaved believers," and the language of "colonization was the best available option."[39]

In the end, the sermons turned out badly for both William Hemphill and George Grier. Their millennial advocacy and attempts to moderate the slave question through an older form of Protestant religion proved insufficient to the monumental task of changing the mind of slaveholding southerners on their most vital economic interest. That these voices were heard at all, though, points to the fact that there were viable alternatives to southern proslavery discourse. How many there were, and why they failed, remain open questions.

NOTES

1. Seceders considered themselves the true heirs of the Covenanter tradition, and thus it is appropriate to label both groups as Covenanters. The ARP distanced themselves from a literal interpretation of these covenant obligations, but still maintained the cell-group devotionals and political piety of the tradition. The term Seceders, which was a slightly more common referent in the South to the ARP, I have avoided for its obvious potential for confusion in a discussion on the Civil War era. For overviews of this history, see Emily Moberg Robinson, "Immigrant Covenanters: Religious and Political Identity from Scotland to America" (Ph.D. diss., University of California, Santa Cruz, 2004); Joseph S. Moore, "Irish Radicals, Southern Conservatives: Slavery, Religious Liberty and the Presbyterian Fringe in the Atlantic World" (Ph.D. diss., University of North Carolina at Greensboro, 2011); Robert Lathan, *History of the ARP Synod of the South* (Harrisburg, 1882); and Samuel Rutherford, *Lex, Rex: or, the Law and the Prince* (London: John Field, 1644).

2. Digital Library on American Slavery, Slavery Petitions Project, PAR 11384203; PAR 11384204. http://library.uncg.edu/slavery/. The petitions themselves are in the South Carolina Department of Archives and History, Columbia. Of the remaining five petitions in this period that relate at all to slaves' religious liberties, three came from just one man, a Baptist minister and slaveholder named Richard Fuller from the Lowcountry. Two others, from Sumter, did not address literacy.

3. Anne C. Loveland, *Southern Evangelicals and the Social Order, 1800–1860* (Baton Rouge: Louisiana State University Press, 1980), 191–93. In the North, radical abolitionists and colonizationists were often at odds, though some overlap occurred. John Stauffer, *The Black Hearts of Men: Radical Abolitionists and the Transformation of Race* (Cambridge: Harvard University Press, 2002), 99–103; Elizabeth Fox-Genovese and Eugene Genovese, *The Mind of the Master Class: History and Faith in the Southern Slaveholders Worldview* (New York: Cambridge University Press, 2005), 234; Stanley Harrold, *The Abolitionists and the South, 1831–1861* (Lexington: University Press of Kentucky, 1995), 27–63, 127–71.

4. Eric Burin, *Slavery and the Peculiar Solution: A History of the American Colonization Society* (Gainesville: University Press of Florida, 2005), 1–56. Various interpretations of colonization supporters exist in large part because of the variety within the movement. Interpretations that variously emphasize the proslavery racist desire to whiten the nation, gradualist attempts to resolve an intractable moral problem, black emigrant desires for freedom, and white and black male attempts to forge a mission of masculine civilization are all true without the other interpretations being wrong. The source of the movement's popularity and problems was that it was genuinely all things to all people, and in so succeeding failed (see Bruce Dorsey, "A Gendered History of African Colonization in the Antebellum United States," *Journal of Social History* 34 [August 2000]: 77–103; and Douglas R. Egerton, "Its Origin Is Not a Little Curious: A New Look at the American Colonization Society," *Journal of the Early Republic* 4 [Winter 1985]: 463–80).

5. Loveland, *Southern Evangelicals,* 213–16.

6. Larry E. Tise, *Proslavery: A History of the Defense of Slavery in America, 1701–1840* (Athens: University of Georgia Press, 1987), 302–5. Tise has also shown that such antislavery sentiment as existed in the Deep South was often couched in the movement of colonization's language and rhetoric. William W. Freehling, *Prelude to Civil War: The Nullification Controversy in South Carolina, 1816–1836* (New York: Harper Torchbooks, 1966), 52, 63–65, 74–75, 122–33, 301–2; Burin, *Slavery and the Peculiar Solution,* 127. For a detailed summary of the South Carolina experience with colonization within a national context, see Lacy K. Ford, *Deliver Us from Evil: The Slavery Question in the Old South* (New York: Oxford University Press, 2009), 299–328.

7. "Contributions" (1825–49), *African Repository and Colonial Journal;* and "Contributions" (1850–65), *African Repository.*

8. "Address on Colonization," July 1, 1840, Hemphill Family Papers, Duke University

9. Ibid., 1–2.

10. Ibid., 3.

11. Ibid., 7–9. These statistics were inaccurate. In reality, Liberians may have suffered the highest first-year morbidity ever recorded in an immigrant population (see Tom W. Shick, "A Quantitative Analysis of Liberian Colonization from 1820–1843 with Special Reference to Mortality," *Journal of African History* 12, no.1 [1971]: 45–59; and Tukufu Zuberi, *Swing Low, Sweet Chariot: The Mortality Cost of Colonizing Liberia in the Nineteenth Century,* trans. Antonio McDaniel [Chicago: University of Chicago Press, 1995], 104, 150–52).

12. "Address on Colonization," 17.

13. Ibid., 14.

14. Ibid.

15. Ibid.

16. Fox-Genovese and Genovese, *Mind of the Master Class,* 201–25.

17. "Rev. E. W. Blyden's Address at the Annual Meeting of the Maine Colonization Society, June 1862," quoted in James H. Moorehead, *American Apocalypse: Yankee Protestants and the Civil War, 1860–1869* (New Haven: Yale University Press, 1974), 106; Bertram Wyatt-Brown, *Lewis Tappan and the Evangelical War against Slavery* (Baton Rouge: Louisiana State University Press, 1997), 84–86.

18. Clifton Jackson Phillips concluded that the ABCFM's African work had no ties to the American slavery debates for missionaries on the ground. However, the impulse to support African missions seems intimately wound up in discussions of antislavery gradualism (see Phillips, *Protestant America and the Pagan World: The First Half Century of the American Board of Commissioners for Foreign Missions, 1810–1860* [Cambridge: East Asian Research Center, Harvard University, 1969], vii, 206–27). David W. Kling, "The New Divinity and the Origins of the American Board of Commissioners for Foreign Missions," *Church History* 72, no. 4 (December 2003): 791–819; Melville B. Cox, *Remains of Melville B. Cox: Late Missionary to Liberia, with a Memoir* (Boston: Light and Horton, 1835).

19. Edward Dorr Griffin, *A Plea for Africa* (1817); for other examples, see Fredrick Freeman, *A Plea for Africa: Being familiar conversations on the subject of slavery and colonization* (Philadelphia: J. Whetham, 1837); Leonard Bacon, *A Plea for Africa* (New Haven: T. G. Woodward, 1825); John Newland Maffitt, *A Plea for Africa* (Boston: E. W. Crittenden, 1830). Slavery and Anti-Slavery, Part I: Debates over Slavery and Abolition, Gale Digital Collections. Quote is from Bacon, *A Plea for Africa,* 9.

20. Griffin, *A Plea for Africa,* 3. For a broader discussion on this theme, see David N. Livingstone, *Adam's Ancestors: Race, Religion, and the Politics of Human Origins* (Baltimore: Johns Hopkins University Press, 2008).

21. Samuel Taggart to William Hemphill, January 1840, Hemphill Family Papers.

22. Orville Vernon Burton, *In My Father's House Are Many Mansions: Family and Community in Edgefield, South Carolina* (Chapel Hill: University of North Carolina, 1985), 404 n. 37; E. E. Pressly to William Hemphill, July 6, 1840, Hemphill Family Papers.

23. Burin, *Slavery and the Peculiar Solution,* 34–56.

24. Joseph Yannielli, "George Thompson among the Africans: Empathy, Authority, and Insanity in the Age of Abolition," *Journal of American History* 96, no. 4 (March 2010): 979–1000.

25. See John Blassingame, *Slave Community: Plantation Life in the Antebellum South* (New York: Oxford University Press, 1972); Eugene Genovese, *Roll, Jordan, Roll: The World the Slaves Made* (New York: Vintage, 1974); and Albert J. Raboteau, *Slave Religion: The 'Invisible Institution' in the Antebellum South* (New York: Oxford University Press, 1978). For a classic example that argues that white ways became the dominant folkways of various regions into which minorities were absorbed, see David Hackett Fischer, *Albion's Seed: Four British Folkways in America* (New York: Oxford University Press, 1989). Daniel L. Fountain, *Slavery, Civil War and Salvation: African American Slaves and Christianity, 1830–1870* (Baton Rouge: Louisiana State University Press, 2010); Michael A. Gomez, *Exchanging Our Country Marks: The Transformation of African Identities in the Colonial and Antebellum South* (Chapel Hill: University of North Carolina Press, 1998).

26. Janet Duitsman Cornelius, *Slave Missions and the Black Church in the Antebellum South* (Columbia: University of South Carolina Press, 1999), 4–22; Donald G. Mathews, *Religion in the Old South* (Chicago: University of Chicago Press, 1977), 185–250.

27. Paul Goodman, *Of One Blood: Abolitionism and the Origins of Racial Equality* (Berkley: University of California Press, 1998); Richard S. Newman, *The Transformation of American Abolitionism: Fighting Slavery in the Early Republic* (Chapel Hill: University of North Carolina Press, 2002); Charles F. Irons, *The Origins of Proslavery Christianity: White and Black Evangelicals in Colonial and Antebellum Virginia* (Chapel Hill: University of North Carolina Press, 2008), 1–22, esp. 55–132; Stanley Harrold, *Subversives: Antislavery Community in Washington, D.C., 1828–1865* (Baton Rouge: Louisiana State University Press, 2003).

28. For examples of many cultural transfers including views of time, place, architectures, death, and religion in eighteenth-century Virginia, see Mechal Sobel, *The World They Made Together: Black and White Values in Eighteenth-Century Virginia* (Princeton: Princeton University Press, 1987).

29. Robert C. Grier owned seven slaves: female age 60; female age 40; female age 30; male age 25; male age 12; male age 9; and male age 1 (1850 Census Slave Schedules, Schedule 2, Abbeville County, South Carolina [September 23, 1850]). Lowry Ware, *Old Abbeville: Scenes of the Past of a Town Where Old Time Things Are Not Forgotten* (Columbia: South Carolina Magazine, 1992); Robert M. Calhoon, "Scotch Irish Calvinists in Conflict: The South Carolina Slave Controversy, 1834–1860," *Journal of Scotch Irish Studies* 2 (2004): 72–75.

30. Digital Library on American Slavery, Slavery Petitions Project, PAR 11380107, Abbeville, S.C. The original document is in the South Carolina Department of Archives and History; Hemphill and Grier are listed as neighbors in the 1850 U.S. Census.

31. Joseph S. Moore, "To the Public: A Transcription of Robert Grier's 1850 Broadside with an Introduction," *Journal of Backcountry Studies* 4, no. 2 (August 2009). The trial records were lost to

fire, but the broadside includes the verbatim transcripts from the trial. The original document is housed at the South Caroliniana Library, University of South Carolina, Columbia. For an analysis of the confrontation between what he calls "backcountry communities in conflict," see Robert M. Calhoon, *Political Moderation in America's First Two Centuries* (New York: Cambridge University Press, 2009), 228–40.

32. Ibid.

33. Ibid.

34. Ibid.

35. David Charles Dennard, "Religion in the Quarters: A Study of Slave Preachers in the Antebellum South, 1800–1860" (Ph.D. diss., Northwestern University, 1983); David B. Chesebrough, *God Ordained This War: Sermons on the Sectional Crisis, 1830–1860* (Columbia: University of South Carolina Press, 1991), 279–94; J. G. A. Pocock, "Languages and Their Implications," in *Politics, Language, and Time: Essays on Political Thought and History* (Chicago: University of Chicago Press, 1989), 11–25.

36. Harrold, *Subversives*, 1–12,146–202.

37. Psalm 68:31. For a discussion of this verse in the colonization movement, see Nicholas Guyatt, "The Outskirts of Our Happiness: Race and the Lure of Colonization in the Early Republic," *Journal of American History* 95, no. 4 (March 2009): 986–1011.

38. Lacy Ford, "Reconfiguring the Old South: 'Solving' the Problem of Slavery, 1787–1838," *Journal of American History* 95, no.1 (June 2008): 95–122; Burin, *Slavery and the Peculiar Solution*, 101–3.

39. Irons, *The Origins of Proslavery Christianity*, 119.

6

THE GREAT INDIAN PENTECOST

Providential Revisions, Indian Evangelization, and the Taking of the American West

JENNIFER GRABER

On a sleepy day in July 1862, Thomas Williamson, missionary to Minnesota's Dakota Indians, sat down to write. In a letter to his supervisor at the American Board of Commissioners for Foreign Missions (ABCFM), Williamson reflected on the moderate success of his day school for Indian children and the small crowd of Dakotas who assembled to hear his Sunday afternoon sermons. Williamson noted that he expected the mission, which counted only a few dozen converts despite two and half decades of effort, to continue unchanged.[1]

Williamson was wrong. Just one month later, in August 1862, four young Dakotas killed a handful of settlers in the village of Acton. After lengthy discussion, their fellow warriors decided to go to war rather than wait for the Americans' retribution. On August 18, the Dakotas embarked on a brutal offensive across southern Minnesota. They killed hundreds of settlers, including many women and children. They took scores of captives. The Dakotas dominated the southern Minnesota frontier for weeks. By September, President Lincoln sent General John Pope, who had been recently defeated at the Second Battle of Bull Run, to assist in the military response to the Indians' attack. Settlers began to repel Dakota offensives. Military reinforcements kept the warriors from seizing a key fort. By the end of September, the army took the upper hand, defeating the Dakotas at the Battle of Wood Creek. Some warriors fled west onto the plains. Others released their white captives and surrendered. By October, military and civilian leaders organized military tribunals for Dakotas who had participated in the war. They established two fortified camps to incarcerate their families. The Dakotas' future in Minnesota was an open question.[2]

Like many Minnesota settlers, missionary Thomas Williamson barely escaped the violence and lost almost everything he had. Minnesota's postwar landscape—riddled with dead white bodies and teeming with fury among the living—forced him and other Protestant missionaries to reevaluate their future work. As the hostilities subsided and the Dakotas in the state were subdued, their ministry took on new dimensions. They evangelized warriors sentenced to death and the more than one thousand Dakota women and children incarcerated at Mankato and Fort Snelling, just south of the capital. To the missionaries' surprise, hundreds of Dakotas converted to Christianity while incarcerated. The growing ranks of Dakota Christians prompted the missionaries to wonder if God had used the uprising to expand his kingdom. They struggled to understand how the conflict, with its devastating violence followed by incarceration and mass execution, could lead to what some were calling "a great Indian Pentecost."[3]

A survey of missionary writing suggests that the U.S.–Dakota War prompted dramatic changes in evangelistic tactics and providential theology. In light of their wartime experiences, the missionaries articulated a new plan for Indian evangelization in line with American visions of westward expansion. At a time when many American preachers employed notions of redemptive violence to explain staggering losses on Civil War battlefields, the Minnesota missionaries used their own encounter with war to fashion a new providentialism suited to future conflicts on the western frontier.[4]

INTERPRETING THE WAR

In August 1862, the ABCFM missionaries interpreted the conflict's early moments through the categories of their evangelical heritage and their religiously infused notions of westward expansion. While sectional and political crises energized many Americans' hopeful gaze to the West, visions of an expanding, religiously unified nation inspired others. As historian Cameron Addis has observed, evangelicalism, anti-Catholicism, and Anglophobia fueled some Americans' ideas about Manifest Destiny. Even so, the West of the early 1860s cannot be characterized by the overwhelming presence of earnest Protestant evangelists building successful missions among native peoples. Historian of the West Ferenc Szasz has shown that white Americans in the West were a religiously heterogeneous mix. These trailblazers encountered a similar diversity among the native peoples who already lived there. Missionaries like Williamson, however, held to a simpler vision of the West's religious situation. He believed that Protestant missionaries brought the truth to Indians. He expected native peoples to accept the gospel and acculturate, bringing themselves out of their heathen savagery. While they were sure that Indians would eventually accept these terms, ABCFM missionaries were among those Americans who believed this transition could best happen by persuasion, not by force.[5]

The missionaries' letters from the first weeks of the 1862 conflict show that they were completely surprised by the Dakota attack. They initially concluded that the violence spelled the end of their missions. In late August 1862, the Dakotas still dominated the southern half of the state. Stephen Riggs, another ABCFM missionary, wrote to his superiors that his family had finally made it to safety. He informed the board that "the Dakota mission is broken up." Riggs's colleague, H. D. Cunningham, also wrote back East about "the end of the labors of the Missionaries among the Dacotas [*sic*]." A few weeks later, Thomas Williamson also wrote to the ABCFM, noting his sadness about the "sudden termination of our missionary labors." The flight from their homes, the sight of dead settlers across the Minnesota landscape, and the destruction of their missions made renewed evangelistic work seem unlikely.[6]

Over the next few weeks—as it became clear that American forces would quell the Dakota uprising—the letters lost their dire forecasts and focused instead on what role the missionaries might play in the war's aftermath. They concentrated especially on promoting a fair process of justice for captured Dakotas and providing specific protections for Christian Dakotas who had not participated in the uprising. Stephen Riggs served as the primary translator in the military tribunals established to deal with captured Dakota warriors. Other ABCFM missionaries began to position themselves as spokesmen for Dakotas who had not participated in the violence and, in some cases, had even saved the lives of white settlers. Thomas Williamson wrote to the press in order to protect "friendly Indians" from the "foolish and wicked" calls for the entire tribe's extermination. Influencing the process of judgment proved to be a complicated task. Most Minnesota editorialists and politicians made public calls for the banishment, imprisonment, or extermination of all Dakotas within the state's borders.[7]

Even as the missionaries tried to influence settlers' opinions, they also struggled to establish a new relationship with incarcerated Dakotas, including those who avoided the conflict and those who were perpetrators. Determined not to let all the Dakotas pay the price for the acts of some, the missionaries pledged their service to the entire Dakota community. As they struggled to comprehend the war and address the needs of imprisoned Indians, the missionaries considered new ways of understanding God's intentions for Indian evangelization, especially the proper methods for Protestant missionary activity. In a series of small revisions, the missionaries moved away from their former strategy of offering the gospel to self-governing Indian peoples and toward a new account of missions that involved providential violence.

These revisions began as the missionaries increasingly focused on the difference between innocent and guilty Indians and how each group ought to be treated. To white audiences, the missionaries insisted that not all Dakotas participated in awful acts of violence. They emphasized that some Dakotas had protested the war and risked their own lives to save white settlers. Those guilty of violence, they insisted, deserved death. The innocent, however, demanded recognition of their courage in resisting their warring relations' actions. Stephen Riggs affirmed this position in his work with the military tribunal and continued to advocate the necessity of the death penalty for warriors who had killed settlers. Both Thomas Williamson and his son John, who was also a missionary, confirmed that those guilty of murder ought to pay with their lives.[8]

The missionaries did not limit their definitions of innocence and guilt to the Dakotas' conduct in war. They soon began to connect actions during the conflict to the Dakotas' religious affiliation prior to the uprising. The missionaries' experiences with converted Indians certainly influenced this reasoning. The missionaries knew that many among the small community of Dakota Christians objected to the war and refused to participate. They insisted that Christian Indians could not be held responsible. Those under the influence of traditional Dakota religion, they then reasoned, were surely the primary instigators of the conflict. To make the connection to religious affiliation clear, the missionaries increasingly attributed primary blame for the war not to Dakota chiefs and warriors, but to the communities' spiritual leaders, namely the medicine men. To be sure, the missionaries had always struggled with these leaders. The war, however, caused the missionaries to see the medicine men not as mere stumbling blocks to the gospel, but as active workers seeking to destroy white civilization. Already by mid-October 1862, Thomas Williamson wrote to the ABCFM that the "conjurors" were the "prime movers in the outbreak." In a hint of the narrative that would emerge, Williamson continued that God would subvert the medicine men's aims and use the outbreak for "extending the righteous kingdom of the Redeemer."[9]

As the missionaries associated traditional Dakota religion with the war effort, they also argued that the Indians' military defeat proved the futility of the Dakota spiritual pantheon. Preaching among the confined survivors, the missionaries claimed that the Dakotas' gods and medicine men had failed. The message seemed to garner at least some consideration. On November 5, John Williamson wrote that he held prayer services at the Dakota prison camp in a tent overflowing with Indians. They renounced their "conjurers and their gods," he reported. The war had been a "course of training" in order to "open their hearts to the truth." His father also reported Dakota responses to his preaching about the war. After an early December Sabbath in another prison camp, Thomas Williamson wrote to Stephen Riggs that he had never preached to such "big and attentive audiences before."[10]

The missionaries articulated this narrative of Dakota spiritual failure as the Dakotas awaited pronouncements about their future. The military tribunals had sentenced more than three hundred warriors to death. President Lincoln was reviewing the trial records, but rumors spread that all those found guilty would soon be hanged. Most Minnesotans begrudged Lincoln's intrusion, wanting instead a quick and dramatic execution. Many believed that a mass hanging would not only satisfy aggrieved white settlers, but also would teach surviving Indians a lesson. In that spirit, most Minnesotans wanted all incarcerated Dakotas—whether they had participated in the conflict or not—to witness the executions. Williamson and Riggs agreed and wrote to the ABCFM's Selah Treat that all the Dakotas should observe the hangings. General Pope went further and argued that the neighboring Winnebagos should also be in attendance. The vast majority of white Minnesotans eagerly awaited word from Washington that the execution of more than three hundred Dakotas could take place as planned.[11]

The missionaries supported the execution of guilty warriors and developed a notion of Indian guilt that mixed acts in war with prior religious association. The hangings, therefore, punished not only the Indians' participation in violent atrocities, but also their refusal to accept the Christian message missionaries had presented for decades. The missionaries' revised notions of God's providence and Indian evangelization were moving toward a new and devastating message: Dakota warriors and medicine men had led their people down the wrong path. The people's gods had not saved them from humiliating defeat. Dakota men hanging from the gallows would show all survivors the peril of rising up against white settlers. The omnipotent Christian God used violent conflict to bring them into his kingdom.

EVANGELIZING THE DAKOTAS

The missionaries pressed their new message in sermons delivered to Dakotas incarcerated in both Mankato and Fort Snelling. They sensed that their efforts were working. On November 28, John Williamson wrote that the Indians realized that the "power of the medicine men" was destroyed. "Their idols," he noted, "by the hundred have been broken, cast away, and buried, as unable to protect them." Williamson took this moment as an evangelistic opportunity, a chance to speak to a people "without a priest and without a god." The ABCFM newspaper, *Missionary Herald,* ran a letter from the young missionary in a similar spirit. The Dakota women and children, he reported, "all say that there is no religion now but that of Jehovah." Hoping to secure a position evangelizing the incarcerated Dakotas when they were moved to a reservation farther west, the younger Williamson implored readers to continue support of the ABCFM mission at such a crucial moment.[12]

Other ABCFM missionaries articulated this message of Dakota failure and Christian victory. Aging missionary Gideon Pond wrote in the *New York Evangelist* that the "real cause" of the war was "pagan resistance to Christianity." Paganism had been overpowered. It "over-did itself and has been signally defeated." Thomas Williamson went even further in his own *Missionary Herald* article. He did not place sole blame on the medicine men, but he argued that these traditional spiritual leaders had quickly turned the war toward their own cause. The medicine men, Williamson wrote, made it "a war not of races, but of religions, of gods." It was the Dakotas, Williamson insisted, not the Christians, who made "this war a religious one."[13]

This message took on a chilling tone as Minnesotans received word that President Lincoln's staff had found thirty-nine Dakotas guilty of killing settlers or raping white women. The president sent execution orders for more than three dozen Dakota men. On the day of the hangings, crowds gathered for a dramatic public spectacle. Fourteen hundred soldiers in full-dress uniforms watched over a gallows specially constructed for the proceedings. More than one thousand spectators observed. According to the *Mankato Record* and other eyewitness accounts, the warriors walked two by two toward the gallows, their faces painted black. The *Saint Paul Pioneer* described the death song the warriors sang as they marched, "a mournful wail" occasionally accompanied by a "piercing scream." Both papers reported that the Dakotas met their deaths with no apparent fear. As the rope was cut and the platform beneath their feet dropped away, the crowd let out a cheer. Soldiers buried the warriors' bodies in a mass grave on the outskirts of town.[14]

Just as Americans clamored for details from Civil War battlefields, they also wanted news from the Mankato gallows. They got it through widely circulated reports from Minnesota newspapers and extended coverage in *Harper's New Monthly Magazine.* When ABCFM missionaries wrote for a wider public audience, however, they deemphasized the Dakotas' demeanor on the gallows and focused, instead, on the Indians' choice for Christ before meeting their deaths. In the days after the hangings, the missionaries reflected on what they understood to be multiple conversions among the condemned Dakota warriors. In subsequent months, they circulated narratives about the death of traditional Dakota religion and the "Indian Pentecost" at work in the prison camps. They hoped these stories would galvanize public support for a new mission to Dakota survivors and other American Indians on the plains.[15]

UNDERSTANDING DAKOTA CONVERSIONS

The missionaries had spent a great deal of time with the condemned in the days before the December 26 execution. Faced with news that they soon would be hanged, the condemned Dakotas had considered their people's future. Many of them spoke to Williamson and Riggs, or to Father Ravoux, a Catholic missionary with a history among the Dakotas. Contemplating their impending deaths and uncertain about their families' futures, twenty-four Dakotas requested instruction from Father Ravoux. The rest chose Williamson as their spiritual advisor. Most of the condemned received baptism in the next few days. Williamson wrote down what he understood to be their conversion narratives.[16]

Missionary-penned narratives intended to convey Indian sentiments present a particularly vexing interpretive task, one that historian Daniel Richter has called "a tricky art." It is especially troubling to attempt this interpretative work with sources from a moment when Americans exerted total power over captive Indians. Historian Erik Seeman has addressed the potential "peril" of this activity in his work on colonial-era Christian Indian deathbed accounts. He has shown how several of these narratives simply bolstered the missionaries' notions of ideal Indian faith. At the same time, Seeman noted examples in which the narratives defied easy interpretation and evidenced Indian ideas and behaviors that would have troubled the missionaries. Scholarly work on captivity narratives reveals a similar impulse in some recorded statements by American Indians. Literary critic Kathryn Zabelle Derounian-Stodola has argued that in some of these texts, Indians "talk back" to settlers, challenging their viewpoints.[17]

Taking this work on death scenes and captivity narratives as inspiration, we can read Williamson's record of Dakota conversion narratives with an eye toward traditional Dakota conceptions of sacred power and approaches to military defeat. They can be understood as something more than the Dakotas' total rejection of their traditions and acceptance of the Americans' religion. To be sure, the Dakotas underwent a dramatic religious transformation in the weeks and months after the war. The question is, what sort of transformation? These narratives show that, at least among those who requested baptism in the days before the hangings, the Dakotas believed that the traditions they once followed had failed them significantly. Capeduta (Scarlet Beaver), for instance, declared that his people needed to forsake their "past ways" to avoid future "trouble." The missionaries were right, it seems, to identify a Dakota willingness to question their traditional spirit beings when faced with catastrophic loss.[18]

But these narratives also reveal that the Dakotas did not throw off their entire understanding of the universe and embrace Christianity to fill the void. Several of the letters show that even as the Dakota showed their willingness to question traditional spirit beings, they did not necessarily alter their notions about how sacred power worked and what it ought to do. Several of the warriors' statements show that they associated an alliance with the Christian God with tangible benefits this new power ought to provide. When Ma{h}piyawisicun (French Cloud) declared that his union with traditional spirits was dissolved, he noted, "We desire that the Great God should remember and have mercy on us." He{h}aka Maza (Iron Elk) stated the Dakotas' expectation even more clearly. "So if the Great God helps us some of us wish to be baptized and thus go to him."[19]

These statements reveal that the Dakotas persisted in their philosophy of sacred power. Or, as historian Kenneth Morrison has written about French–Algonquian contact, new alliances did not mean that understandings of power had changed. Dakotas traditionally believed that sacred power could be manifested in multiple ways. Human beings were expected to respect sacred power and work to harness it for their people's good. If vanquished in war, the Dakotas had an epistemology that required them to consider whether their enemy's supernatural beings had superior power. The loss in war, then, did not completely change their religious worldview, but rather reified their conception of how sacred power worked.[20]

Humility in the face of overwhelming power was particularly appropriate in moments of such loss. By late 1862, the Dakotas had been defeated in battle. Their warriors were about to be executed in a humiliating manner. The survivors would not be able to provide appropriate ritual burial. Such losses demanded explanation, and in this case, a reassessment of their spiritual pantheon. These losses also called for action. But the Dakotas had few options for culturally appropriate responses. They could hardly seek revenge or torture a captive enemy. They were deprived of weapons and were themselves held captive. But the warriors could address these losses and their imminent deaths without fear. This concern comes through clearly in the warriors' conversion statements recorded by Williamson. Dotemena (Round Wind) noted without any apparent worry that he would "soon go to the Great God." Wamniomni hota (Grey Whirlwind) told his sister, "Do not grieve because I must die, I think I will be happy." Even those Dakotas who insisted on their innocence felt compelled to show courage in the face of the gallows. Rdainyankna (Rattling Runner) wrote to his father-in-law that his kin should not grieve because a "brave should be prepared to meet death, and I will do so as becomes a Dakota."[21]

The warriors could also provide for their kin's survival. Indeed, concern for family stability permeates each of the statements that Williamson dictated. Capeduta (Scarlet Beaver) affirmed that he and his followers wished "all our wives and children may follow the law of the Great God." Ma{h}piyawisicun (French Cloud) and He{h}aka Maza (Iron Elk) wrote the same about their "wives and children." Snamani (Sounding Walker) impressed his children to attend missionary school. Tatehihohe (Passing Wind) implored his brother and sister to "pray to the Great God and listen to the missionaries." Hotaninku (Coming Voice) asked his wife to trust in the Great God. Dotemena's (Round Wind's) concern did not stop with his wife: his letter implores her to command their three children and their nieces and nephews to do the same. The Dakotas facing their deaths chose to show no fear on the gallows. They could draw this strength from within. But to secure their kin's survival in an uncertain future, they sought an alliance with the Christians' God.[22]

In his work on seventeenth-century southern New England, historian Richard Pointer has shown that Native Americans put their "own thematic stamp" on the forms of Christianity that emerged among them. He argues that even Puritan-penned documents show that Indian affirmations of Christianity reflected "themes drawn from native spiritual and moral values," including the maintenance of relationships. Pointer has also emphasized the way American

Indians interrogated the Christianity that Puritans purveyed. They asked what biblical passages meant and what sort of rituals they would have to perform if they aligned with the Puritans' God. In the same way, Dakotas in the prison camps considered their community's needs and evaluated the ABCFM missionaries' message. The surviving Dakota statements affirm that the warriors assumed that because the whites had defeated them, the Christian God must have the greatest power. But they still had questions about what this God demanded of them and whether this God would protect their families after the impending executions.[23]

ABCFM missionaries and Dakotas developed competing narratives about the meaning of the war, particularly in their understandings of what it meant for God to work through both military victory and defeat. According to the missionaries, the war, executions, and Dakota conversions were surprising events that confirmed the truth they had known all along. The missionaries had always sought Dakota rejection of their own practices and acceptance of the Christian gospel, but they had never dreamed that it might be accomplished through violence and death. Dakota conversions prompted new providential explanations among the missionaries. The condemned Dakotas, on the other hand, seem to have reasoned from a traditional conception of sacred power that the war had exposed their established spiritual traditions as fatefully weak. Their only hope for survival, then, was an alliance with the ascendant sacred power, the "great God" of the Americans who had defeated them so soundly in battle. This narrative took shape in the lead-up to the executions, but it found a full flowering and dissemination in the months that followed. For the missionaries, it involved a new conception of Indian missions. For Dakota survivors, it included a set of ritual obligations, along with new expectations about their people's future.

SPREADING THE MESSAGE OF PROVIDENTIAL VIOLENCE

The ABCFM missionaries circulated their message about God's work through the war in several eastern periodicals. They reported to readers throughout the country that a truly "pentecostal" work was at hand. They said that in early January 1863, at least 230 of the estimated 300 men left in the Mankato prison camp had announced their desire for baptism. At the larger camp holding mostly women and children, between 300 and 500 Dakotas began to attend religious services. ABCFM missionaries had baptized more than 140 people at the larger camp by the end of April. Episcopal and Catholic missionaries baptized still more. The missionaries claimed that by the time they left the state, all but one Dakota left in the Mankato camp had been baptized. According to historians, the surge of conversions at the prison camps was just the beginning. Later that spring, all the incarcerated Dakotas were removed to a military prison in Iowa or a reservation at Crow Creek in South Dakota. Within a few years, most Dakotas were at least nominal members of Christian congregations.[24]

Stephen Riggs connected the wave of conversions in 1863 to the hangings of late December 1862. He claimed that the inmates in the Mankato camp witnessed the executions through cracks in the prison's log walls. When Riggs preached to these inmates a few days later, he reported that "their fears were thoroughly aroused" and that "it was a good time to unfold to them God's plan of saving from sin." Thomas Williamson also continued his work among the survivors at Mankato, instructing those who requested baptism. By February, he referred to conversions among the survivors as a "mighty work of God."[25]

Riggs's subsequent visits to the Mankato prison confirmed his sense that something truly miraculous was at hand. The prisoners attended daily religious services. Riggs saw them engaged in reading circles, writing letters to family members at Fort Snelling, and reading letters received from relatives. Some townsfolk were skeptical of the Mankato revival. The *Mankato Record* noted that some inmates were baptized into more than one denomination. The article's writer also questioned whether the conversions would last beyond "close confinement." Riggs, however, was convinced. He wrote to the ABCFM that more had happened in the prison camps than in his twenty-six years of missionary work. Considering this success, Riggs recalled his service during the military tribunals. He noted that the commissioners might have been right when they proposed that "the best way to civilize Indians is to imprison them." While Riggs might not have accepted that notion when the trials were under way in October 1862, his experience in the meantime changed everything. What he witnessed in the Indian prisons was "a most amazing work of God's Spirit."[26]

In the end, the missionaries used this narrative about the Christian God overcoming the Dakotas' false gods and idols to argue for a new missionary approach based on forced confinement. "Their own superstition," Riggs reported of the confined Dakotas, "is dashed to pieces like a potter's vessel." The Christian God used war, imprisonment, and difficult conditions on reservations to bring the gospel to the Dakotas. Writing about the Crow Creek reservation, Riggs noted that the Lord used "sword and famine" to evangelize the Indians and that death and sickness served as a portal for religious truth. Gone were the ABCFM methods used from the 1830s through the 1850s. Missions required much more than model farms and day schools. Persuasion was no longer enough. The war convinced Riggs and his colleagues that real conversions resulted when Indians realized their gods had no power and when their material situation left them no possibility for continuing their own cultural traditions.[27]

The Minnesota missionaries convinced ABCFM leaders in the East. Missionary board leader Selah Treat offered his support for the missionaries' providential revision in an introduction to Riggs's memoir. All had seemed lost in August and September 1862, Treat testified, but the work of God was "unexpected and strange." Dakota evangelization, a project that had struggled for years before the war, had become a story of gospel success.[28]

CONCLUSION

Before the 1862 war, Dakotas and whites had been in contact for nearly two hundred years. Their relationships involved myriad negotiations and adjustments over the decades. Even the missionaries who arrived as late as the 1830s established relationships based on at least some measure of cultural give-and-take. The war changed everything. It instigated dramatic religious change for both missionaries and Dakotas. It offered a pattern for understanding American victory and Indian defeat as part of a wider providential purpose. This study, then, not only makes a case for Harry Stout's call for integrating war into our narratives of American religious history, but also specifically demands that historians investigate the way war presented a particular religious challenge to both missionaries and native peoples in contests that stretched across the American plains.

For the missionaries, the war challenged their commitment to an evangelistic program based primarily on education and persuasion. To be sure, missionaries continued to live among plains Indians. They taught in classrooms and offered lessons in planting and plowing. But missionaries such as Riggs and Williamson were changed by war. They moved away from a commitment to evangelical persuasion and toward support of arrangements that forcefully imposed Christian doctrine and structures of white civilization on confined Indian peoples. They cited the prison-camp conversions as their evidence. To native people with no land and no certain future, the missionaries' message about the Protestant God's success and Dakota spiritual failure seemed compelling. Riggs and Williamson were ready to extend this pattern out on the plains. While they never advocated starting a war to accomplish these ends, they certainly accepted an advancing program of physical removal and forced enclosure of Indian nations.

Historian Robert Utley has argued that by 1860, reservations had become the "bedrock" of U.S. Indian policy. Riggs's and Williamson's support of treaties that created Dakota reservations in the late 1850s signals how the missionaries shared in this broad consensus. Utley has also made the case that by 1865, the idea that military force was required to force all western Indians onto reservations had "virtually unchallenged supremacy." The ABCFM missionaries' move toward this militant position reveals the significance of their transformation. Historians hypothesize that most Americans made this move after experiencing the "total war" fought in the last years of the sectional conflict. For Riggs and Williamson, however, it was their own experience of Indian war and spiritual aftermath.[29]

Utley's argument about transitions in the early 1860s is followed by his explanation of the military campaigns against Indians that followed. In 1865, General Pope followed escaped Dakota fighters onto the plains in an effort to bring them to the reservations. Utley argues that these failed military expeditions led to the "conquest of kindness" inaugurated with President Grant's Peace Policy of the late 1860s. Utley is right to observe that the Peace Policy coincided with continued military campaigns to keep native peoples on reservations. But the missionaries central to Grant's "peaceable" approach were hardly immune from the violence happening off the reservations. And they certainly saw evangelistic successes among Indian groups recently devastated by the army. Indeed, it seems that interdenominational infighting about reservation assignments not only betrayed Old World animosities between Christian groups, but also spoke to the missionaries' sense that evangelizing tribes at the moment of defeat offered their best chance at conversion. For Riggs and Williamson, it was not only practical, but part of God's providential plan.[30]

One need only explore the missionary careers of Williamson's and Riggs's children to see how this new providentialism shaped future Indian missions.

John P. Williamson, who had evangelized Dakota inmates at Fort Snelling in 1862, later traveled with the people when they were removed to a reservation at Crow Creek in South Dakota. In 1869, he traveled to the new reservation for the Yanktoni, or Western Dakotas, to serve as one of its first missionaries. Several of Stephen Riggs's children worked as missionaries as well. In 1870, Alfred Riggs founded the Santee Normal Training School under the auspices of the American Missionary Association. While the Santee school was radical in its use of Dakota language in instruction, the curriculum was still intended to Christianize and civilize the captive Dakota population. In 1872, Thomas Riggs took up missionary work among the Teton Lakotas, the westernmost Siouan group. His career coincided with bitter Indian–white conflict that resulted in all the Lakotas settling on reservations. Thomas firmly believed that Indians must acculturate and voiced strong opinions against the Ghost Dance. But his willingness to assent to military force used against American Indians had its limits. As historian Todd Kerstetter has noted, Thomas Riggs provided a sharp critique of the Seventh Cavalry's actions against Big Foot's clan at Wounded Knee in 1890.[31]

As this new providential theology found willing advocates among a new generation of missionaries, it also dominated the historical accounts of emerging Dakota Christianity. Stephen Riggs wrote in his memoir that the Dakotas started the war because they hated Christianity, not because they were almost starving to death and resented living on reservations that restricted their movement. "God, who sits on the throne," Riggs wrote, "had made [the war] result in [the Dakotas'] submission to Him. This was marvelous in our eyes." Historians of the Dakota missions offered a similar line of reasoning. John P. Williamson's biographer wrote that the executions "made a profound impression upon the other prisoners" and that "they felt their gods had failed them." An undated manuscript from around the turn of the twentieth century made similar claims. Presbyterian minister Charles E. McColley wrote that even the innocent Indians' false convictions and sentences served in Mankato were necessary for the "Indian Pentecost." Their confinement, he argued, "counted more important than their personal liberty." Losing the war ushered in a moment in which "the Indians seemed to regard their gods as being defeated." Defeat and confinement convinced the Dakotas that "the God who had given whites such an advantage over the red men must be the great God."[32]

Historian Jill Lepore has written that wars have "victories of wounds" and "victories of words." Her work on King Philip's War details the terrible fighting that tore through seventeenth-century New England communities. Clearly, the British settlers won the victory of wounds. In a similar way, Minnesota's white colonizers eventually won the victory of wounds. Despite terrible losses, they subdued the Dakota people. But Lepore offers us a way to understand the period after the hostilities ceased. She asks us to examine the victories of words. She shows how the English colonists used their position of military victory as a platform for launching a verbal campaign about their own upright actions in the conflict. They overlooked "the elaborate meanings of Indian behavior" to promote a narrative in which the war served as God's judgment against violent Indians.[33]

To some degree, the ABCFM missionaries were key players in white Minnesotans' victory of words. In August 1862, they believed the war was the catastrophic end of their mission. By early 1863, they understood the conflict to be a part of God's providential plan for Indian evangelization. This providential revision required their harrowing personal transformation. It demanded that these mostly mild-mannered missionaries reckon with violence unlike anything they could imagine. Jill Lepore's Puritan ministers were already comfortable with the smiting hand of Jehovah, but the Minnesota missionaries were not. Fleeing their homes, witnessing devastation, and interacting with confined people altered them. The war of words they waged seemed as much about processing their own traumatic experiences as persuading those around them of the conflict's spiritual import. But it anticipated a new language of Indian conflict and evangelization suited for the Indian wars that erupted throughout the American West for the next thirty years.

NOTES

1. Thomas Williamson to Selah Treat, July 2, 1862, American Board of Commissioners for Foreign Missions Papers, Minnesota Historical Society (hereafter MHS).

2. For a good overview of the war, see Duane Schultz, *Over the Earth I Come: The Great Sioux Uprising of 1862* (New York: St. Martin's, 1992). Gary C. Anderson also provides a helpful narrative of the war (see Anderson, *Little Crow: Spokesmen for the Sioux* [St. Paul: Minnesota Historical Society Press, 1986]). For information on two centuries of Dakota–white interactions, see Gary C. Anderson, *Kinsmen of Another Kind: Dakota–White Relations in the Upper-Mississippi Valley, 1650–1862* (Lincoln: University of Nebraska Press, 1984; repr., St. Paul: Minnesota Historical Society, 1997). For a focus on missionaries' interaction with the Dakota, see Linda Marie Clemmons, "Satisfied to Walk in the Ways of Their Fathers: Dakotas and Protestant Missionaries, 1835–1862" (Ph.D. diss., University of Illinois at Urbana-Champaign, 1998).

3. For more traditional accounts of Dakota evangelization, see Robert F. Berkhofer Jr., *Salvation and the Savage: An Analysis of Protestant Missions and American Indian Response, 1787–1862* (Louisville: University of Kentucky Press, 1965); and Bonnie Sue Lewis, *Creating Christian Indians: Native Clergy in the Presbyterian Church* (Norman: University of Oklahoma Press, 2003). I take more recent studies of missionary–native contact as my model for understanding the dynamics of native–missionary exchange (see Emma Anderson, *The Betrayal of Faith: The Tragic Journey of a Colonial Convert* [Cambridge: Harvard University Press, 2008]; Rachel Wheeler, *To Live upon Hope: Mohicans and Missionaries in the Eighteenth-Century Northeast* [Ithaca, N.Y.: Cornell University Press, 2007]; and Richard Pointer, *Encounters of the Spirit: Native Americans and European Colonial Religion* [Bloomington: Indiana University Press, 2007]). I will say more about how I read American Indian "conversion narratives" later in this essay.

4. Harry S. Stout argues that historians of American religion have failed to include episodes of war in their narratives (see Stout, "Review Essay: Religion, War, and the Meaning of America," *Religion and American Culture* 19, no. 2 [Summer 2009]: 275–89). He and Mark Noll have explored the impact of the Civil War on religion (and religion on the Civil War) in recent books (see Harry S. Stout, *Upon the Altar of the Nation: A Moral History of the Civil War* [New York: Penguin, 2007]; and Mark A. Noll, *The Civil War as a Theological Crisis* [Chapel Hill: University of North Carolina Press, 2006]). For more on the way ideas of providence were reconsidered during the war, see George C. Rable, *God's Almost Chosen People: A Religious History of the Civil War* (Chapel Hill: University of North Carolina Press, 2010). Alvin Josephy argues that the 1860s Indian wars are crucial to understanding both the Civil War and the subsequent conflicts on the plains, observing: "During the four years of the Civil War, as a result, more Indians tribes were destroyed by whites and more land was seized from them than in almost any comparable period of time in American history" (see Alvin M. Josephy Jr., *The Civil War in the American West* [New York: Knopf, 1991], xiii). Most scholarship on Protestant responses to Indian wars from the 1860s through the 1890s focuses on eastern Protestants who sat on Indian commissions and led denominational Indian mission boards. It focuses less on the missionaries and agents who worked on the reservations (see Robert H. Keller Jr., *American Protestantism and United States Indian Policy, 1869–82* [Lincoln: University of Nebraska Press, 1983]). This lack of focus on the western Indian wars is surprising given that, in studies of other Indian conflicts, the participants' religious worldviews have received careful exploration (see Joel W. Martin, *Sacred Revolt: The Muskogees' Struggle for a New World* [Boston: Beacon, 1993]).

5. Cameron Addis, "The Whitman Massacre: Religion and Manifest Destiny on the Columbian Plateau, 1809–1858," *Journal of the Early American Republic* 25, no. 2 (Summer 2005): 257; Ferenc M. Szasz and Margaret Connell Szasz, "Religion and Spirituality," in *The Oxford History of the American West,* ed. Clyde A. Milner II, Carol A. O'Conner, and Martha A. Sandweiss (New York: Oxford University Press, 1994), 360.

6. Stephen Riggs to Selah Treat, August 24, 1862, ABCFM Papers, MHS; H. D. Cunningham to Selah Treat, August 29, 1862, ABCFM Papers, MHS; Thomas Williamson to Selah Treat, September 8, 1862, ABCFM Papers, MHS.

7. Carol Chomsky details Riggs's role in the trials (see Chomsky, "The United States-Dakota War Trials: A Study in Military Injustice," *Stanford Law Review* 43, no. 1 [November 1990]: 13–98). Thomas Williamson, "Causes of the War," unidentified newspaper clipping, Thomas Williamson Papers, MHS.

8. Stephen Riggs to Selah Treat, November 24, 1862, ABCFM Papers, MHS; John Williamson to Selah Treat, November 5, 1862, ABCFM Papers, MHS; Thomas Williamson to Selah Treat, November 21, 1862, ABCFM Papers, MHS.

9. Thomas Williamson to Selah Treat, October 17, 1862, ABCFM Papers, MHS.

10. John Williamson to Selah Treat, November 5, 1862; Thomas Williamson to Stephen Riggs, December 5, 1862, Stephen Return Riggs Papers, MHS.

11. Thomas Williamson to Selah Treat, October 17, 1862; Stephen Riggs to Selah Treat, November 24, 1862.

12. John Williamson to Selah Treat, November 28, 1862, ABCFM Papers, MHS; John Williamson, "Results of the Outbreak," *Missionary Herald* 59, no. 1 (January 1863): 14.

13. Gideon Pond, "Religious Aspect of the Indian Raid," *New York Evangelist* 33, no. 11 (March 12, 1863): 2; Thomas Williamson, "Report of the Massacre and Subsequent Religious Interest," *Missionary Herald* 59, no. 7 (July 1863): 201.

14. Schultz describes the hanging in the opening of his book on the war (see Schultz, *Over the Earth I Come*, 1–5). News articles on the hangings were reprinted in *New York Evangelist* 33, no. 3 (January 15, 1863): 7; and *Janesville Daily Gazette* (January 3, 1863).

15. The *New York Times* reprinted an article from the *St. Paul Press* (see "Execution of the Indians in Minnesota, *New York Times*, January 4, 1863, 3; see also Adrain J. Ebell, "Indian Massacres and War of 1862," *Harper's New Monthly Magazine*, June 1863, 1–24). See subsequent paragraphs for specific missionary contributions to interpreting the war and its aftermath.

16. Schultz, *Over the Earth I Come*, 1–5. Father Ravoux recounted his time working with the condemned (see Augustin Ravoux, *Reminiscences, Memoirs, and Lectures of Monsignor A. Ravoux* [St. Paul, Minn.: Brown, Treacy & Co., 1890], 72–81). Catholics emphasized that Ravoux baptized many more Dakotas than did the two Protestant missionaries who had lived among the people for so long. Writers of Catholic periodicals pointed to the Dakotas' overwhelming choice of Ravoux as a way to protest governmental and Protestant mission board policies that marginalized Catholic missionaries (*New York Freedman's Journal and Catholic Register*, February 7, 1863).

17. Daniel K. Richter, *Facing East from Indian Country: A Native History of Early America* (Cambridge: Harvard University Press, 2001), 110–29; Erik R. Seeman, "Reading Indians' Deathbed Scenes: Ethnohistorical and Representational Approaches," *Journal of American History* 88, no. 1 (June 2001): 17–47; Kathryn Zabelle Derounian-Stodola, *The War in Words: Reading the Dakota Conflict through Captivity Literature* (Lincoln: University of Nebraska Press, 2009), 160.

18. Thomas Williamson to Selah Treat, January 29, 1863, ABCFM Papers, MHS.

19. Ibid.

20. Kenneth M. Morrison, *The Solidarity of Kin: Ethnohistory, Religious Studies, and the Algonkian-French Religious Encounter* (Albany: State University Press of New York, 2002), 145.

21. For more on Dakota warfare practices and grieving rituals, see Wilson D. Wallis, *The Canadian Dakota* (New York: American Museum of Natural History, 1947), 21, 31–33; and Jessica Palmer, *The Dakota Peoples: A History of the Dakota, Lakota, and Nakota through 1863* (Jefferson, N.C.: McFarland, 2008), 149–50, 213–14. For expectations about revenge, see Black Eagle and Mazomani's speeches in Mark Diedrich, *Dakota Oratory: Great Moments in the Recorded Speech of the Eastern Sioux, 1695–1874* (Rochester, Minn.: Coyote, 1989), 28, 36. Thomas Williamson to Selah Treat, January 29, 1863, ABCFM Papers, MHS; Diedrich, *Dakota Oratory*, 82.

22. Thomas Williamson to Selah Treat, January 29, 1863. Williamson recorded the Dakotas' testimonies in a December letter to the ABCFM (see Thomas Williamson, December 25, 1862, Thomas Williamson Papers, MHS).

23. Pointer, *Encounters of the Spirit,* 58.

24. Thomas Williamson to Selah Treat, January 20, 1863, ABCFM Papers, MHS; Stephen Riggs to Selah Treat, March 10, 1863, ABCFM Papers, MHS; John P. Williamson to Selah Treat, May 7, 1863, ABCFM Papers, MHS. Another issue is the collection of letters and their translation. The ABCFM missionaries translated and disseminated the Mankato conversion statements. They then accepted letters from and delivered letters on behalf of the remaining prisoners at Mankato and Snelling. They also continued to receive letters once the Dakotas were removed from the state. These letters are only beginning to be translated, and they have not yet been shared widely with scholars. A few from the Iowa military prison are featured in one article (see Sarah-Eva Ellen Carlson, "They Tell Their Story: The Dakota Internment at Camp McClellan in Davenport, 1862–1866," in *Annals of Iowa* 63, no. 3 [Summer 2004]: 251–78).

25. Riggs, *Mary and I,* 185–86; Thomas Williamson to Stephen Riggs, February 22, 1863, Stephen Return Riggs Papers, MHS.

26. Stephen Riggs to Selah Treat, March 26, 1863, ABCFM Papers, MHS; *Mankato Record,* March, 28, 1863. William Beane, a member of Dakota community in Flandreau, South Dakota, has pointed out to me that dedication to kinship ties prompted many Dakotas to take reading and writing lessons from missionaries. Never before their incarceration did the Dakotas depend on writing to communicate with one another. With families separated at the prison camps at Snelling and Mankato, however, letter writing became the primary mode for keeping track of kin. Riggs reported to Selah Treat that he carried hundreds and hundreds of letters back and forth between the two camps (William Beane, phone interview by author, Fall 2009).

27. Stephen Riggs to Selah Treat, March 26, 1863; Stephen R. Riggs, *Tah-koo Wah-kan; or, The Gospel among the Dakotas* (Boston: Congregational Publishing Society, 1869; repr., New York: Arno, 1972), 367, 375–76. The article about the executions in the *Mankato Record* puts some Dakota women at the hanging scene (see "Execution of the Indians in Minnesota," *New York Evangelist* 33, no. 3 [January 15 1863]: 7).

28. Riggs, *Tah-koo Wak-an;* Riggs, *Mary and I*; Selah Treat, introduction to Riggs, *Tah-koo wak-an,* xxxii–xxxiii.

29. Robert M. Utley, *The Indian Frontier of the American West, 1846–1890* (Albuquerque: University of New Mexico Press, 1994), 63, 93, 169.

30. Ibid., 93–96. Other encounters of interest include Quaker Indian agent Lawrie Tatum and his experience with the Kiowas and Comanches during the Red River War; Mormon missionary George Washington Hill's experience among the Shoshone in the 1860s and 1870s; and Congregationalist missionary Mary Collins's experience among the Lakota during the era of the Ghost Dance and massacre at Wounded Knee.

31. Winifred W. Barton, *John P. Williamson: A Brother to the Sioux* (New York: Fleming H. Revell Co., 1919); "The Rev. Alfred R. Riggs," *American Missionary* 70, no. 10 (January 1916): 146–47; J. B. Irvine, "Fifty Years with the Sioux: Pioneer Missionary Work in Central South Dakota," *American Missionary* 76, no. 1 (January 1922): 202–3. Kerstetter's work explores the work of all three of the missionary children mentioned here (see Kerstetter, "Spin Doctors at Santee: Missionaries

and the Dakota-Language Reporting of the Ghost Dance and Wounded Knee," *Western Historical Quarterly* 28, no. 1 [April 1997]: 45–67).

32. Riggs, *Mary and I,* 189–90; Barton, *John P. Williamson,* 60; Charles E. McColley "An Indian Pentecost, undated," reel 2, frame 0377, Dakota Conflict of 1862 Manuscripts Collections, Microfilm edition, MHS.

33. Jill Lepore, *The Name of War: King Philip's War and the Origins of American Identity* (New York: Random House, 1998), 11, 13.

7

PROVIDENCE REVISED

The Southern Presbyterian Old School in the Civil War and Reconstruction

ZACHARY W. DRESSER

The Civil War brought death and destruction to Americans as had no prior event in the nation's history. With 620,000 men falling in combat or succumbing to wounds and infections, the search for an American—North or South—personally unaffected by the war's casualties would be in vain. The devastation encompassed more than human lives, a fact that the southerners who worked to rebuild houses, public buildings, roads, and bridges in the years following the war knew all too well. War tore apart many of the personal and institutional connections that had bound people in antebellum America. Sectionalism and war split most of the national denominations into sectional organizations. Especially in the South, physical edifices crumbled along with the spiritual. Churches were damaged or destroyed, and destitute parishioners struggled to raise funds to repair or rebuild. Civilians and soldiers alike turned to their faith for security in chaotic times, but the scale of destruction and the ubiquity of death posed difficult theological questions.

For decades, the scholarly output concerning the cultural changes wrought in the 1860s was quite slim in comparison to the amount written about political and military events. This situation has begun to change in recent years, and many historians now find that the firsthand experience of unbridled carnage represented, in Louis Menand's words, "a failure of culture, a failure of ideas." The characterization of the era as one of cultural destruction recurs in the literature on the religious impact of the war, which is still relatively slim. Historians frequently speak of religion in the mid-nineteenth century as being in "crisis." Mark Noll labels the war itself as a "theological crisis," and Drew Gilpin Faust argues that widespread suffering induced a "crisis of belief" that "propelled many Americans to redefine or even reject their faith in a benevolent and responsive deity." The selection of the word "crisis" is appropriate in its ability to communicate the seriousness of Americans' sudden inability to use religion as a common language and their doubts about a loving God's providential design. At the same time, it also suggests that the result of these challenges was a kind of intellectual gridlock in which creative solutions were unlikely to be found within tradition. The title of Faust's chapter on the religious impact of Civil War death, "Believing and Doubting," sums up the way in which the subject is now understood. Put simply, some kept believing after the war, and others doubted.[1]

This division into two camps—believers and doubters—is useful insofar as it acknowledges the shaking of cultural foundations that occurred in the Civil War era, but it obscures more subtle transformations that occurred somewhere between faith and disbelief. Historians have demonstrated an overreliance on the writings of northerners who never had a conventional faith in the first place, skewing the historical interpretations too far in the direction of doubt. Ambrose Bierce, Emily Dickinson, Walt Whitman, and Herman Melville were certainly astute critics and observers of wartime culture, but their exceptional capacities for creative, individual thought and their willingness to depart from tradition necessarily set them apart from the majority of Americans. A full accounting of the impact of the Civil War on belief requires historians to alter their approach to the problem and investigate the thoughts of more representative Christians professing traditional beliefs. By expanding the time frame through both the Civil War and Reconstruction, a category of believers emerges who averted crisis by modifying—not fully rejecting—traditional concepts to maintain their faith during changing times. The southern Presbyterian Old School was one such group.[2]

One reason for this expansion of chronological focus is regional setting. Aside from the excellent work on the Lost Cause, the cultural developments of the postwar South have hardly been studied. But with three times as many Confederate soldiers falling in battle as Union troops—adjusted proportionately—and the devastation of the southern landscape, the South must be considered in the measurement of grief caused by the Civil War. And southerners' pain did not end at Appomattox. Current historiography takes for granted that the war itself was the defining event of the mid- to late nineteenth century, but for white southerners the humiliation and suffering provided by defeat extended at least until the end of Reconstruction, a trial almost on par with the loss of the war itself. Adding to the political and military upheaval, the late 1860s and

1870s also presented the faithful with serious new intellectual challenges from science and philosophy, as Darwinism and logical positivism threatened the intellectual defensibility of orthodox Christian belief. It would be difficult to isolate the impact of any of these factors on southern belief; rather, the Civil War, Reconstruction, and new ideas were experienced in tandem by believers working to make sense of a radically new world.[3]

If any group could have weathered the turmoil of the era and emerged intellectually unscathed, it would have been the southern Old School. After splitting along theological lines in 1837, the Presbyterian Church divided again during the sectional crisis. At the 1861 Old School General Assembly, Dr. Gardiner Spring of New York proposed to the mostly northern gathering a pledge of loyalty to the federal government, which easily passed. Southerners saw this action as an intolerable mixture of religion and politics and opted to form their own denomination, the Presbyterian Church in the Confederate States of America.[4] Old School Presbyterians, North and South, placed a heavy emphasis on tradition and orthodoxy. They valued intellectual development and logical argumentation over the passion and zeal of the evangelical revivalists, although the southern branch of the Old School was certainly not as antirevivalist as the northern division could be. As such, despite the destitute conditions of the 1870s, publications like the *Southern Presbyterian Review* remained in print. But even this stalwart institution did not survive the Civil War era unscathed. The intellectual careers of Robert Lewis Dabney and Benjamin Morgan Palmer reveal that the most conservative Calvinist estimations of the way God works in the world changed during this time. Both Dabney and Palmer fundamentally altered their theologies of providence, but the changes in their belief systems by no means weakened their faith. Rather, with the utmost sincerity, they attempted to breathe new life into old forms while remaining true to their theological heritage.[5]

Nearly everyone had some sort of theology of providence during the Civil War, not just the professional theologians. As George C. Rable argues, American Protestants, Catholics, and Jews "shared a providential outlook on life" despite their vastly differing theologies. During every stage of the war, they saw God's involvement in all events. Quoting Rable again, "Everything—storms, harvests, illnesses, deaths—unfolded according to God's will." The language of God's providential control suffused American parlance, even permeating the vocabulary of noted nontraditional believers like Abraham Lincoln. But while providential phrasing could appear in any context for the general population, nineteenth-century American theologians had specific definitions in mind when speaking about the matter. They wrote about "general" and "special" providences. The former category referred to the general plan God had devised to govern the world, such as God's sustained maintenance of nature through consistent laws. God's interventions in history, momentarily breaking the normal order, were known as special providences. Southern theologians separated their formal discourses on providence apart from other technical topics such as grace or predestination, but the questions raised by God's allowing an irreligious North to overthrow a godly Confederacy produced a series of questions beginning in the realm of special providences and spiraling outward. The postwar uncertainty generated in the chastened South motivated Dabney and Palmer to reassess their understanding of the divine's character as well as the very ability of humans to possess religious knowledge.[6]

Dabney and Palmer's approach to the theological problems of the era was informed by a rich tradition of theological reflection on God's role in the world.[7] Dating back to the late colonial period, southern religious thinkers approached theological questions from a perspective that historian E. Brooks Holifield has termed "rational orthodoxy." Rationality, Holifield observes, was "the most noticeable feature of American religious thought in the early nineteenth century." Although the emotional style of eighteenth- and nineteenth-century revivalism is most often seen as the defining characteristic of southern religion, conservative theologians such as Dabney and Palmer sought the experience of the divine primarily through reason. They believed the solution to any theological or philosophical problem could be deduced through argumentation drawing on Scripture, logic, and sensory perception. The world itself had a rational structure that the human mind, by God's design, was able to understand. And, for the Old School, that structure necessarily comported with the doctrines of Reformed theology. If God's power and goodness could not be seen in a particular instance, the believer could trust that with further reflection any supposed irrationality would be revealed as a failing of the theologian's initial thinking and not a reason to doubt the existence of the traditional theistic God. Relying on this tradition, Dabney and Palmer's theological reformulations during the Civil War and Reconstruction never led them away from faith; rather, the two men created a version of orthodoxy both steeped in tradition and applicable to the concerns of the times.[8]

On June 13, 1861, Benjamin Morgan Palmer, the popular minister of First Presbyterian Church, New Orleans, rose before his congregation to deliver a topical sermon entitled "National Responsibility before God." From the lectern, Palmer looked over the packed pews of the South's third-largest congregation, which often attracted visitors who had expressly traveled to hear the pastor's famed orations. The parishioners of this Old School Presbyterian stronghold were likely more restive than they would have been on a typical Sunday in a previous year; it had been only two months since the skirmish in South Carolina at Fort Sumter initiated what these southerners saw as a new war for independence. Palmer sought to galvanize those feelings, emphasizing the seriousness of the moment's political reality. "We must renounce the shallow nominalism which would make such a word as 'nation' a dead abstraction, signifying only the aggregation of individuals," Palmer exhorted. Instead, a nation should be understood as "an incorporated society," possessing "a unity of life resembling the individuality of a single being."[9]

By adopting such an understanding of nationhood, southerners would be able not only to emerge victorious from the war but, more importantly, to stand righteous before the judgment of God. Palmer reasoned that nations, like individuals, have moral responsibilities, and when those obligations are not met, the wrath of God is incurred. In Palmer's words, "each [nation] has its own precisely defined character, fulfils its appointed mission, is developed through a providential training, and is held to a strict providential reckoning." In other words, God acts in history, supporting nations in temporal affairs and, in return, expecting allegiance. When humans transgress this arrangement, God punishes disobedience in this world, not waiting for final judgment. Sometimes punishment is delayed for several generations, but it is "unavoidable" nonetheless.[10]

The Civil War represented for Palmer the dénouement of tensions between the United States and the divine that had been building since the nation's birth. The absence of God's name in the Constitution served as one example among many of the nation's failings to give proper reverence to God in all of its affairs. However, the Confederacy's constitutional recognition of its obligations to God was merely a first step toward righting those wrongs. This decisive turn against past misbehavior, Palmer asserted, meant that the Confederacy would "feel the support of God's immovable Providence." The message was simple: the pious and righteous South should be "prepared to recognize that gracious Providence which will work our deliverance."[11]

Less than a year later, though, New Orleans fell into Union hands, and Palmer fled to Columbia, South Carolina, where he would serve as a professor of theology at the Presbyterian seminary. His dedication to the Confederate cause, however, never flagged. During the war, southern clergymen generally backed the Confederacy through victory and defeat, interpreting results on the battlefield as indications of Providence's mood. In the words of Harry S. Stout, "the clergy were virtually cheerleaders all." Palmer was more energetic than most in his support, and he spent much of the war away from Columbia, speaking and preaching in various venues throughout the South. According to historian James W. Silver, Palmer "ranged up and down the country during the whole of the war, assuming the appearance of a prophet of the Lord. A general in Mississippi declared Palmer to be worth a thousand soldiers to the cause."[12]

Given his firm conviction that Providence would secure Confederate victory, Palmer was understandably devastated by defeat. During the years of war, Palmer lost a beloved daughter to illness, his intellectual inspiration James Henley Thornwell also succumbed to disease, and his South Carolina house and library were burned by the Union army. When Palmer made his way back to New Orleans, an editorial in the *New Orleans Times* from July 17, 1865, noted that he "had lost none of those powers which gave such a charm to his pulpit oratory. He seemed, however, to be more chastened and subdued than he was before."[13]

Reconstruction heaped more misery onto Palmer's life. He had no hope in a nation led by "a man who was a renegade and traitor to his own people," Andrew Johnson. Indeed, Palmer's "only hope" was in the "expectation of seeing the United States go to pieces." The end of the country was near, but not near enough. He feared that "in the meantime, [we] have to go through a terrible ordeal." Although that day did not come, there was no end to Palmer's invective against the North and despair over the South. In an 1872 tirade, Palmer bemoaned the poor South, "breathless and panting in its exhaustion at the close of a long and cruel war with three-fifths of its property practically confiscated by a single stroke of the pen, with its system of labor unhinged and its industry paralysed, overwhelmed with a degree of taxation rendering the poor the envy of the rich, with a band of harpies fattening on the public revenue."[14]

Death seemed to follow Palmer wherever he went. Parishioners constantly asked him for solace and meaning in the death of loved ones. Yellow fever was a particularly heinous menace in New Orleans, taking young infants and healthy adults alike. The 1867 outbreak left him with scarcely a moment's rest from the presence of death and suffering. The pestilence produced particularly distressing deaths, which worked against nineteenth-century notions of the "good death" by forcing a quick burial instead of a prolonged viewing of the deceased. An editorial in the *New Orleans Daily Picayune* described "something so repulsive in the nature of the pestilence itself that even affection does not wish to detain the body from an immediate burial." Scholarly discussion of these disrupted funerary traditions is generally centered during the war itself, but the yellow fever epidemic serves as one example of the continued presence of abnormal death in the South. The personal tragedies that befell Palmer's own family laid the minister low. The death of a daughter in 1875 left only one of his six children alive after Reconstruction. Reacting to her death, Palmer wrote: "For the first time in all my life, I find my public work to be oppressive. I do not understand it. . . . What a pity that faith is not always steady and bright! But one swings so, from faith to sense again and all is dark as before."[15]

As tragedy multiplied, Palmer felt no reprieve. "Each bereavement cuts its way down to the quick," followed by "a return of the old grief, as it rises up to meet the new." In response to the ever-presence of tragedy, Palmer formulated a theology of suffering. He counseled parishioners that "God has not made it a sin to mourn." While grieving freely, the bereaved should consult the biblical story of Abraham's willingness to sacrifice his son, Isaac, which now seemed to Palmer a "form of sacrifice . . . not so peculiar as it seems." The death of a child presented an opportunity for a renewal of Christian "submission and faith." In a memorial sermon, Palmer maintained, "Our blessed Redeemer has sanctified everything which he hath touched, even death." Such a thought was startling, even unbelievable, but Palmer was adamant. Although "cold reason may stagger at the metaphysics of the doctrine," death presented a hidden blessing in forever imprinting the love of the deceased in the memory. Later that year, Palmer wrote about "a depth in the utterances of grief that no philosophy can fathom." Suffering and loss thus forced the believer beyond the rational in order to understand the relationship between human and divine.[16]

The Civil War and Reconstruction failed to destroy the Presbyterian divine's belief in God's active presence in the world. But Palmer's experiences did lead him to revise his understanding of special providence in a way that removed rational certainty. In an 1872 essay entitled "The Tribunal of History," Palmer sought to work out a theory of how God worked through human history. God, not "wholly unmindful of the affairs of earth," nonetheless worked somewhat indirectly, through human agents. Palmer began by reinterpreting the meaning of the creation of humanity in God's own image, a concept with a long trajectory in the history of theology. The image of God here becomes the capacity for understanding divine justice, that is, an innate ability to understand how things ought to work in this world. The fall of Adam, however, clouded human understanding, but it did not destroy the human ability to tap into the knowledge of the true divine order. "This rugged sense of justice," Palmer asserted, "remains, shattered and defaced it may be, warped by passion, obscured by prejudice, blundering through ignorance and mistake into a thousand errors." This sense of justice served as "the corner stone of religion and of law" and held "the very fabric of society together." As such, Palmer reasoned that this sense was the means by which God acted on earth, through human agents endowed with the capability of meting out divine judgment—albeit imperfectly.[17]

The upshot of all this was that Christians could be certain that the divine acted in the world, but unpredictably so. In the short term, Providence worked through humans, whose corrupted faculties and free will lead them not always to act in accordance with divine standards. It was the long term, however, that truly mattered. And only the divine mind could comprehend the true course of events, which extended beyond time into eternity. This world was merely a probationary period, during which both good and evil enjoyed periods of success and neither won entirely. Palmer backed down somewhat from this line of reasoning in the pulpit, but the main point remained the same. He encouraged his parishioners to avoid trying to comprehend the workings of Providence in the world: "No man is able to tell how the thread of his personal history is woven into the web of God's universal Providence. Neither you nor I, can tell why God should, in fatherly discipline, afflict us as He does." Even if someone were to calculate the reasons for personal suffering, Palmer averred, "We must wait until we sit upon the mount of God . . . before we can comprehend either the wisdom or the love of God's dealings with His Saints upon the earth." No longer confident to predict the ways in which Providence operated, Palmer was nonetheless still convinced that God continued to work in the world, and this fact, if little else in the changing world of the South during Reconstruction, could provide vital solace for the southern Christian.[18]

The change in Palmer's understanding of Providence since the outset of the Civil War was not merely a visceral reaction to the disappointments of the war and Reconstruction. It was one part of Palmer's reworking of his religious epistemology—that is, how humans are able to come to knowledge of the divine—in the postwar period. The Reconstruction era was not only a turbulent period in the realm of politics; it was also a period of major transition in the life of the mind. By the 1870s, the Darwinian theory of evolution had gained enough clout that ministers were beginning to wrestle with its implications for faith. Meanwhile, the rise of logical positivism in philosophical circles threatened to undermine the combination of Scottish Common Sense philosophy and inductive method that had allowed for the harmonization of religion and science in the antebellum period.[19]

Along with most other southern theologians in the first half of the nineteenth century, Palmer saw no conflict between the goals of science and religion. Most conservative Christians of the South agreed that through the use of the inductive method—carefully building conclusions from the slow and patient collection of particular and dependable observations—trustworthy facts could be discerned from the natural order. Theologians believed that observation of the natural world, properly constrained by the bounds of induction, provided firm evidence of God's design and ongoing care of the earth, and for many American scientists the end of their fields was to offer empirical proof for the existence of the biblical God.[20]

Palmer, like his antebellum contemporaries, was a true empiricist, believing that the mind was "destitute, at birth, of all knowledge, without power to create within itself a single material of thought, and depending upon experience for all. . . . It is furnished with the senses, the open avenues by which it enters the domain of nature." By compiling the information discovered in nature, the mind could gradually ascend to knowledge of "the most general axioms." True science transcended taxonomy by aiming toward the heavens. Science, philosophy, and theology were all aimed toward the knowledge of God. Scripture, Palmer asserted in 1852, must be included in the investigations of any of these three disciplines. As he put it, "The philosophy . . . which will ignore the Bible . . . has apostatized from" proper methodology. Moreover, Protestantism, in Palmer's mind, was the wellspring of all the major scientific breakthroughs of the age of the Enlightenment. Palmer, again like many other southern theologians, focused on Francis Bacon. "There never could have been a Bacon without the Bible," Palmer wrote. "Francis Bacon was the offspring of the Reformation." All human pursuits of knowledge—science, philosophy, and religion alike—were part of the same intellectual project, which was to be conducted using the same empirical method.[21]

By the 1870s, Palmer's theory of knowledge had undergone fundamental changes. The intelligibility of Providence in human events, as we have seen, was put at a distance, potentially placing the ability to know God in peril. As the questions arising from contemporary geology, Darwinian evolution, and pragmatism revealed seemingly irreconcilable differences with the Bible and Christianity, conservative theologians were forced to take stock of science anew and evaluate whether its conclusions could be trusted to provide information about the divine. For Palmer, nothing could be more misleading in the quest for religious knowledge than science conducted improperly: "It is the shame of bastardy, which Science brands upon her own forehead, and the great scandal which tarnishes her proud name, that she is not, in every stage of her own progress, the interpreter of that God whom she finds in nature, and the witness of His being."[22]

The problem, as Palmer framed it, was that "when we look out upon nature, there is the agency of God, it is true; but that agency, to a large extent, is obscured and hidden from us." Palmer's solution to this dilemma was to devise an epistemological system in which scientific and religious knowledge were both considered true but, at the same time, essentially different types of knowledge. He spoke about this distinction between scientific and religious knowledge using the concept of separate spheres: "Knowledge is acquired by us in one or other of two ways: either by the discoveries of reason, in the sphere of the natural; or by the revelation which is made to faith, in the sphere of the super-natural. The two are entirely distinct; for they relate to different spheres, and are addressed to two distinct faculties of the soul." For Palmer, religious truth existed on "a plane which is higher." It would be impossible to leap to this lofty sphere from the earthly position to which the human mind is bound when confined to the data provided by sensory perception alone. As Palmer put it, "The more successful we are in explaining any natural and secondary causes, all the facts which our senses observe, the further do we put from us the intervention of God."[23]

True religious knowledge, then, could not begin with empirical investigation. Palmer held that it goes "directly to the *heart,*" from the revelation of God. Thus, even though the world appeared to be governed by chance, the believer could trust that "in the religious sphere . . . God shall be in closer personal communication with us." This "closer personal communication" occurred in a faculty each person possesses that was attuned to the reception of religious truth, what Palmer called the "testimony of consciousness." His point was simple: the knowledge stemming from divine revelation was real knowledge and even more trustworthy than that provided by the senses.[24]

This argument marked a significant development. Relying on the thought of Scottish Common Sense philosophers, Old School Presbyterian theologians commonly saw the senses as direct conduits between the objective world and a passive imagination, while frowning on any deductions that moved beyond demonstrable "fact." By collecting many basic units of demonstrable truth, larger truths could slowly be proven. Palmer, like the Scottish Realists, defended the necessity of a priori mental structures in this ascent to truth, arguing that "in every case of deductive reasoning we are pushed back to certain elementary and fundamental principles, so simple we are unable to press behind them." The mind was necessarily active in the process, and Palmer agreed that turning perception into knowledge did not occur automatically.[25]

From here, Palmer's argument broke with tradition. Whereas the Realists used arguments in favor of a priori cognition to contend against the weakness attributed to reason (and hence to religious belief) in Hume, Palmer used these very arguments to supplant the power of reason in favor of revelation. By demonstrating that the mind was active even when receiving data from nature, Palmer secured the ground from which to argue that there was a component of knowledge—scientific and religious alike—that did not appeal to experience. In the case of religious knowledge, this element was the conscience, which had the capacity to receive revelation directly from God. What was communicated in this way was not understood rationally, but by virtue of the authority of this sense alone, it offered "proofs conclusive to the most sluggish understanding." In short, while scientific knowledge was created by both the senses and the mind, religious knowledge was formed by God's activity on the mind alone. Revelation, by relying solely on divine input and not the corrupt data of the world, became the guiding principle behind Palmer's religious epistemology. Palmer had thus constructed an intellectual system that allowed him both to take science seriously and to preserve the demands of faith against the intellectual weather of the times.[26]

In 1860, when war was looking increasingly possible, Robert Lewis Dabney was not nearly as exuberant about the southern cause as was his denominational colleague Palmer. Love for one's nation, Dabney declared to his audience at Hampden-Sydney College, was an admirable and proper sentiment. However, unlike many of his contemporaries, Dabney held that the Christian's duty was to smooth over conflict, to preserve peace, and eschew the divisions that politics often engenders. Prayer, confession of sin, and regular religious duties would serve the Christians' nation the best. For each sin attributable to others within the nation, each sincere Christian could find one to match in his or her own heart. War could do nothing but disturb the two things that matter most in human life: the preservation of the family and the religious work of the church. As a mistake, civil war would be "second only to that of the apostate church which betrayed the Savior of the world." The effects on the church would be calamitous: "[War's] judgment will be rendered in calamities second only to those which avenged the divine blood invoked by Jerusalem on herself and her children." Until war officially broke out, Dabney devoted much of his considerable energies to moderating the passions that were flaring throughout the South.[27]

Dabney, however, was a child of the South, and when the events at Fort Sumter forced his hand, he joined the southern cause with full vigor. More specifically, Dabney was a son of Virginia, born in Louisa County in the eastern Piedmont and educated at Hampden-Sydney, the University of Virginia, and Union Seminary at Hampden-Sydney. While his mind traversed through the gamut of the Western world's ideas, his body stayed firmly planted in the Commonwealth. After seminary, he spent a few years in a rural parish but then found his true calling training the young minds of Virginia's Old School as a professor of theology at his alma mater Union Seminary from 1853 to 1883. Even job offers from Princeton Seminary, the bastion of the Old School's brightest minds, and New York's prestigious Fifth Avenue Presbyterian Church could not pry this Virginian from his home.[28]

So, when war came, Dabney took a stand for Old Virginia in the way he thought he could best serve the cause: by following the troops into battle as a military chaplain. During his four months with the Eighteenth Virginia Volunteers, he witnessed firsthand both the Confederate victory and the horrifying violence at the First Battle of Manassas. Despite his presence at the battle, Dabney assured his sister: "I am a *non-combatant,* and intend to remain so. I have persisted in refusing to get any uniform or side arms." Thus it comes as a surprise that in April 1862, General Stonewall Jackson offered Dabney a position as his chief of staff. Dabney quickly accepted the opportunity to serve Virginia, much to the consternation of the professional soldiers he supplanted in rising to such an office. Jackson was pleased with Dabney's performance, but, as historian Wallace Hettle notes, it was likely because Dabney "never functioned as a general's chief-of-staff; he more closely resembled the personal secretary of a friend." The one time Dabney was given responsibility for conducting military affairs (at the Battles of Seven Days), he passed the duty down the chain of command. Only five months after accepting General Jackson's offer, the unlikely officer who showed up to camp decked out in a knee-length formal coat and a fancy beaver hat returned home for the duration of the war.[29]

The Civil War was a defining event in Dabney's life. According to his most recent biographer: "The war was the dividing line of his mental history and the most significant event of his life. . . . While before the war he had been Virginian first American second, after the War Dabney was Virginian first, Southerner second, and American maybe." His antipathy toward the North and its supposedly dishonorable inhabitants had no end. One former student recollected that he "became so embittered by the ruthless methods of Federal officers like Sheridan and Sherman, and the efforts of Congress to impose Negro rule on the South that he almost went off his mental balance." Moreover, Dabney was forced to suffer the indignity of manual labor in the years immediately following the war. In an 1865 letter, he lamented: "I must work or starve. I would greatly prefer to labor in the gospel rather than in the corn-field, if God . . . will let me. My private income, small before, is now at an end." For the holder of a prestigious professorship and erstwhile Confederate officer, the struggles of Reconstruction life were almost too much to bear.[30]

His postwar writings reveal the spirit of a man possessed, driven by a consuming passion to return to the way things were in the Old South. He became, in the words of historian Charles Reagan Wilson, "a prophet of the past." But as Dabney weathered the storm of Reconstruction, he augmented his logical understanding of tradition with a new appreciation for the role of emotion in both the human psyche and the character of the divine. The role of Providence in the travails of Virginia—which Dabney never doubted—required a new set of tools to explain in a way that also stayed true to orthodoxy.

Given Dabney's admiration of the past, it was fitting that his initial postbellum book was the first biography of his friend Stonewall Jackson, *Life and Campaigns of Lt. General T. J. (Stonewall) Jackson* (1866). This hagiographic treatment of Jackson's life and military career treated the subject as a Christian martyr for a noble, even holy, cause, thus laying a cornerstone for the Lost Cause myth that obsessed the southern mind until well into the twentieth century. A year later, Dabney printed an apologia for his home state entitled *A Defence of Virginia.* First, Dabney argued that northerners milked the southern economy in order to live plush lives of luxury, while southerners endured parsimonious, hardworking lives. The second argument was yet another return to the past, rehearsing a long tradition of using the Bible to justify slavery. These two early publications set the tone for Dabney's subsequent discussions of social and political matters. He spoke out against the reunification of the Presbyterian Church, which had split during the sectional crisis before the Civil War. Public education represented in Dabney's mind the death knell for the traditional, hierarchical family. The only promise capitalism and industrialization held for the South was the fragmentation of southern society and the destruction of republican values. Dabney looked out from his enclave at Union Seminary, and what he saw was not good. Before the war, slavery had assured a stable society built on rank, merit, and Protestant faith. The developments of Reconstruction convinced Dabney that the South was headed for anarchy, racial mixing, and atheism.[31]

The horrors that unfolded before Dabney's eyes during Reconstruction were reminiscent to him of the French Revolution. Southern slaveholders had long been influenced by the memory of the events in France and the waves they made across the Atlantic into Haiti, especially after Nat Turner's revolt and other insurrection scares in the 1830s. For most slaveholders, these fears remained latent possibilities and ended with the war, but thoughts that the Terror had actually resurfaced in history permeated Dabney's postwar writings on social issues. In the introduction to his *Defence of Virginia*, Dabney made the connection explicit, writing, "It will in the end become apparent to the world . . . that the conviction of the wickedness of slaveholding . . . is a legitimate corollary from that fantastic, atheistic, and radical theory of human rights which made the Reign of Terror in France which has threatened that country and which now threatens the United States, with the horrors of Red-Republicanism." A United States devoid of the social hierarchy and stability Dabney believed had been furnished by slavery filled him with a terror that was reflected in his theological and social thought.[32]

C. Vann Woodward summed up nicely the conflict Dabney waged on social and political grounds: "Never, of course, was there the remotest chance of Dabney's goose quill prevailing against the clattering presses" of the New South's proponents. But when it came to religious matters, being stuck in the past was no detriment. Dabney was a disciple of tradition in a denomination that reflected on the history of doctrine. By the time he received his seminary degree in 1846, the role of the conservative Calvinist theologian in America was well defined. At early-nineteenth-century Princeton, the ideal of the full-time professor-theologian was forged. Instead of ministering themselves, the ablest theological minds cordoned themselves off in the seminary, training new generations of conservative ministers and writing endlessly to preserve tradition. The protection of orthodoxy served as the primary end of this system. As Charles Hodge, who set the theological course at Princeton for almost forty years, famously proclaimed, "I am not afraid to say that a new idea never was originated in this seminary." This defensively conservative posture developed in Princeton informed the southern Old School Presbyterians. In the antebellum South,

Robert Jefferson Breckinridge (1800–1871) and James Henley Thornwell (1812–1862) took up the assault on heterodoxy, despite their distance from northern centers of liberal theology and New School Calvinism. Although doctrinal quibbles occasionally arose between the Princetonians and southerners—and even between southerners—the Old School intellectual establishment represented a unified front for the defense of the faith, even as other national denominational ties crumbled during the Civil War.[33]

Dabney's theological writing fits the category of "rational orthodoxy" well, as he applied a thorough rationality to the defense of tradition. Although he was widely published before the war, his main theological and philosophical works appeared after the war. His *Lectures in Systematic Theology* (1878) drew on courses he had been teaching for decades by the time of its publication, but the work evidences no sign that the events and intellectual innovations of the 1860s and 1870s had disturbed his trust in the rationality of Christian belief. *The Sensualistic Philosophy of the Nineteenth Century Considered* (1875) also displays an unwavering confidence in antebellum theological rationality in the face of the criticisms levied by innovative philosophers such as the Positivists Auguste Comte and John Stuart Mill.

While Dabney and other southern conservative theologians affirmed the value of revelation and Scripture, they also thought reason occupied a powerful role in the operation of these traditional sources of religious authority. It was reason by which the human mind could recognize the truth contained in the Bible. In an exposition of the role of reason in theology, Dabney encouraged students to "discard all the false and mischievous ideas generated by the slang of the 'contest between reason and faith.'" For Dabney, "There is no such contest. The highest reason is to believe implicitly what God's word says, as soon as it is clearly ascertained to be God's word. The dictate of reason herself is to believe; because she sees the evidences to be reasonable." Thus, revelation must be filtered through cognition before it becomes valuable. As such, Scripture, by design, is fitted to the capabilities of the human mind: "The claim which the Scriptures address to us . . . is addressed to our reason."[34]

This of course implies that human reason had the power to apply the data from revelation to its proper ends. While Dabney saw reason as necessarily limited in its reliance on revelation to locate truth, his philosophy of mind displayed an optimistic confidence in the natural ability of the mind, operating properly, to cognize truth. "I fearlessly assert," he wrote, "that no erroneous belief on any important question can arise in a sane mind." This ability made it the duty of the responsible Christian to develop a rational belief in the Bible, which could only be done through the logical assembly of evidence. In Dabney's words: "Man is required . . . to believe and love the Bible. . . . He who says he believes, when he sees no proof, is but pretending, or talking without meaning.[35]

Dabney wedded rationalism to tradition, as would be expected of an orthodox theologian. On the one hand, reason operated in conjunction with Scripture as a corrective to scientific and philosophical flights of fancy. On the other hand, as "the laws of thought which necessarily rule in the human soul were established by the same God who gave the Bible," the mind was given the role of first deciphering the categories of proper revelation and then, by those categories, judging the meaning of the revelation contained in Scripture. Thus, rational explanation demonstrated through logical evidence assumed a central place in Dabney's understanding of how humans form religious knowledge.[36]

This approach is evident in Dabney's stance on Providence. That God both designed the world and continually guided its events in time struck Dabney as a matter of "common sense," if God were to be considered perfect. God, as perfectly good and wise, designed a world that required constant intervention in order to maintain a personal relationship with creation. Dabney reached this conclusion first through logical argumentation, and only after this demonstration did he show that his conclusions comported with the Bible. Dabney's refutation of the challenges that Deists and Pantheists presented to the orthodox doctrine of Providence shows the primacy of arguments from reason, rather than Scripture, in his polemical arsenal. His opponents both responded to the problem of theodicy (that is, if God is supremely All-Wise, All-Powerful, and Just, why does suffering exist?) by distancing Providence from day-to-day affairs. Deists—as Dabney understood them—argued that God acted in the world only at the Creation, and then left the world to run through mechanisms of natural law. Pantheists included God in the development of the world, making God mutable and thus imperfect. Dabney, of course, found such positions to be tantamount to atheism. Whereas Dabney's opponents asserted that Providence could be seen only from a broad, general perspective, Dabney, ever the good Baconian, argued that without knowledge of the particular there could be no knowledge of the general. "[A] general class is nothing," he argued, "when separated from particulars which compose it, but an abstraction of the mind." If the means by which God operated in the world on a quotidian basis were "contingent and fallible," then "the providence must be such also." Satisfied by the logical consistency of his argument, Dabney displayed an exuberant confidence in the divine plan directing natural and human history: "A multitude of elements and bodies are here seen connected by most multifarious influences, and yet the complex machine moves on, and never goes wrong. There is a guiding hand!"[37]

However, Dabney's confidence in the ability of logical argumentation to prove the intricacies of dogma, as displayed in the *Lectures in Systematic Theology,* must be put in the context of his other writings from the 1870s. Such contextualization reveals a thinker having doubts about the sufficiency of strict logic to explain the full complexity of human experience and divine action. In the postwar period, Dabney wrangled with how to understand the role of emotion in the human mind, a problem that had not been developed in southern conservative theology until that point. That this problem arose during the trial of Reconstruction should not be surprising.

Emotion is presented as an alternate way to communicate religious truth aside from rigid argumentation in Dabney's *Sacred Rhetoric, A Course of Lectures on Preaching* (1870). In his guidance for future pastors, Dabney asserted that the cultivation of emotion, properly curtailed of its excesses, has its place in religious knowledge. While Jonathan Edwards and other outstanding preachers were able to tap into the resources of emotion through logic, another tactic existed for the average pastor. Dabney called this strategy "descriptive painting," which endowed the orator with the ability to communicate "affecting images of the truth" by involving the "faculty of imagination." It seems that Dabney thought of imagination as the fullest possible use of the human mind, calling it "the imperial faculty of the soul." The mind, Dabney suggested, is capable of creating intricate formulations that logical argumentation strains to put into language, of "construct[ing] complex images out of separate parts, with truth and distinctness." This free-ranging power to combine various sources into something new was what Dabney called imagination. These imaginative processes are the only cognitions possessing the power necessary to tap into the faculty of emotion. In other words, only through the representational powers of the imagination could one experience emotions corresponding to experiences that have not been experienced firsthand. So, just as Paul was able to forecast the emotional needs of future Christian congregations, the average believer could approach unseen "sacred truth" and learn about "the rational attributes and providence of God, or the glories and terrors of the judgment day"—subjects beyond the ken of logic alone—but without falling prey to the fanaticism of evangelical revivalists. "The efficacious . . . movement of the feelings," he wrote in 1887, "is just as essential a part of a true religious experience as the illumination of the intellect by divine truth."[38]

Thus, it was paramount for Dabney that the imagination be put to the service of the gospel, but with logic failing to convey the message fully, he advised that ministers utilize "description" as an alternate mode of exposition. Because the product of the imagination, as a divinely designed mental faculty, is necessarily trustworthy, the orator need only clearly set forth the image held within the mind. Dabney's understanding of this process placed little, if any, stricture on the minister's license to appeal to the Christian's affections in this way. To be successful in this technique, Dabney instructed that a return to Scripture was necessary. While in his systematics lectures Dabney organized Scripture into religious knowledge by filtering it first through reason, here the theologian pointed to Scripture as a starting point for training in the art of description. Nowhere else in the entire Western canon were such brief, unadorned, and yet emotionally affecting narratives to be found. Following this example, eschewing literary flourish for concision, and employing biblical examples whenever possible, the greatest emotional impact could be achieved. Furthermore, by using Scripture as a model for emotive narration, Dabney saw a way to avoid heterodox scriptural hermeneutic methods, notably allegory. As such, Dabney's method offered a way for the defense of doctrinal tradition, while taking emotions seriously as a way of coming to religious knowledge, a position that would have been unthinkable for the antebellum Old School.[39]

As Dabney struggled to articulate the precise role of emotion in genuine religious knowledge, he also began to think about emotion as a way to understand divine action. The problem arose in an 1878 essay in which Dabney took on the question of how the Christian God could willingly ordain some and not others for salvation—a perennial problem within the Calvinist tradition. This question presented a vexing dilemma: "How can [God's] power and wisdom be cleared, save at the expense of his sincerity? Or his sincerity at the expense of his wisdom and power?" Historically, conservatives had tended toward the first pitfall, emphasizing God's power over divine love. At the other end of the theological spectrum, liberals placed great stock in love as God's essential aspect, maintaining that God loved creation enough to grant them free choice in matters of salvation. The issue boiled down to love: either God did not love universally and allowed the unloved to endure eternal torment, or God loved absolutely and wished for all people to be saved through the exercise of their own free will.[40]

However, Dabney found parts of both positions objectionable. The answer, he held, was to be found in proper understanding of God's own emotional composition. For Dabney, the only rational way to make sense of the doctrinal quandary between conservatives and liberals was to modify the rigidly logical approach theologians had taken to understand the aspects of God's character. God had too commonly been depicted in Reformed theology as absolutely simple. That is, in God, thought and action were simultaneously one, so that all of God's attributes blended into a logically consistent whole. If God *did* good, God *was* good, for instance. However, the Bible, Dabney argued, showed a much more complicated God, one endowed with distinct capacities for "wrath, love, pity, [and] wisdom," producing ends that did not always cohere in human reason. This did not give the human power to elicit an emotional response in God capable of changing God's will. Dabney merely maintained that God possessed "active principles" that, while "not passions in the sense of fluctuations or agitations . . . none the less are they affections of his will, actively distinguished from cognitions in his intelligence." Dabney had no problem with the scriptural depiction of a God who was displeased at times, joyous at others. "Why not let the Scriptures mean what they so plainly strive to declare?" Truly orthodox scriptural belief must work to apprehend "that God eternally has active principles directed towards some objective, which combine all the activity of rational affections with the passionless stability of his rational judgments, and which while not *emotions,* in the sense of change, or ebb or flow, are yet related to his volitions."[41]

Despite Dabney's characteristic rhetorical confidence, a sense of confusion is evident regarding how exactly the divine could experience something like emotion, if not true emotion. As the composition of the divine persona was beyond human comprehension in Dabney's estimate, the logic of the theologians had to be given up in favor of an explanatory strategy conforming more closely to human cognitive powers. The answer Dabney found was to look to the Bible as a stylistic guide. The authors of that sacred text had not shied away from using anthropomorphic analogies, leading Dabney to conclude that a bit of anthropomorphism would serve to make scriptural interpretation more accurate and would be easier to understand. The human mind could only cognize that with which it was familiar. "If we are forbidden to think after human norms," Dabney argued, "we cannot think at all." As such, by examining "the most rational and righteous human will," one could, by analogy, "illustrate God's will in its actions touching disputed cases."[42]

To solve the problem at hand, Dabney developed an analogy comparing God's action to that of the most virtuous human he could imagine: George Washington. As arguably the most cherished son of Virginia, Washington was an obvious choice for Dabney. The theologian presented an exegesis of Washington's emotional response when faced with the treasonous acts of John André during the American Revolution. Like God, "Washington had plenary power to kill or to save alive. His compassion for the criminal was real and profound. Yet he signed his death-warrant with spontaneous decision." Washington's compassion was real, but it had to be weighed against duty to country and law. Despite the difficulty of the situation, Washington made the free choice to condemn the criminal to death, all the while feeling remorseful for doing so. If Washington was capable of such a complex arrangement of emotion and duty, could not a perfect God operate similarly? Dabney contended that there was no reason to answer this question in the negative, and a positive response offered the benefit of preserving God's goodness, power, and wisdom in understanding the workings of predestination.[43]

Dabney's theology shows that in the Reconstruction South a rational theology that did not adequately account for the reality of emotion was not reasonable at all. The wild swings of popular mood accompanying the performance of the Confederate army in the field during the Civil War—and the depressing lows privileged white clergy like Dabney felt as their traditional way of life was torn asunder during Reconstruction—created an environment in which even the most logical mind could not avoid the reality of emotion in the human composition. And, as the era's science and philosophy pounded at the gates of orthodox theology, Dabney stood firm in unwavering support of Providence's guidance of earthly affairs. That guidance, however, had to be understood as conducted by a deity whose actions were analogous to the best of humanity's. By working a complex understanding of emotion into his theology, Dabney constructed an orthodox vision that became authoritative among southern conservatives until the early twentieth century.

The lives and intellectual journeys of Palmer and Dabney, while following entirely different courses, both demonstrate that even the most determined believers had difficulty preserving the antebellum formulations unchanged through the trials of the Civil War and Reconstruction. Belief was tested, but it was not defeated. The intellectual journeys of both men show that drawing a strict dichotomy between believing and doubting obscures the nuances that demonstrate how much of antebellum religious thought—like antebellum racial and political thought—survived war and defeat. Perhaps Palmer and Dabney were not even fully cognizant themselves of the changes that had gone on in their theology. After all, major points of doctrine, most notably belief in intervening Providence, appeared fundamentally unchanged. But the ways in which they approached those questions and how they decided what counted as genuine religious knowledge began to look different after the war. If belief itself was not defeated, yet at the least a blow was dealt to the cult of inductive reason practiced among southern Presbyterians before and during the Civil War. The best-laid plans produced by the human mind failed miserably, and Reconstruction-era cultural and economic poverty provided a constant reminder of that failure for decades after the war had ended. Dabney asserted to the end a rational orthodoxy, but he tempered the demands placed upon reason by allowing emotion a place in belief. Palmer similarly maintained a formal attachment to reason, but he granted the divine greater agency in formulating religious knowledge, having seen the failures of human attempts to decipher the will of God and the fragility of human life. Ironically, doubts about human ability only strengthened trust in tradition—both of the church and of southern culture. Dabney and Palmer became warriors for the past because, following Confederate defeat, the past was all they knew to be true.

NOTES

1. Louis Menand, *The Metaphysical Club* (New York: Farrar, Straus, and Giroux, 2001), x. On death and the Civil War, see esp. Drew Faust, *This Republic of Suffering: Death and the American Civil War* (New York: Knopf, 2008), Mark S. Schantz, *Awaiting the Heavenly Country: The Civil War and America's Culture of Death* (Ithaca, N.Y.: Cornell University Press Press, 2008), and Kent A. McConnell, "'There Must Be Tears in the Houses': A Search for Religious Meaning from the Carnage of the American Civil War" (Ph.D. diss., University of Virginia, 2007). Faust, *This Republic of Suffering,* 210.

2. Randall Fuller, *From Battlefields Rising: How the Civil War Transformed American Literature* (New York: Oxford University Press, 2011), Faust, *This Republic of Suffering,* 196–208, George M. Frederickson, *The Inner Civil War: Northern Intellectuals and the Crisis of the Union* (New York: Harper and Row, 1965). Mark Noll has explained that a literalistic reading of Scripture created a crisis in antebellum religion, as Christians in each section were unable to use their common religion to solve the problems of slavery. This gridlock in scriptural interpretation contributed to a theological crisis that not only restricted creative religious answers to the problems of the Civil War but fueled the carnage. The challenges of defeat and Reconstruction threatened to lead southerners into another, perhaps more difficult theological morass, as declarations of God's allegiance to the Confederacy were seemingly proven false. However, most postwar southerners were able to

modify their conceptions of the divine, ever so slightly, to allow for the perseverance of traditional forms of religion (see Noll, *The Civil War as a Theological Crisis* [Chapel Hill: University of North Carolina Press, 2006]).

3. Charles Reagan Wilson, *Baptized in Blood : The Religion of the Lost Cause, 1865–1920* (Athens: University of Georgia Press, 1980). Daniel Stowell addresses questions of faith and doubt, but the primary thrust of his book is the institutional rebuilding of the southern church after the war (see Daniel W. Stowell, *Rebuilding Zion: The Religious Reconstruction of the South, 1863–1877* [New York: Oxford University Press, 1998]). For statistics on wartime death, see Faust, *This Republic of Suffering*, xi.

4. The 1837 schism, ostensibly over theology, was tacitly a sectional split, given the preponderance of Old Schoolers located in the South and New Schoolers in the North. On the 1861 division and the Gardiner Spring Resolution, see Ernest Trice Thompson, *Presbyterians in the South*, vol. 1, *1607–1861* (Richmond: John Knox Press, 1963), 551–71; John Halsley Wood Jr., "The 1861 Spring Resolutions: Charles Hodge, the American Union, and the Dissolution of the Old School Church," *Journal of Church & State*, 47 (Spring 2005): 371–87.

5. Morton Smith, "The Southern Tradition," in *Reformed Theology in America: A History of Its Modern Development*, ed. David F. Wells (Grand Rapids, Mich.: Eerdmans, 1985), 189–207.

6. George C. Rable, *God's Almost Chosen People: A Religious History of the American Civil War* (Chapel Hill: University of North Carolina Press, 2010), 1, 2. On Lincoln and Providence, see Allen C. Guelzo, *Abraham Lincoln: Redeemer President* (Grand Rapids, Mich.: Eerdmans, 1999), 152–53, 318–20, 325–39.

7. One of the most influential in that tradition, James Henley Thornwell, passed away in 1862. It took both Dabney and Palmer to attempt to fill his shadow for the Southern Presbyterian Church. Palmer wrote a biography of Thornwell during Reconstruction, *The Life and Letters of James Henley Thornwell* (Richmond, 1875). For modern scholarship on Thornwell, see, for instance, James O. Farmer, *The Metaphysical Confederacy: James Henley Thornwell and the Synthesis of Southern Values* (Macon, Ga.: Mercer University Press, 1986); and Mark J. Larson, "A Champion of the Original American Republican: The Political Thought of James Henry Thornwell," *Journal of Presbyterian History* 82 (November 2004): 258–70.

8. E. Brooks Holifield, *The Gentleman Theologians: American Theology in Southern Culture, 1795–1860* (Durham, N.C.: Duke University Press, 1978), For rational orthodoxy, see ix, 3–4, 77–110, 186–99. The quote is found on page 3.

9. Haskell Monroe, "Bishop Palmer's Thanksgiving Day Address," *Louisiana History* 4 (Spring 1963): 105–18, 106. Benjamin Morgan Palmer, "National Responsibility before God," in David B. Chesebrough, *"God Ordained This War": Sermons on the Sectional Crisis, 1830–1865* (Columbia: University of South Carolina Press, 1991), 201–20, 202.

10. Ibid., 203, 206.

11. Ibid., 219.

12. The literature on religion in the American Civil War is extensive. On the clergy, Providence, and nationalism, see esp. James W. Silver, *Confederate Morale and Church Propaganda* (Tuscaloosa, Ala.: Confederate Publishing, 1957); Noll, *The Civil War as a Theological Crisis;* Harry S. Stout, *Upon the Altar of the Nation: A Moral History of the Civil War* (New York: Penguin, 2006), quote on page xviii. Silver, *Confederate Morale and Church Propaganda*, 78.

13. Thomas Cary Johnson, *The Life and Letters of Benjamin Morgan Palmer* (Richmond: Presbyterian Committee of Publication, 1906), 74.

14. Palmer to Robert Lewis Dabney, February 25, 1867, William Smith Morton Library, Union Presbyterian Seminary, Richmond, Va.; Palmer, "The Tribunal of History," *Southern Presbyterian Review* 23 (April 1872): 245–62, 248.

15. On the notion of the "good death," see Faust, *This Republic of Suffering,* 3–31. *Daily Picayune,* October 6, 1867, quoted in Johnson, *Life and Letters,* 297. On Palmer's work with the victims of yellow fever in New Orleans, see ibid., 298–29. Palmer to Mrs. Edgeworth Bird, ibid., 512–13.

16. Palmer to Mrs. Lonsdale, March 23, 1876, in Johnson, *Life and Letters,* 493–94; "Tribute to the Memory of Mrs. S. L. Hutson," *Southern Presbyterian,* June 1873, in Johnson, *Life and Letters;* "The Companionship of Grief," *Southwestern Presbyterian,* November 5, 1873.

17. "Tribunal of History," 250, 251.

18. Ibid., 254; Palmer, "Christians Sometimes Left to Themselves," *A Weekly Publication Containing Sermons, December 3, 1876* (New Orleans: Clark & Hofeline, 1876), 111.

19. On Darwinism in America, see Jon H. Roberts, *Darwinism and the Divine in America: Protestant Intellectuals and Organic Evolution, 1859–1900* (Madison: University of Wisconsin Press, 1988); and Ronald L. Numbers and Lester D. Stephens, "Darwinism in the American South: From the Early 1860s to the Late 1920s," in *Darwinism Comes to America,* ed. Numbers (Cambridge: Harvard University Press, 1998), 58–75. On the impact of positivism on American religious thought, see Charles D. Cashdollar, *The Transformation of Theology, 1830–1890: Positivism and Protestant Thought in Britain and America* (Princeton, N.J.: Princeton University Press, 1989).

20. On this arrangement, see Theodore Dwight Bozeman, *Protestants in an Age of Science: The Baconian Ideal and Antebellum American Religious Thought* (Chapel Hill: University of North Carolina Press, 1977).

21. Palmer, *The Love of Truth, the Inspiration of the Scholar: An Address Delivered before the Philomathean & Euphemian Literary Societies of Erskine College, at the Annual Commencement, August 9th, 1854.,* 11; Palmer, "Baconianism and the Bible," *Southern Presbyterian Review* 6 (October 1852): 226–53, 238; Bozeman, *Protestants in an Age of Science,* 63; Palmer, "Baconianism and the Bible," 251, 250.

22. Palmer, "The Church, the Kingdom of Truth," *A Weekly Publication Containing Sermons, October 1, 1876,* 7.

23. Palmer, "Christians Sometimes Left to Themselves," 106; Palmer, "The Church, The Kingdom of the Truth," 6; Palmer, "Offense of the Cross, Unreasonable," *A Weekly Publication Containing Sermons, November 18, 1876,* 87; Palmer, "Christians Sometimes Left to Themselves," 106.

24. Palmer, "The Church, the Kingdom of Truth," 11; Palmer, "Christians Sometimes Left to Themselves," 106.

25. Bozeman, *Protestants in an Age of Science,* chaps. 1 and 2; Palmer, "Testimony of Consciousness," *A Weekly Publication Containing Sermons, February 11, 1877,* 223.

26. Palmer, "Truth, the Law of the Intellect," *A Weekly Publication Containing Sermons, April 1, 1877,* 315.

27. Robert Lewis Dabney, "The Christian's Best Motive for Patriotism," in *Discussions,* 4 vols. (1890–97; repr., Carlisle, Penn.: The Banner of Truth Trust, 1982), 2:401–6. On Dabney's campaign for moderation, see Sean Michael Lucas, *Robert Lewis Dabney: A Southern Presbyterian Life* (Phillipsburg, N.J.: Presbyterian and Reformed Publishing, 2005), 105–8.

28. Morton H. Smith, *Studies in Southern Presbyterian Theology* (Phillipsburg, N.J.: Presbyterian and Reformed Publishing Company, 1962), 183–85; Charles Reagan Wilson, "Robert Lewis Dab-

ney: Religion and the Southern Holocaust," *Virginia Magazine of History and Biography* 89 (January 1981), 79–89, 80–81. On the rise of Princeton Seminary and its status in the nineteenth century, see Mark A. Noll, *Princeton and the Republic, 1768–1822: The Search for a Christian Enlightenment in the Era of Samuel Stanhope Smith* (Princeton, N.J.: Princeton University Press, 1989); and John W. Stewart and James H. Moorhead, eds., *Charles Hodge Revisited: A Critical Appraisal of His Life and Work* (Grand Rapids, Mich.: Eerdmans, 2002).

29. Dabney to his mother, July 19, 1861, in *Life and Letters of Robert Lewis Dabney,* ed. Thomas Cary Johnson (Richmond, Va.: Presbyterian Committee of Publication, 1903), 239; Wallace Hettle, "The Minister, the Martyr, and the Maxim: Robert Lewis Dabney and Stonewall Jackson Biography," *Civil War History* 49 (December 2003), 353–69, 360. On the wartime relationship between Dabney and Jackson, see Hettle, esp. 359–62.

30. Lucas, *Robert Lewis Dabney,* 130; Samuel Hall Chester, *Memories of Four-Score Years* (Richmond, Va.: Presbyterian Committee of Publication, 1934), 77. Quoted ibid., 132; Johnson, *Life and Letters of Dabney,* 295.

31. Wilson, "Robert Lewis Dabney," 81. On Dabney and education, see Dabney, "Secularized Education," in *Discussions,* 3:272–94. On capitalism and industrialization, see, for instance, Dabney, "Principles of Christian Economy" in *Discussions,* 1:1–28; Dabney, "Labor Unions, the Strike, and the Commune," in *Discussions,* 3:295–322; and Lucas, *Robert Lewis Dabney,* 187–92.

32. *Defence of Virginia,* 21–22; see also Dabney, "The Crimes of Philanthropy," *The Land We Love,* December 1866, in *Discussions,* 4–5:53–70, 56–57; "Free Schools," *Southern Planter and Farmer,* January 1879, in *Discussions,* 4–5:260–80, 261–62; "Commendation of the Study of Philosophy," lecture at the University of Texas, December 1885, in *Discussions,* 4–5:281–93, 292.

33. C. Vann Woodward, *Origins of the New South, 1877–1913* (Baton Rouge: Louisiana State University Press, 1951), 174; Archibald A. Hodge, *The Life of Charles Hodge* (London: T. Nelson and Sons, 1881), 521; John W. Stewart, "Introducing Charles Hodge to Postmoderns," in *Charles Hodge Revisited,* ed. Stewart and Moorhead, 1–40; E. Brooks Holifield, *Theology in America: Christian Thought from the Age of the Puritans to the Civil War* (New Haven: Yale University Press, 2003), 370–94.

34. On reason's operation in southern biblical interpretation, see Bozeman, *Protestants in an Age of Science,* 72–109; Dabney, *Syllabus and Notes of the Course of Systematic and Polemic Theology Taught in Union Seminary, Richmond, Virginia* (Richmond: Shepperson & Graves, 1871), 143–44, 141.

35. Dabney, *Syllabus and Notes,* 136–37, 141.

36. Ibid, 141.

37. Ibid., 52, 280, 284. For Dabney's full doctrine of Providence, see ibid., 276–91.

38. Robert Lewis Dabney, *Sacred Rhetoric, A Course of Lectures on Preaching Delivered in the Union Theological Seminary of the General Assembly of the Presbyterian Church in the U. S., in Prince Edward, Va.* (Richmond, Va.: Presbyterian Committee of Publication, 1870), 243, 245, 243, 244–45; Dabney, "Spurious Religious Excitements," *Presbyterian Quarterly* (October 1887), in *Discussions,* 3:1–20, 1.

39. Ibid., 67–69. For more on Dabney's understanding of the cultural and religious value of literature, see "On Dangerous Reading," *Richmond Watchman and Observer,* 1849, in *Discussions,* 2:158–69; and "John Milton," *The Land We Love,* April, May, June, and July 1867.

40. Dabney, "God's Indiscriminate Proposals of Mercy, as Related to His Power, Wisdom, and Sincerity," *Princeton Review* 50 (July 1878): 33–67, also in *Discussions,* 1:282–313, quotes on 282,

286–87. For another take on this essay, see Thomas E. Jenkins, "The Character of God in American Theology: 1800–1900" (PhD diss., Yale University, 1991), 358–66.

41. Dabney, "God's Indiscriminate Proposals of Mercy," 289–90, 290, 291, 292, 293.

42. Ibid., 297, 298.

43. Ibid., 285.

8

EMANCIPATION AND AFRICAN AMERICAN MILLENNIALISM

MATTHEW HARPER

It would be hard to overestimate the millennial importance of emancipation to African American communities during and after the Civil War. Nineteenth-century black Protestants attempted to locate themselves within God's plan for human history—past, present, and future—by writing their own experience into biblical and supernatural narratives. For them, the clearest intersection of divine history and human history was the emancipation of southern slaves in 1862–65. The event carried many theological meanings. It proved to them that God was on their side and at work in the world. The event and its many commemorations emboldened their belief that God had already begun a plan to vindicate and elevate the race. Antebellum black voices had prophesied the end of slavery, and African Americans saw in the Civil War the fulfillment of not only those prophecies but also biblical prophecies and signs of things to come. When black Protestant leaders struggled to interpret God's purpose for the race in a particular situation, they returned to emancipation as the surest example that divine history and human history were inseparably intertwined.

When emancipation came to Wilmington, North Carolina, in February 1865, black residents piled millennial meaning onto the event. On February 22, the Fourth and the Thirty-Seventh U.S. Colored Troops, among others, occupied the city. The following Sunday, local African Americans gathered, as they usually did, for a sunrise prayer meeting at the Methodist church on Front Street. The church, a congregation of the Methodist Episcopal Church, South (ME South) had white and black members; it had a white pastor, even though the eight hundred black members easily outnumbered the two hundred white members. Many of the church's services were biracial with segregated seating, but the sunrise prayer service, a long-standing tradition, was attended almost exclusively by the church's African American members. On that Sunday, it was no ordinary prayer service. "The whole congregation was wild with excitement," observed the church's white pastor, "with shouts, groans, amens, and unseemly demonstrations." A black leader named Charles chose the scripture lesson from Psalm 9: "Thou hast rebuked the heathen, thou hast destroyed the wicked, thou hast put out their name for ever and ever." Charles told the people to "study over this morning lesson on this the day of Jubilee." After the scripture reading, a black U.S. Army chaplain, Rev. William H. Hunter, stood up to speak. Born a slave in North Carolina, Hunter was freed at an early age and moved to New York. He later attended Wilberforce University and was ordained an AME minister. Chaplain Hunter had arrived with his regiment only days before, and he brought with him news that the world now looked very different. When he spoke, an observer noted Hunter stretching "himself to his full size and displaying to the best advantage for a profound impression his fine uniform." He proclaimed, "One week ago you were all slaves; now you are all free." The congregation responded with "uproarious screamings." Hunter continued, "Thank God the armies of the Lord and Gideon has triumphed and the Rebels have been driven back in confusion and scattered like chaff before the wind."[1] The emancipation of southern slaves clearly held theological meaning for black believers—as a day of reckoning and judgment, a divinely appointed climax of history.

Leaders referenced multiple biblical accounts: the Day of Jubilee, the Exodus story, Gideon's victory, and the Psalms of David. Yet not one at that sunrise meeting made reference to the apocalypse, the millennium, or the Second Coming of Christ. Is the prayer service, then, an example of black millennialism? In arguing that it is, as this essay does, we must first make two observations about the nature of nineteenth-century black millennialism. First, black millennialism was about much more than the millennium. It was a belief in the intersection of human history and divine history that gave African American believers a window on the future. Even though this sacred historical design culminated in an earthly redemption, black millennialism involved multiple biblical stories and not just narrowly futuristic ones like the millennium or the return of Christ. Second, because nineteenth-century black millennialism differed from most forms of white millennialism, scholars might miss its importance or assume that African Americans abandoned their millennial hopes after Reconstruction, which they did not. African American Protestants developed distinct though diverse understandings of the sacred historical design—an eschatology—that centered on emancipation and loomed large in black conversations during and long after the Civil War. This essay uses the experience of African American communities in eastern North Carolina, like those at the sunrise prayer service, to chart the contours of black millennialism and to explain the many theological meanings of emancipation.

Antebellum slaves prophesied and prayed for an end to slavery. Like other American Protestants, black Protestants believed in a providential God, a being actively at work in human affairs, showing favor to some and displeasure to others. As Albert Raboteau put it, they believed in a "God of History, a God who lifted up and cast down nations and peoples, a God whose sovereign will was directing all things toward an ultimate end, drawing good out of evil."[2] This belief in Providence led nineteenth-century Protestants—white and black—to look for divine meanings in all earthly affairs. This was especially true in major events like war, natural disaster, or national politics.[3]

For black Protestants, however, emancipation was a providential event of a different order of magnitude. Black southerners expected God to emancipate them, and when freedom came, they considered it an answer to prayer and a fulfillment of prophecy. When the Twenty-Seventh Massachusetts Regiment landed in northeastern North Carolina, an elderly slave woman greeted the troops with dancing, telling them: "Bless the Lord, Massa! I've been praying for you these forty years! I thought you never coming at all! but you come at last! Bless the Lord."[4] Rev. Morgan Latta, born a slave south of Raleigh, recalled the reaction to emancipation on his and neighboring plantations: "I heard the shouts all over the plantations, 'We are free!' 'Free from slavery!' 'God has heard our prayers. We have been praying for twenty-five or thirty years that we should be free, and God has answered our prayers at His own appointed time; He has bursted the bonds of slavery and set us all free.'"[5] Slaves anticipated emancipation and the war.

The most famous of black prophets from eastern North Carolina was David Walker, whose 1829 antislavery pamphlet panicked planters across the South. Walker reminded slaveholders that "God rules in the armies of heaven and among the inhabitants of the earth," and "being a just and holy Being will at one day appear fully in behalf of the oppressed, and arrest the progress of the avaricious oppressors." Walker's words were prescient: "for although the destruction of the oppressors God may not effect by the oppressed, yet the Lord our God will bring other destructions upon them—for not unfrequently will he cause them to rise up one against another, to be split and divided, and to oppress each other, and sometimes to open hostilities with sword in hand."[6] Albert Raboteau surely had Walker in mind when he wrote, "Black Christians warned antebellum America (in terms strikingly prophetic of the Civil War) that it stood in peril of divine judgment unless it quickly repented the sin of slavery."[7]

Northern free black clergy likewise wrote about the Civil War as divine punishment for slavery. "The God of the Universe is a just God," wrote a minister in 1862, "and he is pouring out his wrath upon the country in political dissension, rebellion and cruel war: to avenge for the many wrongs inflicted upon an oppressed and helpless race." They expected freedom to come from the war, and described that expectation in millennial terms, a "future glory" to soon follow the present tribulation: "ere long the bright sun of our destiny will break forth from behind the dark cloud of oppression and adversity."[8] The Emancipation Proclamation confirmed their expectations. When northern whites grumbled against the proclamation, one minister retorted, "It is the Lord's doings, and who shall hinder it?" Emancipation was prophecy fulfilled: "The time has come; it is written by the prophet Jeremiah."[9] Emancipation-era black ministers and David Walker believed in a divinely orchestrated history; they prophesied a coming day of judgment, where God would punish wrongdoers. Clearly, their warnings were a kind of eschatology. But to what kind of eschatology did Walker and other nineteenth-century black Protestants subscribe?

Nineteenth-century African American eschatological thought defied the theological categories of white Protestantism. When analyzing eschatology, scholars normally zoom in on millennial beliefs, and they categorize them as premillennial, postmillennial, and amillennial. These categories refer to the dating of the Second Coming of Christ vis-à-vis his prophesied thousand-year reign of peace. Premillennialists believed Jesus would return to earth before the millennium. Archetypal premillenialists, the Millerites, climbed hilltops on October 22, 1844, because they expected Jesus's dramatic return. Other premillennialists were less certain about the date but shared the Millerites' conviction that the Second Coming was imminent. Some, like dispensational premillennialists, who gained popularity in the twentieth century, spelled out clearly how the apocalypse would unfold: first, a dramatic return of Jesus Christ to rapture the faithful into heaven; then a seven-year period of tribulation when Satan would be unleashed on the world; then another return of Jesus Christ, this time as a victor riding on a white horse to defeat Satan and inaugurate the millennium.[10] Whether they believed Jesus was coming next Tuesday or after a seven-year tribulation, premillennialists expected a sharp break between the present and the future.

Postmillennialism, the dominant strain of eschatology among late-nineteenth- and early-twentieth-century white Protestants, led followers not to mountaintops but to soup kitchens and settlement houses. These white Protestants expected the Second Coming of Christ to follow an earthly millennium. Earlier this belief found expression in notions of Manifest Destiny, that God had preordained American prosperity and expansion.[11] But by the 1880s and 1890s, northern white Protestants interpreted the millennial reign of Jesus described in the Revelation to St. John figuratively as the world's destiny to achieve peace and justice through the progress and perfecting of human institutions. The earthly work of the church would usher in a golden age, the millennium, after which Jesus would return.[12] So they put their energy into bringing about the millennium through social reform, working in sanitation efforts, education, temperance, and orphanages. Unlike premillennialists, they saw continuity between the present and the future.

A third option, amillennialism, uncommon among American Protestant thinkers, eschewed debates over the timing of the millennium. Amillennialists rejected the belief in a literal millennium. Rather, they understood the Book of Revelation's prophecy symbolically as referring to Christ's rule in their own day and not to the apocalypse or some future golden age. The millennium, they argued, had arrived at Jesus's First Coming in Palestine and would end with his Second Coming at the end of human history. Amillennialists, like Lutheran and Dutch Reformed immigrants, were not looking for the millennium in city slums or on hilltops. The millennium, they believed, was in the church or in the hearts of believers.

Black Protestants agreed on the millennium no more than white Protestants did. As historian Timothy E. Fulop argues, late-nineteenth-century black millennialism "exhibits great variety." African Methodist Episcopal (AME) minister T. G. Steward's 1888 *The End of the World* displayed classic tenets of premillennial thought, envisioning the return of Christ before the coming millennium. Many racial "uplifters" held to postmillennialism, believing that their work to educate, reform, and evangelize would usher in the millennium. James Walker Hood, the only black author to pen a theological commentary on Revelation during the period, sided with amillennialism. And as Fulop writes, an ever-greater diversity of opinion existed in debates over what, not when, the millennium would be.[13]

Most black Protestants held views of the end times that did not fall neatly into these categories. Rather, they blended elements from premillennialism, postmillennialism, and amillennialism. For example, Hood, whose formal writings were amillennialist, in other venues sounded like Walker, making dire warnings of an imminent day of judgment akin to those of premillennialists. In his addresses to other ministers and congregations, Hood routinely connected the earthly work of God's people with a future golden age, clearly a postmillennial way of thinking. Black theologians, pastors, and laypeople simply did not feel confined by existing eschatological categories.

Some of the difficulty in categorizing black millennialism lay in black Protestants' peculiar mix of hope and sorrow. Unlike many premillennialists, African American Christians almost never despaired over the future of the world. One North Carolina Baptist, Rev. C. J. W. Fisher, admitted that "the world appears so corrupt that Christians sometimes think it is going over into the hands of the devil." But Fisher told his audience that appearances could be deceiving and that Christianity, not the devil, was gaining power in the world.[14] Fisher and his colleagues did not easily retreat into an otherworldly passivity. Rather, they fully expected to be vindicated and see progress in their own day. This hope in earthly progress differed significantly, however, from the postmillennialism of white reformers. Black Protestants tempered their hope with a good deal of mourning. They sang mournful slave spirituals and lamented the persistent forms of oppression that marred their experience of freedom. Black churchgoers had reason to doubt the inevitability of human progress. They were decidedly less optimistic and held more sober assessments of human nature than did most white postmillennialists.

For this reason, many black Protestants make a better comparison with seventeenth-century Puritans. New England Puritans were, one could argue, postmillennialists. They believed in earthly progress; they named their children Increase and Truth Shall Prevayl; they placed Christ's return after the millennium. Yet a firm belief in human depravity tempered their optimism. God Himself, not human progress, would inaugurate a *literal* millennium with favor upon his chosen people, the New Israel. Puritans, especially those that immigrated to America, were prone to believe themselves the heirs of Israel's promise. Their journey to the New World mirrored the arrival of Israel in the Promised Land. Black Americans, too, believed that God, in a decisive moment of history, would usher in a new era, and show special favor to a specific people. But for them, as Albert Raboteau has argued, "the Christian imagery is reversed." Crossing the Atlantic, for African American Christians, was not the start of the millennium but the beginning of tribulation. Raboteau continues: "This is, as Vincent Harding remarked, one of the abiding and tragic ironies of our history: the nation's claim to be the New Israel was contradicted by the Old Israel still enslaved in her midst."[15] African Americans' belief in the destiny of their race to rise from slavery to prosperity ran counter to white American nationalism and eschatology.

Because nineteenth-century black thought did not fit well into the categories of white eschatology, we must find a different way to talk of black eschatology. First, we must move beyond a narrow focus on the millennium. Lots of stories mattered just as much: Flood, Jubilee, Exodus, Exile, Crucifixion, Resurrection, Pentecost, etc. Black Protestants found eschatological meaning in stories that many white Protestants treated as merely historical or allegorical. African American believers saw these stories as ongoing, living stories likely to be replayed in nineteenth-century America.

According to twentieth-century black theologian James Cone, the reading of biblical stories enabled black people to be "taken from the present to the past and then thrust back into their contemporary history with divine power to transform the sociopolitical context." That is, in many African American religious traditions, the people do more than retell stories. They relive them. Black Protestants, in the words of Cone, "break the barriers of time and space as they walk and talk with Jesus in Palestine."[16] Slave spirituals expressed this living experience of the past:

> Were you there when they crucified my Lord?
>   Were you there when they crucified my Lord?
> Oh! Sometimes it causes me to tremble, tremble, tremble.
>   Were you there when they crucified my Lord?

In this song, the singers ask one another if they have witnessed the Crucifixion. The question assumes that it would have been possible for nineteenth-century Americans to have actually been there. The song collapses all the distance of time and space, such that African Americans in the nineteenth century might find themselves outside Jerusalem early in the first century A.D. Black believers were not confused; they fully understood that the Crucifixion was an event from a different era and different place. Rather, they adopted a hermeneutic that did not confine stories to their historical context.

The experience of straddling the past and the present empowered black believers to resist the oppression of their own day. It had real-world application. Cone explains its relevance to twentieth-century black religion: "Through the experience of moving back and forth between the first and twentieth centuries, the Bible is transformed from just a report of what the disciples believed about Jesus to black people's personal story of God's will to liberate the oppressed in the contemporary context."[17] We can similarly characterize nineteenth-century black Christianity. By placing their experience in the stories of Old Testament Israel or of Jesus, black Protestants resisted the dominant narratives of their day that worked to subjugate African Americans. By placing themselves inside stories of the past, black Protestants were able to offer interpretations of the present and predictions of the future that differed from those offered by their oppressors.

Southern slaves' identification with the Hebrews in Egypt, Moses, and the Exodus is well known.[18] Freed slaves saw themselves in the Old Testament story of the Hebrews' flight from Egypt. After four hundred years of bondage, the Hebrews followed Moses out of Egypt into the Sinai desert. As they fled, God caused Moses to part the Red Sea to provide an escape from the Egyptian army. After the Israelites passed through on dry land, the waters returned to drown Pharaoh's soldiers. Black southerners relived this story in their own experience of freedom from slavery as occasioned by the military defeat of their enemies. Rev. L. S. Burkhead, the white pastor of Front Street Methodist Church in Wilmington, explained his black congregation's excitement: "They had just crossed the 'Red Sea' dry-shod. In their estimation Pharaoh's hosts had been engulfed in ruin—gone down in a sea of blood! Hence they rejoiced with exceeding rejoicing."[19] That black Americans, like ancient Hebrews, had experienced a dramatic emancipation served only to confirm their belief that Africans or African Americans were God's chosen people and would relive the Exodus story.[20]

Black identification with Israel went beyond the story of Exodus. In the sunrise meeting at Front Street Methodist Church, Chaplain Hunter called the Union forces the army "of Gideon," and Charles, the lay leader, quoted from Psalm 9. In both cases, these leaders identified emancipation with the military exploits of Israel. Two years later, black political leaders in eastern North Carolina used the military conquest of Canaan as evidence that African Americans would gain suffrage and political power.[21]

Similarly, black Americans routinely appropriated the Day of Jubilee, a feature of Israel's Levitical law, to narrate their own struggle for land and economic justice. The leader at the sunrise prayer meeting called the Sunday following the capture of Wilmington "the day of Jubilee." Rev. Burkhead noted that many black worshippers referred to emancipation as "their great jubilee."[22] Levitical law commanded ancient Israel to celebrate every fiftieth year as Jubilee. That year began with priests' trumpets announcing a Day of Atonement, a day when all slaves were freed, all debts were forgiven, and all the property the wealthy had amassed was returned to its original owner. The practice of Jubilee no doubt brought significant upheaval to the social and economic order. The commandment was intended to remind ancient Israelites that land and people belonged to God and not to those who held title. Black Americans greeted the social and economic upheaval of emancipation as their own long-awaited Jubilee.

Former slaves clearly associated the Day of Jubilee with both the millennium and government plans for property redistribution. Passersby heard communities of freed slaves singing:

> Old master's gone and the darkies stayed at home;
> Must be now that the kingdom's come and the year of jubilee.[23]

A black Union soldier camped near the North Carolina–Virginia border linked the coming Jubilee with the millennium: "So soon as the general jubilee is proclaimed throughout the Southern regions—so soon as this rebellion, originating from the power of slavery, is subdued, then we will have a glorious millennium of peace in this once slave-cursed country."[24] One group of African Americans in Mississippi put a precise date on the coming Jubilee/millennium. They heard a story that the Freedmen's Bureau had a "Great Document" sealed with four seals, which would be broken on New Year's Day 1866, when the federal government would deliver its "final orders" for land confiscation and redistribution. In this dramatic retelling of St. John's vision in Revelation, the federal government took on a divine authority. The opening of the document reminded black southerners of millennial prophecy, and the contents of the document reminded them of Jubilee.[25]

Black Protestants at times understood themselves to be in exile, identifying with the Israelites' suffering in Assyrian or Babylonian captivity. They appropriated stories of Jewish preservation during exile and prophecies of an end to exile and a return to glory. Months after the sunrise prayer meeting, black residents of Wilmington prepared to elect representatives for the state's first Freedmen's Convention. The organizers for the Wilmington meeting published this call in the papers: "Freedmen of North Carolina, Arouse!! . . . These are the times foretold by the Prophets, 'when a Nation shall be born in a day.' . . . The time has arrived when we can strike one blow to secure those rights of Freemen that have been so long withheld from us."[26] This call appropriated Isaiah's prophecy in which the Lord asks a rhetorical question: "Can a nation be born in a day?" The Lord casts aside the obvious answer (that such a project would take years) and announces plans to bring Israel back from exile and restore the nation in a day. The prophecy of building a nation in a day came accompanied with a promise from God. The passage from Isaiah reads, "'Shall I bring to the birth, and not cause to bring forth?' saith the LORD."[27] The organizers of Wilmington's mass meeting claimed Isaiah's prophecy for themselves; they planned to build a nation in a day, to leap immediately from emancipation to political action. In emancipation, God had brought the race to the moment of birth. As the prophecy promised, God would not fail to finish the job.

Placing themselves within biblical stories helped black Protestants to chart their future. They could appropriate the plot of biblical narratives—reliving the plight of enslaved Israelites, for instance—and take comfort in the well-known resolution that lay ahead. Burkhead noted black worshippers' confidence in the future. By seeing emancipation as an event in these ancient biblical stories, African Americans at Front Street Methodist "now looked ahead with protruding eyes and swelling hearts to the dazzling lights of their coming glories." Burkhead mocked them for the quick jump from reading ancient stories to imagining a future that he considered quite fanciful. That future included full participation in the body politic on terms of equality and "fine churches and residences . . . and plenty to eat and drink and wear." The theologically inspired visions of the future differed within black religious communities, though almost all included acquisition of land, education, and political power. What Burkhead found both laughable and dangerous was the power of black eschatology to counter the logic of subordination.[28] By placing themselves in biblical stories, and thus in a promise of better days, black Protestants contested the racial narratives of the day that forecast the future of blacks in America as one of slavery, perpetual childhood, dependence, or doom. Emancipation became the sign from heaven that they were living out a much different story. And there were many stories from which to choose.

African Americans' predictions of the future carried more real-world significance than theologians have typically attributed to eschatological thought. German theologian Jurgen Moltmann laments that eschatology in Western

Christian theology became "a loosely attached appendix that wandered off into obscure irrelevancies." Because theologians talked about the Second Coming and the millennium as events that broke into human history at the end of time from somewhere outside human history, it was possible for Christians to segregate their eschatological beliefs from the rest of their religious lives. Although Moltmann does not believe in an imminent Second Coming or a sudden rapture, he protests against the definition of eschatology as the study of the distant future. "Eschatology," he argues, "means the doctrine of Christian hope. . . . From first to last, and not merely in the epilogue." With Moltmann's definition, believers would not relegate hope to some distant age but let hope "suffuse everything here" and now.[29] James Cone notes that black people talked about this kind of Christian hope long before Moltmann and his German colleagues did.[30] Nineteenth-century black Protestants wrote their experiences into stories about the future, just as they did with stories about the past. For them, as for Moltmann, eschatology was not just about distant events. It held the power to transform the present.

Rev. Burkhead of Front Street Methodist certainly observed the power of black millennialism to transform the present. African Americans in Wilmington did not end their celebrations with the sunrise prayer meeting. An hour or so after the service, Burkhead gathered together the lay white leaders of the church to discuss the "never-to-be-forgotten sunrise prayer-meeting" he had just witnessed. As they met, Burkhead could still hear "the shouting and general demonstrations of joy at the jubilee . . . along the streets in the vicinity of Front Street Church." The celebrations continued throughout the day. During the regular morning service, when Burkhead led worship for the white church members, the congregation heard the noises of celebration outside. That afternoon, Burkhead preached before the church's black members, and he picked a somber passage of scripture in a vain attempt to calm the passions of the congregation. The worshippers were so excited, Burkhead wrote, that "an impassioned appeal would have almost thrown them into convulsions; at least they would have raised an uproar."[31]

In the days and weeks that followed that "tumultuously jubilant" sunrise prayer service, Burkhead noticed profound changes in the city's black population. "On all the streets of our City might be seen the exhibitions of the spirit of the newly acquired boon of freedom," he wrote. African Americans had for some time outnumbered whites in Wilmington, but with their newly acquired freedom, they seemed to increase in number. Burkhead observed, "The whole city seems to be alive with 'Africans.'" Some rural blacks made their way into the city when they heard news of the Union occupation. But long-standing residents made their presence known in new and bold ways. They flagrantly violated rules of deference to whites. Black women, for example, no longer ceded the sidewalk to white women. Burkhead complained: "They sing and shout; and preach and pray; and drink and swear; and fiddle and dance; and laugh and yell—'Ye-ah, ye-ah, the bottom rail on the top at last!'" The sudden change in the behavior of African Americans, whom white southerners thought they knew well, mystified Burkhead and others. Burkhead was shocked to observe how quickly his black parishioners' experience of emancipation had begun "to unsettle all their former principles and ideas of subordination."[32] He blamed the sudden change on African Americans' "pure 'anti-slavery gospel' dashed with the radical spirit of political intrigue." Black Protestants did not confine millennialism to the appendix of human history. It mattered in the moment.

Emancipation clearly mattered for African American church history. The tale of a prominent player in North Carolina history illustrates how significant emancipation was for some denominations. In 1863, Rev. James Walker Hood, a northern free black preacher, left a comfortable pulpit in Connecticut, and took a train south to North Carolina in the middle of intense fighting. Delayed by a shifting war front and frozen rivers, Hood arrived in January 1864 and immediately began planting churches right behind the troops. His missionary efforts often took place fewer than fifteen miles behind the frontlines. In Washington, North Carolina, he and his congregation twice had to retreat as Confederate forces advanced, only to resume missionary activities when Union forces regained control of the town. Such plucky tactics did not go without reward. In 1864, when he arrived in North Carolina, Hood was the only member of the African Methodist Episcopal Zion (AMEZ) Church in the state. Less than ten years later, he presided over 366 churches in North Carolina with upward of 20,000 members.[33]

Hood was not alone. Hundreds of missionaries from northern denominations organized independent congregations of freedpeople during and after the war. Few black believers worshipped without white oversight in the antebellum South, but 90 percent of all black churchgoers attended independent black congregations by the 1870s. It was a boon for northern church plants in the South, but southern whites had trouble understanding the mass exodus from their churches. In fact, Burkhead soon found Hood at the doorstep of his parsonage in Wilmington, and Burkhead praised Hood's "practical spirit." But there was no secret as to why Hood was in Wilmington: he was planting independent black churches. Burkhead watched as his own congregation fell apart in 1865. Six hundred members of Front Street Methodist petitioned to join the AME, and in doing so, fought to take the church property with them. Lay black leaders and Chaplain Hunter presented petitions to the military authorities in Wilmington claiming that they represented a majority of the congregation and should have the right to select their own pastor and to use the church building. For more than a year, Burkhead and white officials in the ME South fought legal battles to retain their control over the pulpit and the church property. Military officials arbitrated the dispute by declaring that the African American congregation had use of the building one-half of each day. In 1866, white Methodist leaders appealed that decision to Andrew Johnson's administration, and control of the property reverted to the ME South. The black congregants then marched a few blocks north to build the city's first AME church.[34] Emancipation marked a new way of doing church for black southerners.

An editorialist for the *Christian Recorder* considered the significant growth of the AME Church in 1865 as evidence that the church had entered "upon a new epoch, and is destined to illuminate her pathway by the dazzling splendor of millennial glory." The editorial boasted of church plants all across the country, especially in the South. "In Virginia and the Carolinas," the writer explained, "she [the AME Church] now follows in the war path of Grant, Sherman and Sheridan, applying the Balm of Gilead to the wounded and dying soldier, and publishing salvation to the forsaken and heartbroken contraband."[35] The church organizers who oversaw this influx of black worshippers into northern denominations ascribed eschatological significance to emancipation. Hood viewed the growth of black churches following emancipation as the fulfillment of prophecy, a sign that black Americans were rising to meet an important destiny, and the first fruits of "the millennial glory of the Christian Church."[36]

African American millennial beliefs predicted significant church growth, but they may have also caused it. Much of the postemancipation church growth came from Christian slaves' move for religious independence, abandoning the white oversight they endured in their days in slavery. Still, many contemporaries observed a rather remarkable upsurge in conversions among freed slaves. Historian Daniel Fountain argues that scholarly consensus on slave religion has overestimated the number of Christian slaves. His findings, taken from a thorough survey of extant slave autobiographical material, suggest that the majority of African Americans did not become Christians until after emancipation. A small but important core of African American Christians, slave and free, prayed for and prophesied freedom in ways that eerily matched the conditions of wartime emancipation. When non-Christian slaves came to witness the fulfilled prophecies of their converted peers, they flocked to the church, and Christianity vaulted from an important minority faith to the majority faith among black Americans. The truth of black millennial claims garnered new converts to the faith. These conversions were both evidence of the millennial importance of emancipation to believers and an outcome of those same millennial beliefs.[37]

The importance of emancipation did not fade with time. Over time, black Americans turned again and again to recall emancipation, and in recalling it, they reaffirmed the glorious future that awaited them. Black communities commemorated the event each year in public celebrations across the state and the nation. These parades and festivals, with their marching militia units, floats, songs, and speeches, were meant, according to W. Fitzhugh Brundage, to "counter the dominant white version of the past." Black ministers, whose "powerful influence" often dictated the forms of the celebrations, "cast both the distant and recent past as scenes in a familiar spiritual drama." In their orations, ministers and other leaders looked back on emancipation as a divine act of redemption and many "anticipated . . . an even more profound, imminent, and millennial transformation in the status of black people."[38] These frequent commemorations ensured that emancipation's eschatological significance among black Protestants waxed rather than waned in the decades following the Civil War.

Those commemorations became hotly contested. During and immediately after the Civil War, blacks and whites held widely divergent views on emancipation. While the black congregation at Front Street Methodist interpreted emancipation as Jubilee, Exodus, and the sign of good things to come, Burkhead and his white parishioners considered the social upheaval "a tribulation" to be patiently endured. The white and black members of the church shared much of the same theological worldview. They invested the past with providential meaning, and their theological expectations for the future gave them the ability to weather the present. But their radically different interpretations of emancipation left them unable to speak to one another.[39] And with the passage of time and regular commemorations, the white and black memories of emancipation became irreconcilable. Religious southern whites mourned the Confederate defeat as God's chastisement of his beloved people while southern blacks hailed it as God's long-delayed deliverance.

These mutually exclusive memories of emancipation fueled political and violent clashes, even after Reconstruction collapsed. In Oxford, North Carolina, on January 1, 1874, the African American community gathered to celebrate emancipation. The day involved a parade led by black militiamen in full regalia through the town center. The marching of black soldiers to remember emancipation seemed appropriate because, for many black North Carolinians, freedom came when the black soldiers did. It also reminded ex-Confederates of their recent military defeat, and the white community in Oxford balked. County officials rushed in to stop the parade. The black community subsequently brought suit, and the state's Supreme Court ruled that "the laws allow great latitude to do public demonstrations, whether political, social or moral."[40] The ability to publicly celebrate emancipation allowed black North Carolinians to continue to ascribe theological meaning to the historical event.

At one emancipation celebration, C. R. Harris, an AMEZ minister from North Carolina, explained what was at stake in his providential interpretation of emancipation. At the 1892 Agricultural and Industrial Fair in Alexandria, Virginia, Harris said, "[Emancipation] will also remind us of that truth, so signally impressed by the lessons of the civil war, that God hears the cry of the oppressed, of whatever color or clime, and in due time comes to deliver them."[41] This religious confidence countered depressing news when it came, as it often did in the 1890s; remembering emancipation lent weight to black claims that God was actively working on their behalf.

Within African American discourse, emancipation became a benchmark in time. Laurie Maffly-Kipp writes that late-nineteenth-century race histories "hinged on the acts of civil war and emancipation as the harbingers of a worldwide spiritual and social transformation." In black Americans' retelling of world history, the "climax . . . came with the issuing of the Emancipation Proclamation." As early medieval Christians (and eventually most of the world) marked time by the birth of Christ, African Americans marked time by emancipation. Within black communities, the years 1863–65 held a place akin to the B.C./A.D. divide. African American writers reported events and race progress in relation to emancipation: "Ten years since emancipation" or "only thirty-five years after slavery," or "only a generation from slavery." Titles from African American literature like Katherine Tillman's *Thirty Years of Freedom: A Drama in Four Acts* (1902) or her *Fifty Years of Freedom, or From Cabin to Congress: A Drama in Five Acts* (1910) and James Weldon Johnson's poem "Fifty Years" (1917) bear this out.[42]

The memory of emancipation, for African American thinkers, was largely about hope. Hope for what? Black eschatology had two primary answers: an end to race prejudice and a special role for the African race within Christian history. These two hopes, or strains of thought, sometimes went hand in hand; but at other times, they existed in tension with each other and fueled debate among black religious leaders. These debates existed within and between denominations and within and between local congregations.

The hope for an end to racism found biblical support in Acts 17:26: "God hath made of one blood all nations of men for to dwell on the face of the earth." This verse, black Protestants argued, supported their claim of the monogenetic origins of the human race and laid out God's intentions for all races to dwell together in harmony. Some saw evidence around them of the eroding of white racism. Others considered it black Americans' duty to Christianize the nation, and thus rid it of race prejudice. Expounders on this eschatological theme found further proof in John's vision in Revelation of "a great multitude, which no man could number, of all nations, and kindreds, and people, and tongues," all gathered around God's throne.[43]

The second and competing theme in black eschatology—belief in a special role or destiny for the race—drew heavily on Psalm 68:31: "Princes shall come out of Egypt; Ethiopia shall soon stretch forth her hands unto God." In this verse, black ministers interpreted Ethiopia and Egypt as the entire "Negro race." For some, it was a prophecy that those of African descent would turn from their "sin; idolatry—forgetfulness of God" and embrace Christianity. Many interpreted the passage as an imperative for black Americans to evangelize Africa, and others envisioned a future black ascendancy to rival the powerful nations of the world. Many hopes stemmed from this oft-quoted verse in Psalm 68.[44]

Many nineteenth-century black Christians held comfortably in tandem the two themes within black eschatology—race destiny and an end to racism. Others, however, saw them in conflict. The belief in a special destiny for Africans or African Americans necessitated some sort of race essentialism. Even though most black ministers affirmed the monogenetic origins of the human race, beliefs in race destiny implied that the races had distinctive aggregate character traits and peculiar God-ordained futures. Some black Protestants were uncomfortable with the race essentialism of their colleagues and shied away from proclaiming a separate black destiny. Other leaders thought it hopeless to reform America from the inside and staked their millennial hopes not on an end to racism in the United States but in solidarity with people of color around the world. The millennial themes that black Protestants emphasized and the conclusions they made at times diverged widely.[45] Even the black parishioners of Front Street Methodist disagreed. Some seized on emancipation as an opportunity for autonomy; they rejected Burkhead's authority and demanded an independent black church. Others came out of the gallery to sit among whites in the front pews, frustrating Burkhead and signaling that a new era of racial equality and integration had begun.[46] Despite these differences, the method behind black eschatology was remarkably regular. African American Christians wrote themselves into biblical narratives, found evidence of God's favor in current events, and predicted a triumphant future. Despite their different emphases, black Protestants agreed that the future looked bright, not merely because of favorable political circumstances but because of God's plan for human history. Emancipation, the growth of black churches, and Christianity's power to end prejudice all signaled a new God-ordained era of progress and racial justice.

African American members of Front Street Methodist, and later of St. Stephen's AME, began to witness that new era, in part. Wilmington's black majority, especially its upwardly mobile black middle class, could point to substantial gains since emancipation. By 1898, black-owned businesses lined the streets, and a progressive biracial coalition controlled the city council. In the same year, however, Wilmington witnessed the only successful coup d'état perpetrated on United States soil. A mob of armed white men burned black businesses, ransacked black churches, exiled the mayor and city council, and installed their own leaders in government.[47] John C. Dancy, the collector of customs in Wilmington and perhaps the city's most influential person of color, was among the exiled. Dancy had not been at the Front Street Methodist sunrise prayer service thirty-three years earlier, but he was the most prominent black Methodist in town and no doubt worshipped with several who had been there. Two years after the coup d'état, when North Carolina disfranchised black voters, Dancy wrote to his fellow Methodists, calling on them to remember God's work in emancipation. That work of Providence still gave African Americans in Wilmington a millennial hope. He wrote, "The density of this darkness only foreshadows the brightness of the approaching dawn."[48] Confronted with disfranchisement and unprecedented racial violence during a period now known as the nadir of American race relations, black Protestants continued to see intersections between human history and divine history and to forecast a brighter future. The memory of emancipation nurtured their millennial hopes, even in the darkest hour.

NOTES

The author would like to thank the Summer Seminars program at Calvin College for its support in the writing of this essay.

1. Rev. L. S. Burkhead, "History of the Difficulties of the Pastorate of the Front Street Methodist Church, Wilmington, NC, for the Year 1865," *An Annual Publication of Historical Papers Published by the Historical Society of Trinity College,* series VIII (1908–9): 37–43; Ps. 9:6, King James Version (hereafter KJV). Reginald F. Hildebrand, *The Times Were Strange and Stirring: Methodist Preachers and the Crisis of Emancipation* (Durham: Duke University Press, 1995), 36–40; Richard R. Wright Jr., ed., *Centennial Encyclopedia of the African Methodist Episcopal Church* (Philadelphia: Book Concern of the A.M.E. Church, 1916), 122.

2. Albert J. Raboteau, *A Fire in the Bones: Reflections on African American Religious History* (Boston: Beacon, 1995), 17.

3. See Randall Miller, C. R. Wilson, and Harry Stout, eds., *Religion in the American Civil War* (New York: Oxford University Press, 1998); Mark A. Noll, *The Civil War as a Theological Crisis* (Chapel Hill: University of North Carolina Press, 2006); and *America's God: From Jonathan Edwards to Abraham Lincoln* (New York: Oxford University Press, 2002).

4. W. P. Derby, *Bearing Arms in the Twenty-Seventh Massachusetts Regiment of Volunteer Infantry during the Civil War, 1861–1865* (Boston: Wright and Potter Printing, 1883), 94–95, quoted in Joe A. Mobley, *James City: A Black Community in North Carolina, 1863–1900* (Raleigh: North Carolina Division of Archives and History, 1981), 2. Here I have taken the liberty to edit the derogatory dialect transcription that nineteenth- and early-twentieth-century whites sometimes used when recording the words of African Americans. I have changed the spelling but none of the words.

5. Morgan London Latta, *The History of My Life and Work* (Raleigh, N.C.: Edwards and Broughton, 1903), 169–70.

6. David Walker, *Walker's Appeal, in Four Articles; Together with a Preamble, to the Coloured Citizens of the World, but in Particular, and Very Expressly, to Those of the United States of America, Written in Boston, State of Massachusetts, September 28, 1829* (Boston: David Walker, 1830), 6–7.

7. Raboteau, *A Fire in the Bones,* 12.

8. *Christian Recorder,* November 15, 1862.

9. Ibid., October 11, 1862.

10. Ronald Numbers and Jon Butler, eds., *The Disappointed: Millerism and Millenarianism in the Nineteenth Century* (Knoxville: University of Tennessee Press, 1993). Dispensationalism began in the early nineteenth century, but did not gain significant popular following until after the publication of the Scofield Reference Bible in 1909. Dispensational premillennialism is today the most popularized and most visible eschatology of conservative American Protestants.

11. Timothy Miller, *Revivalism and Social Reform: American Protestantism on the Eve of the Civil War* (1957; Gloucester, Mass.: Peter Smith, 1976).

12. Their faith in human progress and in the essential goodness of human nature inspired the Progressive reforms of the early twentieth century and faltered in the face of the two world wars that followed. Please see James H. Morehead, *World without End: Mainstream American Protestant Visions of the Last Things, 1880–1925* (Bloomington: University of Indiana Press, 1999); Susan Curtis, *Consuming Faith: The Social Gospel and Modern American Culture* (Columbia: University of Missouri Press, 2001).

13. Timothy Fulop, "The Future Golden Day of the Race: Millennialism and Black Americans in the Nadir, 1877–1901," *Harvard Theological Review* 84, no. 1 (1991): 75–99; A. G. Steward, *The End of the World, or Clearing the Way for the Fullness of the Gentiles* (Philadelphia: A.M.E. Church Book Rooms, 1888); James Walker Hood, *The Plan of the Apocalypse* (York, Pa.: P. Anstadt, 1900).

14. *Proceedings of the Joint Sessions of the Baptist Educational and Missionary Convention, the Ministerial Union, the Hayes-Fleming Foreign Missionary Society, and the State Sunday School Convention of North Carolina* (hereafter NCBEMC Proceedings) (October 1894): 17.

15. Albert Raboteau, "African-Americans, Exodus, and the American Israel," in *African-American Christianity: Essays in History,* ed. Paul E. Johnson (Berkeley: University of California Press, 1994), 9.

16. James H. Cone, *God of the Oppressed* (1975; Maryknoll, N.Y.: Orbis, 1997), 102–3.

17. Ibid., 103.

18. See Eddie Glaude, *Exodus! Religion, Race, and Nation in Early Nineteenth-Century Black America* (Chicago: University of Chicago Press, 2000).

19. Burkhead, "History of the Difficulties," 44.

20. Raboteau, *A Fire in the Bones,* 12. Rev. Morgan Latta, of Raleigh, North Carolina, for example, invited a direct comparison between ancient Hebrews and African Americans: "People have said that God was not just, allowing other nationalities to predominate over them [Hebrews] and hold them as slaves. . . . God works things to suit Himself, and if God, in His own mysterious ways, in managing things, has promoted the Hebrews to prosperity, then it is prima facie evidence that the same God that promoted the Hebrews will promote the negro race" (*History of My Life and Work,* 53–54).

21. See, for example, Report of Speech by Edwin Jones, August 22, 1867, Letters Received, Oaths of Office, and Records Relating to Registration and Elections, 1865–1869, ser. 1380, Post of Wilmington, Record Group 393 Pt. 4, National Archives, quoted in Eric Foner, "Reconstruction and the Black Political Tradition," in *Political Parties and the Modern State,* ed. Richard L. McCormick (New Brunswick, N.J.: Rutgers University Press, 1984), 62.

22. Burkhead, "History of the Difficulties," 44.

23. Quoted in Steven Hahn, "'Extravagant Expectations' of Freedom: Rumour, Political Struggle, and the Christmas Insurrection Scare of 1865 in the American South," *Past and Present* 157 (November 1997): 136.

24. *Christian Recorder,* October 1, 1864.

25. S. D. Barnes to Lieutenant E. Bamberger, December 30, 1865, cited in Edward Magdol, *A Right to the Land: Essays on the Freedmen's Community* (Westport, Conn.: Greenwood, 1977), 141.

26. *Wilmington Herald,* September 8, 1865, quoted in William McKee Evans, *Ballots and Fence Rails: Reconstruction on the Lower Cape Fear* (Athens: University of Georgia Press, 1995), 87.

27. Isa. 66:6–9, KJV.

28. Burkhead, "History of the Difficulties," 44–45.

29. Jurgen Moltmann, *Theology of Hope: On the Ground and the Implications of a Christian Eschatology* (New York: Harper and Row, 1965; trans. 1967 by James W. Leitch), 15–16.

30. Cone, *God of the Oppressed,* 116.

31. Burkhead, "History of the Difficulties," 43–44.

32. Ibid., 64–65.

33. James Walker Hood, *One Hundred Years of the African Methodist Episcopal Zion Church, or the Centennial of African Methodism* (New York: AME Zion Book Concern, 1895), 185–88, 289–300.

34. Burkhead, "History of the Difficulties," 47–50, 56, 61, 73.

35. *Christian Recorder,* April 1, 1865.

36. Hood, *One Hundred Years,* 55–56; see Katherine Dvorak, *African American Exodus: The Segregation of Southern Churches* (Brooklyn, N.Y.: Carlson, 1991). See also Paul Harvey, *Freedom's Comin': Religious Culture and the Shaping of the South from the Civil War through the Civil Rights Era* (Chapel Hill: University of North Carolina Press, 2005), 8–19.

37. Daniel Fountain, *Slavery, Civil War, and Salvation: African American Slaves and Christianity, 1830–1870* (Baton Rouge: Louisiana State University Press, 2010), 6–40, 93–114. Fountain's thesis is a formidable challenge to the consensus that the practice of Christianity was the center of slave culture. Fountain's survey results may be less significant than they first appear. In revivalistic evangelical Protestantism, converts almost always narrate the earlier parts of their lives as ones of irreligion, even if Christianity profoundly shaped their ideas and practices before conversion. Moreover, slave narratives, starting with Olaudah Equiano's, took as their genre model the spiritual autobiography, substituting the moment of freedom for the climactic moment of conversion. Many slave autobiographies purposely equate conversion with freedom; Fountain's data tell us as much about the conventions of a genre and of a revivalistic faith as they do the numerical strength of Christianity. Nevertheless, historians will have difficultly refuting Fountain's claim that emancipation itself was the event that placed Christianity at the center of black cultural life.

38. W. Fitzhugh Brundage, *The Southern Past: A Clash of Race and Memory* (Cambridge: Belknap Press of Harvard University Press, 2005), 89, 94. See also Kathleen Clark, *Defining Moments: African American Commemoration & Political Culture in the South, 1863–1913* (Chapel Hill: University of North Carolina Press, 2005).

39. Burkhead, "History of the Difficulties," 64–65.

40. Laura Edwards, *Gendered Strife and Confusion: The Political Culture of Reconstruction* (Urbana: University of Illinois Press, 1997), 194.

41. C. R. Harris, "The Negro's Mission in America," *African Methodist Episcopal Zion Quarterly* 3, no. 1 (October 1892): 48.

42. Laurie F. Maffly-Kipp, "Mapping the World, Mapping the Race: The Negro Race History, 1874–1915," *Church History* 64, no. 4 (December 1995): 610–26; *Star of Zion,* passim; J. A. Whitted, *A History of the Negro Baptists of North Carolina* (Raleigh: Edwards and Broughton Printing, 1908), 164. I am indebted to Andrea N. Williams for alerting me to the way African American literature used emancipation to track time.

43. Acts 17:26, KJV; Rev. 7:9 KJV; see, for example, editorial, *Star of Zion,* January 26, 1899; "Dangerous Advice," *Star of Zion,* November 17, 1898; Butler Harrison Peterson, "Is the Negro Morally Depraved as He Is Reputed to Be?" in *Twentieth-Century Negro Literature, Twentieth Century Negro Literature, or, A Cyclopedia of Thought on the Vital Topics Relating to the American Negro, by One Hundred of America's Greatest Negroes,* comp. D. W. Culp (Toronto, Canada: J. L. Nichols,

1902), 240; Latta, *The History of My Life and Work,* 198–99; *Journal of Freedom,* September 30, 1865; George W. Clinton, *Christianity under the Searchlight* (Nashville, Tenn.: National Baptist Publishing Board, 1909), 54–56; Francis Grimke, "Christianization of America," in *Twentieth Century Negro Literature,* comp. D. W. Culp, 431–33.

44. Fulop, "Future Golden Day of the Race." A particular reading of history accompanied these interpretations of Psalm 68. In numerous race histories, black Americans wrote of a mythic glorious past that placed their ancestors in the ancient civilizations Egypt and Ethiopia, civilizations that predated and outstripped the West. And as Raboteau argues, it was "surely as legitimate a fictive pedigree as white American claims of descent from Greco-Roman civilization" (Albert J. Raboteau, "'Ethiopia Shall Soon Stretch Forth Her Hands to God': Black Destiny in Nineteenth-Century America," in *African American Religious Thought: An Anthology,* ed. Cornel West and Eddie Glaude Jr. [Louisville, Ky.: Westminster John Knox Press, 2003], 397–413). Laurie Maffly-Kipp explains, "African participation in ancient history was a useful counter to the white claim that the Negro had always been, and would remain, a degraded race" ("Mapping the World, Mapping the Race," 618). See also Maffly-Kipp, "Redeeming Southern Memory: The Negro Race History, 1874–1915," in *Where These Memories Grow: History Memory, and Southern Identity,* ed. W. Fitzhugh Brundage (Chapel Hill: University of North Carolina, 2000), 170, 179, 184. According to Maffly-Kipp, these race histories exhibited the many tensions within the black community. Often writers were well-educated, middle-class northern blacks who criticized southern blacks for their primitive spirituality. Moreover, these black elites rarely held approval for the actions and beliefs of the black masses. Race historians also disagreed among themselves. And in one sense, their histories removed Negro history from the realm of a personal God favoring His people to a liberal understanding of inevitable progress. But Maffly-Kipp concludes that race historians had more in common than not. Their common message was that African Americans had a prominent place in history and the future, and their common purpose was to foster the building of a successful free black community.

45. See Glaude, *Exodus!,* 12–15.

46. Burkhead, "History of the Difficulties," 78.

47. LeRae Umfleet and the 1898 Wilmington Race Riot Commission, *1898 Wilmington Race Riot,* Office of Archives and History, North Carolina Department of Cultural Resources (2006); Timothy Tyson and David S. Celeski, eds., *Democracy Betrayed: The Wilmington Race Riot of 1898 and Its Legacy* (Chapel Hill: University of North Carolina Press, 1998).

48. John C. Dancy, "Disfranchisement," *AME Zion Quarterly Review* 14, no. 4 (December 1905): 85.

9

A SHARECROPPER'S MILLENNIUM

Land and the Perils of Forgiveness in Post–Civil War South Carolina

SCOTT NESBIT

Francis L. Cardozo read the hand of God on the Lowcountry landscape. "Providence," he told his fellow delegates in South Carolina's 1868 Constitutional Convention, "has not only smiled upon every effort for abolishing" the "hideous form" of plantation slavery. Providence also "has given unmistakable signs of disapprobation" wherever large plantation holdings continued, by "blasting the cotton crops in that part of the country." Providence seemed to be reshaping the state's agricultural and cadastral map before his eyes, replacing staple production with fields of grain and replacing extensive plantations "of no service to the owner or anybody else" with a "system of small farms, by which not only my race, but the poor whites and ninety-nine hundredths of the other thousands will be benefitted." Cardozo called upon his colleagues to participate in this divine work by allowing large debts taken out during the war to be collected, action that could force hundreds of large, indebted planters into forfeiture.[1]

By invoking a providential reading of the present and recent past, Cardozo was placing the convention's actions in the middle of what historian Laurie Maffly-Kipp has called "an eschatological saga," a narrative that interprets the community's past, present, and future together by invoking the unfolding of God's judgment and millennial kingdom in the world. Historians have debated the meanings of these narratives and how African Americans employed them in the political contexts of Reconstruction. Maffly-Kipp has emphasized the extent to which black millennial innovations created "collective stories" that placed the black past and destiny in world-historical context. Timothy Fulop has suggested that these black millennial stories developed in three ways: a cultural millennialism that emphasized the role of the United States as a redeemer nation, a millennial Ethiopianism that posited a pan-African future, and a progressive millennialism that emphasized the role of the church, missions, and reform in giving birth to the millennium on earth. Matthew Harper has recently distinguished between two biblical narratives in the political and religious thought of North Carolina blacks: the Jubilee, a narrative imploring southern blacks to remain on the land, and the Exodus, a narrative that fit with the vibrant emigrationist politics of the post-Reconstruction period. This historiography has brought to light the constant pull in black thought between envisioning a South where blacks might find their own land and displacing their hopes for land elsewhere. Yet black hopes for a southern millennium in many accounts remain simply hopes, central to black religious thought yet peripheral to Reconstruction political debates and disconnected from mechanisms for enacting political and economic change.[2]

Black Christians put the millennium at the center of the debate on land policy. As historians Michael Walzer and Eddie Glaude Jr. have argued, by the close of the Civil War African Americans had produced a long tradition of millennial political thought dependent upon the Exodus narratives. Freedpeople participated in the Exodus story in what ways they could. Some appealed to federal authorities for the right to work their own land independent of whites. If these appeals failed, some had little recourse within the Reconstruction political system. Yet blacks in South Carolina were not simply dependent on congressional action for land redistribution; they held political control of state legislative bodies that had the power to enact redistributive policies. Black politicians debated how they would reshape the southern landscape in providential and millennial terms. In doing so, they confronted the ways in which black millennial narratives—whether cultural, Ethiopian, or progressive, and whether narrated as the Jubilee or an Exodus—played out in space, especially in debates over lowcountry landholding patterns and in how (and whether) blacks should live in proximity to former slaveholders.[3]

Though many black Carolinians could see God's hand in their past, present, and future, they offered conflicting solutions to the spatial problem of living and laboring near powerful whites. The problem was complex and one that many believed must be solved in order to enact God's kingdom after slavery. Black and white southerners still called each other neighbors. Continued proximity in emancipation called for new ways of relating. Emancipation, many black Christians believed, had replaced hierarchical bonds of subservience with new relations. Some blacks and a number of white army officials and politicians believed that freedmen's relations with whites should be tempered by charity; charity toward whites, for these Carolinians, meant forgiving slaveholders, enabling them to escape bankruptcy and foreclosure on their plantations. For others, including Cardozo, the true application of Christianity meant allowing God's judgment against the sin of slavery to run its course, allowing unrepentant former Confederates to reap judgment and fall into bankruptcy, opening up their lands for redistribution. For still others, particularly those without access to political or economic power, forgiveness of former slaveholders was altogether impossible. Charity in this case meant putting space between former slaves and former slave owners because violent whites made the practice of Christian love impossible; charity toward one's oppressors, some found, could lead to greater violence and even death.[4]

Each of these millennial hopes for the South's future offered a distinct spatial arrangement. Black narratives of Jubilee, in which slaves might possess their former master's land, eroded quickly in Reconstruction. By the emergence of Radical Reconstruction in 1867–68, such hopes had given way to competing visions. Cardozo interpreted blight and Civil War destruction as divine judgment on the landscape. He sought to participate in this judgment by allowing distressed properties to come under foreclosure. His opponents instead hoped for a South fit for Christian charity and a land miraculously healed of racial antagonism. In such a postslavery South, capital and labor could find peace in the profits made possible by a reinvigorated plantation system. Both these visions were shattered by increasing levels of racial violence. By 1870, black farmers across South Carolina believed that they could find no peace in the state. In cooperation with the American Colonization Society, they sought millennial space abroad. Throughout Reconstruction, black Carolinians deployed religious narratives for specific political and economic purposes, linking their desires for the future of the landscape with narratives of God's millennial kingdom and proposals for resolving the problem of living in proximity to former slave owners. They projected their millennial visions both out of religious conviction and out of more worldly calculations; they turned ordinary neighborhoods and political debates, in the words of theologian Charles Marsh, "into theaters of complex theological drama." And they saw God's kingdom breaking into a cotton-producing landscape scarred by war and burdened with debt.[5]

Cardozo's assessment, that God had "blasted" the state since 1860, was not far from the truth. South Carolina's financial problems from 1865 to 1868 were severe. Much of Charleston lay in ruins in the first months of 1865, and little escaped fire in Columbia in mid-February. Planting season arrived on Sherman's heels, by mid-April. The 1865 cotton crop was weak—less than a tenth of what had been produced in 1860—and encumbered by taxes. Emancipation had destroyed South Carolinians' liquid capital investments in enslaved men and women. Postwar South Carolinians saw widespread foreclosure and default on debts contracted in the tenuous antebellum credit system. In the words of one South Carolina judge, "the property is gone, the labor is very uncertain, the debts remain." Formerly enslaved men and women entered freedom in poverty, susceptible to violence and fraud, and hoping for the possibility of purchasing the land many had worked their entire lives.[6]

Property owners' holdings in the state had been devastated by the war and its aftermath. Capital invested in enslaved men and women composed nearly 60 percent of agricultural investments in the Lower South by 1860, and close to half of the cotton region's total wealth. The devastation of Sherman's army, though exaggerated in local rumors and later accounts, was real. Much of Charleston lay in ruins by the war's end, and nearly every building in Columbia had gone up in flames in 1865. In addition to the widespread devastation wrought by Sherman's army, drought and disease destroyed a tremendous proportion of the state's crops in the first years of Reconstruction.[7]

The State of South Carolina was required to pay sizable back taxes to the federal government in order to fund the United States' war effort. In the summer of 1861, Congress levied a direct tax on every state, whether it had seceded or not, to pay for the war. South Carolina's assessed contribution was to be in excess of $350,000. By 1863, the U.S. military in conjunction with the Bureau of Internal Revenue seized land and cotton as payment for the tax, leading to the "rehearsal for Reconstruction," the confiscation of land from former Confederates on the Sea Islands.[8]

Former planters who had abandoned their lands as they fell into Union hands claimed that their presidential pardons entitled them to all lands that had not been directly confiscated as part of the U.S. Treasury Department's seizure of land in payment of the direct tax. Under the auspices of Gen. Oliver O. Howard, many of these lands, especially on Port Royal, St. Helena, and other islands occupied since early in the war, had already been sold. Islands closer to Charleston and coastal lands in Charleston County, on the mainland, had yet to be disbursed. These lands, especially the valuable property on Edisto Island, were the subject of hot debate. On September 23, 1865, former planters who had fled the island applied to President Johnson for protection of their property rights. They had earlier found little luck in petitioning General Howard or his counterpart in the U.S. Army Quartermaster office, Rufus Saxton. Against their claims lay the demands of the formerly enslaved men and women who currently held possession of the land under the authority of Gen. William T. Sherman's Field Order 15.[9]

Johnson responded favorably to the former planters, who appealed to him by the mechanism the president perceived to be his most powerful tool for Reconstruction: the executive pardon power. Johnson quickly ordered Maj. Gen. Oliver O. Howard to meet with both sets of claimants to find a "mutually satisfactory" arrangement. When Howard arrived on Edisto Island on the evening of October 19, he was met by hundreds of men and women lining the street to the Episcopal church at the center of the island, with hundreds more waiting inside. Howard told the gathered men and women that the ex-Confederates' plantations were to be given back to their former owners. When the freedmen and women began shouting, the major general became flustered and asked them to lay aside any bitterness they harbored and work for their masters.[10]

One freedman responded to Howard's news in light of scripture and his dashed expectations, replying that "he could forgive his old master, as he hoped he would be forgiven." Still, he had lived his whole life with a basket over his head, and "now that it had been taken off and air and sunlight had come," he could "not consent to have the basket over him again." Forgiveness was one thing, giving up the land another. A committee of freedmen led by Henry Bram, Ishmael Moultrie, and Yates Sampson quickly drew up their reaction to federal revocation of the land: "We are at the mercy of those who are combined to prevent us from getting land enough to lay our Fathers bones upon. . . . You ask us to forgive the land owners of our island," they wrote Howard, an amputee from wounds received in battle. "You only lost your right arm in war and might forgive them. The man who tied me to a tree and gave me 39 lashes and who stripped and flogged my mother and my sister . . . that man I cannot well forgive." Howard was insistent. The government "considers a forgiven man in the light of a citizen restored to rights of property excepting as to slaves. . . . The duty of forgiveness is plain and simple. Forgive as we hope to be forgiven of Him who governs all things."[11]

Freedmen and women had placed a tremendous hope in acquiring land, hope that was widely been associated with the Jubilee—as one freedman on Edisto Island called it, "air and sunlight." After federal land reform stalled,

Major General Howard perceived that if former slaves were to work for their old masters and live in proximity to them, all concerned would be required to engage in social relations no longer ordered by the hierarchies of slavery. They would meet as moral equals, able to engage in an exchange between laborers and holders of capital. He and the freedmen on Edisto Island both knew, however, that former slaveholders had incurred tremendous moral debts to those they held as slaves. In order for labor to proceed on land owned by a former slaveholder, freedmen and women would be forced to assume that moral debt. Howard's insistence that freedmen and -women forgive was an insistence that they set their master free from his debt to them. They were to proclaim their master's Jubilee. Many left the island instead.[12]

These moral debts and allowances meant everything on Edisto Island but were not the only debts held in the state. Much of the crushing personal debt carried by South Carolinians and other southerners into the postwar era was a direct result of the combination of hazardous borrowing practices before the war and uncompensated emancipation. The 1850s boom throughout the cotton-growing South had increased planters' hopes of favorable rates of return on their principal investments, enslaved workers. Speculation ensued. The Thirteenth Amendment abolished slavery, but left untouched the debts incurred in the slave trade. Moreover, personal indebtedness and default on those debts grew alarmingly across the South after the Civil War. Antebellum cultural prohibitions on debt and declaration of bankruptcy exploded in the Civil War. What had simply been called "embarrassment" before the war seems not to have been nearly so embarrassing afterward.[13]

Debtors continued to hold property, however, and this made them a distinct, even privileged, minority. Far more men and women in South Carolina, including the vast majority of the formerly enslaved, held no real property; their destitution was more pressing. Accounts of starvation among freedmen circulating at the time and in the years immediately following Reconstruction were exaggerated, though at the time, the situation seemed dire to all parties involved. By 1866, Governor James L. Orr warned Maj. Gen. Oliver O. Howard, superintendent of the Freedmen's Bureau, that "thousands, white and black, were bound to suffer" if the bureau's program of aid were not expanded.[14]

There was suffering, but by January 1868 black South Carolinians had become beneficiaries of congressional changes. Congress rejected the state constitution of 1865. Andrew Johnson, who had extended official magnanimity toward former Confederates in 1865 and 1866, was impotent in the face of the legislative branch's power to override his veto. Black men had begun voting to form new state constitutions throughout the South. In South Carolina, the black majority voted overwhelmingly for African Americans to represent them in the convention. At the opening gavel in early 1868, men of at least some African descent occupied 70 of the 124 convention seats in a meeting dominated by Republicans.[15]

Cardozo had reason to believe that his vision of a transformed South would take hold in the convention. His description of a renovated South had deep roots in Republican opposition to plantations, their respect for contractual obligations between debtors and creditors, and their belief in the virtue of small landholdings. It was just as grounded in the aspirations freedmen held for the land they had worked. And it was steadfast in its opposition toward former slave traders and Confederates. He thought it obvious that "nine-tenths of the debts were contracted for the sale of slaves. I do not wish we should go one inch out of the way to legislate either for the buyer or the seller. They dealt in that kind of property, they knew its precarious tenure, and therefore, let them suffer." In arguing to allow debts to be collected and foreclosures to proceed, Cardozo created a forceful mix of political and religious arguments for the breakup of the plantation system by foreclosure that resonated with many at the Convention.[16]

Francis Cardozo's background made him particularly suited to carry this mix of political and religious ideologies into the convention. Cardozo grew up in Charleston, the son of the prominent Jewish economist Isaac N. Cardozo and a free woman of color. He was educated successively at the school for free black children in the city and after apprenticeships in carpentry went on to extensive theological training at universities in Glasgow, London, and Edinburgh, winning competitive scholarships for Latin and Greek along the way. By 1864, Cardozo moved to Connecticut to take up the pastorate of the Temple Street Church in New Haven.[17]

Once in Connecticut, Cardozo quickly made inroads in Congregationalist and black abolitionist circles. He joined the National Convention of Colored Men in Syracuse in 1864 and by the following year had volunteered his services to the American Missionary Association. He was immediately charged with the uncomfortable task of investigating an accusation of impropriety between his brother, Thomas, who had been serving in Charleston for several months, and a former student in New York. Despite Francis's request for leniency toward his brother, the AMA quickly relieved Thomas of his duties and replaced him there with his theologically astute brother.[18]

Francis Cardozo threw himself into the administrative work of starting a school and assessing his new pupils and teachers. He arrived in the summer and by October 1 had organized a school of 950 students and oversaw nearly two dozen teachers. He quickly proved himself politically adept, managing to earn commendations from AMA officials and endorsements for his school from prominent local whites. This maneuvering was particularly impressive given the level of Cardozo's distrust of most ex-Confederates. He refused to preach at the Second Presbyterian Church mission on account of the racism he attributed to its pastor, and he had participated in the Colored People's Convention in Charleston in 1865 that repudiated the Black Codes and other work of the conservative government that year. Cardozo was a theologian thoroughly interested in the practicalities of making emancipation work in his native state by entering directly into politics.[19]

Despite the goodwill Cardozo had generated among freedmen in Charleston, among elite free people of color, and even from a few Carolinian whites, it quickly became clear that his position in favor of allowing foreclosure of plantations generated antagonism. A number of white delegates to the convention along with more than a few black delegates were increasingly uncomfortable both with Cardozo's political proposal and the religious terms in which he couched it. To these delegates, Cardozo's blunt exhortation to "let them suffer" lacked Christian love.[20]

No delegate was more strident in the attack on Cardozo than William J. Whipper, a black lawyer representing Beaufort with unimpeachable abolitionist credentials and heritage. His uncle, also named William Whipper, had long been a fixture in the push for civil rights in the North, a leader in early strategies for moral suasion, and a vocal proponent of "color-blind" political activism. The elder Whipper combined elite, relatively conservative reform ideology with an acute business sense; by the late antebellum period, some estimated his lumber holdings in Columbia, Pennsylvania, to be worth twenty thousand dollars. Neither wealth nor hopes for a color-blind politics were able to shield William Whipper from racism, though; the lumber mill offices he managed with his partner, Stephen Smith, were attacked by a mob just as his activism began.[21]

The younger Whipper, too, took a decidedly active role in antebellum reform, though he seemed to carry few hints of his uncle's commitment to nonviolence. William J. Whipper first embarked in a career of political activism while training as a lawyer in Ohio and later Michigan. He voted for a friend in a local political race in 1859, challenging prohibitions against black suffrage and was race-baited during his friend's trial for voter fraud. Two years later, Whipper carried a barely concealed, three-foot iron club with armed accomplices onto a train as part of a failed conspiracy to ambush agents carrying an escaped slave south from Ohio. Though thrown from the moving train when discovered, he was unharmed. Once the U.S. Army began recruiting African Americans, he volunteered, fighting at Cold Harbor and Petersburg before witnessing Gen. Robert E. Lee's surrender at Appomattox. Whipper thought little of Grant's exquisitely orchestrated surrender ceremony. A few years later, the delegate Whipper recalled that "when General Lee surrendered," he "would have hanged every leader of the rebellion. I would have given them a short, shrift, and a speedy death."[22]

Whipper would become one of the wealthiest members of the convention. In addition to whatever wealth he was able to leverage from his family's lumber business in Pennsylvania, Whipper quickly set up a livable if undistinguished legal practice in Beaufort. Whipper, a widower by 1868, began to woo Frances "Frank" Rollin, a member of the Brown Society, who split her time between Charleston, where her father owned a lumber manufactory, and her family's Beaufort county plantation. Rollin had participated fully in Charleston's elite society for people of color, even if the family's considerable wealth had been ruined by the war. She was a Charleston power broker in her own right with piercing intelligence and ambition, enough to come to the notice of Martin Delany, who asked the twenty-year-old to author his biography. Just after the convention, Whipper married Rollin. By 1872, but probably earlier, Whipper came to own a rice plantation along the Ashepoo River; at the convention, he decided protect the Lowcountry's plantation geography from Cardozo and his allies.[23]

Whipper's motivations for opposing Cardozo were surely complex. He had long been committed to civil rights for blacks in the United States and had an established record of risking personal injury on behalf of his own rights and the rights of others. While few would have called him devout—he had reportedly twice faced court-martial, first for gambling, then for insubordination—Whipper was long accustomed to thinking and talking about worldly affairs in reference to Christianity and its obligations. After having been invited to lecture on slavery in a Methodist church in Ohio as a young man, Whipper found that the local minister had refused, for the second time, to announce the lecture publicly. Exasperated, Whipper demanded in a letter to the evangelical *Anti-Slavery Bugle,* "How long will such Christianity prevail?" He had gone to great pains to take care of some of the most vulnerable around him, adopting an orphaned child who had followed the Thirty-First Pennsylvania Infantry on its marches through Virginia. Whipper was certainly not the only wealthy delegate at the convention, either. Cardozo himself recorded five thousand dollars in property in the 1870 census and was accused by some members of the convention of seeking to profit from the low real estate prices. Wealthy delegates of color lined up behind Cardozo's and Whipper's sides in even numbers during the debate. Still, Whipper's personal interest in land as wealth was clear. His speeches emerged both in order to advance his own prosperity and out of a widely held millennial vision of the South as a place where whites and blacks might live together in peace.[24]

Whipper's vision of a reconstructed South relied on the redemptive power of time and forgiveness. For Whipper and many others, the time for judgment against Confederates had passed. He argued that when he first arrived in the state, he "was zealous to see the leaders of the rebellion hung, and every man engaged in it disfranchised and their lands confiscated." But by 1868, he claimed, the time for legitimate punishment had passed. Instead of legislating out of "vengeance," "prejudices, and hatreds," he told the delegates, "all these things should be forgotten now." Bringing up the past in judgment now was "wrong, cruel, and unjust." Whipper attacked Cardozo's proposal, accusing the minister from Charleston of "appealing to the prejudice" of black members of the convention by mentioning slavery in order to attack a measure that would redound to "the general good," and "to the prosperity of all the people of the State, black or white." If the lands were brought to foreclosure, Whipper envisioned a South brought lower than it already had been, a lurid picture seemingly borrowed from the Old Testament, a place where "whole families" were "thrown upon the cold charities of the world," where the "innocent" suffer, and where land monopolists, a "merciless set of legalized robbers" who care nothing for cultivation, "gobble up the land" itself.[25]

In describing forgotten wrongs, Whipper was picking up on language that some black Carolinians had used from the beginning of Reconstruction. The first resolution passed by delegates to the Charleston Colored People's Convention in 1865 imagined the South Carolina landscape as the Kingdom of Heaven, where sins are forgotten and peace reigns. "Resolved," they wrote, "that as the old institution of slavery has passed away, that we cherish in our hearts no hatred or malice toward those who have held our brethren as slaves," the convention's resolution added, "but we extend the right hand of fellowship to all, and make it our special aim to establish unity, peace, and love amongst all men." Whipper applied this line of thought directly to land-use policy in the Reconstruction state.[26]

This vision led to a far different policy prescription than that offered by Cardozo. Where Cardozo believed proximity to white southerners meant that former slaves and free blacks should do what they could to attack planters' real holdings, Whipper spoke of proximity to whites as an opportunity to exercise Christian virtue. Cardozo imagined black freeholders enjoying a precarious independence, in which antagonism between laborers and those who owned land persisted beyond emancipation. Whipper proposed the possibility of a clean moral break between antebellum and postbellum worlds. Such a break would allow a transformation in social relations even if the plantation system remained intact. This fictive social peace, he imagined, would be imperiled only if black southerners made it so by legislating against encumbered plantations and offering them to sale to the highest bidder. Where Cardozo believed that planters were reaping the just desserts of their sin, Whipper attacked Cardozo for transgressing the bounds of charity. To demand that debtors "ought to suffer" did not conform to Whipper's "idea of Christianity." Christianity, Whipper told the convention, instead demanded that he "forgive a man" whenever he believed "he is repentant."[27]

It was his claim that Christianity demanded forgiveness of those who had bought and sold slaves that Cardozo disputed. Cardozo instead argued that true Christian forgiveness was not unilaterally given, but was only granted after the sinner confessed his sin and repented. As Cardozo stated flatly, "I do not believe they have repented." By invoking the need for repentance in this way, Cardozo dodged the charge of vindictiveness that haunted all black public officials who attempted to limit ex-Confederate power through land reform or disfranchisement. Instead, he charged his opponents with reckless misunderstandings of the relationship between mercy and justice.[28]

Cardozo's opponents attempted to gain a moral upper hand by replacing his strict construal of forgiveness with a seemingly more generous plan. Whipper's speech at the constitutional convention, accusing Cardozo and his ally Richard H. Cain of vengeance, seemed to win over a number of delegates; the following day, Cain disassociated himself from "any desire of vindictiveness" against slaveholders. A combination of black and white delegates quickly—but barely—carried the vote petitioning the military district commander, Gen. Edward R. Canby, to suspend executions on debts; most whites voted for the petition; one-third of the black delegates supported it as well, providing the crucial votes needed to pass the petition. In the end, General Canby followed the suggestion of the Convention in disallowing executions on outstanding debts for three months.[29]

Black politicians chose between different models of forgiveness that corresponded to vastly different visions for a millennial South. They chose between Cardozo's position of strict justice and Whipper's attempt to demonstrate magnanimity in concert with white Carolinians. As they did so, they chose a South Carolina whose property owners were protected from their debts instead of one that had the potential to open new land up for freedmen to purchase. Surprisingly, African Americans provided the margin of victory for the stay law, disallowing any immediate confiscation of property. William Whipper, like Cardozo, believed that polities might reflect God's will for the land. Unlike the minister from Charleston, he pressed for policies of magnanimity; these policies elided the strict justice Cardozo demanded. They also implied a specific spatial organization for the postwar South, in which planters—including Whipper himself—might control wide swaths of the Lowcountry and the labor of its population.

Arguments over forgiveness and the spatial relations of Reconstruction were bound as tightly in the neighborhoods of the Upcountry as they were in the halls of the state convention, though by the 1871 it was not clear that the landscape imagined by either Cardozo or Whipper was still possible. In York and surrounding counties, debate over the forgiveness of debts and forfeiture of land had given way to more pressing issues. The Ku Klux Klan had begun a massive wave of violence against African American men and women to eliminate sites of opposition to white supremacy, all in the name of local peace. Amos T. Akerman, a former Confederate judge who quickly rose in the Grant administration to the newly created position of attorney general, reflected to an army officer after his visit to the Upcountry that "I feel greatly saddened by this business. It has revealed a perversion of moral sentiment among the Southern whites which bodes ill to that part of the country for this generation. Without a thorough moral renovation, society there for many years will be—I can hardly bring myself to say savage, but certainly very far from Christian." Violence on the land ended predictions of the South as a millennial space.[30]

On April 1, Rufus Bratton, a local surgeon and ex-Confederate officer, called a "Public Meeting of the Blacks," demanding that York County freedmen sign a resolution calling for the resignation of Republican officeholders at the local and state level. The resolution's stated purpose was reconciliation between the county's whites and blacks, "the perpetuation of kind feelings and true friendship among all classes—both white and black." Another former Confederate officer made very clear at the meeting how such reconciliation was to be obtained. It was folly "to talk about peace, harmony, and true friendship," he told those in attendance, until white men ruled, and so he "advised the colored people to vote for it because it was a peace measure."[31]

The head of the York County Union League, Rev. Elias Hill, had been skeptical of the "peace negotiations" between whites and blacks in Yorkville, in the midst of Klan terror. Still, he thought there was a possibility that "it would be the means of compromising or pacifying the whites." June Moore, a nephew of Hill and one of his closest followers, had even participated in a meeting held in February to determine what the points of contention were between white and black men in York County, but the peace meetings did little to quell the violence.[32]

His role as leader of the Union League, minister, and teacher marked Hill out for Klan attack. That was what Rufus Bratton and the other men said as they broke into Hill's cabin on the night of May 5. They beat Hill as they asked questions: "Who did that burning?" "When did you hold a night-meeting of the Union League?" "Haven't you been preaching political sermons?" "Will you quit preaching?" Hill reported these and other questions to the congressional investigators. "Wasn't I willing to die? Didn't I preach?" After threatening Hill's life and beating him, the six attackers seized Hill, and in his words, "gathered around and told me to pray for them. I tried to pray. They said, 'Don't you pray against Ku Klux, but pray that God may forgive the Ku-Klux. Don't pray against us. Pray that God may bless us and save us.'" Elias Hill did not pray for his attackers that night. He "couldn't speak to pray" on account of the beating he had received.[33]

The Klan's use of the language of forgiveness extended Christian admonitions to "love your enemies" and "pray for those who persecute you" to debased conclusions. Hill's reaction to this brutality was twofold. In speaking about his activities to the congressional investigators, Hill affirmed his allegiance to the faith to which he had devoted much of his life. He also planned to leave the country.

Hill's view of Christianity seemed to imply the forgiveness of enemies. Less than three months after his beating, Hill explained, "I have good-will, love," and even "affection" toward whites, he told congressional investigators, "but I fear them." He could not "believe it possible, from the past history and present aspect of affairs," for his people "to live in this country peaceably, and educate and elevate their children to that degree which they desire."[34]

The guilt of southern whites did not give Hill much hope for York County, so he decided to emigrate. Although at first he considered moving west or taking advantage of the southern Homestead Act, he decided against it, instead contacting the American Colonization Society in order to move to Liberia. Hill told the Philadelphia press that he preferred a place where "the lands were rich." There, he believed, "cotton could be grown and free schools established." As importantly, "there was no animosity or prejudice against his race." In order to practice what he called "love universal," the enactment of the millennial kingdom of God on earth, Hill and the freedmen of York County required space from whites, who had proven themselves unremittingly hostile to peace.[35]

Along with Hill, at least seventy families from York County had decided to emigrate, displacing their hope for God's kingdom. Among them were members of Elias Hill's family and many others from his neighborhood of Clay Hill. The departure was a direct result of the violence—two-thirds of the families who left had either been victims of Klan violence or were relatives of victims. Altogether 135 men, women, and children from York County boarded the *Edith Rose* on November 7, 1871, for Liberia. As word of Hill's arrival in Liberia reached Clay Hill, it became clear that nearly every family in the neighborhood contemplated emigrating. J. D. Currence of Clay Hill believed that two hundred more settlers from the area would soon emigrate; he then revised his estimate to five hundred. Hill had hoped "that the times will eventually come that those who want to go away now may stay, finding that they can live in peace." Hill himself had "lost hope entirely" in the virtue of his neighbors. Others, he admitted, "are still hoping."[36]

Hill created and put into practice a theology of redemption and emigration. The text of his inaugural sermon on reaching Liberia, Romans 10:1, intertwined the history of enslaved men and women with the Exodus of the Israelites: "Brethren, my heart's desire and prayer to God for Israel is, that they might be saved." For Elias Hill, Christianity demanded practices of universal love. Since whites abused him and his neighbors so severely, they made these practices impossible. In order to practice Christianity—love universal—Hill sought to leave, literally, the country of his bondage. Bringing about the millennium, he believe, would occur not in the United States, where all he saw was violence and grief, but in Africa.[37]

Like the freedmen and women on Edisto Island, Francis L. Cardozo, and William J. Whipper, Elias Hill had ambitious plans for bringing about spatial patterns suitable for Christian practice in a society without slavery—a geography for the Kingdom of God. Each of the geographies proposed was built out of two spatial patterns: a landholding pattern constructed out of the existing plantation system and a pattern emerging from proximity and labor relations that demanded that black southerners either come to terms with whites as moral equals in the marketplace—in some formulations, forgive them—or emigrate. For Cardozo, forgiveness for slave traders was possible only after divine judgment on the slave regime and the plantation system of landholding that made it so profitable, and after slaveholders themselves had repented. Whipper argued that forgiveness ought to be extended without reservation, even to former Confederates, and that Cardozo's hoped-for judgment was simply an unchristian desire for vengeance. Politics that would conform to God's vision were first of all politics that would leave the spatial status quo intact. These hopeful times, in which black Carolinians could credibly believe in a southern millennium, quickly vanished. A few years later, in the midst of Klan violence, Elias Hill argued that Christian practice could not exist in the U.S. South as he knew it because ex-Confederates would continue to abuse those who practiced true Christianity. Only a transatlantic exodus from slavery, for Hill, could create the conditions by which he and other freedmen and -women might build a millennial society based on universal love.

NOTES

I would like to thank the editors of this volume, as well as Edward Ayers, Robert Jackson, Christopher Loomis, Robert Nelson, Logan Sawyer, Peter Slade, Joshua Yates, and the participants in the Early American Seminar at the University of Virginia, for their patient and helpful readings of various forms of this essay. The Institute for Advanced Studies in Culture at the University of Virginia supported this research.

1. South Carolina, *Proceedings of the Constitutional Convention of South Carolina, Held at Charleston, S.C., Beginning January 14th and Ending March 17th, 1868,* vol. 1 (Charleston: Denny and Perry, 1868; New York: Arno, 1968), 116–18, hereafter *Proceedings* (1868).

2. I use "millennium" and its derivatives in this essay to mean the coming of God's Kingdom into the world and the process by which that Kingdom is brought about, both God's own work of judgment and blessing and the work of men and women to bring about a society marked by harmony and peace. Laurie Maffly-Kipp, *Setting Down the Sacred Past: African American Race Histories* (Cambridge: Harvard University Press, 2010), 9, 11; Timothy Fulop, "'Future Golden Day of the Race': Millennialism and Black Americans in the Nadir, 1877–1901," *Harvard Theological Review,* 84, no. 1 (January 1991): 75–99; Matthew Harper, "Living in God's Time: African-American Faith and Politics in Post-Emancipation North Carolina" (Ph.D. diss., University of North Carolina, 2009), 110–60.

3. Michael Walzer, *Exodus and Revolution* (New York: Basic, 1985), Eddie Glaude Jr., *Exodus! Religion, Race, and Nation in Early Nineteenth-Century Black America* (Chicago: University of Chicago Press, 2000).

4. On space, moral hierarchy, and proximity, see Yi-Fu Tuan, *Space and Place: The Perspective of Experience* (Minneapolis: University of Minnesota Press, 1977), 34–50; Charles Taylor, *Sources of the Self: The Making of Modern Identity* (Cambridge: Harvard University Press, 1989), 25–52, 111–14; Henri Lefebvre, *The Production of Space,* trans. Donald Nicholson-Smith (1974; Malden, Mass.: Blackwell, 1991), 59–65.

5. This essay has benefitted from the work of scholars analyzing "lived theology," with its focus on taking seriously the theological innovations of "everyday saints and sinners." It looks for theological articulations outside religious newspapers, tracts, and ecclesiastical contexts to find how millennial visions infused putatively secular spaces. Charles Marsh, *God's Long Summer: Stories of Faith and Civil Rights* (Princeton, N.J.: Princeton University Press, 1997), 3; Peter Slade, *Open Friendship in a Closed Society: Mission Mississippi and a Theology of Friendship* (Oxford University Press, 2009). On millennial (or utopian) spaces and political economy, see David Harvey, *Spaces of Hope* (Berkeley: University of California Press, 2001), 133–81.

6. Jacqueline Glass Campbell, *When Sherman Marched North from the Sea* (Chapel Hill: University of North Carolina Press, 2003), 58–74; Susan O'Donovan, *Becoming Free in the Cotton South* (Cambridge: Harvard University Press, 2007), 24–34; Ulrich Bonnell Phillips, *American Negro Slavery: A Survey of the Supply, Employment and Control of Negro Labor as Determined by the Plantation Regime* (New York: Appleton, 1918), 205–27; Willie Lee Rose, *Rehearsal for Reconstruction: The Port Royal Experiment* (Indianapolis: Bobbs-Merrill, 1964), 381–82; Simkins and Woody, *South Carolina during Reconstruction* (Chapel Hill: University of North Carolina Press, 1932), 257; "The Stay Law: Letter from Judge Aldrich," *Barnwell (S.C.) Sentinel,* reprinted in *Charleston Daily Courier,* July 6, 1866, quoted in Elizabeth Lee Thompson, *The Reconstruction of Southern Debtors: Bankruptcy after the Civil War* (Athens: University of Georgia Press, 2004), 1.

7. Roger L. Ransom and Richard Sutch, *One Kind of Freedom: The Economic Consequences of Emancipation* (New York: Cambridge University Press, 1977), 52; these figures may have been conservative. See Gavin Wright, *Old South, New South: Revolutions in the Southern Economy since the Civil War* (Baton Rouge: Louisiana State University Press, 1986), 19. On the vexed question of the extent of Sherman's destruction, see Campbell, *When Sherman Marched North;* John Bennett Walters, "General William T. Sherman and Total War," *Journal of Southern History* 14, no. 4 (November 1948): 447–80; Mark Grimsley, *The Hard Hand of War: Union Policy toward Southern Civilians, 1861–1865* (New York: Cambridge University Press, 1995); Charles Royster, *The Destructive War: William Tecumseh Sherman, Stonewall Jackson, and the Americans* (New York: Knopf, 1991); and Edward Caudill, *Sherman's March in Myth and Memory* (Lanham: Rowman and Littlefield, 2008), 75–79.

8. Carol K. Rothrock Bleser, *The Promised Land: The History of the South Carolina Land Commission, 1869–1890* (Columbia: University of South Carolina Press, 1969), 4–5; E. Merton Coulter, *The South during Reconstruction, 1865–1877* (Baton Rouge: Louisiana State University Press, 1947), 10; Rose, *Rehearsal for Reconstruction.*

9. Rose, *Rehearsal for Reconstruction,* 350–52.

10. Eric L McKitrick, *Andrew Johnson and Reconstruction* (New York: Oxford University Press, 1988), 144–45; Rose, *Rehearsal for Reconstruction,* 352–53; Mary Ames, *From a New England Woman's Diary in Dixie in 1865* (Springfield Mass.: Plimpton, 1906), 95–96; Leon Litwack, *Been in the Storm*

So Long (New York: Knopf, 1979) 405; Edward Magdol, *A Right to the Land: Essays on the Freedmen's Community* (Westport, Conn.: Greenwood, 1977), 160–64.

11. Ames, *Diary in Dixie,* 96; Committee of Freedmen on Edisto Island, South Carolina, to the Freedmen's Bureau Commissioner, and the Latter's Reply, October 20 or 21, 1865, and October 22, 1865, in *Freedom: A Documentary History of Emancipation, 1861–1867,* ser. 3, vol. 1, *Land and Labor, 1865,* by Steven Hahn et al. (Chapel Hill: University of North Carolina Press, 2008), 440–42.

12. Ames, *Diary in Dixie,* 96; Steven Hahn, *A Nation under Our Feet: Black Political Struggles in the Rural South from Slavery to the Great Migration,* 136–38; Harper, "God's Time," 110–60.

13. Walter Johnson, *Soul by Soul: Inside the Antebellum Slave Market* (Cambridge: Harvard University Press, 2001), 26–27; Gavin Wright, *The Political Economy of the Cotton South: Households, Markets, and Wealth in the Nineteenth Century* (New York: Norton, 1978), 144–46; William J. Cooper, "The Cotton Crisis in the Antebellum South: Another Look," *Agricultural History* 49, no. 2 (April 1975): 381–91; Thompson, *Southern Debtors,* 5; Scott A. Sandage, *Born Losers: A History of Failure in America* (Cambridge: Harvard University Press, 2005), 208–12; Charles Warren, *Bankruptcy in United States History* (1935; New York: Da Capo, 1972), 106–8; Richard Holcomb Kilbourne Jr., *Debt, Investment, Slaves: Credit Relations in East Feliciana Parish, Louisiana, 1825–1885* (Tuscaloosa: University of Alabama Press, 1995), 75–80; Dan T. Carter, *When the War Was Over: The Failure of Self-Reconstruction in the South, 1865–1867* (Baton Rouge: Louisiana State University Press, 1985) 102–3, 142; David Silkenat, "Suicide, Divorce, and Debt in Civil War–Era North Carolina" (Ph.D. diss., University of North Carolina, 2007).

14. Roger L. Ransom, *One Kind of Freedom,* 52–54; James L. Orr to O. O. Howard, July 9, 1866, quoted in Martin Abbott, *The Freedmen's Bureau in South Carolina, 1865–1872* (Chapel Hill: University of North Carolina Press, 1967), 40–41.

15. Thomas Holt, *Black over White: Negro Political Leadership in South Carolina during Reconstruction* (Urbana: University of Illinois Press, 1979), 35.

16. *Proceedings* (1868), 116–17.

17. Eric Foner, *Freedom's Lawmakers: A Directory of Black Officeholders during Reconstruction* (New York: Oxford University Press, 1993), 39–40; William J. Simmons, *Men of Mark: Eminent, Progressive and Rising* (Cleveland, 1887), 428–29; Lerone Bennett Jr., *Black Power U.S.A., the Human Side of Reconstruction, 1867–1868* (Baltimore: Penguin, 1969), 157–58.

18. Richard Gergel and Belinda Gergel, "'To Vindicate the Cause of the Downtrodden': Associate Justice Jonathan Jasper Wright and Reconstruction in South Carolina," in *At Freedom's Door: African American Founding Fathers and Lawyers in Reconstruction South Carolina,* ed. James Lowell Underwood and W. Lewis Burke Jr. (Columbia: University of South Carolina Press, 2000), 38; F. L. Cardozo to George Whipple and M. E. Streiby, August 18, 1865, American Missionary Association Archives, Amistad Research Center, Dillard University, New Orleans (hereafter AMAA); Thomas Cardozo to "My Dear Friends in the Rooms," August 17, 1865, AMAA; Joe M. Richardson, "Francis L. Cardozo: Black Educator during Reconstruction," *Journal of Negro Education* 48, no. 1 (Winter 1979): 73–83.

19. F. L. Cardozo to George Whipple and E. M. Streiby, December 2, 1865, AMAA; Richardson, "Cardozo," 78–79; *Proceedings of the Colored People's Convention of the State of South Carolina, Held in Zion Church, Charleston, November, 1865. Together with the Declaration of Rights and Wrongs; An Address to the People; A Petition to the Legislature, and a Memorial to Congress* (Charleston: South Carolina Leader, 1865), 7, hereafter *Colored People's Convention* (1865).

20. See Holt, *Black over White,* 127–28.

21. Tunde Adeleke, "Afro Americans and Moral Suasion: The Debate in the 1830s," *Journal of Negro History* 83, no. 2 (Spring 1998): 127–42; Howard H. Bell, "The American Moral Reform Society, 1836–1841," *Journal of Negro Education* 27, no. 1 (Winter 1958): 34, 39; R. G. Dun & Co., vol. 79, p. 131, in Juliet E. K. Walker, "Racism, Slavery, and Free Enterprise: Black Entrepreneurship in the United States before the Civil War," *Business History Review* 60, no. 3 (Autumn 1986): 353. By 1853, Dun & Co. estimated the elder Whipper's worth at twenty thousand dollars.

22. J. R. Oldfield, "A High and Honorable Calling: Black Lawyers in South Carolina, 1868–1915," in *A Question of Manhood: A Reader in U.S. Black Men's History and Masculinity,* ed. Darlene Clark Hine and Earnestine Jenkins (Bloomington: Indiana University Press, 2001), 190; "The Ruined Ballot Box," letter to editor, *Anti-Slavery Bugle,* April 23, 1859, in *Black Abolitionist Papers, 1830–1865* 11:698; Carole Ione, *Pride of Family: Four Generations of American Women of Color* (New York: Summit, 1991), 164; John E. Vacha, "The Case of Sara Lucy Bagby, A Late Gesture," *Ohio History* 76, no. 3 (1976): 222–24; William F. Cheek, *John Mercer Langston and the Fight for Black Freedom, 1829–65* (Urbana: University of Illinois Press, 1996), 373–74; William Seraile, *New York's Black Regiments during the Civil War* (New York: Routledge, 2001) 84; Frederick H. Dyer, *A Compendium of the War of the Rebellion* (New York: T. Yoseloff, 1959), 3:1727; *Proceedings* (1868), 130.

23. Ione, *Pride of Family,* 130–32, 162; Foner, *Freedom's Lawmakers,* 227; James H. Tuten, *Lowcountry Time and Tide* (Columbia: University of South Carolina Press, 2010); Eric Foner, *Nothing but Freedom* (Baton Rouge: Louisiana State University Press, 1983), 91.

24. Ione, *Pride of Family,* 164–66; Foner, *Reconstruction,* 360–61; "Piety at Charleston," *Anti-Slavery Bugle,* October 30, 1858, *Black Abolitionist Papers, 1830–1865,* 11:394; Holt, *Black over White,* table 5; *Proceedings* (1868), 148. Of the twelve wealthiest delegates of color in the convention, six voted with Whipper and six voted with Cardozo on the issue of debt relief.

25. *Proceedings* (1868), 122, 124–25, 127–31.

26. *Colored People's Convention* (1865), 13, 16

27. *Proceedings* (1868), 122–23

28. Ibid., 125.

29. *Proceedings* (1868), 130, 148; Holt, *Black over White,* 129. The final vote was 57–52.

30. Allen W. Trelease, *White Terror: the Ku Klux Klan Conspiracy and Southern Reconstruction* (New York: Harper and Row: 1971), 402; William McFeely, *Grant: A Biography* (New York: Norton, 1981) 367–68; Amos T. Akerman to Gen. Alfred Terry, November 18, 1871, Akerman, Letter Books of Amos Tappan Akerman, 1871–1876, Accession #1165, Albert and Shirley Small Special Collections Library, University of Virginia, Charlottesville.

31. United States, Congress, *Joint Select Committee on Condition of Affairs in the Late Insurrectionary States, Report of the Joint Select Committee Appointed to Inquire into the Condition of Affairs in the Late Insurrectionary States, so Far as Regards the Execution of the Laws, and Safety of the Lives and Property of the Citizens of the United States and Testimony Taken, South Carolina,* 1872 (hereafter *KKK Report*). 1348.

32. Ibid., 1410; John Fabian Witt, *Patriots and Cosmopolitans: Hidden Histories of American Law* (Cambridge: Harvard University Press, 2007) 128–29.

33. *KKK Report,* 1406–8

34. Ibid., 1412–13; 1410.

35. Ibid., 1412; "A Remarkable Man for Liberia," *African Repository,* 47, no. 9 (September 1871): 280; Edward W. Blyden, "Visit to Arthington," *African Repository* 65, no. 2 (April 1889): 44.

36. "Departure of our Fall Expedition," *African Repository* 47, no. 12 (December 1871): 353, 356–60; *KKK Report,* 1410; Witt, *Patriots and Cosmopolitans,* 131, 135; *KKK Report,* 411.

37. Elias Hill, "Letter from Rev. Elias Hill," *African Repository* 48, no. 4 (April 1872): 116.

10

"TWO DIVISIONS OF THE SAME GREAT ARMY"

Ecclesiastical Separation by Race and the Millennium

CHARLES F. IRONS

In the decades before the Civil War, white southern evangelicals worked strenuously to bring black southerners into their churches. They succeeded to a remarkable degree, in some states bringing more than one-half of the enslaved and free black populations into congregations controlled by whites. Writing in 1908, Rev. J. A. Whitted depicted the escape of African American Baptists in North Carolina from these forcibly integrated religious communions following the Civil War as an eschatological event, rejoicing that Carolina blacks at last had their prayers answered and were able to "worship God under [their] own vine and fig tree." While the pioneering black Baptist historian described independent black worship as fulfillment of the millennial prophecies in Micah chapter 4, however, he also made room in his account for black believers who remained in white-controlled churches.[1] Referring specifically to a Raleigh congregation, he acknowledged that "when the time came for a separation," there were some black Baptists who "refused to go out from their white brethren, and remained with them for several years afterward." Whitted even conceded that there were some men and women who *never* completed the ecclesiastical exodus. "So strong was the relation" between some blacks and whites, he added, "that many retained their membership among the white brethren until their death."[2] Whitted thus described the millennial landscape in racially complex terms, populated by both independent black congregations and biracial, white-controlled churches. While the minister and historian wrote from a distance of more than forty years and had his own reasons for offering charitable words for whites in the 1880s, Whitted was nonetheless writing in an established tradition.[3] From the earliest days after emancipation, southern black evangelicals used a version of postmillennialism to frame their ecclesiastical choices in such a way as to minimize conflict both among African Americans and between black and white believers.

The African American Baptists who comprised a majority of churched black southerners rarely described their views on the millennium in formal theological treatises, especially in the chaotic months following the Civil War. Scholars who have written about black millennial theology have therefore tended to focus on northern blacks and on a later period. Timothy Fulop, to cite only the most prominent example, surveyed black millennialism from 1877 through 1901 and drew his evidence primarily from northern divines.[4] But historians have begun to explore southern freedpeople's eschatology and have demonstrated the value of extending the analysis of millennialism and providentialism to the newly emancipated as well. Matthew Harper and Scott Nesbit, for example, have even suggested that understanding black southerners' theological commitments is the key to understanding their political sensibilities during Reconstruction. In Harper's estimation, black southerners' conviction that God was using them to help bring about the millennium "guided their collective action from emancipation to the beginning of the Jim Crow era."[5] Harper concentrates primarily on partisan politics, but some of the first and most important collective actions that freedpeople undertook were ecclesiastical rather than political—none more important than the formation of independent black-run churches. While there are several fine studies of the process through which southern black churchgoers withdrew from white-controlled congregations following the Civil War, scholars who have examined ecclesiastical separation by race have not tended to give attention to black eschatology.[6] Whitted's use of imagery from Micah, however, is a reminder that many black churchgoers understood the formation of independent churches as a development with significance for the future, and this essay represents a step toward recapturing how and with what consequences freedpeople placed themselves in a divine narrative swiftly winding to its conclusion.

Black Baptists did not always conform their ideas about the millennium to conventional theological categories. In the early Reconstruction period, they tended to agree that God was working in history through human agents to build a more just, equitable society, making their perspective functionally postmillennialist. Despite this emphasis on the dawning of a new, divinely sanctioned social order, however, black southerners in the immediate postwar period did not provide many details about when and how that order would unfold. In this sense, it is difficult to distinguish postwar black optimism in general from more theologically grounded understandings of an approaching millennium. As Harper concedes, black eschatology was ultimately more about hope for the future than a specific timeline for Christ's return. He nonetheless labels African Americans' postwar outlook as a form of postmillennialism and discerns in it two defining expectations of freedpeople: "an end to race prejudice and a special role for the African race within Christian history."[7] Though her subjects are largely northern authors, Laurie Maffly-Kipp concurs that black Americans at the time believed that "as a community," they "would play a central role in the steady progress toward the end of time." She suggests that in the late nineteenth century, as white violence escalated, black divines retained their millennial sensibilities but came to disagree as to whether racial distinctions would endure at the end of human history.[8] This question about the role of racial distinctions in the millennium is an important one, for it clarifies the theological implications of black southerners' actions vis-à-vis the formation of independent churches. When they decided whether to form independent churches, African American Baptists asked themselves how racial separation, in worship of all places, might be a part of God's plan for a perfectly just, perfectly reconciled world.

Black Baptists in Virginia and North Carolina, the two states from which the evidence in this account is drawn, adopted a millennial framework for thinking about racial separation that justified division but also left considerable room for interracialism. Specifically, they expressed confidence in the gradual resolution of mankind's thorniest problems (including interracial conflict) and emphasized the need to invest in evangelism and education in order to hasten the fulfillment of human history. Black Baptists recognized both independent and biracial churches as potential paths to racial reconciliation, a move that alleviated conflict among one another about whether or not to leave white-controlled churches. Furthermore, since black Baptists perceived both practical and theological reasons to continue cooperating with white Baptists, they typically left biracial churches without permanently condemning whites. After separation, African Americans proved willing to collaborate with even openly racist whites on evangelism and education. For their part, southern white Baptists did not attribute millennial significance to emancipation or to the ecclesiastical changes that followed. As Daniel Stowell, Charles Wilson, and others have pointed out, white southerners generally regarded the war and Reconstruction as seasons of chastisement for God's chosen people rather than decisive steps toward the *telos* of human history.[9] Nonetheless, dispirited whites facilitated African Americans' formation of a distinctive form of millennialism by accepting black initiatives to divide churches by race and by entertaining the hope that independent black churches would accelerate the conversion of other black southerners.

Freedpeople made ecclesiastical choices after Appomattox that challenge some elements of Reconstruction historiography while affirming others. Enough black southerners chose to remain either in the same church with whites or in jurisdictions sanctioned by whites, for instance, to qualify the academy's emphasis on freedpeople's search for autonomy as they "looked out from slavery."[10] The diverse choices former slaves made about where to worship, meanwhile, affirm scholars' increasing awareness of divisions within postwar black communities.[11] Likewise, attention to the persistent efforts churchgoing blacks made to remain in relationship with churchgoing whites extends our understanding of interracialism, especially within religious spaces.[12] Finally, the fact that at least a few black southerners translated their postmillennial views into an integrationist, optimistic political program illuminates for historians yet another way in which Americans' religious sensibilities shaped their understandings of citizenship and belonging in the postwar period.[13]

There were limits to the extent to which African American Baptists could reduce conflict over church separation by appealing to shared millennial concepts. For one thing, black churchgoers who shared a similar theology with one another might nonetheless differ as to how best to conduct ecclesiastical relations with whites. Even those who believed that a more egalitarian "millennial dawn" was spreading, for instance, might still disagree about the possibility for short-term improvement of their position within white-dominated churches or about the prudence of separating from whites. Furthermore, though it is beyond the scope of this paper, there is considerable evidence that the "theological big tent" regarding ecclesiastical separation shriveled as the racial politics of Reconstruction intensified. After an initial burst of black religious organizational activity in 1866 and 1867, the pace of growth of black churches slowed somewhat through 1870, when it rapidly accelerated again. The experience of electoral politics and the withdrawal of white northerners from the South confirmed for the remnant of black southerners within biracial churches what a majority of churched blacks had already realized—that the millennium was a long way off if reckoned by the racist attitudes of white Americans. By 1870, black southerners in separate churches responded to the terror of white violence and to disappointment from the departure from the region of most of their white, northern allies by questioning the religious sensibilities of those African Americans who remained in faith communities with whites.[14]

The fact that a significant minority of black Baptists in Virginia and North Carolina continued to worship with whites through at least 1867 indicates that freedmen were not unanimous in their expectations for postemancipation race relations. Scholars such as Steven Hahn have suggested that many black southerners failed to create independent churches for several years primarily because they lacked the "opportunities and resources" to do so (access to a meeting site or a minister, for example).[15] Hahn's claim is likely accurate in some instances, especially for the rural areas on which he focused. But the piecemeal pace at which black men and women withdrew from individual congregations—that is, from situations in which they possessed both the opportunity and the resources to strike out on their own—is sufficient proof that black choices were at least as determinative as more practical barriers in restricting the flow of black members out of white churches. Not all black Baptists agreed that racial solidarity and separation was the best policy for freedmen to pursue at the outset of Reconstruction.

Scenarios like that which played out in Hephzibah Baptist Church outside of Wendell, North Carolina, revealed fault lines within black communities on how closely freedpeople should fellowship with whites. In 1866, white members "agreed that the church grant her colored members a letter in a body and constitute them into a separate church." More than three-quarters of the black members promptly formed Good Hope Baptist Church, but more than forty still remained with the whites in Hephzibah as late as 1872.[16] Similarly large contingents of African Americans left Buck Marsh and Mill Swamp Baptist Churches in Southside Virginia between 1867 and 1868, but between 10 and 15 percent of black members stayed in those churches indefinitely.[17] Twenty-eight black men and women from Southampton and Isle of Wight Counties actually joined white-controlled Tucker Swamp Baptist Church in October 1867, yet another instance suggesting that inertia and poverty were not the only things keeping black members in white-dominated churches at substantial levels in the months following the war.[18]

According to church records, in fact, at least one-third of southern black Baptists hesitated for two or more years before transferring their membership to an all-black church. There were slightly more than fifty thousand black Baptists in full membership in Virginia in 1860, and the State General Association calculated that twenty-eight thousand had gone out by 1867 (leaving approximately 44 percent).[19] The Portsmouth and Dover Associations had contained the state's storied semi-independent black churches before the war, several of which boasted more than one thousand members by 1860. These associations experienced the most significant losses of black members when these large congregations quickly shifted from semi-independence to full autonomy.[20] For churches that were already semi-independent, there appear to have been fewer relational or theological barriers to separation. North Carolina boasted fewer semi-independent black Baptist churches, and the number of black Baptists who remained in white-dominated churches after the war was correspondingly higher. For instance, in 1867, the Chowan Baptist Association retained 1,726 of the 3,175 black members it listed in 1861 (54 percent); Cape Fear Baptist Association documented an increase in the number of black members from 656 in 1860 to 708 in 1867 (a gain of 8 percent); and the Raleigh Baptist Association still had 818 of its 883 antebellum black members in 1867 (93 percent).[21] That so many North Carolina and Virginia African Americans were not ready to leave their antebellum churches helps to explain why most black Baptists adhered to an understanding of the end times that had a place for both integrated and racially homogeneous churches.[22]

White Baptists aided in the formation of an African American version of millennialism broad enough to reduce conflict among blacks and between whites and blacks in two related ways. First, whites accepted separation between the races as an arrangement consistent with good order and Gospel principles. When whites not only granted blacks' petitions for autonomy but also gave clerical assistance and donations of property to fledgling black churches, many black witnesses saw white charity for the first time and had reason to be especially sanguine about the future. Second, whites provided theological ways of understanding separation as a spiritual advance, one that would hasten the universal conversion that was a hallmark of the millennium. In each of these instances, whites might have imagined a millennium with more racial hierarchies intact than did their black coreligionists, but these differences did not prevent whites and blacks from finding common ground in the midst of the potentially volatile process of ecclesiastical division.

White Baptists in North Carolina and Virginia allowed, and ultimately encouraged, blacks to strike out on their own ecclesiastically. An astoundingly high proportion of black Baptists who wanted separate churches sought whites' sanction for the new congregations, and whites explicitly and repeatedly sanctioned separate worship. Whites at the Baptist General Association of Virginia, for instance, devoted considerable time and energy at both their 1865 and 1866 meetings to discussing how to respond to the "sudden and radical changes which have taken place in the relations which existed between the white and colored people, politically and socially." By 1866, white delegates from across were ready to adopt a report offered by Addison Hall, concluding:

> In regard to the separate organization of churches composed of colored people, we think this should be left to their free choice. They should not be compelled to sever their present church relations, nor to disconnect themselves from our congregations, but as it is most likely they will prefer to do so, no hindrance should be thrown in their way, but facilities and encouragements afforded them to accomplish their object. A place in our houses of worship should always be afforded, and material aid be rendered them in building their own houses of worship when they desire it.[23]

North Carolina whites were just as decisive in their acquiescence to separation. In May 1866, delegates to their state convention resolved that "whenever the numbers and abilities are sufficient, the colored members in our churches should be encouraged and assisted to organize separate and independent churches and Associations."[24] Those whites in North Carolina's twenty-odd local associations who had not already passed similar resolutions in advance of the state convention's action generally did so within a year.[25]

White Baptists affirmed the policy of separation when dealing with members of individual churches. Black Baptists in Hampton, Virginia, began meeting independently of white church members at the same time that they asked formal permission of their parent church to do so. A special committee from the Dover Association "recommended, that inasmuch as the colored members have organized themselves into a distinct body, they may be dismissed from said church, excepting such as may voluntarily declare their preference for their former connection."[26] The course that whites and blacks in North Carolina's Mud Creek Missionary Baptist Church pursued in the fall and winter of 1867–68 appears to have been even more collaborative than was that in Hampton. On January 5, 1868, "According to previous arrangement, a meeting was held at the Baptist House of worship in this place for the purpose of organizing a church composed of the colored members by the Hendersonville Baptist Church, regularly dismissed therefrom a few months since for the said purpose." White

Elder N. Bowen presided over the meeting and extended the new congregation the right hand of fellowship. "Being thus formally organized and recognized," the church then proceeded to elect deacons to be ordained at a future date by a white presbytery.[27]

White Baptists routinely assisted black Baptists in acquiring a place to build new sanctuaries, which was a powerful gesture in the ravaged postwar South. In one sample of thirty-seven black Baptist churches in North Carolina founded in 1868 or earlier, white Baptists donated the land on which ten of the congregations built their churches. The actual incidence of white bequests may have been higher, as not every church preserved information about the origin of its land.[28] Sometimes, as in the case of Keathern Baptist Church, "the old building was given to the negroes" when whites moved to a new structure. White-controlled churches acted corporately in other ways as well. In Forestville Baptist Church, whites "met and drew up plans to give these negroes [who had been members of their congregation] a church site," and in Hephzibah Baptist Church, whites raised and donated twenty-five dollars "to the colored brethren to purchase a church site." At other times, individual white Baptists acted alone. Between Wendell and Zebulon, "a former slave owner, Bill Richardson, gave" to one group of black Carolinians "a small plot of land to be used for church and school." In Salisbury, there was "a white man, a Mr. Dixon, who gave an acre of land for the 'development of colored freedmen forever.'"[29] These examples show two things: first, that black Baptists could point to substantial signs of white charity and second, that a surprising interracialism characterized even the most fundamental act of black ecclesiastical separatism, the act of erecting separate houses of worship.

White Baptists portrayed these new racially separate churches as temporal expedients that would encourage the further Christianization of black southerners, giving a theological rationale for the existence of segregated worship. Some of this thinking had deep roots in the antebellum mission to the slaves, when white evangelicals realized that they were able to recruit more black church members when they allowed those converts some independence.[30] In the middle of the Civil War in 1863, delegates to the Baptist General Association of Virginia voted to accept a report that showed the relationship between white support for antebellum missions to the slaves and postbellum white acceptance of independent black congregations especially clearly. The committee charged with studying the "religious instruction of colored people" reported:

> Some years ago, an experiment was entered upon by our brethren in several cities and towns of Virginia, for organizing the colored members of our churches, into separate worshipping congregations, assembling in a house of worship, owned by trustees, for the use and benefit of such congregations, with a regular pastor, and the privilege of conducting all matters of Gospel discipline among themselves, subject, of course, to the supervision of the church, thus organizing them into separate congregations. This experiment has succeeded far beyond their expectations, and furnishes abundant evidences of the divine favor.[31]

Providence would not have allowed separate churches to produce so many converts, Virginia whites reasoned, if God disapproved of racially homogeneous worship. North Carolina whites also determined at the close of the war that the sort of "evangelical comparative advantage" that racially separate congregations had offered in the mission to the slaves should justify congregations with even more autonomy after emancipation. Writing on behalf of the Sandy Creek Association in September 1865, William White urged other whites to accept the movement by some African Americans for separate churches by observing that "it is a suggestive fact, that colored Churches in our large towns have not only become self-sustaining, but, in many instances, efficient and liberal in sustaining the cause of Home and Foreign Missions."[32]

Even when white Baptists did not necessarily believe that acquiescing in separation would advance the kingdom of God, they were charitable to their separating black coreligionists in an effort to retain control over them. Most whites thought that they needed to retain some influence over black churches in order to prevent them from becoming incubators of social disorder. Whites from Virginia's Albemarle Association in 1866, for instance, freely acknowledged their interest in trying to control the religious education of blacks whether or not separation occurred: "If we properly care for their wants—if with prayerful pains-taking effort, we seek to enlighten their minds and train them to virtuous and religious living, we shall then, as heretofore, have the best working population of the world," they concluded. "But, neglecting these important duties, we shall be constantly surrounded by dangers, the very contemplation of which is appalling."[33] Whites in the Tar Heel State's Sandy Creek Association even more bluntly acknowledged the prudential reasons for wanting to retain influence over their black coreligionists; "Religious instruction will prevent a conflict between the two races, which can only be made harmonious by compulsion or by the influence of holding the same religion," they agreed. "While it may be alleged that this is a more selfish than religious view of the subject, your Committee do not claim for it precedence over the paramount duty of Christians to preach the Gospel to every creature."[34] Whites did not always acknowledge that their perspective was "more selfish than religious," but until whites and blacks became habituated to separation by the 1870s, whites tended to accompany all of their statements endorsing division with proclamations of their intent to continue educating freedmen generally and black ministers in particular, often with codicils warning against northern intervention. Whites in Virginia's Baptist General Association, for instance, pledged in June 1865 "to resist and counteract all influences tending to alienate the confidence and affections of this class of people from the white population."[35]

White Baptists in the Sandy Creek Association penned a rare eschatological discussion of racial separation in an open letter to a black church in 1867. It is likely that whites included such language precisely *because* they were writing for a black audience since whites at that time did not feel the same optimism about the future as did their black coreligionists. Mount Zion Baptist Church, referred to in the letter as "the colored Baptist church in Chapel Hill," was among the first independent black churches in the state and claims a founding date of 1865. The fledgling congregation of black worshippers wrote (probably in early 1867) to Sandy Creek for the association's blessing and guidance. In response, the white leaders of the association not only reiterated their support for independent black churches, but they also described the process of ecclesiastical segregation as part of a providential plan. "This is an important period in the history of the church that we have reached," white Baptists assured the community at Mount Zion; "The church in the South, at least, is, we think, beginning to wake up to a sense of her high and holy mission." The white leaders then went on to describe separation as an undisputed blessing that would enable blacks and whites to help achieve a truly Christian society. "And thus an effectual door, we trust, is opening for us to discharge a duty that we feel we owe you and for you to take a position in which you can labor more effectually in the Lord's vineyard," they exhorted. "We will be two divisions of the same great army evincing our zeal for the Master's cause by laboring separately, when we can, but harmoniously, feeling that we have one common Master, one common Mission and one common Hope—in a word—that we are brethren."[36]

Many black Baptists were willing in the 1860s to accept this rosy characterization of black and white ecclesiastical relations. They accepted that black and white Baptists had certain solidarities based on faith that would only deepen following emancipation. But this millennial sensibility was not simply accommodationist. Since most black Baptists believed that the obliteration of distinctions on the basis of race was an attribute of the Redeemer's kingdom they were helping to build, they felt paradoxically empowered to rebuke white Baptists for racist actions within the church while constrained to respect the ecclesiastical processes of white-dominated churches. Those same white churches, as flawed as they appeared to be in the 1860s, would nonetheless be building blocks in the realization of the beatific vision.

Leading black churchmen in the immediate postwar period chose to believe the best about their white brethren in part because so many of them benefited directly from the patronage of leading southern whites. In an excellent unpublished paper on William Gibbons, the first black pastor of Charlottesville's First African Baptist Church, Scott Nesbit showed that "Gibbons's awareness of his subordination to whites, in law and custom, was the social education that paralleled any formal literacy that Gibbons gained as a child."[37] Most of the first native-born black Baptist leaders in Virginia and North Carolina after emancipation had also enjoyed privileged status under slavery and were enmeshed in patronage relationships with southern whites. Henry Cowan, beyond doubt the most prolific organizer of black churches in North Carolina, had been the body servant of Confederate Gen. Joseph Johnston during the Civil War; John Jasper of Virginia—later the most famous minister of either race in the Commonwealth and a cofounder of the Colored Shiloh Baptist Association—preached in hospitals at the request of the Confederate government and, according to his white biographer, "had grown up with that pleasing pride that the coloured people who lived in prominent families had about white people"; and Richmond's James H. Holmes, first black pastor of the largest Protestant church in the nation, was a protégé of proslavery ideologue Robert Ryland.[38] Another North Carolina black Baptist leader, L. W. Boon—cofounder of the state convention in 1867 and missionary to blacks in the northeastern portion of the state—also enjoyed the special confidence and patronage of white Baptists, who commissioned him as early as 1866 as a special missionary to black Carolinians.[39] The confidence southern whites placed in the leadership abilities of these men may help explain why the first cohort of native-born black leaders was able to assert the necessity of ecclesiastical segregation without impugning too much the spiritual integrity of the whites in whose churches they had felt so oppressed. Indeed, few black Virginians or North Carolinians declared that they were leaving white-dominated churches because of whites' apostasy.[40]

Another important reason why African American Baptist leaders were willing to give their white coreligionists the benefit of the doubt was because they had credible evidence that God was changing the hearts of white Baptists and swiftly bringing His kingdom to fruition—and that God had given black southerners a central role in the process of redeeming white Americans. For generations afterward, black Christians would regard emancipation as incontrovertible evidence that God had intervened directly on behalf of black Americans, representing both a great work accomplished and an invitation for freedmen to participate in the further process of redemption.[41] North Carolina freedman Friday Jones, for instance, firmly believed that God had directed Abraham Lincoln's steps: "No other man did the will of God as he did; it seemed as if he was intended to liberate us. He arose and declared that slavery should be abolished. This was power that God gave him. His heart failed him, but God pressed him on." Moreover, Jones understood that emancipation created special responsibilities for freedpeople, exhorting individual readers of his short biography to believe in God and exhorting blacks that, "All that we can do is to live close to the cross as a race."[42] At a meeting in June 1865 in still-smoldering Richmond, black Virginians meeting to organize the Colored Shiloh Baptist Association also acknowledged God's hand in emancipation and invoked a steady stream of millennial images. They compared themselves to the Israelites released from captivity to rebuild the temple under Nehemiah, to Israelites on the day of Jubilee, and—in one memorable instance—to Simeon after the birth of Jesus. All were confident that, after a long delay, the Gospel was breaking loose in Virginia "in all the refulgence of the Redeemer's kingdom."[43]

Northern black ministers who came south to help organize new churches, many of whom had southern roots, shared the integrationist perspective of many of the highly acculturated southern blacks with whom they worked. Even when they helped black southern Baptists to separate from their white coreligionists, these ministers insisted publicly that integration in just terms, rather than problack nationalist self-determination, was their object. Many ministers, such as Virginia-born Peter Randolph, thus pursued an apparently paradoxical course of preaching integration and achieving separation. Randolph returned to his native state from Massachusetts as soon after Appomattox as possible for the express purpose of helping to organize black churches. Though an interloper of sorts, he nonetheless served as the delegated spokesman for Richmond's black Baptists in their initial discussions with Richmond's white Baptists about how much separation blacks hoped to achieve. Richmond whites initially made a bid to keep African American Baptists in association with them. On behalf of his brethren, Randolph agreed, provided, "*First,* that they would take back all they had claimed and said against the Baptists of the North. And *second,* that they would meet us as Christian brethren, and not as slaves." In sum, Randolph claimed that there would be no need for separation if whites acknowledged black equality.[44] Whites could not accept these terms, and so black Baptists from Virginia's capital city promptly formed their own churches and association.

African American Baptists for the first several years after emancipation consistently demanded that whites treat them as equals as a condition of continued fellowship, though few were as bold as early as Randolph. Within white-controlled churches, some of the black protests remain murky and appear in the records only as "general disaffection of the colored membership."[45] At other times, especially when all-black associations gave black Baptists a venue in which to speak more freely, the issue was more pointed. In 1870, a select committee from the Colored Shiloh Baptist Association consisting of leading men from across Virginia—William Troy, James H. Holmes, I. W. Smith, William McKenzie, Spencer Green, and George N. Corprew—discussed how to respond to the fact that whites demanded access to black churches' pulpits without being willing to reciprocate. Citing a passage that had been a favorite of black and white abolitionists (Acts 17:26), the group made a bold stand against racism within the broader church:

> WHEREAS the Word of God declares that God has made of one blood all the nations of men who dwell on the face of the earth, thereby acknowledging the natural equality of the creation of all men: therefore, Resolved, That it is the sense of this Association that it is a condescension of manhood and ministerial dignity for the ministers of this Association to invite into their pulpits those who will not extend the same courtesy to them, the color alone being the excuse or barrier, and not the prejudices of their congregations.

Black Baptists were striving for justice within a millennial framework that empowered them to make stands against whites while obligating them to maintain contact with whites and to respect the authority of bigoted white churchmen. The day following the bold resolution above, one of the Shiloh Association's gifted preachers, E. G. Corprew, occupied the pulpit of the white First Baptist Church in Charlottesville, and the clerk of the black association entered into the minutes the conviction that such interracialism was part of God's plan: "He also desires to say that his heart was filled with joy at the good feeling that was manifested between the white and colored people at Charlottesville, and sincerely desires to see that spirit of brotherly love and friendly intercourse pervade the entire State."[46] Members of North Carolina's Cedar Grove Association, one of the first black associations in that state, also tried to balance firm convictions about human equality with an olive branch for well-meaning whites. In a brief published address to the world, they praised God for his providential delivery from slavery and called African Americans to a ministry of reconciliation. "We believe that it is the duty of all professing Christians to show by their lives and works that they are what they profess to be, the colored in particular. Therefore, we hope that our colored brethren will exhibit no unkindness toward our white friends; yet, while wishing all mankind well, they are opposed to any white person's having the whole control of the colored Churches, but gladly receive advice from all."[47]

Blacks who did form independent churches did not hastily sever all ecclesiastical ties with whites and instead preserved several tangible signs of unity. North Carolina black Baptists invited whites to help them organize their state convention in 1867, for instance, an act of deference and goodwill noted with pleasure by the (white) secular press.[48] In Nelson County, Virginia, members of the newly formed Hebron Baptist Church voted in 1867 to continue to be represented in the white Albemarle Baptist Association by delegates chosen from the white church from which they had withdrawn. Whites regarded the request as a "manifestation of returning confidence and affection on the part of our colored brethren towards their white brethren."[49] Black Baptists' persistent willingness to retain or develop new formal relationships with white Baptists, despite repeated humiliations, is astounding. In 1873, for instance, a white minister visiting the annual meeting of the Colored Shiloh Baptist Association expressed regret that white Baptists had refused to seat a black delegate at the previous year's General Association meeting (it is not clear if this expression of regret rose to the level of an apology). The African American Baptists did not retaliate but promised that their doors were "always open" for interracial cooperation on the grounds of equality. Then, R. Wells, the very man who had been denied a seat at the General Association meeting, "said[,] let the past be buried. Our hearts and hands are opened to our white brethren. He hoped the time would soon come when all distinction on account of color in the Christian church will have passed away."[50]

Enough white northerners acted as if "distinctions on account of color" were passing away to sustain hope among African Americans that white southerners might also be redeemed. White northerners may not have been able to organize many churches among freedpeople in the South, but they did provide very substantial support for and leadership of educational initiatives. Black Baptists in North Carolina and Virginia each placed enormous stock in education (so much that they deemed it "the handmaid of Religion in the great work of receiving immortal souls from the thralldom of sin"), and white northerners worked with black southerners to found biracial institutions devoted to the education of black ministers. The North Carolina state convention officially supported Shaw University, and white northern Baptist and Shaw founder H. M. Tupper was a welcome member of the education board of the convention, pastor of a black church, and friend to all.[51] Despite the involvement of proslavery white minister Robert Ryland, black Virginia Baptists resolved in 1870, "That we favorably recommend the Colver Institute of Richmond to our ministers, and beg them to avail themselves of the advantages of this institution. We also recommend the Rev. J. C. Corey, principal of the above named school, as an efficient teacher, full of zeal and love for the cause of humanity and education."[52] Historians now disagree on the proportion of white interlopers in the postbellum South who professed religious motivation for their educational work, but this question is somewhat immaterial to the issue of how black southern evangelicals envisioned possibilities for interracial interaction. For at least a few black southerners, white northerners offered evidence that a more egalitarian order was dawning.[53]

Black Baptists worked not only with white northerners but also with white southerners on evangelism, an issue even more pressing than education for the coming of the millennium. The Gray's Creek Colored Baptist Association in North Carolina was one of several associations that expressed an eagerness to work with whites on African missions, which had been a point of interracial cooperation even before the Civil War. In 1872, based on the biblical promise to "ask of me and I will give thee the heathen for thine inheritance, and the uttermost parts of the earth for thy possession," members of the association "*Resolved*, That we go speedily to work for their recovery from their idols and superstitious worship, by giving of our substance to preach to the benighted land of Africa" and "*Further Resolved,* That we co-operate with the Baptist State Convention and the Southern Baptist Convention in this great work."[54] Members of the same association further demonstrated solidarity with white Baptists by recommending denominational newspapers published by whites in North Carolina and Virginia. These clerics were excited about the *Home and Foreign Journal* because it gave them "information of what is doing in the foreign fields."[55]

Indeed, some of the most prominent black ministers of North Carolina and the Commonwealth continued throughout Reconstruction to behave in ways that only make sense given their religiously inspired commitment to interracialism and their millennial expectations of the future. At times, black Baptists appeared "radical" because of their insistence on human equality, at times "accommodationist" because of their willingness to build partnerships with whites. Fields Cook, a prominent member of Richmond's First African Baptist Church before he took a pastorate in Alexandria, made his grand appearance on the public stage when he went to Washington, D.C., with three others in June 1865 to lodge a formal complaint about the Union Army's treatment of black Richmonders. The group wanted to be sure that "justice was done to all classes" and argued that African Americans were deserving of government protection (and, by extension, citizenship) in part because "more than 6,000 of our people are members in good standing of Christian churches, and nearly our whole population constantly attend divine services."[56] After this brave start, the only common thread in the rest of Cook's public life was a passionate commitment to Christian brotherhood. He was so radical in 1868 that he bolted the more moderate wing of the Republican Party, along with white firebrand and minister James Hunnicutt. Cook and Hunnicutt demanded, among other things, equal opportunity for whites and blacks to hold office. Just a few months later, Cook no longer seemed very radical, however. He was so conservative that he ran afoul of his own party when he fought to preserve voting rights for former Confederates, arguing that "every citizen who wished to unite in reconstructing the State ought to be received and made welcome with us."[57] Cook believed that his willingness to restore voting rights to whites in hopes of creating a color-blind society cost him his political career—and cost Republicans control of Virginia. "Myself and all others who dared speak in favor of the removal of disabilities were denounced as conservatives," he complained, despite the fact that his "views of Republicanism have always been that every man should have equal rights, and hence, the white as well as the black, and the black as well as the white, nothing more, nothing less." Cook then revealed his roots as a minister of the Gospel and his millennial hopes for Virginia, renouncing partisan politics and pledging to "do all I can to convince others to do likewise, as now is the time to have reconciliation and peace in this State. Let us then, black and white, try to make it permanent and forever, is my prayer."[58]

In conclusion, black Baptists held theological positions in the immediate postwar period that justified but did not require the formation of independent black churches. While a majority of black believers commenced after emancipation to build the most important postwar black institutions, churches, others preferred to remain in fellowship with whites. Members of both groups, however, hewed to a millennial vision in which they had a special calling to teach their white coreligionists to embrace human equality and to build a more just church polity. Furthermore, even blacks in separate jurisdictions continued to welcome their white brethren's cooperation and financial assistance on matters of eschatological significance, namely missions and education.

This brief overview of ecclesiastical negotiations following emancipation suggests two new approaches to the study of black southerners' churches. First, the local is far more vital than the global. In order to understand precisely why some freedpeople chose to remain in affiliation with whites while others chose to strike out independently, for example, scholars will need to penetrate below the level of aggregate statistics, and below even the level of individual denominations. They will begin to find meaningful answers, from which they may well be able to make fruitful generalizations, only at the level of individual congregations, townships, and even families.

Second, we must approach churches in a far more sophisticated manner and acknowledge their status as intermediary institutions, simultaneously public and private. In more purely private contexts such as households, freedpeople immediately sought separation from whites after emancipation in order to protect their families from abusive whites. In public venues such as streetcars, railroads, statehouses, and the metaphorical spaces of party politics, freedpeople pursued integration (or at least equal access) because in so doing they laid claim to full citizenship. Freedpeople in the South's churches felt both the push of white condescension and the pull of interracialism. Perhaps more importantly, however, black churchgoers in the postwar period also tried to embody in their religious institutions a vision of the beloved community, one which they hoped would soon become fully realized across the nation and around the world. The new churches they formed, as well as the existing churches they attempted to redeem, offer rich possibilities for the continued study of conflicting black aspirations in the postwar period.

NOTES

1. Micah 4, esp. 4:1–5.

2. J. A. Whitted, *A History of the Negro Baptists of North Carolina* (Raleigh: Edwards and Broughton Printing, 1908), 14–15.

3. Whitted favored accepting funds from white Baptists at the turn of the century, for example, which might have made him depict interracialism more favorably. On the other hand, writing in the "nadir," he knew well that one of the key promises from Micah, that "none shall make them afraid," went unrealized.

4. Timothy E. Fulop, "'The Future Golden Day of the Race': Millennialism and Black Americans in the Nadir, 1877–1901," *Harvard Theological Review* 84, no. 1 (January 1991): 75–99. Fulop focuses most directly on millennialism, but many other scholars have addressed the late-nineteenth-century merger of black nationalism with millennial themes of uplift and progress, with the same general bias toward later and more northern sources. See, for example, Laurie Maffly-Kipp, *Setting Down the Sacred Past: African-American Race Histories* (Cambridge: Belknap Press of Harvard University Press, 2010); Wilson Jeremiah Moses, *The Wings of Ethiopia: Studies in African American Life and Letters* (Ames: Iowa State University Press, 1990), esp. 141–43; David W. Blight, *Frederick Douglass' Civil War: Keeping Faith in Jubilee* (Baton Rouge: Louisiana State University Press, 1989), 8–10, 77, 109–11; and Edward L. Wheeler, *Uplifting the Race: The Black Minister in the New South, 1865–1902* (Lanham, Md.: University Press of America, 1986), esp. 47–50.

5. Matthew J. Z. Harper, "Living in God's Time: African American Faith and Politics in Post-Emancipation North Carolina" (Ph.D. diss., University of North Carolina, 2009), 5. See also the essays by Scott Nesbit and Matthew Harper in this volume.

6. Especially William E. Montgomery, *Under Their Own Vine and Fig Tree: The African American Church in the South, 1865–1900* (Baton Rouge: Louisiana State University Press, 1993); Katharine L. Dvorak, *An African American Exodus: The Segregation of the Southern Churches* (Brooklyn: Carlson, 1991). For more general studies that also treat the separations, see Daniel W. Stowell, *Rebuilding Zion: The Religious Reconstruction of the South, 1863–1877* (New York: Oxford University Press, 1998); and the collected essays in Donald G. Nieman, ed., *Church and Community among Black Southerners, 1865–1900* (New York: Garland, 1994).

7. Harper, "Living in God's Time," 15, 19.

8. Maffly-Kipp, *Sacred Past,* 216.

9. Stowell, *Rebuilding Zion,* 33–48; Charles Reagan Wilson, *Baptized in Blood: The Religion of the Lost Cause, 1865–1920* (Athens: University of Georgia Press, 1980).

10. The long-standing emphasis on black southerners' search for autonomy in Reconstruction historiography reached its apogee in Steven Hahn, *A Nation under Our Feet: Black Political Struggles in the Rural South from Slavery to the Great Migration* (Cambridge: Belknap Press of Harvard Uni-

versity Press, 2003). For the challenge to move beyond an emphasis on black agency, with special attention to religion, see John C. Rodrigue, "Black Agency after Slavery," in *Reconstructions: New Perspectives on the Postbellum United States,* ed. Thomas J. Brown (New York: Oxford University Press, 2006), 40–65.

11. Among scholars of postwar black religion, only a few have offered a sustained discussion of divergent theological reactions to emancipation *within* southern black communities. For an exception, see Reginald Hildebrand, *The Times Were Strange and Stirring: Methodist Preachers and the Crisis of Emancipation* (Durham, N.C.: Duke University Press, 1995).

12. For the antebellum period, Randolph Ferguson Scully, *Religion and the Making of Nat Turner's Virginia: Baptist Community and Conflict* (Charlottesville: University of Virginia Press, 2008); Erskine Clarke, *Dwelling Place: A Plantation Epic* (New Haven: Yale University Press, 2005); Sylvia Frey and Betty Wood, *Come Shouting to Zion: African American Protestantism in the American South and British Caribbean to1830* (Chapel Hill: University of Chapel Hill Press, 1998); Mechal Sobel, *The World They Made Together: Black and White Values in Eighteenth-Century Virginia* (Princeton: Princeton University Press, 1987); John B. Boles, ed., *Masters and Slaves in the House of the Lord: Race and Religion in the American South, 1740–1840* (Lexington: University Press of Kentucky, 1988). For the postwar period, see Paul Harvey, *Freedom's Coming: Religious Culture and the Shaping of the South from the Civil War through the Civil Rights Era* (Chapel Hill: University of North Carolina Press, 2005); and Paul Harvey, *Redeeming the South: Religious Cultures and Racial Identities among Southern Baptists, 1865–1895* (Chapel Hill: University of North Carolina Press, 1997).

13. Derek Chang, *Citizens of a Christian Nation: Evangelical Missions and the Problem of Race in the Nineteenth Century* (Philadelphia: University of Pennsylvania Press, 2010); Harper, "Living in God's Time"; Edward J. Blum, *Reforging the White Republic: Race, Religion, and American Nationalism, 1865–1898* (Baton Rouge: Louisiana State University Press, 2005); Martin, *For God and Race.* See also a parallel study of black benevolent societies in the same period: Stephen Kantrowitz, "'Intended for the Better Government of Man': The Political History of African American Freemasonry in the Era of Emancipation," *Journal of American History* 96, no. 4 (March 2010): 1001–26.

14. Scattered accounts of black southerners refusing to worship with black Democrats are the most unequivocal example of this phenomenon ("Treatment of Negro Bolters," *Documents Relating to Reconstruction,* no. 3, ed. Walter Fleming [Morgantown: West Virginia University, 1904], 35).

15. Hahn, *Nation under Our Feet,* 231

16. "The Churches of the Wake Baptist Association," chap. 10 of *History of the Wake Baptist Association* ed. *Claude R. Trotter (Raleigh: Irving-Swain Press, 1976);* and *Minutes of the Sixty-Seventh Annual Session of the Raleigh Baptist Association . . . 1872.* (Raleigh: Edwards and Broughton, 1872).

17. See *Minutes of the Seventy-Sixth* through *Eightieth Annual Sessions of the Portsmouth Baptist Association* (various publishers, 1867–71).

18. *Minute Book of the Tucker[’s] Swamp Baptist Church, 1858–1906,* Virginia Baptist Historical Society, Richmond.

19. *Minutes of the Baptist General Association of Virginia . . . 1867* (Richmond: Dispatch Steam Power Presses, 1867), 56.

20. Dover did not break down its members by race in 1867 but lost roughly 10,000 of its prewar membership according to its entry in the General Association minutes cited above; Portsmouth recorded 377 black members in 1867, out of an 1860 African American membership of 5,190. For Portsmouth, see *Minutes of the Seventy-Sixth Annual Session of the Virginia Portsmouth Baptist As-*

sociation . . . 1867 ([?]: printed for Rev. C. T. Bailey, 1867). By way of comparison, the Albemarle Association retained 3,102 of its 4,457 black members (*Minutes of the Seventy-Sixth Anniversary of the Albemarle Baptist Association . . . 1867* [Charlottesville: James Alexander, 1867]).

21. *Minutes of the Sixty-First Annual Session of the Chowan Baptist Association . . . 1867* (Raleigh: Hufham & Hughes, 1867); *Minutes of the Annual Session of the Cape Fear Association . . . 1867* (Raleigh: Mills & Hughes, 1867); *Minutes of the Sixty-Second Annual Session of the Raleigh Baptist Association . . . 1867* (Raleigh: Biblical Recorder Publishing Co., 1867).

22. The Methodist Episcopal Church, South, retained 54,172 African American members in 1867, out of 171,857 black members in 1860 (31.5 percent). Totals for the two most important conferences for the area considered in this study were slightly lower; the North Carolina and Virginia Conferences tallied a combined total of 19,113 black members in 1860 but only 4,383 in 1867 (23 percent) (*Minutes of the Annual Conferences of the Methodist Episcopal Church, South for the Years 1860* and *1867* [Nashville: SM Publishing House, 1861, 1867]). In brief, the semi-independent mission churches that Methodists maintained for black members before the war proved especially vulnerable to recruitment by AME and AMEZ missionaries.

23. *Minutes of the Baptist General Association of Virginia . . . 1866* (Richmond: Dispatch Steam Press, 1866), quotations 25 and 26.

24. *Proceedings of the . . . Baptist State Convention, of North Carolina . . . 1866* (Raleigh: Biblical Recorder Book and Job Printing Establishment, 1866), 19.

25. *Minutes of the . . . Chowan Baptist Association . . . 1866* (Raleigh: Biblical Recorder and Job Printing Establishment, 1866), 9; and *Minutes of the One Hundred and Seventh Session of the Sandy Creek Baptist Association . . . 1865* (Raleigh: Biblical Recorder Book and Job Printing Office, 1866),10; for associations that followed the state convention's lead (sometimes citing the state resolution), see *Minutes of the . . . Cape Fear Association . . . 1867*, 5; and *Minutes of the . . . Raleigh Baptist Association . . . 1867*, 9.

26. *Minutes of the 78th, 79th, 80th, 81st and 82d Annual Meetings of the Dover Baptist Association . . . 1862, 1863, 1864, 1865 and 1866. Condensed* (Richmond, Va.: Laughton & Fore, 1866).

27. *Mud Creek Missionary Baptist Church (East Flat Rock, N.C.), 1868*, North Carolina Baptist Historical Society, Winston-Salem. For white ordinations of black ministers, see, for example, *Proceedings of the . . . Cape Fear Baptist Association . . . 1870* (Lumberton, N.C.: Robesonian Office, 1871), 16.

28. See also Harvey, *Redeeming the South*, 49–50.

29. This sample is drawn principally from M. W. Williams and George W. Watkins, *Who's Who among North Carolina Negro Baptists: With a Brief History of Negro Baptist Organizations* (n.p., 1940); Trotter, *History of the Wake Baptist Association;* and *The Centennial Celebration of the Middle District Missionary Baptist Association, 1871–1971* (Wilmington, N.C.: n.p. [1971]), but it is supplemented by a variety of newspaper articles and programs from the vertical files housed in the North Carolina Baptist Historical Society in Winston-Salem, N.C., viz., "Cedar Grove Dedicates New Edifice," *Winston-Salem Chronicle,* August 6, 1998; "New Beginning for Negro Worship Emerges," *Goldsboro News Argus,* April 26, 1985; "First Calvary," *Salisbury Post,* July 21, 2001; Ilong Baptist Church 1993 Directory; "Nazareth Baptist Church Founded Here in 1867," *Asheville Times,* December 15, 1993.

30. Charles F. Irons, *The Origins of Proslavery Christianity: White and Black Evangelicals in Colonial and Antebellum Virginia* (Chapel Hill: University of North Carolina Press, 2008), 169.

31. *Minutes of the Baptist General Association of Virginia, for the Sessions of 1861, 1862, and 1863* (Richmond: MacFarlane & Fergusson, 1863), 77.

32. *Minutes of the . . . Sandy Creek Baptist Association . . . 1865,* 10.

33. *Minutes of the . . . Albemarle Baptist Association . . . 1866* (Charlottesville: James Alexander, 1866), 20.

34. *Minutes of the . . . Sandy Creek Baptist Association . . . 1865,* 10.

35. Quotation from *Minutes of the Baptist General Association of Virginia . . . 1865* (Richmond: Gary & Clemmitt, 1866), 12; see also *Proceedings of the . . . Baptist State Convention, of North Carolina . . . 1865* (Raleigh: Biblical Recorder Book and Job Printing Office, 1866), 16; *Proceedings of the . . . Baptist State Convention, of North Carolina . . . 1866* (Raleigh: Biblical Recorder Book and Job Printing Establishment, 1866), 19; *Minutes of the Baptist General Association of Virginia . . . 1866,* 25–26.

36. *Minutes of the . . . Sandy Creek Baptist Association . . . 1867,* 11. In an internal debate about the merits of separation—i.e., one not intended for black readers—whites were not as confident about the spiritual efficacy (see *Proceedings of the . . . Baptist State Convention, of North Carolina . . . 1867* [Raleigh: Hufham & Hughes, Printers, 1867], 18).

37. Scott Nesbit, "The Education of William Gibbons" (2004), unpublished manuscript in the author's possession.

38. On Cowan, see Whitted, *History of the Negro Baptists,* 11. William E. Hatcher, *John Jasper: The Unmatched Negro Philosopher* (1908; Documenting the American South, 2000), 99. For an excellent discussion of black Richmond leaders indebted to white patronage and therefore more willing to cooperate with whites, see Adolph H. Grundman, "Northern Baptists and the Founding of Virginia Union University: The Perils of Paternalism," *Journal of Negro History* 63, no. 1 (1978): 26–41.

39. *Minutes of the . . . Chowan Baptist Association . . . 1866,* 9, 12.

40. Please contrast the antebellum denunciations of white spiritual integrity, for example, Henry Brown, *Narrative of the Life of Henry Box Brown* (1851; Documenting the American South, 1999).

41. For a recent discussion of how freedpeople interpreted emancipation as divine deliverance, see Daniel L. Fountain, *Slavery, Civil War, and Salvation: African American Slaves and Christianity, 1830–1870* (Baton Rouge: Louisiana State University Press, 2010), 93–114.

42. Friday Jones, *Days of Bondage* (1883; Documenting the American South, 1999), 17–18.

43. *Minutes and Proceedings of the Colored Shiloh Baptist Association of Virginia . . . 1865* (Richmond: Republic Book and Job Office), 5, 9.

44. In his later summary of the ensuing debate, which stretched out over three meetings, Randolph issued one of the most scathing criticisms of southern whites found in the formal record surrounding the creation of new black churches. This gloss postdates the debate itself, and it shows how, by the 1890s, Randolph had moved to a much more strident advocacy of all-black churches. "We chose rather to grope our way in the dark, than to have thrust upon us the kind of preachers we had had in the dark days of slavery, men who could neither sympathize with us, nor preach us the full Gospel" (Peter Randolph, *From Slave Cabin to the Pulpit: The Autobiography of Rev. Peter Randolph: The Southern Question Illustrated and Sketches of Slave Life* [1893; Documenting the American South, 2000], 94–96).

45. *Minutes of the . . . Cape Fear Association . . . 1867,* 17.

46. *Minutes of the . . . Colored Shiloh Baptist Association of Virginia . . . 1870* (Richmond: V. L. Fore, 1870), 11–12, 16.

47. *Proceedings of the State Baptist Convention, Colored, of the State of North Carolina . . . 1870* (Raleigh: W. J. Edwards, 1871), 7.

48. "Quite a Pleasing Event," *Raleigh Register,* October 25, 1867.

49. *Minutes of the . . . Albemarle Baptist Association . . . 1868* (Charlottesville: James Alexander, 1868), 18.

50. *Minutes of the . . . Colored Shiloh Baptist Association of Virginia . . . 1873* (Richmond: Geo. W. Gary, 1873), 7.

51. On support of Shaw, see *Proceedings of the State Baptist Convention, Colored, of the State of North Carolina . . . 1870* (Raleigh: W. J. Edwards, 1871), 8–12; for an associational resolution, see *Minutes of the . . . Shiloh Baptist Association, Col'd. . . . 1875* (Henderson, N.C.: Harrell's Job Office, 1875), 12–13.

52. *Minutes of the . . . Colored Shiloh Baptist Association of Virginia . . . 1870,* 8.

53. The classic work is Joe M. Richardson, *Christian Reconstruction: The American Missionary Association and Southern Blacks, 1861–1890* (Athens: University of Georgia Press, 1986). For the tension over the significance of the role of religion in white northerners' service in the South, see Blum, *Reforging the White Republic,* and Chang, *Citizens of a Christian Nation* on the one hand; and, on the other, Ronald E. Butchart, *Schooling the Freed People: Teaching, Learning, and the Struggle for Black Freedom, 1861–1876* (Chapel Hill: University of North Carolina Press, 2010).

54. *Minutes of the . . . Gray's Creek Colored Association . . . 1872* (Raleigh: Edwards & Broughton, 1872), 9. On black participation in African missions, the best starting place is Sylvia M. Jacobs, ed., *Black Americans and the Missionary Movement in Africa* (Westport, Conn.: Greenwood, 1982).

55. *Minutes of the . . . Gray's Creek Colored Association . . . 1870* (Fayetteville, N.C.: Presbyterian Office, 1870), 5.

56. "The Richmond Freedmen," *New York Tribune,* June 17, 1865.

57. "The Virginia Election," *Daily National Intelligencer,* May 29, 1869.

58. "Why the Radical Party Failed in Virginia," *Charleston Courier,* July 17, 1869. On Reconstruction Richmond and Cook's early role, see Elsa Barkley Brown, "Negotiating and Transforming the Public Sphere: African American Political Life in the Transition from Slavery to Freedom," *Public Culture* 7 (1994): 107–46; and John O'Brien, "Reconstruction in Richmond: White Restoration and Black Protest, April–June 1865," *Virginia Magazine of History and Biography* 89, no. 3 (July 1981): 253.

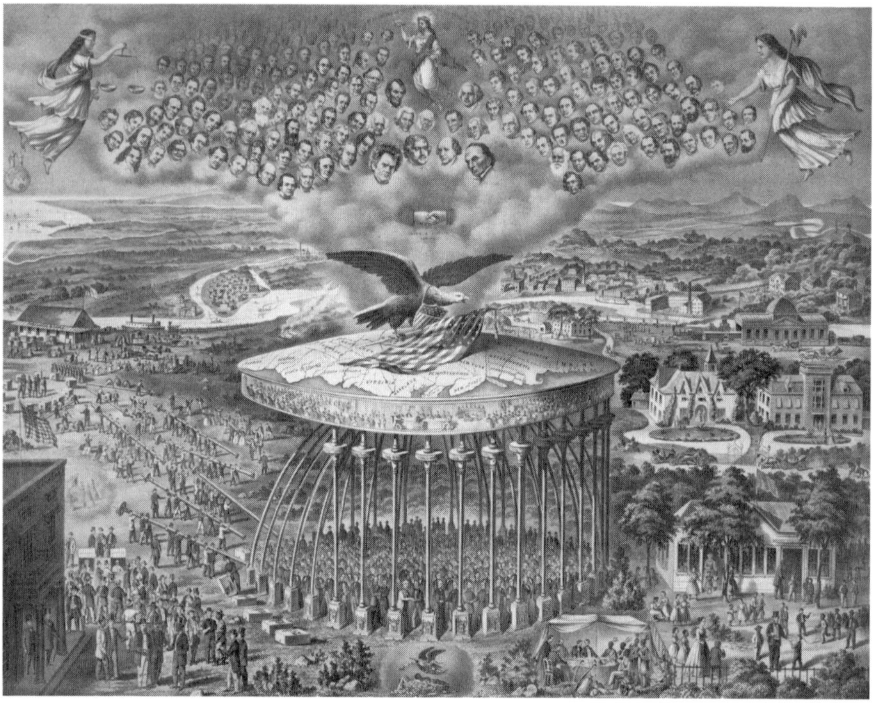

"Reconstruction" was a millennial dream.

Reconstruction, ca.1867, by J. L. Giles. Courtesy of the Library of Congress Prints and Photographs Division Washington, D.C.

11

"TO DOUBT THIS WOULD BE TO DOUBT GOD"

Reconstruction and the Decline of Providential Confidence

EDWARD J. BLUM

"Reconstruction" (1867) was a millennial dream. It was also, in the hands of artists Horatio Bateman and J. L. Giles, a providential prophecy in pictorial form. Printed in 1867 just after Congress had passed the Fourteenth Amendment, this political cartoon imagined a sacred transformation of the United States. The national union of the antebellum era—upheld by pillars of slavery—was undercut first by Confederate secession and then by federal emancipation. The reconstructed nation would be built upon new pillars of justice, liberty, and education. Harmony would replace hate. Northern and southern whites would shake hands on the earth below, and in the sky above, whites from the nation's past would populate heaven. Universal education would link blacks and whites in games and grammar. Universal suffrage would enfranchise African American men, and bodies and souls would be recognized as equal. A white baby and a black baby would coo next to one another in cradles side by side. The eagle of liberty would fly above and protect them carrying a bannered proclamation: "all men are born free and equal."

This vision was far more expansive than most historical accounts of Reconstruction. In addition to the transition from slavery to freedom, the contested political issues of citizenship and suffrage, the importance of education, and the desire for sectional reconciliation, Bateman and Giles incorporated women, Native Americans, technology, and the West. They pictured women in the voting ranks, conjured a United States that would respect Native American rights and dignities, and mapped a successful Reconstruction in the East moving to the West through canals, roads, and railroads. This West, though, was devoid of conflict—from either infamous Indians or polygamous Mormons. This was a millennial manifest destiny that linked white, black, and red, male and female, citizen and student, North and South, East and West.

Even further, Bateman and Giles translated Reconstruction from the natural to the supernatural. Religion was central to their rendering of the new United States. Above their prophesied Reconstruction, in the upper left side, the goddesses of liberty and justice preside over the new world. In the center, Jesus offers political, social, and religious instruction with his golden rule: "DO TO OTHERS AS YOU WOULD HAVE OTHERS DO TO YOU."[1]

Although central to the vision and spirit of "Reconstruction," issues of postwar faith have been largely neglected not only by Reconstruction historians, but also by scholars of American religion. For Eric Foner, religion is something done within churches and by church leaders. For David Blight, religion is something that merely gets mixed with nationalism during civic ceremonies. For Steven Hahn, religion is one element of black political formation, but not elemental to it. For Heather Cox Richardson, religion is effectively unessential. Her pathbreaking *West from Appomattox* discusses the lobster industry of Maine, but not the Latter-day Saints.[2]

While there are some excellent works of religious history on the time period—especially from Paul Harvey, Daniel Stowell, James Moorhead, James Bennett, Charles Reagan Wilson, Reginald Hildebrand, and Clarence Walker—scholars of American religions have yet to connect religion to the crucial issues of the era.[3] A survey of American religious history textbooks shows that Reconstruction hardly gets mentioned, except for the creation of autonomous black churches.[4] Marie Griffith's reader of primary documents on American religions, for example, has five documents on slavery, abolition, and the Civil War, but none on Reconstruction.[5] Specific studies of providentialism and millennialism, such as Nicholas Guyatt's *Providence and the Invention of the United States,* Catherine Albanese's *America: Religions and Religion,* or Ernest Tuveson's *Redeemer Nation,* gloss over Reconstruction in favor of supposedly bigger game like the American Revolution or the Civil War.[6]

But religion was central to Reconstruction, and Reconstruction fundamentally altered religions in the United States. If we follow Bateman and Giles by moving expansively throughout the United States, we find that Reconstruction was a crucial moment in the history of American religions. Religious language, concepts, ideas, and sentiments were key to the debates of the era. Political speeches, soldiers' diaries, political cartoons, labor newspapers, feminist critiques, and oral histories were full of religious expressions and ruminations.

Moreover, the destruction of southern slavery and the rebuilding of the nation compelled new appraisals of faith for nearly all Americans. Because slavery and the nation had been lodged so powerfully and so complexly in the religious cultures of Americans before the war, emancipation and Reconstruction wrought religious adjustments and transformations. The religious changes reverberated throughout the land. From the rural South to the urban North, from those who labored with their hands to those who struggled with their pens, from environmentalists to industrialists, from Democrats to Republicans, from Utah's Mormons to the Ghost Dancers of the Plains, and to the Golden Coast's immigration battles, Americans during and after the Civil War altered their perspectives on God's actions in history, the nation, and the world.

THE SOUTH

Most obviously, emancipation and Reconstruction drastically altered the religions of the South. For African Americans, slavery's end had been prophesied in song, in visions, and with blood. Nat Turner believed that God had called him to arms for freedom's sake. Frederick Douglass found faith in northern flight and came to love the Christianity of Christ and hate "the slaveholding, the woman-whipping, the mind-darkening, the soul-destroying religion that exists in the southern states of America." When liberation came, it seemed a fulfillment of the Exodus narrative and the liberating art of Jesus. Slaves sang out: "Slavery's chain done broke at last, / Going to praise God till I die." In Little Rock, Arkansas, a black minister cheered that God was transforming the sacred geography of the nation: "God has marked it out with his finger; . . . [H]ere, where we have been degraded, will we be exalted."[7] Within years of the war's end, moreover, the vast majority of African Americans religiously voted with their feet. They exited hierarchical biracial churches and joined all-black congregations.[8]

Reconstruction did not result in the exaltation of blacks in the South, however. The dreams of the 1860s devolved into the nightmarish nadir of the 1890s. Yet providential memories, interpretations, and rituals of emancipation stuck with African Americans. As historian Matthew Harper has shown, African Americans in North Carolina wrapped their theological and political worldviews around emancipation. Even after the terrible Wilmington massacre of 1898, African Americans held fast to the power of emancipation. "We have seen gloomier times than the present," Alexander Walters wrote for the *Star of Zion* in December 1898, and "we were brought triumphantly through by the God of battles."[9] Interviews in the 1920s and 1930s with former slaves revealed the longevity of providential understandings of emancipation. Concepts of black agency and God's intervention conjoined into a cosmic explanation for liberty. As one former slave recalled: "When de war was over de people jus' shouted for joy. . . . 'Twas only because of de prayers of de cullud people, dey was freed, and de Lawd worked through Lincoln."[10] Clayborne Gantling explained: "I tell you chile, it was pitiful, but God did not let it last always. I have heard slaves morning and night pray for deliverance. Some of 'em would stand up in de fields or bend over cotton and corn and pray out loud for God to help 'em and in time you see, He did." The experience of the 1860s—that God was present and acting among them—transformed into inspirational memories and prophetic hopes for another sacred invasion.[11]

The belief that providence brought emancipation was not some way of concealing or avoiding human agency. Black providential interpretations never exempted humans from action—either for right or for wrong. African Americans never saw God behaving alone. Providence worked in tandem with human action, and human action could, at times, energize God. The belief that God's intervention was connected to black activity for freedom became a constitutive part of the prophetic hope that David Chappell identified in his study of the political worldviews of African Americans in the civil rights movement. They, as Chappell notes, were "conspicuous for their unwillingness to let social processes work themselves out."[12]

Southern whites, of course, had a much more conflicted relationship with emancipation and Reconstruction. Most wanted neither, and they had vested significant faith in both the institution of slavery and their national independence. First responses to emancipation were ferocious.[13] Southerners demonized Lincoln for his preliminary Emancipation Proclamation of September 1862. They hunkered down to fight longer and harder, and they claimed that if Lincoln had his way, the South would be awash in a racial apocalypse. When both slavery and the Confederacy came crashing down by 1865, many southern whites were left spiritually confused. One white writer recorded, "The first Sunday we went to church the sadness and dreariness of everything was piercing."[14] Ella Gertrude Clanton Thomas was brought to her knees in prayer and defeat in 1865. Abolition showed this Georgian "how intimately my faith in revelations and my faith in the institution of slavery had been woven together—true I had seen the evil of the latter but if the *Bible* was right then slavery *must be*— Slavery was done away with and my faith in God's Holy Book was terribly shaken. For a time I doubted God. The truth of revelations, all—everything."[15]

Since slavery was lodged in the heart of southern white religions, emancipation necessitated religious responses. Military loss led some to wonder if God was on their side.[16] Southern whites groped to find God's meaning. Even before the war was over, a Lost Cause ideology was emerging that explained defeat as God's chastening. Although slavery was rarely given as an example of southern sins, there was a growing sense that perhaps God desired the removal of slavery. "I some times think that this is rong to one a slave for the Bible ses that a man shal eat bred by his swet of his brough," one Confederate from North Carolina wrote to his sister.[17] A young man in South Carolina explained in 1865 to John Trowbridge, a traveler from the North, "I think it was in the decrees of God Almighty that slavery was to be abolished in this way, and I don't murmur." These southerners wondered about God's will, acknowledging that emancipation and the war had upended their certainties of right and might.[18]

Yet there were plenty of others who murmured and much more. Southern whites did not abandon proslavery ideology or go quietly into the night. It was so fastened to their conceptions of this world and of God's teachings that proslavery ideology continued even after slavery's demise. As Luke Harlow has observed in his study of Protestants in Kentucky, many continued to believe that slavery was divine. Proslavery Christianity, Harlow has contended, "remained an animating ideological force" that provided the basis for their reactions to civil rights legislation and calls for denominational reconciliations.[19] Slavery may have been dead legally in the United States, but it continued to provide providential explanations for American history. It was a means for southern whites to claim moral rightness in a nation that ratified its legal wrongness. Writing for *Scott's Monthly Magazine* in 1868, Russ James argued that in Africa, blacks were "barbarous, idolatrous, and utterly depraved. *As a southern slave,* he . . . obtained a knowledge of the true God."[20]

With chattel slavery constitutionally devastated in 1865, though, a window opened for new white-supremacist providential interpretations of the place and status of blacks in the United States. The white-supremacist theology that emerged redefined the very nature of humanity and human difference, the locus of original sin, and God's designs for the nation. Proslavery may have been biblically just and it certainly continued as a vibrant social, political, and religious philosophy longer than historians have recognized, but it offered little to post-emancipation questions of social interactions, politics, schooling, and sexuality.

The new white supremacy saw God's providential design in permanent human difference and hierarchy, not just in slavery. In 1876, one southern white wrote, "This line of demarcation between the races is not accidental or the result of outward surroundings; it has been fixed by the finger of God."[21] Rather than locate difference in the biblical curse of Canaan, which provided justification for racial enslavement, the new white supremacists looked further back in sacred time to be more applicable to the modern postslavery world. Suggesting now that people of color were pre-Adamites, white supremacists located difference not in God's curse, but in God's designs. The pre-Adamites, or as Charles Carroll theorized, the "beasts of the field," were created by God before humans; they were inferior and subject to human control. True humans—those made in the image of God with bodies, minds, and souls—were white people.[22]

This new theology for the new era shifted sin around. Original sin was not about general disobedience to God's will or the desire for knowledge. It was specific, particular, and racial: the sin of integration and its child, interracial sexuality. Eve did not just listen to a serpent or eat some fruit. She interacted, perhaps sexually, with a pre-Adamite serpent who was rendered a person of color in these formulations. A. Hoyle Lester wrote: "Eve, poor woman, yielded to the evil machinations of this seductive deceiver. She rose from the mossy couch a wiser but fallen creature, and returned to the presence of her lawful companion disrobed of virtue, that precious jewel, the brightest ornament of her sex."[23] Charles Carroll agreed and disagreed. He did not believe the first sin was an act of interracial sex, but rather one of equal interracial interaction. Eve sinned by listening to the ideas of her black female servant. "The beast of the field which tempted Eve was a *negress,*" Carroll concluded, "who served Eve in the capacity of maid servant." Eve fell by becoming "confidential and familiar" with her servant. The "negress" seduced Eve, and Adam through Eve, to challenge the words of God. The ultimate sin, Carroll concluded, was social equality. "This reveals the startling fact that it was man's social equality with the negro that brought sin into the world." The past was now prophetic for the present. "This being true, it follows that man's social equality with the negro will keep sin into the world, and will bring upon man the just condemnation of God." Equality—political, social, and religious, the types of equality radical Republicans seemed to usher in after emancipation—will breed the final great evil:

interracial sexuality, "itself the most infamous and destructive crime known to the law of God."[24]

Carroll characterized God's relationship to human history as one of anger over interracial sexuality. "The Bible is largely a history of the long, destructive conflict which has raged between God and man, because of man's social, political, and religious equality with this beast, and the amalgamation to which these crimes inevitably lead." The great flood of the Book of Genesis resulted from amalgamation, Carroll continued, and so too did the Israelites' fall from grace. And now, in the United States, God's wrath may be coming, and it would alter everything in the nation. When amalgamation happens, "the nation's relation to God, its relation to the earth and the animals has completely changed."[25]

These white-supremacist theologies, with their new accounts of sin, providence, and divine wrath, had political and social answers for the postemancipation world. Abolition was providential to some and an apocalyptic nightmare for others. When historians locate the connections among religious ideologies, fears of interracial interactions, and opposition to the civil rights movement—as Jane Dailey and Paul Harvey have done brilliantly—they are beholding an ideological world created in response to the power of emancipation. The new white supremacy made new providential certainty out of providential uncertainty by forecasting millennial doom.[26]

Abolition and Reconstruction forced reconsiderations of southern religions. The faith of slaves changed dramatically with freedom and citizenship. They could now have their own churches with their own leaders, deacons, and Sunday school classes. They could explain and experience God's hand in American history not just through redemptive suffering, but with shouts of jubilation and wonder over emancipation. God had intervened to bring freedom. God had intervened to make them citizens. And not God alone, but God activated by their prayers and actions. The nadir was a confusing time religiously, but hope had a tangible past that was continually remembered. Southern whites, alternatively, were left to cast about for new religious answers to their losses. They had lost slavery; they had lost national independence; they had lost, in some moments, the rights to govern themselves during radical Reconstruction. Wondering about God's hand in American and southern history, some turned to a new white supremacy that adjusted original and national sin. The United States was now in jeopardy—not over slavery, but over integration and interracial sexuality. The theological battle lines were set for twentieth-century struggles over God's relationship to the nation, civil rights, and southern religions.

THE NORTH

Emancipation and Reconstruction also remade the North in numerous millennial and providential visions. Southern whites, in part, inherited their apocalyptic racial prophecies from northern Democrats during the Civil War. Politically abandoned by southern whites, northern Democrats were in bad shape during the 1860s. A minority party, they were overwhelmed by executive power and Republican congressional majorities. Winning elections amid war was extremely difficult, but in 1863 and 1864, they thought they had their ticket: racial fears. In what Forrest Wood long ago called the "first white backlash" against civil rights advances, Democrats conjured fears of interracial sex to turn whites away from the Republican Party. Visual imagery was central to this push, as antimiscegenation pamphlets carried drawings of black men and white women kissing.[27]

"Miscegenation—or the Millennium of Abolitionism," a political cartoon from 1864, drew concepts of interracial sexuality into the lexicon of millennialism, and then drew millennialism into the genre of sarcasm. In "Miscegenation," concepts of heaven, paradise, and God's will were mocked to undermine the work of emancipation and the Republican Party. This millennium would have obese black women holding hands with white men, black men hugging and kissing white women, whites serving blacks, and the president of the nation bowing to interracial marriage. An African American woman speaking to Lincoln expresses joy that "de hebenly Miscegenation times was cum." Horace Greeley, sharing ice cream with a black woman, reveled, "We have at last reached our political and social Paradise." At the far right, a German figure—symbolic of the world watching what would become of the United States—exclaimed: "Mine Got, vat a guntry, vat a beebles!"[28]

Democrats used millennialism as mockery, in part, because it and other proclamations about God's providence were so frequently used by their opponents, the Republicans. The majority of voting northern whites cast their political allegiances with the Republican Party, and the Republicans voiced strong and certain feelings about God's relationship to slavery and the nation. Almost uniformly after 1863 Republicans heralded emancipation as God's sacred work in the world. But when it came to what freedom required and what the relationship of the government would be to freed African Americans, Republicans fell apart and God's designs seemed lost or confused. Republicans' mix of certainty, confusion, and splintering over God's directions for Reconstruction, coupled with southern white resistance, tempered millennial aspirations significantly. Providential certainty for emancipation failed to unite Republicans in the postwar era, and their plans for Reconstruction floundered with lack of religious specificity.

White Republicans joined African Americans in hailing emancipation as evidence of God's providence and forecasting the coming of the millennium. Time and again, they heralded emancipation as divine. Senator Charles Sumner asserted that with emancipation, "it seemed as if the millennium was at hand"[29] Theodore Tilton wrote to Susan B. Anthony: "The millennium is on the way. . . . Three cheers for God!"[30] At the very end of 1863, James Jessee, a soldier from Illinois, wrote in his diary that the "liberation of this oppressed and down trodden race" was God's "glorious object." "To doubt this," he asserted with certainty, "would Be to doubt God." What caused providential perplexity for many southern whites became a spiritual bedrock for many white Republicans.[31]

Although abolition was universally beloved by Republicans, they fractured on the problems of postslavery. With Reconstruction, the Republicans could never agree on what southern reinstatement or freedom for slaves truly meant. Would former slaves receive land? Would they be entitled to vote? How and when would southern states be readmitted into the union that was worth dying and killing for? What, exactly, did God require for all of this?[32]

No one articulated the Republican shift from providential certainty to uncertainty more clearly than Abraham Lincoln. His Second Inaugural Address, in fact, trafficked directly in that movement. A master of misdirection and rhetorical sleights of hand, Lincoln may have attempted to pull off one of epic providential proportions on that rainy day in March 1865, one that has fooled historians far more than the people of his age. Of the origins of the war, an issue difficult to explain in the 1860s and contested by generations of historians, Lincoln set certainty amid confusion. "All knew," he said of the slave interest, that it "was, somehow, the cause of the war." Lincoln asked his audience to agree that slavery was "one of those offenses" that God had willed now "to remove." Now that slavery was virtually vanquished, God's intention, plans, and demands were unclear. Lincoln spoke in vague generalities and hid behind biblical and mystical language. "The prayers of both could not be answered," he continued of the war. "That of neither has been answered fully. The Almighty has His own purposes." Over and over in the speech, Lincoln invoked certainty about the end of slavery and then used God to account for confusion. The days were so uncertain and God was so unclear—except for heaven's hatred for slavery—that "if God wills that" the war "continue . . . as was said three thousand years ago, so still it must be said 'the judgments of the Lord are true and righteous altogether.'" Even in his call for charity and firmness in the right, Lincoln couched it in providential uncertainty and human passivity—"as God gives us to see the right." In this formulation, the judgments of the Lord and the Almighty's purposes had revealed themselves against slavery, but beyond that they were unknowable and untraceable. God's will, or at least in Lincoln's presentation of it, offered no roadmap for the next four years.[33]

Lincoln's Second Inaugural has been celebrated as his "greatest speech." Its supposed theological profundity, humility, and twin calls for racial justice and sectional harmony have become cherished. Scholars quote Frederick Douglass, who told Lincoln late in the day that it "was a sacred effort." Historian Mark Noll contrasted Lincoln with the ministers of his age and found that "none probed so profoundly the ways of God or the responses of humans to the divine constitution of the world. None penetrated as deeply into the nature of providence. And none described the fate of humanity before God with the humility or the sagacity of the president." It became, Noll pointed out, one of America's "semisacred texts."[34]

Scholarly adoration for Lincoln's speech has been used to chastise American religion of the time, especially since his inaugural was met by many Americans with confusion, irritation, and disappointment. Whether it has been Harry Stout moaning that so few white northerners or white southerners challenged the moral actions of their sections or Noll lamenting the ways Protestant spokesmen tied faith to the nation, historians have found it tragic that Lincoln's generation did not understand him.[35] But responses to the Second Inaugural revealed far more than spiritual shallowness or the all-consuming power of civil religion. Numerous reports expressed frustration with providential musings in a time when what was needed was political clarity. Many newspapers were disappointed that Lincoln offered no roadmap for the future, and several highlighted the religious confusion of the speech. The *Richmond Examiner* reported, "It reads like the tail of some old sermon, and seems to have no particular meaning of any kind, at least, if any meaning lurks in it we fail to perceive it." England's *Spectator* teased that Lincoln "seems to be one of those 'foolish things of the world' which are destined to confound the wise, one of those weak things which shall 'confound the things which are mighty.'" The *Daily Illinois State Register* charged Lincoln with praying "into the arcana of God's council." In their responses, Americans revealed their hopes for moral and political direction in strange and troubling times. In short, the responses showed that the acceptance of abolition as God's work did not provide political or religious vision for the future and left Americans without a compass to navigate their futures or at least know what the president's plans were. Responses showed that Americans wanted, but had little, clear direction.[36]

In life, Lincoln's providential uncertainty was perplexing. In his death, providential certainty and uncertainty came together to comprehend his assassination. Although clearly distraught by the president's assassination on Good Friday in 1865, many northern whites responded by suggesting that it was part of God's confusing providence, the Almighty's purposes that Lincoln had sought to render unintelligible. Frederick Douglass acknowledged that it was the "inscrutable wisdom of Him who controls the destinies of nations" that allowed Booth to kill Lincoln. New York lawyer George Templeton Strong searched for God's certain direction, but knew that he and America were on uncertain ground. Ruminating on the sermon he heard on the Easter Sunday after Lincoln's death, Strong recorded in his diary his fragile providential interpretations: "The thought that had occurred to me and to many others" was: "Perhaps Lincoln had done his appointed work; his honesty, sagacity, kindliness, and singleness of purpose had united the North and secured the suppression of rebellion. Perhaps the time has come for something beside kindliness, mercy, and forbearance, even for vengeance and judgment."[37]

Lincoln's inaugural and his death were inauspicious starts to Reconstruction, and they set the providential terrain as one of uncertainty. And, of course, we know that a sterner executive failed to materialize. The early years of post-Lincoln Reconstruction were fraught with political conflict that further splintered providential views in the North. Andrew Johnson had few friends, but the Democrats who rallied to him envisioned him as a "godsend." "The designs of Heaven begin now to be visible throughout," one Democrat pronounced at a party convention in July 1865.[38] Even in the summer of 1868, after Johnson had narrowly avoided removal from office, several spiritualists prophesied that he would win the Democratic nomination for president.[39]

Providential conflicts emerged in Reconstruction as various designs for remaking the nation clashed. Radical Republicans were diametrically opposed to President Johnson and former Confederates in their vision of God's designs for the nation after slavery. Thaddeus Stevens and his radical Republican colleagues were not confused about God's will for the postslavery and postwar nation. The Almighty's ways were clear to them, and they would not budge. The God of the Bible, of providence, and of the millennium directed the nation to racial justice for African Americans and to sacred punishment for slaveholders and the disloyal. Stevens believed that God would pour wrath upon the nation if it did not bring true freedom to African Americans, and this freedom must come through land and education. Stevens announced to Congress in December 1865: "The time to which they looked forward with anxiety has come. It is our duty to complete their work. If this Republic is not now made to stand on their great principles, it has no honest foundation, and the Father of all men will still shake it to its center."[40]

In his congressional speeches, Stevens reworked the relationship among the Bible, God's will, and race in the United States. Passages that had once been used to justify black enslavement were now cast against disloyal southern whites. The logic from the tale of Cain and Abel, Stevens concluded, was that southern whites should not be forgiven. They should be driven off their land and exiled. Stevens also invoked Exodus, not just as a motif of liberation, but also as a biblical roadmap for postslavery societies. Following their liberation, "God commanded the men and the women to borrow from their confiding neighbors 'jewels of silvers and jewels of gold and raiment.' They obeyed him amply, and spoiled the Egyptians, and went forth full-handed." Stevens promised divine punishment if the United States failed to follow this model: "If we refuse to this down-trodden and oppressed race the rights which Heaven decreed them, and the remuneration which they have earned through long years of hopeless oppression, how can we hope to escape still further punishment if God is just and omnipotent?" The outcomes would be devastating: "It may come in the shape of plagues or of intestine wars—race against race, the oppressed against the oppressor. But come it will."[41]

The arm of radical Reconstruction moved from the North to the South often in the form of white women. Emancipation and Reconstruction made possible a titanic shift in home missions. Missionaries and teachers ventured South in the hundreds and perhaps thousands to bring schools and faith to former slaves. No longer did Protestant missionaries have to justify themselves to white owners. No longer would they use "Negro catechisms" that stressed obedience to whites as God's divine agents on earth. No longer would they counsel acceptance of violence and brutality. New books and primers stressed freedom and responsibility. They stressed God's designs for liberty.[42]

Many missionaries experienced their trip as God's kingdom coming to the world. Watching former slaves and northern whites in Florida interact as friends—sharing tobacco, for instance—Esther Hawks concluded in her diary in mid-1864 that "the end of the war was near for the millennium had begun!"[43] Remembering her work among freedmen and -women in Kentucky, one female graduate of the University of Michigan put her feelings to verse: "No more talks about our Lord / No more searchings for his word, / No more longings for his grace, / She hath seen him face to face."[44] After speaking with a group of African Americans, one missionary in South Carolina reimagined the South as a sacred location, "Such interviews, even in the *lowly cabin*—seem *quite* on the *verge of Heaven.*"[45]

The radical talk of heaven requiring change in citizenship and voting did not translate to equality for all Americans. Although unable to vote, white feminists in the North had supported the Republican Party and abolition. When the Fourteenth Amendment cast citizenship in male terms and then the Fifteenth Amendment protected black male suffrage, however, their millennial hopes crashed. Elizabeth Cady Stanton viewed the political task as bigger than race or nation: "The work of the hour is a broader one than the reconstruction of the rebellious states. . . . It is the realization of what the world has never yet seen, a genuine Republic." Stanton fumed with righteous rage at the Fourteenth Amendment and deployed the racist language that at other times she deplored: "Now, as the celestial gate to civil rights is slowly moving on its hinges, it becomes a serious question whether we had better stand aside and see 'Sambo' walk into the kingdom first." Historian Kathi Kern shows in her work on the emergence of Stanton's *Woman's Bible* that these Reconstruction struggles paved the way to her feminist theological innovations, and perhaps just as importantly, the general rejection of them.[46]

Providential certainty and optimistic millennial expectations floundered in the 1870s, in part, because uncertainty had been wedged into the religious political thought and because there were no clear resolutions to the postwar problems. Several of the biblical battles of the antebellum era were resolved—slavery died and emancipation was accepted, for most Americans, as a sacred good. The place of African Americans and the rights of individuals within the nation, however, were not settled in the late 1860s or the 1870s. Southern whites continued to express dissatisfaction with the federal government, with their rights, and with the status of African Americans. Some southern whites continued to turn to militancy and insurgency as their answers to federal law. African Americans had achieved citizenship and black men the right to vote, but clearly they were embattled, terrified, and it seemed as if their gains could easily be wiped away. Feminists had believed the great day of equal rights had come only to be closed out of the kingdom. All of the confusion and uncertainty tempered providential visions and millennial aspirations. This paved the way for a remodeled premillennialism to reemerge publicly and for a new fashion of labor radicalism to shift millennial questions from the literal of when Jesus would return to the metaphorical of what his words and spirit meant for the age.

Emancipation and the first days of Reconstruction fired few premillennial visions in the North. In the antebellum period, premillennialism was a dynamic movement with new religious leaders, prophecies, and magazines. William Miller's predictions had failed time and again, and the Millerites never fully rebounded from the Great Disappointment of 1844. One prophetic calculus placed the date of Christ's return in 1866, but English writers made more of it than American ones did.[47] Abraham Lincoln received several letters of premillennial prophecy, but none that he took seriously. One squarely linked abolition and racial equality to Christ's physical return. In February 1863, George F. Kelly wrote to Lincoln worried that the president was wondering "if God has forsaken us." "He has not," Kelly assured Lincoln, but warned "God is just." If Lincoln wanted to retain God's favor, he must "adopt the plans called, Radical." The Lord had given Kelly a vision that Jesus was going to destroy slavery and save the nation. "Have not the honest hearted been longing for the Second 'Jesus' to Save this nation and the world—Doesent the times look like he was wanted even *now*," Kelly wrote. This was not just Christ in spirit, but in person. Jesus had returned. He had come to save the Union, to liberate the slaves, and to crush white supremacy. "Have ye not heard that in one of the New England States 'God has raised him up in 'humble life'—did He not do even So with His former Servant; who toiled with the people more than thirty years." Lincoln wasn't convinced, and wrote "crazy-man" on one of Kelly's letters.[48]

Premillennialism stormed back into public and political spheres in the 1870s. This time it was on center stage and grew steadily into the twentieth century. Reconstruction was once again an important element of the equation. Dwight Moody—an unlettered former shoe salesman known on the streets of Chicago as "Crazy Moody"—led titanic revivals in 1876 and 1877 that captured the nation's attention as much as the presidential election or Custer's disaster at Little Big Horn. In northern newspapers and magazines, he became the focus of thousands of print pages. Moody taught a gospel of individual conversion that distanced faith from the realms of politics and society. "Don't flatter yourselves that the world is going to get any better," he told one audience, the "world is on the rocks." Moody envisioned humanity aboard a sinking ship and reported that God had told him, "Moody, save all you can." Moody's premillennialism was appealing at the end of Reconstruction because it was vague, general, and dislodged from American events. Christ would return at some given point, but Moody made no claims about its timing. In addition, Moody's preaching was decidedly apolitical in an era of political strife, and his goal was to alleviate conflicts—between man and God, among denominations, and between North and South. For Americans of the mid-1870s, this kind of vague, harmonious premillennialism was certainly more appealing than the providential certainty that had deluged the nation in blood and failed to resolve so many problems.[49]

Premillennialism took another twist, one that once again turned from the concrete to the ethereal, with the emergence of a much smaller movement that became known as Seventh-Day Adventism. Founded officially in 1863, the organization shifted attention on Christ's return from the corporeal to the spiritual, from the certain to the uncertain. Christ had returned in the 1840s, just not to the earth. He had moved into a new spiritual kingdom, and the battle between him and Satan was one of confusion, perfidy, and obfuscation. Ellen White, the chief leader of the movement in the end of the nineteenth century, regularly discussed how Satan was trying to delude humanity in such ways that the times were difficult to interpret and understand.[50]

At the same moment that Moody was rising in popularity, labor activism emerged on a national scale. Portions of it, too, responded to the postslavery and postwar nation with refashioned providential and millennial conceptions. Before the Civil War, labor activism was episodic and confined to particular urban areas. It had a complicated relationship with slavery, attempting at times to distance itself from chattel slavery and the abolitionist movement while at other times claiming that "wage slavery" was akin to the peculiar institution.[51] With the end of the Civil War, millions of men flooded the job market in the Northeast, and then the economic depression of the 1870s undercut the economy. A growing number of workers sought to unite and push back against powerful industrialists and businessmen. The Knights of Labor emerged as the largest and most dynamic movement. Founded in 1869, the Knights swelled to more than seven hundred thousand members in 1886. They hoped to unite all who labored—male and female, white and black. The Knights called for an eight-hour workday, for graduated income taxes, for government ownership of telegraphs and railroads, for public land for citizens, and for equal pay for women. Those who opposed them called the Knights "visionaries and lunatics." Just as abolitionists were mocked in the antebellum era for trying to create an "abolition millennium," the Knights were derided for trying to instill a "labor millennium."[52]

Union leaders fought back with their own views of God and heavenly plans for society.[53] Terence Powderly, the leader of the Knights and a son of Irish Catholic immigrants, never shied away from characterizing the labor battle as a religious one. He retooled religious ideas and millennialism to dismantle attacks upon labor. Powderly insisted that the Knights were far more realistic than everyday Christians. Take their designs for human society. The Knights merely wanted an eight-hour workday or equal pay for women. Christians pray, "Thy kingdom come. Thy will be done, as it is in heaven." This prayer, Powderly continued, meant that American Christians wanted society to be "an abode of bliss; where love reigns supreme; where poverty, sin, death and crime are unknown; where all things are enjoyed in common by all the inhabitants thereof." The Knights, alternatively, would never presume "to ask that this earth should become better than such a heavenly place."[54]

When Powderly spoke of the millennium, he approached it in a restrained capacity. He either brought it to the genre of sarcasm or recognized the limitations of its use. Even after their rapid fall after the Haymarket Square disaster of 1886, Powderly told all who would listen: "Yes, the Knights of Labor are breaking up, and they will continue their appointed work of breaking up until universal rights shall prevail; and while they may not bring in the millennium, they will do their part in the evolution of moral forces that are working for the emancipation of the race." Several years later, Powderly mocked the idea that material prosperity was a marker of God's providence. "Too frequently," he wrote for the *Labor Day Annual* in 1893, "the system in which we are now rushing on toward the millennium displaces mechanics, laborers and miners, so rapidly that they are forced into crime in order to get bread."[55]

Slavery and emancipation, the Civil War and Reconstruction, informed and tempered Powderly's religious approach to labor activism. Emancipation became a touchstone of sacred reality that could be wielded against any and all opponents. While on a speaking tour through Maine in 1884, Powderly was challenged by a Catholic priest who commanded him, "Do not speak in my state again until I give consent." In his defense, Powderly turned not to the Bill of Rights, but to emancipation: "I became indignant, lost my temper, and told him that there were a few people in the state of Maine who did not belong to him, that human slavery had been abolished, and that it was a piece of presumption on his part to assume that Maine was all his."[56] On other occasions, Powderly even justified potential labor violence as an improvement over the old system of slavery. When charged with fomenting revolution, Powderly responded: "How much worse can a nation be with a bomb in every man's hand than to have every man's hand bound in chains? Who would not prefer a nation of men who would rather fight than be slaves to a nation of creatures who would rather be slaves than fight?" The Knights were insistent: liberty was God's plan for humanity, not slavery: "Of what avail to longer cry, 'Servants, obey your masters,' when it is written in the full light of heaven's day that many of the masters are devils incarnate, whose only God is gold, and whose reward for labor is hell upon earth?"[57]

Perhaps the most significant impact of the Civil War on the Knights' religion was in the reinterpretation of hard labor from a curse to a blessing. According to the Bible, when Adam and Eve were cast from the Garden of Eden, they were in part cursed that in "the sweat of thy face shalt thou eat bread." In the antebellum era and that of the Civil War, abolitionists transformed this into a condemnation of slaveholders, individuals who, as Lincoln put it in his Second Inaugural, "dare to ask a just God's assistance in wringing their bread from the sweat of other men's faces." Slaveholders were vile, this logic insisted, because they failed to endure the curse themselves and altered it for other humans. With slavery dead, the Knights of Labor turned this scripture from a sacred necessary evil to a positive good. Upon initiation, a new member would be asked three questions to which she or he must answer in the affirmative. The second was, "Do you obey the Universal Ordinance of God, in gaining your bread by the sweat of your brow?" Moments later, the foreman for the local group would tell the initiate: "In the beginning God ordained that man should labor, not as a curse, but as a blessing; not as a punishment, but as a means of development, physically, mentally, morally, and has set thereunto his seal of approval in the rich increase and reward."[58] Finally, Powderly shifted the emphasis from when Jesus would return to if his words were truly preached what would happen to the vessel of his message. "If the Sermon on the Mount were preached in many a church today, and the identity of the divine author concealed," Powderly conjectured, "fashionable pews would be emptied, the minister of God would be censured and warned never again to repeat the ravings of an utopist. In the church where the minister is the only friend to the poor, it shows that he has preached in vain not to have made more converts to the doctrine of Christ crucified."[59]

The end of slavery and Reconstruction shifted the terrains, languages, expressions, and experiences of providentialism and millennialism in the North.

In their attack upon emancipation, Democrats mocked Republicans as millennial dreamers who wanted to upend white supremacy with interracial marriage and friendship. Lincoln tied God's purposes solely and certainly to emancipation, but left the rest of the issues to God's almighty and unknowable purposes. After Lincoln's death, Republicans struggled to locate providential certainty, even while radicals cried out for racial justice as God's clear call. Some feminists felt betrayed by the Fourteenth and Fifteenth Amendments and cried corruption in the kingdom. As Reconstruction faltered and flailed in the 1870s, premillennialism made stirring comebacks, this time in amorphous, apolitical, spiritualized versions. Finally, the new and expansive Knights of Labor rewrote God's laws and transformed labor from a curse to a positive good. They juxtaposed the realism of their goals with the utopian vision of the Bible and positioned themselves as the truest Christians. Democrats, radical Republicans, feminists, and workers had differing visions for the postwar nation, but slowly each gave ground on the idea that to doubt their agenda was "to doubt God." Human events and God's millennial plans seemed either dislodged from one another or confusing enough to be acknowledged as uncertain. Providential confusion and millennial splintering stood in even starker relief if we follow the advice of 1872 presidential candidate Horace Greeley and "go west."

THE WEST

The end of slavery and Union victory substantially refigured providentialism and millennialism in and about the American West. For those in the East, the providential and millennial meanings of the West were reassessed, while those living west of the Mississippi River (or soon to be living there) were compelled to reappraise their sacred worldviews. Biblical meanings poured into the West. The region was reinterpreted as a new Promised Land, a new Eden, and a new location of Christ's return. The West shifted from a location of profane sectional disunity to a place of sacred national reunion, as conflicts over the West shifted from concerns about slavery to concerns about industrial development. The millennial worldviews of many western Mormons and Indians were remade by Reconstruction, while problems of race and citizenship spun the Golden Coast into violence, judicial battles, and federal legislation.

The West promised so much to Americans throughout the nineteenth century. Before the Civil War, it was a grand but complicated symbol of providential design for the nation. In 1835, Lyman Beecher preached not only that the "Millennium would commence in America," but also that the fates of America and Christianity would be "decided in the West." The West must be won by American Protestants, Beecher insisted, for its vast resources were surely a sign of God's favor and call. If Catholics were to somehow prosper there, it would be a victory for the Antichrist. The West was awash in potential and peril, both financially and spiritually. Proponents of "manifest destiny" characterized the West as heaven's bastion of riches set aside for white Americans to claim and tame for the glory of God.[60]

Antebellum providential views of the West, however, were troubled. First, the myth of emptiness was exactly that—a myth. Indians and Mexicans lived there, and violence against them seemed to indicate the immorality of whites, not their divine racial superiority.[61] Second, by the late 1840s and 1850s, the Church of Jesus Christ of Latter-day Saints had found refuge in the West, and their new religious teachings, especially that of plural marriage, disgusted many in the monogamous East. Third, slavery colored providential visions of the West. For proslavery forces, the expansion of slavery was imperative and part of the "divine trust" that Benjamin Palmer described. For antislavery forces, the expansion of slavery would only grow the "millennium of sin and misery" brought on by slavery.[62] For many slaves, movement to the Southwest was terrifying. It meant removal from family and quite possibly the auction block. According to Henry Bibb, the "soul drivers" who planned on moving him and his family to New Orleans took him on a journey only explainable as a journey through and to hell.[63]

Emancipation demolished the problem of slavery in the West, but not the other dilemmas. Providential conflict over the West shifted from slavery to the environment, industry, and development. For some, the West became an edenic bastion distanced from the sins of human conflict. In Albert Bierstadt's *The Sierra Nevada in California* (1868), sunlight beams through the clouds onto mountains, trees, and animals. There are no people, and hence there is no political or social conflict. The frustrations of Reconstruction are nowhere present. The *Overland Monthly,* a new magazine started in 1868, heralded the West as an "Eden" where individuals "Would walk, a child, through Nature's wild, / And hear His voice and answer Him." John Muir believed the West's terrain and foliage showed the "glorious traces of the thoughts of God, and leading on and on into the infinite cosmos" and should therefore be protected from human corruption.[64]

The environmentalists, however, were matched by another providential vision that focused on industrial and technological development. In this approach, technology displaced humanity as God's engine of change, and the railroad was that engine. Praise for God's providence, for example, was present at the completion of the transcontinental railroad in 1869. After a series of prayers that thanked God for linking "the Atlantic of Thy strength to the Pacific of Thy love," the golden spikes were driven into the ground of Promontory Point, Utah. One of the spikes was engraved with a prayer that joined national harmony to development: "May God continue the unity of our Country as the Railroad unites the two great Oceans of the world."[65] The railroad was accomplishing what others could not, what politicians promised but failed to deliver: it was aiding America's divine destiny by uniting the nation. John Gast's *American Progress* of 1872, an image often wrongly used to teach manifest destiny in the antebellum period, showcases the angel of American progress moving east to west. She leads railroads, strings the telegraph, and emboldens white settlers to build farms on the prairie. Indians and bison flee, knowing all too well what becomes of them with whites' arrivals.[66]

The railroad became an actor in God's divine drama, a supreme symbol of millennial destiny. When John McDowell Leavitt, president of Lehigh University, turned to fiction to save the American people from sin and decadence with his mid-1880s novel *Kings of Capital and Knights of Labor,* he declared: "The locomotive is . . . the prophet of peace, the messenger of civilization, the herald of the millennium, the conqueror of humanity, and the John the Baptist of Christianity, raising the valleys, leveling the mountains, and making the crooked straight and the rough plain for the monarch of the universe."[67]

As whites debated whether God's kingdom in the West must be protected from human activity or advanced through human action, some African Americans of the 1870s found in it a potential escape from the horrors of the postwar South. As millennial hopes waned with each Klan attack, with each legislative defeat, and with each season's mounting debts, a group of black southerners refigured the West as a heavenly, rather than hellish, space. The Exoduster movement of the late 1870s was filled with providential hopes and millennial rhetoric. Its leading spokesmen, Henry Adams and "Pap" Singleton, declared that God would damn African Americans if they remained in the South. They turned to the Book of Daniel and found a God who helps those in terrible trouble. This God was leading them west. John Solomon Lewis recounted of arriving in Kansas: "I looked on the ground and I says this is free ground. Then I looked on the heavens, and I says them is free and beautiful heavens. Then I looked within my heart, and I says to myself I wonder why I never was free before?" Lewis made sure that the first action of his family was to thank God: "When I knew I had all my family in a free land, I said let us hold a little prayer meeting; so we held a little meeting on the river bank. It was raining but the drops fell from heaven on a free family, and the meeting was just as good as sunshine. We was thankful to God for ourselves and we prayed for those who could not come." Years later, mobility once again was branded as part of God's plans as African Americans of the "Great Migration" sang hymns as they traveled out of Dixie land.[68]

Slavery's destruction and increased attention on the West brought Mormons into the national gaze as never before. Mormonism emerged as a unifying enemy in the postwar years that bound northern and southern Protestants in concerted local and federal action. As early as the 1850s, Republicans and Democrats had denounced Mormons and polygamy. Amid heightened sectional tensions in the late 1850s, one southern leader wrote to President James Buchanan that the only way to "supersede the Negro-Mania" and avert civil war would be through "an Anti-Mormon Crusade."[69] The new Republican Party of the 1850s was especially vocal in its opposition to Mormon polygamy, which it branded with slavery the "twin relics of barbarism" that needed to be destroyed.

Emancipation rid the nation of one relic, and with the Civil War over, attention quickly turned to the second. Anti-Mormon writers depicted the Church of Jesus Christ of Latter-day Saints as a national enemy perhaps more pernicious than the Confederacy. "The elements of a second rebellion are in active progress in Utah," claimed one anti-Mormon writer in 1866, "and, as in the case of the slavery rebellion, the great danger lies in the failing to place a proper estimate upon the power of those elements for mischief, and to take the proper precautions in time." But the author was convinced that "religious fanaticism is more active, and, when hostile, more dangerous, than political ambition; hence the arrogant and intolerant spirit, and the bitter hostility of the Mormons, are more worthy [of] the serious attention of our statesmen than would be the opposition of so many mere political traitors."[70] Anti-Mormonism became a binding tie amid intrapolitical and interpolitical conflict. Democrats and Republicans, northerners and southerners, swelled the chorus of anti-Mormonism in the 1870s, 1880s, and 1890s.[71] The Republican Party of the late 1860s and early 1870s was deeply fractured over both how to legislate the South and over the failures of Grant's presidency. They knew exactly what to do regarding polygamy, and in the 1860s, 1870s, and 1880s, Congress, the president, and the Supreme Court united in outlawing plural marriage. Arguments against polygamy also linked

Republicans and Democrats. In President Grover Cleveland's annual message to Congress in 1885, he contrasted the miserable "homes of polygamy" with "our homes, established by the law of God, guarded by parental care, regulated by parental authority, and sanctified by parental love." Democrats and Republicans connected in their sacred and legal assault on polygamy, in large part by turning to the protection of women and children. God's designs that the nation protect women became a providential tie for southern and northern whites and brought them into concerted effort against Mormons.[72]

Mormons refused to take this treatment lying down. Perhaps the most millennial-minded of all Americans in the Civil War era, with newspapers named *Millennial Star* and with almost constant discussions of visions, revelations, and prophecies in their sermons, newspapers, letters, and diaries, Mormon faith went on a roller-coaster ride in the eras of the Civil War and Reconstruction.[73] Emancipation, the end of hostilities, and federal legislation against them compelled Mormons to reassess nearly every facet of their faith and relationship to the government. The millennial and providential implications were titanic, and Mormonism emerged with less prophetic certainty, more flexibility toward the nation, but still rigid in antiblack racism.

For Mormons in Utah Territory, the Civil War was a godsend. Federal troops who had been stationed there since the Mountain Meadow massacre in 1857 were removed from the territory. Even more, the war became more evidence of the divine inspiration of their founder, Joseph Smith. In 1832, amid the South Carolina nullification crisis, Smith had prophesied that the "days will come that war will be poured out, beginning at that place. For behold, the Southern States shall be divided against the Northern States. . . . And thus with the sword" all the earth would feel God's vengeance. Amid the chaos, God would have his select people—the Mormons—save the nation and the world.[74] Mormons were elated with the sectional crisis. Even before South Carolina initiated the military conflict in 1861, Mormons viewed the election of Lincoln as the fulfillment of Smith's words. In late November 1860, one Mormon in Utah wrote in his diary: "There is tremendous excitement prevails in the U.S. concerning the Election of Lincoln. The south is angry; the North is no better and from what I can see they are both hastening to fulfill the Prophecy of Joseph Smith Jr." Time and again, diarists saw in the war and its escalation evidence of end times. "There has been many severe Battles fought between the North and South at Gettysburg, Chattanooga, Chickamaugua, and other places," one diarist penned in September 1863. "Many thousands have been slain. . . . In fact as far as I can judge every thing is working out right for the redemption of Zion and the onward progress of God's great Kingdom in the last days."[75] The war brought Mormon millennial hopes for autonomy to a fever pitch, in part because it had taken federal military attention away from Utah. Heber C. Kimball explained to a group of Mormons, "the yoke is off our neck and it is on theirs, and the bow key is in. The day is not far distant when you will see us free as the air we breathe. President Young is our leader. . . . He can govern this people with his hands in his pockets."[76] Abolition and the arming of slaves further confirmed Smith's prophecy.

Reconstruction, though, turned Mormon elation to depression, rage, and eventually some prophetic capitulation. Mormons complained vehemently when they were accused of disloyalty. Brigham Young told one federal official that he could "go to hell" if he required an oath of allegiance from Mormons.[77] Mormons were understandably angry about antipolygamy legislation and expected a federal invasion. John D. Lee fumed when President Grant warned of a new civil war "where Mayson & Dixon will not be the line of demarkation, as it was in the last struggle." The writing was on the wall. Grant was calling for a war against Mormons. Lee penned in his diary: "He that hath an Ear, let him hear & observe the signs of the Times. Cal. offered 20,000 Troop to wipe Mormonism out of Utah."[78] Mormons, like former Confederates, were being legislated upon by radical Republicans hell-bent on imposing their will over local democracy and the Constitution as it was.

Emancipation, Union victory, and increasing civil rights for African Americans posed serious problems for Mormon prophecies, teachings, and actions. They could no longer purchase Native Americans as slaves, which Young had recommended in the early 1850s as a means to educate and convert local Indians.[79] Black citizenship, male suffrage, and uplift, moreover, bucked Mormon cosmological understandings of racial difference. The Church of Jesus Christ of Latter-day Saints had clear visions of the links between blackness and the sacred. Whiteness was divine and blackness was cursed.[80] Brigham Young brought the white and divine association to the realm of politics. On the eve of Civil War, he preached that "the Anglo Saxon Race were the pure Ephriamites and the[y] might kick and flounce like the Wild Bull in the net, but the Lord would cuff [them] from one side to the other and Chasten them and finaly gather them out, for they were of the seed of Abraham."[81] Mormonism's divine whiteness was matched by its rendering of blackness as sinful. Mormon leaders taught that black slavery would continue forever. In December 1860, as one

Utah diarist recorded, Brigham Young preached of slavery in ways that echoed a century later in the rhetoric of George Wallace on segregation: "Touched on Slavery; said it always was so and would be. The inferior would always be in subjection to the superior. The blacks thro Cain and Ham would be servants of servants until every son and Daughter had receved the[i]r blessings thro and belonging to the Holy Priesthood."[82]

Whereas national schism and titanic warfare in the East confirmed so many Mormon prophecies, Reconstruction was an exercise in frustration. The Union ended the war and elevated African Americans from slaves to citizens, and then the Fifteenth Amendment protected black male suffrage. Mormons were furious. How could the United States support African American political rights and waste money on sinful blacks holding back Utah's statehood because of the religious choice of polygamy. Brigham Young denounced the meddling tendencies of northern Republicans in establishing southern "schools for the freedman," and Mormon newspapers routinely mocked voting rights for nonwhites. The *Deseret News* complained, "The Mexican greasers, barbarians of Russian America, Chinese, Indians, and Negroes, and all inferior races are to have the right of suffrage before white people." By putting the federal government behind rights for blacks and not in favor of Mormons, the United States was denying God's providential order. The *Millennial Star,* published in England, complained that federal treatment had the effect of "thrusting" the Saints, "personages of royal birth and lineage . . . a long way below the negro," and then later accused northern Republicans of attempting to reverse "the social, political and civil relations of the blacks and whites" by placing "the white man's head under the nigger's heel."[83]

Reconstruction was a strange time for Mormons. The war had ended, and they had not saved the United States, much less the world. In fact, the reconstructed nation had turned its legislative power against them.[84] Mormons continued to interpret new wars and violence as evidence of Smith's prophecies, such as Charles Lowell Walker cheering when "Custer and a few of his relatives were killed, also about 300 of his men." To Walker, "this is a begining of the fullfiling of the Revelation given to Joseph Smith in the Last days: the Remnants that is left of the Land will marshall themselves and shall become exceeding angry and shall vex the Gentiles with a sore vexation." As the years went on and as the final part of Smith's prophecy failed to be realized, however, Mormons stopped linking the Civil War with the immediate coming of Armageddon. Mormon Sunday school literature, in fact, counseled a direct shift in teaching the prophecy. They instructed teachers to shift from the word "then" to "thus" when discussing the casual links between war and end times. "This changes the significance from the casual element to the time element. The general war was to come after this special [time] and was not to be related necessarily."[85]

Attacked as traitors, denied statehood, and shut out from federal elections, Mormons compromised over the issue of polygamy. Once again, the shift was set in the visionary. Claiming to have had a revelation from God, President Wilford Woodruff declared in the Manifesto of 1890 that Mormons would no longer recognize plural marriage and that they would obey the laws of Congress. The East could cheer: the first relic of barbarism had died in 1865; now the second had fallen in 1890.[86]

Mormon millennial and providential teachings were shaken and then reconfigured in Reconstruction. They upheld white supremacy by continuing to bar African Americans from the priesthood. They looked to violence as a sign of the millennium, and when it failed to come, Mormons altered their interpretation of Smith's prophecy. Amid increasing persecution, they dreamed of saving the nation but banned the practice of polygamy.

The year 1890 was a momentous one in American religious history, not just for Mormons, but also for many Native Americans on the plains. Four days after Christmas, a federal force led by Colonel James Forsyth, a Civil War veteran and friend of George Custer, opened fire on Sioux Indians, killing about 150 of them at Wounded Knee, South Dakota. The atmosphere had been tense, in part, because a new Indian prophetic movement had rallied many to believe the Second Coming of Christ was at hand and that sacred forces were about to roll back the whites. The Ghost Dance, the prophecies of Wovoka, and white fears were products of Reconstruction, and contested notions of providence and the millennium preceded and followed the gunfire.

For many Native Americans, the era of Reconstruction was filled with one frustration after another. Fighting among the whites in the Civil War had not ended white-Indian conflict, but it had significantly reduced it. With war's end, America's military gaze once again turned westward. Perhaps even more devastating than the federal military, however, was the loss of the buffalo. In the early 1870s, American hunters and tourists, along with Indians themselves, decimated the bison population. This radically altered Indian life on the plains, for so many had directed their entire lives around the bison herds.[87] In response, a new millennial movement emerged that promised a reversal in the trajectory of history. It taught that what had been would return, and what was would be no more. The Ghost Dance movement was based on the idea that Christ and the buffalo would come back while the whites would disappear, and it connected Christ's return with that of the buffalo.[88]

The Ghost Dance was a millennial movement that combined traditions from native faiths with those from Christianity. This was nothing new, but the Second Coming of Christ had a new face on the prairies in the 1880s. Clouded in mystery, the life, visions, and representations of Wovoka or Jack Wilson spoke to the changes wrought by Reconstruction in Native American sacred worldviews. Born in the 1850s and raised among whites and Indians, Wovoka had a series of religious experiences in the 1870s, 1880s, and 1890s. He taught a sacred renewal of lost Indians, land, buffalo. This new millennial vision imagined the sacred invading this world and overwhelming the white destruction that was so devastating during the years of Reconstruction.

The Coming of Christ was central to fears and hopes for this Indian millennium. Jesus was everywhere in reports of Wovoka and his Ghost Dance. Whites derided it as a "Messiah Craze" and denounced Wovoka as an "Indian who impersonated Christ." Ethnographer James Mooney reported, "He has been denounced as an imposter, ridiculed as a lunatic, and laughed at as a pretended Christ." Wovoka, for his part, seemed slippery when it came to his affiliation with Jesus. Usually he declared himself a prophet or visionary, but on occasion linked himself to Jesus, writing on the back of a photograph in 1917, "I am the only living Jesus there is. Signed, Jack Wilson."[89]

After Wounded Knee, Wovoka and other plains Indians struggled to keep hope alive. In 1891, whisper campaigns shot through the West that the messiah was present and the time of reckoning was uncertain but soon. "Do not tell the white people about this," one letter instructed, "Jesus is now upon the earth. He appears like a cloud. The dead are all alive again. I do not know when they will be here; maybe this fall or in the spring. When the time comes there will be no more sickness and everyone will be young again." With hope was despair. Wounded Knee and later Wovoka's death ushered in new spiritual sadness for many Native Americans.

Even farther west, the dramas of Reconstruction took another turn along the Golden Coast. California had its own distinctive racial and religious character in large part because of the influx of Chinese immigrants following the Gold Rush of the late 1840s and 1850s. They were a confusing group to classify and could not easily be regarded as similar to other groups in the United States. The Chinese were considered nonwhite, they were immigrants, and they were, for the most part, non-Christian. Their presence was vital to the providential elements of economic development, but frightening to the millennial hopes for a Christian republic. During the Civil War and radical Reconstruction, several eastern Protestants heralded the coming of Chinese immigrants. These whites viewed God as uniting the world under the canopy of America, and missionary organizations hoped not only to Christianize Chinese immigrants, but also to bring them into the nation as full citizens. In the spring of 1863, heralding both emancipation and the Pacific Railway Act, the recording secretary for the American Baptist Home Mission Society (ABHMS) cheered the integration of the world in the United States: "It is Europe, it is Asia, it is Africa, it is all of these brought together upon our own continent."[90] A variety of missionary organizations reached out to Chinese Americans. Moreover, missionary organizations counterpoised their alleged equality with the hierarchies made by other American institutions. In the midst of the Klan hearings, anti-Chinese violence, and racially restrictive local voting laws, white missionary organizations proclaimed the universality of Christianity: "Wherever man hates his fellow, or race is hostile to race," one ABHMS board member told the committee in 1871, "remind the people that God is the just and loving Father of us all, and that his searching eye is upon us."[91]

In the 1870s, things fell apart. In San Francisco, political, racial, and religious fires burned as white Protestants, Irish Catholics, and Chinese Americans jousted for control of the developing region. West Coast Protestants joined their East Coast counterparts throughout the 1860s and damned Catholics as a "class of people largely ignorant, degraded, and vicious." The anti-Catholic drawings of Thomas Nast in *Harper's Weekly* had their western cousins in new tabloids like the *Jolly Giant.* In response, Irish Catholics turned on Chinese Americans. According to James Buchard, a part-Indian Presbyterian minister turned Catholic priest, the Chinese should not be allowed to fill California because they were an "inferior race." They were "pagan," "vicious," and "immoral." Moreover, the missionaries were wrong. They could not be Christianized. They "are incapable of rising to the virtue that is inculcated by the religion of Jesus Christ." Catholics took the American fixation on the West and posed this question to Protestants: Would you rather have your beloved West populated by Catholics or by pagans?[92]

Western religious and racial trauma followed the course of conflict in other parts of Reconstruction America as sexualized racism incited violence, and elicited federal action. In the late 1870s, the specter of interracial sexuality was mapped onto western race relations and new cartoons trafficked in fears of white women forming families with Chinese men. Violence was everywhere on the West Coast, moreover. In November 1876, the very same month the nation would fall into a panic over the presidential election, a mass anti-Chinese meeting in San Francisco featured a mock gallows where a prominent Protestant missionary to the Chinese was hung in effigy. The crowd set fire to the effigy, and a local judge asked, "If the country's flag was to be defended, to whom would Chinese admirers look—to Chinamen or Irish?" Locals predicted that the next executions would not be done in effigy. Throughout these years, symbols of violence were matched by actual violence: more than three hundred Chinese Americans were driven out from their homes, communities, and businesses.[93]

In the West, providential problems and millennial musings stood in stark relief. An even more complex mosaic of racial and religious conflicts filled the decades after the Civil War with religious conflict. Whether in the case of the Mormons, the Indians of the plains, or the Catholics, Protestants, and Chinese Americans in the West, the course of Reconstruction was one of religious conflict, violence, and the imposition of federal power. Religion was remade in the Reconstruction West as providential certainty and millennial hope were often transformed to prophetic uncertainties and millennial despair.

CONCLUSION

By the 1890s and the early twentieth century, providentialism and millennialism in the United States looked and felt different than they had before the Civil War. Emancipation and Reconstruction created new grounds for religions to walk upon, to talk upon, and to debate upon. In the process, northerners and southerners, easterners and westerners, women and men, blacks, whites, natives, and Mormons fashioned new religious conceptions of themselves, their gods, their governments, their laws, their movements, their hopes, and their fears. In at least three ways, emancipation and Reconstruction helped reshape providentialism and millennialism for the early twentieth century.

First, religion lost some of its antebellum authority. The possibilities of disbelief expanded because providential claims were so ubiquitous and full of conflict.[94] Since so many Americans were claiming that to doubt this or to doubt that was to doubt God, and since many of these assertions were irreconcilable, some Americans became jaded with providential explanations. Certainty gave way to speculation. For monotheists in the Christian tradition, God certainly could not be on everyone's side. The divine could not be for and against polygamy; it could not be for and against civil rights; it could not be for and against industrialization. This led providentialism and millennialism further into the genres of sarcasm and mockery. Mark Twain regularly lambasted providential explanations. "Trusting in Providence is a very good thing," he wrote in one draft of *Life on the Mississippi*, "but a chart and a compass are worth six of it, any time. Statistics have shown this to be true."[95] Ambrose Bierce jabbed in his 1911 *Devil's Dictionary* at providence as "unexpectedly and conspicuously beneficial to the person so describing it" and the millennium as "the period of a thousand years when the lid is to be down, with all reformers on the under side."[96] Turning religion into the realm of sarcasm paved the way for twentieth-century agnostics, most prominently Clarence Darrow, H. L. Mencken, and Sinclair Lewis, to gain popularity by mocking the faithful and certain.

Second, religion reworked itself by making ambiguity and flexibility work. Those who took providence and the millennium seriously shifted from certainty to circumspection or from outspokenness to whispers. They built ambiguity into their faiths, allowing for greater flexibility and durability. Modernists, for instance, shifted their postmillennialism from the tangible and corporeal to the realm of ethics and ideals. One explained that Jesus "fulfilled prophecy, *not because he is the fulfiller of prophetic predictions but because he is the fulfiller of prophetic* ideals."[97] Dispensational premillennialism refused to map God's biblical timeline onto human history with absolute certainty, but conjectured wildly as to the links between human affairs and the Lord's plans. When *The Fundamentals* of fundamentalism were published, the pamphlets said little of the end times, Christ's Second Coming, or the millennium. Amid World War I, for instance, the editor of the *Christian Herald*, declared, "We are living in a time of prophetic fulfillment, though just now how far that fulfillment may reach no man knows."[98]

Mormons, who had once been so certain that the Civil War was a divine sign of the end times, now built caution and unspecific time lines into their teachings. Their instructions for teaching Smith's 1832 prophecy in Sunday school now included: "*A Caution:* When we consider prophecy, whether ancient or modern, it is necessary to submerge the idea of time and relationship. This prophecy does not say exactly when the general war will take place, but only that it will take place. Between the time of the prophecy and the war twenty-nine years elapsed; between the 'Civil War' and the world war more than half a century; and between the two world wars about twenty years. Prophecy, therefore, pays little attention or no attention to the element of time."[99]

Third, and linked to the widespread acceptance of some forms of ambiguity and flexibility, there was a shift from focusing on when Jesus would literally return to metaphorically if he returned what would he think and how would he be treated. These works typically clouded Jesus in mystery and referenced him as a "stranger." The Jesus figure of Charles Sheldon's *In His Steps* (1896) was a "tramp" and "stranger" who appeared out of nowhere. W. E. B. Du Bois penned story after story about Jesus showing up in the United States of the early twentieth century only to be lynched for his radical teachings of racial integration and economic equality. Upton Sinclair had Jesus emerge as a stranger in Southern California to address issues of economic greed, labor activism, and racism.[100]

Religions shaped Reconstruction, whether in Lincoln's providential ruminations, Powderly's claims for working-class superiority, African American mobility and hope, new rationales for white supremacy, or westward expansion and conflict. And Reconstruction transformed religions in the United States. When the Civil War began, many Americans were certain about God's designs for the nation, even though their sacred certainties were in dire conflict. Emancipation and Reconstruction shattered the old America, and in its place something new had to be made. As prophetic visions, providential promises, and millennial dreams failed to be realized fully, all types of Americans recast their faiths. Southern whites found new explanations for slavery and race. Many northern whites became religiously tentative. Premillennialists stormed back with assured ambiguity. Mormons banned polygamy to keep pace with suffrage rights for black men. Labor activists transformed biblical curses into sacred blessings, and Native Americans on the plains mourned new iterations of failed prophecies. Just as America was never the same after emancipation and Reconstruction, neither were its religious expressions.

NOTES

1. "Reconstruction," in *American Political Prints, 1766–1876: A Catalog of the Collections in the Library of Congress,* ed. Bernard F. Reilly Jr. (Boston: G. K. Hall, 1991), 572; Horatio Bateman, *Explanation of Bateman's National Picture of Reconstruction* (New York: Bateman, 1867); Mark Elliott, *Color-Blind Justice: Albion Tourgée and the Quest for Racial Equality from the Civil War to* Plessy v. Ferguson (New York: Oxford University Press, 2006), 26; Edward J. Blum, *Reforging the White*

Republic: Race, Religion, and American Nationalism, 1865–1898 (Baton Rouge: Louisiana State University Press, 2005), 1–2.

2. Eric Foner, *Reconstruction: America's Unfinished Revolution, 1863–1877* (New York: Harper and Row, 1988); David W. Blight, *Race and Reunion: The Civil War in American Memory* (Cambridge: Harvard University Press, 2001); Steven Hahn, *A Nation under Our Feet: Black Political Struggles in the Rural South from Slavery to the Great Migration* (Cambridge: Harvard University Press, 2003); Heather Cox Richardson, *West from Appomattox: The Reconstruction of America after the Civil War* (New Haven: Yale University Press, 2007).

3. Daniel W. Stowell, *Rebuilding Zion: The Religious Reconstruction of the South, 1863–1877* (New York: Oxford University Press, 1998); Paul Harvey, *Freedom's Coming: Religious Culture and the Shaping of the South from the Civil War through the Civil Rights Era* (Chapel Hill: University of North Carolina Press, 2005); Paul Harvey, *Redeeming the South: Religious Cultures and Racial Identities among Southern Baptists, 1865–1925* (Chapel Hill: University of North Carolina Press, 1997); Reginald F. Hildebrand, *The Times Were Strange and Stirring: Methodist Preachers and the Crisis of Emancipation* (Durham, N.C.: Duke University Press, 1995); James B. Bennett, *Religion and the Rise of Jim Crow in New Orleans* (Princeton: Princeton University Press, 2005); James H. Moorhead, *American Apocalypse: Yankee Protestants and the Civil War 1860–1869* (New Haven: Yale University Press, 1978). The finest study on the religion of the Lost Cause remains Charles Reagan Wilson, *Baptized in Blood: The Religion of the Lost Cause, 1865–1920* (Athens: University of Georgia Press, 1980). Katharine L. Dvorak, *An African-American Exodus: The Segregation of the Southern Churches* (New York: Carlson, 1991); Clarence E. Walker, *A Rock in a Weary Land: The African Methodist Episcopal Church during the Civil War and Reconstruction* (Baton Rouge: Louisiana State University Press, 1982). Molly Oshatz, *Slavery and Sin: The Fight against Slavery and the Rise of Liberal Protestantism* (New York: Oxford University Press, 2011), makes some important connections among debates over slavery, the Civil War and Reconstruction, and providential, millennial, and theological considerations.

4. In *God and Race in American Politics,* for instance, Mark Noll titled his chapter on Reconstruction "The Origins of African-American Religious Agency" (Mark A. Noll, *God and Race in American Politics: A Short History* [Princeton: Princeton University Press, 2008], chap. 2). Martin Marty, *Pilgrims in Their Own Land: 500 Years of Religion in America* (New York: Penguin, 1985), 221–46; Mark A. Noll, *A History of Christianity in the United States and Canada* (Grand Rapids, Mich.: Eerdmans, 1992); Winthrop S. Hudson, *Religion in America* (New York: Scribner, 1965), chap. 9.

5. The sources covering the decades after the war are limited to "Science, Immigration, and Consumer Capitalism" (R. Marie Griffith, ed., *American Religions: A Documentary History* [New York: Oxford University Press, 2008], pt. 4).

6. Catherine L. Albanese, *America: Religions and Religion* (Belmont, Calif.: Wadworth, 1981); Nicholas Guyatt, *Providence and the Invention of the United States, 1607–1876* (Cambridge: Cambridge University Press, 2007); Robert N. Bellah, *The Broken Covenant: American Civil Religion in Time of Trial* (Chicago: University of Chicago Press, 1992); Ernest Lee Tuveson, *Redeemer Nation: The Idea of America's Millennial Role* (Chicago: University of Chicago Press, 1968); Harry S. Stout, *Upon the Altar of the Nation: A Moral History of the American Civil War* (New York: Viking, 2006).

7. Quoted in Blum, *Reforging the White Republic,* 49.

8. Dvorak, *An African-American Exodus*; Walker, *A Rock in a Weary Land*; Hildebrand, *The Times Were Strange and Stirring*.

9. Quoted in Matthew James Zacharias Harper, "Living in God's Time: African-American Faith and Politics in Post-Emancipation North Carolina" (Ph.D. diss., University of North Carolina, Chapel Hill, 2009), 243.

10. Quoted in Dvorak, *An African-American Exodus*, 81.

11. Quoted in Daniel L. Fountain, *Slavery, Civil War, and Salvation: African American Slaves and Christianity, 1830–1870* (Baton Rouge: Louisiana State University Press, 2010), 93.

12. David L. Chappell, *A Stone of Hope: Prophetic Religion and the Death of Jim Crow* (Chapel Hill: University of North Carolina Press, 2004), 45.

13. Chandra Manning, *What This Cruel War Was Over: Soldiers, Slavery, and the Civil War* (New York: Vintage, 2007), 103–8.

14. Quoted Dvorak, *An African-American Exodus*, 82.

15. Quoted in Harvey, *Freedom's Coming*, 22.

16. Jason Phillips, *Diehard Rebels: The Confederate Culture of Invincibility* (Athens: University of Georgia Press, 2007), 25.

17. Quoted in Manning, *What This Cruel War Was Over*, 171.

18. John Townsend Trowbridge, *The South: A Tour of Its Battle-fields and Ruined Cities* (Hartford, Ct.: L. Stebbins, 1866), 291.

19. Luke Edward Harlow, "From Border South to Solid South: Religion, Race, and the Making of Confederate Kentucky, 1830–1880" (Ph.D. diss., Rice University, 2009), chap. 6.

20. Quoted in John David Smith, *An Old Creed for the New South: Proslavery Ideology and Historiography, 1865–1918* (Westport, Ct.: Greenwood, 1985), 20.

21. Civis, *The Public School in Its Relations to the Negro* (Richmond: Clemmitt & Jones, Steam Printers, 1877), 8, in *Anti-Black Thought, 1863–1925: "The Negro Problem,"* ed. John David Smith, vol. 4 (New York: Garland, 1993).

22. Edward J. Blum, *W. E. B. Du Bois, American Prophet* (Philadelphia: University of Pennsylvania Press, 2007), chap. 4; Mason Boyd Stokes, "Someone's in the Garden with Eve: Race, Religion, and the American Fall," *American Quarterly* 50, no. 4 (December 1998): 718–44; David N. Livingstone, *Adam's Ancestors: Race, Religion, and the Politics of Human Origins* (Baltimore: Johns Hopkins University Press, 2008).

23. A. Hoyle Lester, *The Pre-Adamite, or Who Tempted Eve?* (Philadelphia: Lippincott, 1875), 25, in *Anti-Black Thought, 1863–1925: "The Negro Problem,"* ed. John David Smith (New York: Garland, 1993), vol. 6. For more on the importance of sexuality in studying American religious history, see Ann Taves, "Sexuality in American Religious History," in *Retelling U.S. Religious History*, ed. Thomas Tweed (Berkeley: University of California Press, 1997), 27–56.

24. Charles Carroll, *The Tempter of Eve, or The Criminality of Man's Social, Political, and Religious Equality with the Negro, and the Amalgamation to Which These Crimes Inevitably Lead* (St. Louis: Adamic, 1902), 414, 402, 406, in *Anti-Black Thought, 1863–1925: "The Negro Problem,"* ed. John David Smith (New York: Garland, 1993), vol. 6.

25. Ibid.

26. Jane Dailey, "Sex, Segregation, and the Sacred after Brown," *Journal of American History* 91, no. 1 (June 2004): 119–44; Paul Harvey, *Freedom's Coming*.

27. Forrest G. Wood, *Black Scare: The Racist Response to Emancipation and Reconstruction* (Berkeley: University of California Press, 1968).

28. "Miscegenation—or the Millennium of Abolitionism" (New York: G. W. Bromley & Co., 1864), Library of Congress.

29. Edward Lillie Pierce, ed., *Memoir and Letters of Charles Sumner,* vol. 4 (Boston: Roberts Brothers, 1893), 124.

30. Quoted in Ellen Carol DuBois, *Feminism and Suffrage: The Emergence of an Independent Women's Movement in America, 1848–1869,* 2nd ed. (Ithaca, N.Y.: Cornell University Press, 1999), 53.

31. Quoted in Manning, *What This Cruel War Was Over,* 119.

32. For more on this confusion, see Moorhead, *American Apocalypse.*

33. Ronald C. White Jr., *Lincoln's Greatest Speech: The Second Inaugural* (New York: Simon and Schuster, 2002).

34. Mark A. Noll, *America's God: From Jonathan Edwards to Abraham Lincoln* (New York: Oxford University Press, 2002), 426.

35. Harry S. Stout, *Upon the Altar of the Nation: A Moral History of the American Civil War* (New York: Viking, 2006).

36. White, *Lincoln's Greatest Speech,* 190–98. "Arcana" in Oxford English Dictionary.

37. Quoted in Blum, *Reforging the White Republic,* 20–21, 27.

38. Quoted in Eric McKitrick, *Andrew Johnson and Reconstruction* (New York: Oxford University Press, 1988), 74.

39. Frederick A. Aiken to Andrew Johnson, June 27, 1868, in *The Papers of Andrew Johnson,* vol. 14, *April–August 1868,* ed. Paul H. Bergeron (Knoxville: University of Tennessee Press, 1997), 274–75.

40. Thaddeus Stevens, "Reconstruction," in *The Selected Papers of Thaddeus Stevens,* ed. Beverly Wilson Palmer, vol. 2, *April 1865–August 1868* (Pittsburgh: University of Pittsburgh Press, 1998), 53. For more on religion and radical Republicans, see Victor B. Howard, *Religion and the Radical Republican Movement, 1860–1870* (Lexington: University Press of Kentucky, 1990).

41. Thaddeus Stevens, "Damages to Loyal Men," in *The Selected Papers of Thaddeus Stevens,* ed. Palmer, 2:278, 284–85.

42. Jacqueline Jones, *Soldiers of Light and Love: Northern Teachers and Georgia Blacks, 1865–1873* (Chapel Hill: University of North Carolina Press, 1986); Joe M. Richardson, *Christian Reconstruction: The American Missionary Association and Southern Blacks, 1861–1890* (Athens: University of Georgia Press, 1986); Ronald E. Butchart, *Northern Schools, Southern Blacks, and Reconstruction: Freedmen's Education, 1862–1875* (Westport, Ct.: Greenwood, 1980).

43. Gerald Schwartz, ed., *A Woman Doctor's Civil War: Esther Hill Hawks' Diary* (Columbia: University of South Carolina Press, 1994), 63.

44. M. Waterbury, *Seven Years among the Freedmen* (Chicago: T. B. Arnold, 1891).

45. Reverend W. J. Richardson to Reverend George Whipple, July 3, 1863, American Missionary Association Manuscripts, South Carolina, Roll 1.

46. Kathi Kern, *Mrs. Stanton's Bible* (Ithaca, N.Y.: Cornell University Press, 2001), 110–11.

47. Daniel Walker Howe, *What Hath God Wrought: The Transformation of America, 1815–1848* (New York: Oxford University Press, 2007), 289–92; Albanese, *America: Religions and Religion,* 298–301; Ronald Numbers and Jonathan Butler, eds., *The Disappointed: Millerism and Millenari-*

anism (Bloomington: Indiana University Press, 1987); David Pae, *Two Years After and Onwards, or the Approaching War amongst the Powers of Europe* (London: Houlston and Wright, 1864), 45.

48. George F. Kelly to Abraham Lincoln, February 24 and 25, 1863, and George F. Kelly to William H. Seward, October 26, 1863, Abraham Lincoln Papers, Library of Congress.

49. Blum, *Reforging the White Republic,* chap. 4; W. H. Daniels, ed., *Moody: His Words, Work, and Workers* (New York: Nelson and Phillips, 1877), 476.

50. Marty, *Pilgrims in Their Own Land,* 321–24; Ellen G. White, *The Great Controversy between Christ and Satan* (Battle Creek, Mich.: Seventh-Day Adventist Publishing Association, 1878).

51. David R. Roediger, *The Wages of Whiteness: Race and the Making of the American Working Class* (London: Verso, 1991).

52. Harry J. Carman, Henry David, and Paul N. Guthrie, eds., *The Path I Trod: The Autobiography of Terence V. Powderly* (New York: Columbia University Press, 1940), 102; "The English Labor Lesson," *Nation,* February 27, 1890, 172

53. Clark D. Halker, *For Democracy, Workers, and God: Labor Song-Poems and Labor Protest, 1865–95* (Urbana: University of Illinois Press, 1991); Herbert G. Gutman, "Protestantism and the American Labor Movement: The Christian Spirit in the Gilded Age," *American Historical Review* (October 1966): 74–101.

54. Terence V. Powderly, *Thirty Years of Labor: 1859–1889* (1890; New York: Augustus M. Kelley, 1967), 357–58.

55. T. V. Powderly, "Prison Contact Labor—A Remedy," in *Labor Day Annual,* ed. Powderly and A. W. Wright (Philadelphia: Labor Annual Publishing Company, 1893), 43.

56. Carman, David, and Guthrie, eds., *The Path I Trod,* 346–47.

57. Powderly, *Thirty Years of Labor,* 356.

58. Carman, David, and Guthrie, eds., *The Path I Trod,* 48–50.

59. Powderly, *Thirty Years of Labor,* 357.

60. Lyman Beecher, "A Plea for the West," in *A Plea for the West* (Cincinnati: Truman and Smith, 1835), 7–40; Reginald Horsman, *Race and Manifest Destiny: The Origins of American Racial Anglo-Saxonism* (Cambridge: Harvard University Press, 1981); Laurie F. Maffly-Kipp, *Religion and Society in Frontier California* (New Haven: Yale University Press, 1994); Henry Nash Smith, *Virgin Land: The American West as Symbol and Myth* (Cambridge: Harvard University Press, 2007).

61. Guyatt, *Providence and the Invention of the United States,* 200.

62. Ibid., 250, 240.

63. Henry Bibb, *The Life and Adventures of Henry Bibb, an American Slave* (1849; Madison: University of Wisconsin Press, 2001), 92; Walter Johnson, *Soul by Soul: Life inside the Antebellum Slave Market* (Cambridge: Harvard University Press, 1999), 23.

64. Richardson, *West from Appomattox,* 117–19.

65. Quoted in James P. Moore Jr., *Prayer in America: A Spiritual History of Our Nation* (New York: Random House, 2007), 192.

66. Amy S. Greenberg, *Manifest Manhood and the Antebellum American Empire* (Cambridge: Cambridge University Press, 2005).

67. John McDowell Leavitt, *Kings of Capital and Knights of Labor* (New York: Powers and Le Craw, 1886), 311.

68. Nell Irvin Painter, *Exodusters: Black Migration to Kansas after Reconstruction* (1976; repr., New York: Norton, 1992), 4; Milton C. Sernett, *Bound for the Promised Land: African American Re-*

ligion and the Great Migration (Durham: Duke University Press, 1997); Kevin Boyle, *Arc of Justice: A Saga of Race, Civil Rights, and Murder in the Jazz Age* (New York: Holt, 2004), 2.

69. Quoted in Leonard J. Arrington and David Bitton, *The Mormon Experience: A History of the Latter-day Saints,* 2nd ed. (Urbana: University of Illinois Press, 1992), 165.

70. Mrs. C. V. Waite, *The Mormon Prophet and His Harem: An Authentic History of Brigham Young, His Numerous Wives and Children* (Cambridge: Riverside, 1866), iii–iv.

71. Gaines M. Foster, *Moral Reconstruction: Christian Lobbyists and the Legislation of Morality, 1865–1920* (Chapel Hill: University of North Carolina Press, 2007); Patrick Q. Mason, "Opposition to Polygamy in the Postbellum South," *Journal of Southern History* 76, no. 3 (August 2010): 541–78.

72. Mason, "Opposition to Polygamy in the Postbellum South," 549.

73. Grant Underwood, *The Millenarian World of Early Mormonism* (Urbana: University of Illinois Press, 1993).

74. Joseph Smith, *The Doctrine and Covenants of the Church of Jesus Christ of Latter-Day Saints* (Bedford, Mass.: Applewood, 2009), 304.

75. A. Karl Larson and Katharine Miles Larson, eds., *Diary of Charles Lowell Walker* (Logan: Utah State University Press, 1980), 147, 242; Robert Glass Cleland and Juanita Brooks, eds., *A Mormon Chronicle: The Diaries of John D. Lee* (San Marino, Calif.: Huntington Library, 1955), 283–84, 295.

76. Quoted in Arrington and Bitton, *The Mormon Experience,* 171.

77. Leonard J. Arrington, *Brigham Young: American Moses* (New York: Knopf, 1985), 297.

78. Cleland and Brooks, eds., *A Mormon Chronicle,* 2:372–73.

79. Arrington, *Brigham Young,* 221; Juanita Brooks, "Indian Relations on the Mormon Frontier," *Utah Historical Quarterly* 12 (January–April 1944): 1–48; Sondra Jones, "'Redeeming' the Indian: The Enslavement of Indian Children in New Mexico and Utah," *Utah Historical Quarterly* 67, no. 3 (Summer 1999): 220–41.

80. Richard Abanes, *One Nation under Gods: A History of the Mormon Church* (New York: Thunder's Mouth, 2003), 12, 17, 47–57, 484–85 nn. 47–48; Richard Lyman Bushman, *Joseph Smith: Rough Stone Rolling* (New York: Knopf, 2005); Noel A. Carmack, "Images of Christ in Latter-day Saint Visual Culture, 1900–1999," *BYU Studies* 39, no. 3 (2000): 26 and 69 n. 28. 1 Nephi 13:15 and 11:13. See Carmack, "Images of Christ in Latter-day Saint Visual Culture, 1900–1999," 28–30.

81. Larson and Larson, eds., *Diary of Charles Lowell Walker,* 153

82. Ibid., 154–55. Armand Mauss, *All Abraham's Children: Changing Mormon Perceptions of Race* (Urbana: University of Illinois Press, 2003), chaps. 8 and 9.

83. Newell G. Bringhurst, *Saints, Slaves, and Blacks: The Changing Place of Black People within Mormonism* (Westport, Ct.: Greenwood, 1981), 152.

84. Sarah Barringer Gordon, *The Mormon Question: Polygamy and Constitutional Conflict in Nineteenth-Century America* (Chapel Hill: University of North Carolina Press, 2002).

85. *Gospel Doctrine Sunday School Lessons for the Church of Jesus Christ of Latter-day Saints* (Salt Lake City: Deseret Sunday School Union Board, 1940), 73. For a use of "then" as the means of describing the links, see "A Revelation and Prophecy by the Prophet," *True Latter-Day Saints' Herald* 11, no. 6 (December 1, 1864): 161–62.

86. Gordon, *The Mormon Question,* 220, 243.

87. Richardson, *West from Appomattox,* 127.

88. Don Lynch, ed., *Wovoka and the Ghost Dance* (Lincoln: University of Nebraska Press, 1997).

89. Ibid., 12–13, 18, 190, 238.

90. Derek Chang, *Citizens of a Christian Nation: Evangelical Missions and the Problem of Race in the Nineteenth Century* (Philadelphia: University of Pennsylvania Press, 2010), 17.

91. Ibid., 29.

92. Joshua Paddison, "Anti-Catholicism and Race in Post-Civil War San Francisco," *Pacific Historical Review* 78, no. 4 (2009): 505–44.

93. Jean Pfaelzer, *Driven Out: The Forgotten War Against Chinese Americans* (New York: Random House, 2007); Paddison, "Anti-Catholicism and Race in Post-Civil War San Francisco."

94. James Turner, *Without God, Without Creed: The Origins of Unbelief in America* (Baltimore: Johns Hopkins University Press, 1985).

95. Mark Twain, *Life on the Mississippi* (1883; New York: Penguin, 1984), 204n.

96. Ambrose Bierce, *The Unabridged Devil's Dictionary* (Athens: University of Georgia Press, 2000), 164, 189.

97. James H. Moorhead, *World Without End: Mainstream American Protestant Visions of the Last Things, 1880–1925* (Bloomington: Indiana University Press, 1999), 42.

98. George M. Marsden, *Fundamentalism and American Culture: The Shaping of Twentieth-Century Evangelicalism, 1870–1925* (New York: Oxford University Press, 1980), 119, 145–46.

99. *Gospel Doctrine Sunday School Lessons,* 73

100. Charles M. Sheldon, *In His Steps* (1896; New York: Grosset and Dunlap, 1935); Upton Sinclair, *They Call Me Carpenter: A Tale of the Second Coming* (Chicago: Paine, 1922); Blum, *W. E. B. Du Bois, American Prophet,* chap. 4.

CONTRIBUTORS

EDWARD J. BLUM is an associate professor of history at San Diego State University. He is the author or editor of six books, all of which explore the intersections of religion and race in American history. His first, the multiple-prize-winning *Reforging the White Republic: Race Religion, and American Nationalism, 1865–1898* (2005), demonstrates how religion fueled sectional reconciliation on the basis of white supremacy. Most recently, Blum and Paul Harvey trace the way images of Jesus have reflected American understandings of race in *The Color of Christ: The Son of God and the Saga of Race in America* (2012).

RYAN CORDELL is an assistant professor of English at Northeastern University. His scholarship focuses on the intersections between literary and religious culture in antebellum America. He is also active in the digital humanities and is currently building a digital edition of Nathaniel Hawthorne's short story "The Celestial Railroad."

ZACHARY W. DRESSER is a visiting assistant professor in the religion and culture department at Virginia Tech. His dissertation, "The Theology of Reconstruction: White Southern Ministers in the Aftermath of the Civil War," explores the role of religious thought in the social and political actions of nineteenth-century southerners. By applying the framework of liberation theology, Dresser demonstrates how white southern ministers responded to the challenges of Civil War defeat and Reconstruction by reinterpreting existing orthodoxies.

JENNIFER GRABER is an associate professor of religious studies at the University of Texas at Austin. Her first book, The *Furnace of Affliction: Prisons and Religion in Antebellum America* (2011), examines the intersection of religion and prisons in the early American republic. Her current project focuses on religious transformations prompted by conflicts between settlers and Indians in the American West. Graber is a part of the Young Scholars in American Religion Program sponsored by the Center for the Study of Religion in American Culture.

MATTHEW HARPER is an assistant professor of history and the director of African/African-American studies at the University of Central Arkansas. Harper is at work on his first book, which demonstrates how millennial theology shaped the politics of African Americans in the postemancipation South.

CHARLES F. IRONS is an associate professor of history at Elon University. His first book, *The Origins of Proslavery Christianity: White and Black Evangelicals in Colonial and Antebellum Virginia* (2008), argues that white evangelicals' ideas about slavery grew directly out of their interactions with black evangelicals. His current project carries this treatment into the period after emancipation by answering why the rate at which African American members of biracial communions left to form their own churches varied so widely from community to community.

JOSEPH MOORE is an assistant professor of history at Gardner-Webb University. He is currently at work on his first book, a study of American Covenanters, a Presbyterian sect he tracks from seventeenth-century Scotland and Ireland to nineteenth-century America.

ROBERT K. NELSON is the director of the Digital Scholarship Lab at the University of Richmond. His current research uses a text-mining technique called topic modeling to uncover themes and reveal historical patterns in massive amounts of text from the Civil War era. He is currently completing two projects from this research. One is a digital project that will publish and analyze multiple topic models of Civil War–era archives including the *Richmond Daily Dispatch* and the *New York Times.* The other is an essay that analyzes these models to produce a comparative analysis of Union and Confederate nationalism and patriotism.

SCOTT NESBIT is a doctoral candidate in history at the University of Virginia and the associate director of the Digital Scholarship Lab and the University of Richmond. His dissertation explores how Americans used the language of forgiveness in religious and political contexts between the 1850s and 1870s, especially concerning slavery, emancipation, and sectional conflict. Nesbit has been active in the digital humanities, directing projects that include an interactive map on the end of slavery, entitled *Visualizing Emancipation,* which is available free for public use.

JASON PHILLIPS is an associate professor of history at Mississippi State University. His first book, *Diehard Rebels: The Confederate Culture of Invincibility* (2007), explains Confederate soldiers' constant faith in victory and reexamines the aftermath of the defeat in the South. His essay here is drawn from his current book project, which reconsiders how Americans imagined the future during the sectional crisis and introduces cultural prophecy as an analytical category that is the opposite of historical memory. Phillips is also editing a book of essays that showcase innovative work at the intersection of southern history and literature.

NINA REID-MARONEY is an associate professor of history at Huron University College. From 2007 to 2012, she was coinvestigator on the Promised Land Project, a Community-University Research Alliance (funded by the Social Sciences and Humanities Research Council of Canada) that focused on African Canadian communities in the nineteenth century. She is the author of *Philadelphia's Enlightenment, 1740–1800: Kingdom of Christ, Empire of Reason* (2000); and *The Reverend Jennie Johnson and African Canadian History* (2013); and is coeditor of *The Promised Land: History and Historiography of Black Experience in Chatham-Kent's Settlements* (2013).

BEN WRIGHT is a doctoral candidate in history at Rice University.